HOW TO HUSTLE AND WIN PART 2

Rap, Race and Revolution

FOREWORD by STIC.MAN of DEAD PREZ

SUPREME UNDERSTANDING

 Published by Supreme Design Publishing. PO Box 10887, Atlanta, GA 30310.

Originally released as **Rap, Race and Revolution: Solutions for Our Struggle.**

Supreme Design Publishing books are printed on long-lasting acid-free paper. When it is available, we choose paper that has been manufactured by environmentally responsible practices. These may include using trees grown in sustainable forests, incorporating recycled paper, minimizing chlorine in bleaching, or recycling the energy produced at the paper mill.

Supreme Design Publishing is also a member of the Tree Neutral™ initiative, which works to offset paper consumption through tree planting.

Publisher's Cataloging-in-Publication Data

Understanding, Supreme.

How to hustle and win, part 2 : rap, race and revolution / Supreme Understanding ; foreword by Stic.man.

p. cm.

ISBN: 978-0-9816170-9-1

1. African Americans—Social conditions—1975-. 2. Conduct of life. 3. Social change. 4. Urban poor. I. Stic.man, 1975- II. Title.

E185.615 .U528 2010

305.896—dc22

2010922185

Wholesale Discounts. Special discounts (up to 55% off of retail) are available on quantity purchases. For details, visit our website.

Individual Sales. Supreme Design publications are available for retail purchase, or can be requested, at most bookstores. They can also be ordered directly from Amazon or via mail order (see information at the back of this book)

Visit us on the web at www.SupremeUnderstanding.com or www.BestBlackBooks.com

DEDICATION

To my queen Mecca. You keep me energized to deal with this world.

To my daughters Nena and Nilani. You keep me motivated to change the world before you have to suffer in it.

To the Five Percent. Without you, I would be reading this book in a cell instead of writing it.

Finally, to the forces who work tirelessly to destroy us. Without you, people like me would be unnecessary.

PREFACE

10TH ANNIVERSARY EDITION

"The devil sure do stay busy" - Somebody's Grandma

Peace! Since we've first published this book, so many amazing things have happened. This should be a great moment - our 10th anniversary edition of a self-empowerment guide that has quite literally changed the world. Nearly every successful artist and athlete I respect has read this book or heard of it!

Bigger than that, there are the millions of people, much like yourself, who may not have a platform (yet!), who have been impacted by this book and the two dozen titles that followed it!

6 DOPE THINGS WE'RE PROUD OF AT SDP

At Supreme Design Publishing, we take pride in producing high-quality nonfiction books. They're well-researched and designed to produce great changes in any reader, through a process of nonformal education inspired by my doctoral dissertation on the learning-centered culture of the Five Percent in America.

When we change lives, we change communities. We've won a few awards and our books earn amazing reviews from all walks of life. This book has been translated into Spanish (by readers!) and will soon be in French. It's used in university courses across the country. It's been spotted in quite a few big artists' videos. Yet i's bigger than rap videos!

Here are six things we're proud to see over the past decade:

1. Getting the blessing of ancestor Dick Gregory as the "change in the wind" the community needed before his transition
2. Contributing to getting political prisoner Mumia Abu Jamal off death row and into general population
3. Assisting former drug kingpin "Freeway" Ricky Ross in his transition to community change activist, educator, and author
4. Empowering hundreds of businesses, schools, community centers, and parents with the resources they needed

5. Ensuring that thousands of Black and brown people (prolly some white folks too) didn't go back to prison, **thanks to a greater understanding of self, allowing them to raise families!**
6. Changing tens of thousands of lives through the gift of self-directed learning and a roadmap to success that works! Ina language most of us can relate to!

YET HERE'S WHAT'S CRAZY...

Our books are banned in prison! Yes, in prison systems across the country. Not just the self-empowerment guide, even science-based texts like *The Science of Self* are banned!

You don't just get a reprimand for reading our books, **you go to the hole!**

Solitary confinement. 23 hour lockdown.

For inhumane stretches of time. For *reading self-help literature?*

WHAT YOU SHOULD KNOW

Here's what anyone should know about these books.

1. **There's never been an incident of violence or unrest related to our books or their readers.** Yet these books are considered a "security threat" because they "threaten the functioning" of some facilities. What functions are being threatened by inmates reading and becoming study-oriented and wanting to improve themselves and help others?
2. **The books don't increase criminality!** Despite the attention-catching headlines, this book shows people how and why NOT to be criminal, and how to live righteously. They explore the risks of poor choices and how to live wisely for a better future. Who does this threaten?
3. **Mental health goes UP when people read.** When they read empowering literature, they are less likely to engage in self-destructive behavior and spend less time stressing and reacting!
4. **Recidivism goes DOWN when you read our books.** When young warriors enter the prison system and encounter our books and the guidance that comes with them, they rarely reoffend! Is this ultimately what threatens the functioning of these facilities? That prisoners don't come back?

5. **Book banning is like slavery!** In fact, since prison remains the only legal form of slavery not abolished by the Constitution or its Amendments, perhaps literate and self-motivated people are indeed a threat to the functioning of the system.

Prisons are profitable - **is recidivism the goal?** Are we being targeted for cutting into the free labor that keeps this industry in business? Who thinks this is wrong?

Is this why Michelle Alexander's *The New Jim Crow* was once banned in prisons as well? Was it dangerous for Black people to learn that prison was modern day slavery because it might shake some out of accepting that lot as their life? What do our books do that warrants them still being on this ban list?

If Prison Isn't Slavery, Why is Literacy so Dangerous?

Why are inmates treated so harshly simply for owning *The Science of Self*, a scientific text full of references on geneology, astronomy, and evolutionary history? Or a health text called *The Hood Health Handbook*? Or a history book on ancient Black civilizations?

What do the prisoners forced into solitary as a "security threat group" for owning a book called *Knowledge of Self* or *Black God* have to denounce about themselves to get free? It just sounds crazy.

These books are used in universities and schools, so we're sure they don't espouse hatred - only self love and self development. They're also nonfiction works full of references. So what's really happening here?

We know prison education program push profits over people and typically don't help. Our books do. Is that the problem?

Are educated Black and Hispanic (or Indigenous/Native) people *that scary* - **that books teaching ancestral values and self-empowerment must be *banned* - and people who have done nothing else "wrong" must be thrown in 23 hour SOLITARY CONFIEMENT *simply for having them in their possession*?**

Let's Make a Change!

All that to say - time for our books and readers to be given a break!

If you're of moral conscience, you know there's no good reason for any of it.

I considered editing each line that some official had cited as their "evidence" these books could cause problems, but I soon realized I could rewrite the books in full and they'd still end up blocked somehow.

That's when I realized this was a **First Amendment** kind of situation, and predominantly Black and Hispanic people are being stripped of their civil and human rights! Meanwhile, you can find white nationalist literature like *Mein Kampf* in many prison libraries! Something is seriously wrong here!

Rather than spend our time trying to change these books any further, I'd like to raise a demand for prisoners to be given their rights, including the right to educate themselves and read empowering literature that changes lives.

How to Get Involved

Lend your voice against the squashing of literacy among those who can benefit most from it - those incarcerated and with opportunity to truly "rehabilitate" themselves, end recidivism, and help others to grow as they have. You can sign a petition supporting this cause at supremedesignonline.com/petition

At our site you'll find other ways to get involved with our campaign to increase literacy and entrepreneurship everywhere its needed most!

For those without internet access, you can write in at Supreme Design, PO Box 10887, Atlanta GA 30310 with a SASE for a reply by mail.

Other Ways to Support Supreme Design

Supreme Design is dedicated to "Reinventing the World" by raising solutionaries, people who find the answers and apply them to all problems we encounter. We build the future by teaching tomorrow's leaders. We've built a righteous family around our endeavors, and we thank you for your support and companionship.

Want to support our mission? There's plenty of ways to spread awareness and empowerment:

1. Share our social and our site with anyone you think would benefit!
2. Sign up for our emails and share them too
3. Write reviews and comments promoting what we do
4. Join our sales and promotional teams
5. Write a blog or post a video about what you've learned from us!

---

6. Take people to a bookstore that carries our books
7. Visit a local library and request our books
8. Develop lesson plans or programs using our books
9. Start a bookclub or study group using our books
10. Introduce the books to a college or university professor
11. Donate our books to an indepenent Black school
12. Donate our books to a local homeless or women's shelter
13. Donate our books to halfway house or group home
14. Incorporate our books into your own media projects
15. Mention one of our books every chance you get!

We love when you talk and post about us! Tag us or email us when you do. We want to support you back!

Want early access to everything we do, including our events and book releases? Join our promotional team! You can get an idea of what we're looking for by reading the blogs at our site and following our social media where we post opportunities to work with us!

You can also contribute to our books by sharing your own local solutions and success stories. We have some very specific needs and guidelines! For details on our upcoming projects and what we're looking for (as well as everything above), visit supremedesignonline.com and get started!

How to Learn the Solutionary Way

Ready to see real change? We do! How? Teaching and learning what works. That's what it means to **#BeSolutionary!**

We started with the curriculum – you all showed us it could be used anywhere – so now we're building an educational system that you can access anywhere – a true school without walls! For our needs!

We're working on homeschooling programs and children's curriculum, as well as real-world learning for adults – teaching industry, science, law, art, and mathematics.

Currently, you can take advantage of their #homeschooling #independentpublishing and #buildyourbusiness programs.

Homeschooling: www.ourbestschools.com

SelfPublishing: www.provenpublishing.com

BuildYourBusiness: www.righteousfamily.com

TSI in its early stages, but growing daily. It's a member of Righteous Family, a business network geared towards entrepreneurship and the rebuilding of our communities. Sign up at righteousfamily.com

Start a Bookstore!

Did you know you can start a bookstore for your local community, with as little as $60? Yes! When you visit supremedesignonline.com and take advantae of one of our package deals, you can use the books to build your dream #homeschoolinglibrary or #lendinglibrary.

You can just as easily start a bookstore, out of your living room, the trunk of your car, a rolling cart, an ice cream truck, the corner of someone's barbershop or convenience store, the possibilities are endless.

Why not hit hair salons and festivals with books in your bag? You could even go to door to door like a Mormon, except you're pushing knowledge of self and better health! Who doesn't want that?

The books kinda sell themselves. We even provide you some materials that can help. You've just gotta get yourself out there! Social media is cool, but really getting "social" goes much further! Use your talents to promote yourself as an entreprepreneur because this could be part of your path upwards! You could turn your experience into a book that could sell alongside ours!

Selling books isn't bad money either. For example, our best package deal can make you $520 off an investment of $200. Not bad huh?

Feeling rich-poor? Want to save even more? Use my promo code RIGHTEOUSFAMILY when you order and you'll get 10% off anything at the site, including the already discounted package deals.

Want your own promo code? If you join our sales and marketing team, you can get cashback on your own (discounted) purchases AND 5% of all sales made using your code. You can also help us start some local bookclubs and study groups!

We're putting out a ton of new guides and handbooks to success (in every area of life) so you'll be seeing our books everywhere soon. Why not be a part of the process?

We're really pushing to bring books and self-knowledge back! Remember the days when people discussed books in barber shops and hair salons – and sold them on street corners? We're bringing that era back in a new way – with you! **Let's make it happen!** Peace to the Gods and Earths, and all the Righteous Family across the Universe!

Foreword

STIC.MAN OF DEAD PREZ

Rap, Race and Revolution. These three powerful things have dramatically effected and inspired my life. As an emcee and producer and one half of the revolutionary but gangsta duo dead prez, rap has being my passport to the world, my language and my livelihood.

As child of the seventies growing up in the racist rural south in Wakulla County, Florida, the realities of race and racism helped to sharpen and define my quest for self understanding and self determination. My discovery of the legacy of the revolutionary strides of the 60's has critically shaped my worldview and given my work significance and purpose among the masses of my people. The revolutionary struggle has given my rage direction and my mind maturity. When we think of the continuing struggle it is how these three powers interface that will determine the development of our movement.

Supreme Understanding has brought forth a brilliant work in this 2nd volume, *Rap, Race and Revolution,* a book that I'm sure will have the same phenomenal success as his initial work in this series, *How to Hustle and Win.* The relevance of this kind of work should not be understated.

Supreme's point of view represents a true bridge of understanding because of the way he condenses *volumes* of information – using satire, humor, pimpology, revolutionary theory, metaphysical/mathematical analysis – all into an easy to follow, hip hop-toned conversation aimed at inspiring and empowering the masses to discover their own knowledge of self and the world around us…And then challenging us all to ACTUALIZE this information to empower our people.

I am honored to play a small role such as writing this foreword, as a comrade, and as a fan of the author. I think that Supreme represents a new kind of authorship that is creative, conscious, activist and brutally honest. His work is consistently well-researched and well-written.

Supreme's lifestyle is also a great demonstration of his ideas in action. The grind that this brother has put in to push his books in the community has been a great inspiration to me in seeing the power of the people and guerilla marketing in action. We have to have the winner mentality to be effective and I give thanks for Supreme's dedication, his insights and his creative swagger.

If you enjoyed Supreme's first work *How to Hustle and Win*, then get ready for the next level: *Rap, Race and Revolution*. Your world is sure to change for the better.

- Stic.man of dead prez,
Author of *The Art of Emcee-ing* and
Editor-in-chief of *.AMMO* magazine
www.BossUpBU.com

TABLE OF CONTENTS

PART TWO

THE "APARTHEID WALL"
PALESTINE
Rap, Race and Revolution

Introduction

RETURN TO THE THE BASICS

> *"Anytime you see someone more successful than you are, they are doing something you aren't." Malcolm X*

CAN THE GAME BE WON?

Whether you know it or not, you're playing the game. The "game" is not "a" game, as in the dope game, the real estate game, the corporate game, or the music game. "The" game is the summation of all those different enterprises. Together, they are known as "life" or "the real world." All of these seemingly different enterprises are bound by very similar principles, as well as similar odds for success. How can you tell if you're playing the game? You are. It's just that simple.

Whether you're hustling to keep your job, keep the bills paid, please your spouse, or sell a bird...or a CD...you're hustling. To "hustle" simply means to work strategically towards success when the odds are against you. In a white man's world, most of us are hustling. Although unfortunately, some of us are too brainwashed to know it. And in this game, you would think that having enough hustle would ensure that you win. But so many of us can hustle...Why aren't more of us winning?

How can you tell if *you're* winning the game? Okay...do you:

- ❑ Know what your life will be like five years from now?
- ❑ Have the resources to provide for yourself and your family without constant worries?
- ❑ Have a means of income doing something you "want" to do?
- ❑ Have peace at home, peace at work, and inner peace?
- ❑ Have the sense of calm that results from understanding the world you live in, and why things are the way they are?

- ❑ Have the ability to make sure that your grandchildren won't have to suffer and struggle?
- ❑ Know – with certainty – that your rights, priviliges, and luxuries cannot be taken from you?
- ❑ Enjoy freedom from injustice, oppression, profiling, and discrimination?

I KNOW almost no one made it past the first few criteria, but here's one for all of you content, wealthy fools who believe money is the key to every door: If you're such a winner, where's your power to change conditions for others? Now that you're so much better off, why isn't the world a better place? Are you even WORKING on that goal?

Ah…and that's the point. The ones who THINK they're winning are usually the biggest losers of all. Things only get better because of people who realize they need to do things differently. And chances are good that you're one of those people.

But I totally understand the self-absorbed losers who don't know they're losing. After all, this society has scammed you from day one, so it's no surprise that you believe in the illusion. Let me unveil the myth for you:

Modern society, especially America, with its "American Dream," is set up like any scam. The majority of the participants are meant to lose, while a few are ALLOWED to win (by the perpetrators of the scam) so that the losers will continue to have hope. The losers, no matter how much they're losing, continue to keep the faith that one day, they too can win big. It's like a pyramid scheme, complete with a million-dollar dream, where a bunch of losers at the bottom believe foolishly that they can make their way to the top by putting more folks below them at the bottom.

Is it really possible for everyone to "win" and "make it"? Could everyone be rich? How? Who would be the poor people that make others above them rich? Who would do all the work? It's impossible. That's like every team winning the Superbowl. It's simply not how the game works.

No, the game is a gamble, like the lottery. You know the odds are a million (or more) to one, but you keep playing, inspired by the trailer park couple who were on the news last night for winning the $47 million jackpot. But, for you, by the time you win $600, you've spent at least $1200 on tickets. Ask anyone who's "won" on the lottery recently whether they've won more than they've put in. If they're honest, you'll see how the game works.

An even better analogy is the casino. The next time you get to visit a casino, you can save a lot of money just by walking around a while and "doing the knowledge" (being observant). Take a seat by the slot machines and you'll see a dozen people blow through ten to twenty dollars in no time. Of course, the machines don't display how much money you're wasting. They covert your cash to a number of credits and only display that. You don't even have to pull the arm anymore. With the digital machines, you just press a button. Boop, boop, boop, and in 3 minutes, you've blown eighty dollars. That's not an exaggeration. That's more like an average. And that's just the dollar slots. Let's not even talk about the card tables! But it's no different from our predicament in America. Most of us lose, but they let a few win to inspire the rest of us losers with a false sense of hope. We think we're winning, but you know the old saying: "The house always wins."

But when you watch others winning, it seems easy. Teenagers watching dopedealers and cubicle workers watching corporate hustlers see the possibility of "doin it big." They don't get to see the other side of the game, because people don't like to talk about how much they've lost. People will usually only tell you about their wins. So we perpetuate the myth. And the idea that you can possibly win entices you into foolish moves that set you back worse than before you started.

I realized that if we could learn by observing the failures of others we wouldn't gamble our lives away. We could avoid bullsh*t gambles like the lottery as well as more serious gambles where you're risking your life or freedom.

So I wrote a book that explores both the successes *and the failures* that we usually don't hear about. This book talked about the myths and illusions that surround us. The book provided practical guidelines for success based in real life. And since my target audience was hustling anyway, the book was written to show you *How to Hustle and Win.*

Rap, Race and Revolution

This book, *Rap, Race and Revolution, Part Two*, continues the tradition of *How to Hustle and Win, Part One.* As the title suggests, this book continues to address the themes of street culture and the hiphop generation; race as a persistent factor in our lives; and the need for us to create revolutionary change in both our personal lives and our communities. Both *How to Hustle and Win* and *Rap, Race and Revolution* address the various and unique conflicts that confront all of us, as well as practical solutions for those problems.

One reason for the different titles was to help bring that message to a variety of audiences. While the title of *Part One* grabbed a lot of people's attention (you may have been one of them), it also scared a lot of folks off. Meanwhile, a lot of people who aren't interested in race or revolution may pick up *Part One* before they take a look at this book.

But on a deeper level, *Rap, Race and Revolution* says a lot. When you say the title, the first two words sound like "rat race," don't they? That's intentional. After all, that term quite accurately describes our situation, no matter whether we're rich or poor, street or legit, male or female, or even Black or white. It's pretty much how this whole society works. And very few (if any) of us are meant to win, no matter how hard you hustle...unless, of course, you're hustling for revolutionary change.

If you think about it, both the rat race and revolution are cycles. Picture the circular nature of a race circuit. Now think of the rat race we run in American society: We "need" money (the cheese), so we work hard (to make someone else rich). We then make enough money to survive, while spending the rest on things we don't really need. At this point, we're back needing money, so we keep working. And the cycle repeats. Throughout this whole process however, we stay motivated with the idea that one day we'll be rich or famous. Right.

On the other hand, the word "revolution" itself also refers to the circular motion of a cycle. But it's not a cycle where the end brings you right back to the beginning again (See *Part One*, "The Cycles of Life"). Instead, the process of revolutionary change is more like a spiral. Although the principles that govern in remain consistent, it grows (improves) as it continues. So at 46, you'll go through some of the same processes you went through at 26, but hopefully you'll have stepped your game up by then. Similarly, we can change the world the same way we change a single hood. And we can change the hood the same way we can change a single person. But we have to begin by changing ourselves. So the revolution begins with you.

The question is, which one is for you? The rat race or the revolution?

Is this Book for You?

If you're reading this and you're still not sure about whether you're the type of person who would benefit from this book, I'll give you a few hints on how to tell. This book is meant for you if:

- ❑ You read *Part One* and you loved it. Duh.
- ❑ You've always been intelligent, but hated school because they only taught bullsh*t.
- ❑ You see the injustices and wrongs going on all around you, and it's driving you nuts.
- ❑ You want to change something in the world or in yourself, but haven't figured out how.
- ❑ You know you're not just another "nigga."

- ❑ You're trying to turn your life around, but without church or the military!
- ❑ You're not waiting on Jesus to come back and save you.
- ❑ You wonder why other people are such followers and hypocrites.
- ❑ You know there's more to life than this.
- ❑ You're ALWAYS questioning things.
- ❑ You're able to take responsibility for the things that are happening in your life (without blaming it on someone else or "the devil")
- ❑ You're not scared to challenge the things most people believe.
- ❑ You want better for yourself, your family, and/or your people.
- ❑ You're not struggling to survive, but you want to understand and help others who are.
- ❑ You're not in the ghetto, but you can relate to the struggle, and you know you have a role in changing things for others.
- ❑ You're white, but you sincerely want to contribute to the global struggle of people of color and poor people.
- ❑ You're a woman looking for a book that digs deeper than the bullsh*t love stories and ghetto drama that's being marketed to you.
- ❑ You're a parent or elder who wants to understand and relate to our children.
- ❑ You're an activist, academic, or revolutionary that loves reading about social transformation.

If you responded "yes" to any of these questions, then do yourself a favor and read this book from cover to cover. If nothing in here sparks your mind, then either you know it all already, or you're braindead.

What's in this Book?

I tried to make this book an all-you-can-eat for your brain. There's stuff in here that you'll think is stupid, stuff that's funny, and stuff that will make you want to cry or knock somebody the f*ck out. At the end, my goal is to reverse the way we've been destroyed.

In *Part One*, I introduced you to the nine principles of a successful life. To illustrate those principles, there were dozens of stories and commentaries, each emphasizing a different life lesson. This book is a continuation of that education. The essays included in the five chapters of *Part Two* illustrate the last five principles of those nine.

The nine principles are:

Mind over Matter: Be aware. Examine what you know, and how you know it. Know who you are, and where you're going.

Manifestation and Presentation: Once you know better, do better, speak better, choose better, and live better.

Reconsider and Reevaluate: Seek understanding. Find clarity, vision, and perspective on yourself, life, and the world.

Create a Culture of Success: Transform a strong vision into a strong lifestyle and long-term agenda.

Identify your Strengths: Find your power within, in life, and in the world…and focus on developing it.

Expansion and Distribution: Broaden your horizons, spread your reach, and find balance in all you do.

Leadership and Greatness: Be yourself, lead yourself, and put the weight of the world on your shoulders.

Kill Yourself So You Can Live: Eliminate the weaknesses in yourself and the world around you, while developing the strength and discipline it will take to do so.

Seal the Deal: Choose the best paths, envision the future, ensure survival, and achieve success.

The problem with many so-called "self-help" books is that they're not practical. It's very hard to apply some of those philosophical ideas and cliché sayings to daily life, especially if daily life is a struggle. So the laws by themselves aren't necessarily going to save you life. You have to understand the many life lessons that fall under each of those nine principles. That's the reason why this book is filled to the brim with so much content.

Each chapter covers a variety of issues (women, money, crime, etc.), but the lessons in each book will all fall under one of those nine laws. If you can successfully use these laws to guide your life, you're destined to win before you even begin. *Part Two* will cover the the last five principles. *Part Two* picks up in halfway through the fifth principle where *Part One* leaves off, and completes the journey with the ninth principle.

How to Read this Book

You can start from the beginning and work your way to the end, or you can find interesting headings in the Table of Contents and hop around from essay to essay. This book can be read in any order.

When you come across a word you don't know, first see if you can figure out the meaning based on the rest of the sentence. If not, grab a dictionary or go to www.dictionary.com

The same thing goes for any person, place, event, or idea that's new to you. Look it up. If you don't feel like grabbing a book, Wikipedia it.

Bring it with you wherever you go. Instead of smoking a cigarette or text messaging when you're bored or waiting for something, *read.*

Find a partner or two who can get a copy of the book to read as well. Or just buy copies for others. When you meet, talk about what you're reading and what you think about it. This develops your brotherhood, your minds, and your ability to communicate.

Don't hide the book. Unless you're a total clown, you shouldn't be scared to be seen with a book. If you *are* a total clown, *this* book should earn you at least 50 cool points when people see you with it.

Take notes. Highlight. Circle important sections. But only if this is *your* book. Otherwise the owner's gonna be pissed.

Work to understand every idea that is discussed in this book. If you can do that, I guarantee that you'll be more knowledgeable than the average college graduate.

I didn't make everything easy. Some of this book is written in very simple language that anyone can understand. Other parts are meant to be more difficult. If this book didn't challenge every reader, I wouldn't be proud of writing it.

Finally, I didn't make everything obvious. Some of the life lessons in this book have already appeared many times in your life, but you may have missed them. Don't miss the lessons in this book. I may use the Pequot Indians or the Black Mafia to explain a point, but those lessons could apply to everything from a business deal to the check-out line at the supermarket. Keep your eyes open as you read.

Yes, *Part Two* is a little different from *Part One*. That's why it's *Part Two*. It's a natural progression, so some of the concepts are more advanced. Some of the reading is longer or more involved. And yes, some of the philosophy is more political and revolutionary. What did you expect? Me hustlin backwards and talking bout snitchin again?

Oh, and perhaps most importantly, these books are about practical application, not abstract ideas, theories, and philosophy. As the Buddha said over 3,000 years ago, "An idea that is developed and put into action is more important than an idea that exists only as an idea." With that said, let's begin.

Guns and Ammo

BEGINNING WHERE WE LEFT OFF

"The strongest people in the world aren't the most protected; they are the ones that must struggle against adversity and obstacles – and surmount them – to survive."

Without the aid of guns, knives, steroids, or a gang of thugs riding with you, you alone are infinitely strong. Within you there is the infinite potential for unprecedented greatness. As said before, the decision is up to you to act on that potential or let it wither away and die within you. All of us were born great, but few of us live great.

What are your strengths? What are your talents?

It may be these strengths and talents that one day propel you to greatness. Then again, there may be some undiscovered part of you that will only emerge when you are ready to see it and develop it.

But the conditions we live in give us an overwhelming feeling of powerlessness. We see life as a series of problems rather than opportunities, and because we are tired of struggling, many of us quit halfway through.

Out of these feelings of powerlessness and hopelessness, we develop other emotions, attitudes, and behaviors that further our self-destruction. We show our immense frustration with our oppression when we fight and act out, when we escape into the highs of various drugs, when we zone out completely and give up on being successful.

But in doing so, we reinforce our powerlessness even further.

Instead, we can reverse the cycle by denying our fears and cultivating the infinite power within us.

FOR BEGINNERS

If you haven't read *Part One*, don't stress out. This ain't a novel with a storyline you have to follow. You can jump in right here, or anywhere else in this book for that matter. But as you may know, every chapter normally begins a brief quiz. The quiz not only sets the stage for what you'll learn in that chapter, but it gives you some insight into yourself. So, although this is the second half of a chapter that began in *Part One*, I'm still going to throw in a quiz right here. The following questions come from a historically important work known as the Proust Questionnaire. These questions will tell you a lot about how you think, so compare your answers with others when you're ready.

1. Your most noticeable characteristic?
2. The quality you most admire in a woman?
3. The quality you most admire in a man?
4. What do you most value in your friends?
5. What is your biggest flaw?
6. What is your favorite occupation?
7. What is your dream of happiness?
8. What, in your mind, would be the greatest of misfortunes?
9. What would you like to be?
10. In what country would you like to live?
11. Who are your heroes in real life?
12. Who are your favorite heroines of history?
13. What is it you most dislike?
14. What historical figures do you most despise?
15. What natural gift would you most like to possess?
16. How would you like to die?
17. What is your present state of mind?
18. Which vices do you give in to the most?
19. What is your motto?

Were those questions tough to answer? They should be. But if you felt stuck, hopefully this book will help you find the answers you didn't have. I just hope you didn't answer like Soulja Boy did. Oh, you didn't hear? Well, when I first wrote about Soulja Boy and other young rappers (see *Part One*, "Young Money"), he was only 16. I gave him the benefit of the doubt because he was so young. Since then, he's shown us exactly what this industry is about…and how f*cked up our next generation may be…if we don't start doin something soon.

BET journalist Toure was interviewing rappers for his show, *The Black Carpet*. To switch things up, he used questions from the Proust Questionnaire. When it was Soulja Boy's turn, Toure asked him, "What historical figure do you most hate?" He was stumped.

Toure tried to help him by adding, "Others have said Hitler, bin Laden, the slave masters..."

According to Toure's blog on XXLMag.com, Soulja Boy responded: "Oh wait! Hold up! Shout out to the slave masters! Without them we'd still be in Africa. We wouldn't be here to get this ice and tattoos."

Just sip on that for a minute. No…take your time. Let it sink in. Yes…this is how a lot of us think. Really. I don't even wanna say anymore. I'm done. You see what our situation is. On to *Part Two*, y'all.

The Fifth Principle

"Identify Your Strengths" means: Find your power within, in life, and in the world…and focus on developing it.

What You'll Learn

- Why so many of us are hopeless, and what we can do about it.
- What Blacks and Hispanics have in common…and it ain't chicken.
- Why Europeans sent *priests* into Africa first.
- The truth about the industry that Pimp C *almost* told.
- The true story of Thanksgiving…and that ain't turkey blood.
- 10 reasons we can't come up, and the 18 words that keep us down.
- How to get your money right…and have it make money for you.

If Einstein was Black

If Albert Einstein grew up Black, in the hood, he'd be probably turn out to be a crackhead and a deadbeat dad. If Thomas Edison grew up Black, in the ghetto, he'd probably be a crack dealer. And that would be it.

Their life stories would never make it into your school textbooks, and the world would never even know they existed. Unless maybe they were arrested in some high profile case. You think I'm exaggerating? Let me elaborate.

Albert Einstein

Einstein didn't even say his first words until he was four years old. He was quiet, but still a terrible student throughout his schooling years. He regularly cut class. In college, people called him "a slacker."

He graduated college, which he called a "torturing duty," thanks to a friend who let him copy class notes. Upon his graduation, he commented:

> For a dreamer like me, university studies were not always a blessing. If we are forced to constantly eat selected meals, we can permanently spoil our stomach and lose our appetite. Luckily, in my case, this intellectual

> depression, after the completion of my studies, lasted no more than a year.

Einstein's daydreamin ass couldn't stomach the rigmarole of the formal educational system, but he was passionate about pursuing studies in his own interests. He focused his attention intensely into things he was fascinated by, or which he wanted to understand. If he were alive today, he'd probably watch nothing but the Discovery Channel. Then again, he'd probably do a little more than just watching TV. But then again, probably none of that if he grew up in the hood.

He would have been diagnosed with autism, ADHD, and dyslexia (which he was), but he'd be pushed into a Special Ed. program, where he'd be ignored by teachers and harassed by other students until eventually dropping out of a high school he'd have no hope of finishing anyway. Then working some minimum dead-end wage job, while still yearning to understand a vast world that was totally, impossibly, out of his reach, **Einstein would be a drug addict in no time.**

> **Did You Know?**
>
> Housing projects were designed as "housing experiments" (thus the name "projects"). They were used to see how poor people would respond to living in cramped conditions.
>
> As Bro. Akil says in the important book *From Niggas to Gods*, there are OBVIOUS natural consequences to putting hopeless creatures into conditions so cramped and desperate that few have enough resources to survive. Studies show that if you put enough rats into small boxes with nothing else to do, they'll have babies, but then they'll run out of room. Eventually they'll begin killing each other, and even eat their young. And that's what the projects, the ghetto, the hood, and the TRAP, are all about!

Thomas Edison

On the other hand, Thomas Edison was the definition of a hyperactive child. He never stopped asking questions, couldn't sit still, and had a hard time focusing on school work (he daydreamed too). As a result, the young Edison constantly disrupted classes. His teacher thought he was slow, that he "could not grasp anything," and labeled him retarded! His mom, sensing a flaw in the formal system of education, decided to homeschool him. Since his parents had tons of books at home, he read what he was interested in and basically taught himself.

This course of instruction evolved into Edison's passion for scientific inquiry. He became a tireless researcher, often working late nights, and sleeping on a bench in his laboratory. Totally obsessed with his work, he would sometimes forget to eat. His wandering mind actually helped to look at situations from many different perspectives, allowing him to find answers and explanations for some of the most challenging problems.

But in the ghetto today, a Thomas Edison (or better) is born every minute. And kids like him who can't sit still, who want more than what their teacher can offer, who have endless questions...what happens to them? They get shot down and shut down. And their lives spiral out of control til they're shot down or locked up. Edison would have been a clever-ass dope boy, I bet. He'd probably come up with ingenious new ways to cook, market, and conceal his product. He'd probably make a ton of money selling to ghetto Einsteins before being taken down. But besides an episode of BET's *American Gangster*, you'd never hear about him.

"He who teaches speaks to the future."
Ptahhotep

If you read *Part One*, you know that (A) We ain't stupid by far, and most of us have incredible untapped intellect (see "9 Signs We Ain't Stupid") and (B) Our people are constantly misdiagnosed with made-up shortcoming (see "Mental Illnesses in the Black Community"). But we can reverse that. We gotta start looking for untapped talent in the young people around us. And let's start showing them alternate routes to success. School won't work for everybody. But those of us who can't hack it in school don't have to be failures all around. That little knucklehead down the block may be the best auto mechanic, painter, airplane pilot, landscaper, business owner, jeweler, sculptor, or plumber ever...they just need to be shown the way. If not, all our Einsteins and Edisons are going to waste.

Without guidance and opportunities, we're all bound to fail.

Movies to See

Tsotsi; The Professional; Always Outnumbered, Always Outgunned; Akeelah and the Bee; The Longshots

All of these movies are about the way that taking a younger person under your wing can have a profound effect on the life and attitude of even the most hardened person. While *Tsotsi* is about a South African thug ending up with a stolen baby and *The Professional* is about a hitman taking responsibility for an orphaned girl, all of these movies show the transformational power of mentoring. Even if you don't feel like you're worthy of such a role, trust me...no matter how f*cked up you are, there's somebody young who could benefit by having you around. And in the process, you'll become less f*cked up!

Ready to Die

As I walked down an unfamiliar street late one winter night, the cold wind cut at my face. Still hot from the vodka I'd just finished in the park with Sun, the chill didn't seem to faze me much. What did bother me was that I was 16, still "stuck" in Jersey City, and wondering if I would ever get out. Life seemed especially bleak, even when I was drunk.

The street seemed empty until, from the shadows, a voice called me out. I was still drunk and couldn't see clearly, but I figured I knew whoever it was. I didn't. Two older guys in bubble goose coats approached quickly and the first one, a light-skinned dude with cornrows, asked me, "Where the weed at?"

As I opened my mouth to answer, he sucker-punched me and grabbed my chain. By instinct along, I swung back and hit him in the jaw. That's when I remembered I was wearing some soft-ass winter gloves. Sh*t! I didn't have any time to take them off, so I kept swinging as hard as I could. But the other dude, a skinny dark-skinned dude with wild eyes, had already snuck behind me and started takin shots at my ribs. I was stuck.

Number One, almost a foot taller than me, stopped boxing with me and started wrestling. He was able to put his arm around the back of my neck and put me in a headlock. As if on cue, the crackhead-lookin one behind me started digging into my pockets. I had to act. I was going to kill them both. I didn't think I had any other choice. I just wasn't okay with getting robbed (even though I was broke and the chain was fake). I drew the knife I kept in the sheath at my waist and – without thinking anymore about it – I stabbed Number One in his thigh. He winced in pain and let me go. As I fell backwards, I slashed at his neck, determined to kill him. I missed, catching his cheek, but not doing any life-threatening damage.

When I hit the pavement with a thud, they were shocked, but the teenage crackhead quickly picked me up, threw me on the hood of a nearby car, and they both started beating the sh*t outta me. While one punched, the other tried to wrestle the knife from my hand, but I just wouldn't let go. I knew what would happen if I did. But after they had beaten me halfway unconscious, I'd lost some of my resolve and my grip loosened. They yanked the knife from me. I knew what would happen next. My time was up. The cold night air didn't feel so cold anymore. Everything become slow and the world around me went silent. My life didn't flash before my eyes, though. I guess I wasn't living much of a life to reminisce about. But I was ready. I was ready to die. **I had nothing to live for anyway**. I imagined what it would feel like to get stabbed to death. And I braced for it.

And then nothing.

Those two guys didn't kill me that night (obviously). Number Two wanted to, but Number One seemed scared. He talked his friend out of it and they stomped me out pretty good instead. I swear I had the print from a Timberland boot imprinted into my temple for a day or two.

But I wasn't dead. I just didn't know why I wasn't happy to have lived. I understand what that despair was all about now. Maybe you can relate. Maybe you've felt that way at one point. Maybe you still do.

Well, are you ready to die? You may think you are. But why? Is it:

- ❑ Because you feel you have seen and done everything there is to see and do?
- ❑ Because you have stopped valuing your own life and just don't give a f*ck what happens to you anymore?
- ❑ Because you are fearless and willing to sacrifice anything, including yourself, for a greater cause?
- ❑ Or because you're just trying to keep up with everyone else who claims the same thing?

I'm still ready to die. But my reason today isn't the same reason as when I was 16. Back then, I WANTED to die. I hated my life. **I hated the world**. I didn't see a future for myself, and so I didn't see the point of wasting any more time in a life that didn't want me. That was why I did so many self-destructive things day after day. Whether it was starting sh*t with cops or jumping across rooftops, I wasn't defying death...I was courting it. I was trying to bring it to me. From drinking the pain away to smoking my lungs black, I didn't care about the long-term consequences because I didn't expect to see the long-term of anything. I planned to die before 21. So I gave the world every chance I could to kill me off and save me the extra misery.

Things are different now. I've learned why I was so hopeless, and I've focused all my energy into destroying the forces that made me that way. I found the knowledge of myself, and dedicated my life to fighting the people who took it away from me and left my mind in such chaos. I have a family now. I have a lot to live for now, actually. So I don't WANT to die. I'm not chasing death. But I still don't fear it.

My dedication to this truth I'm sharing with you is just that real. I'm not playing when I say the people in power will do anything they can to stop you when you do what I do. But I'm okay with that. I'm ready. After all, if I didn't have the truth and my own free mind to tell it, I might as well be dead anyway.

As David Walker said in his *Appeal* over 100 years ago:

> In preference to such servile submission to the murderous hands of tyrants...I count my life not dear unto me, but I am ready to be offered at any moment. For what is the use of living, when, in fact, I am dead?

Or as Huey P. Newton said about 40 years ago:

> The first lesson a revolutionary must learn is that he is a doomed man. Unless he understands this, he does not grasp the essential meaning of his life.

Or as Tupac Shakur said about ten years ago:

> It always happens, all the niggas that change the world die. They don't get to die like regular people, they die violently.

So come on with it. I'm ready. After all, if I'm going to die, I'd rather die because of hope, than die because of hopelessness...any day.

If you're going to risk your life, do it for hope, not hopelessness.

---

15 Ways to Say "F*ck the World"

In *Part One*, I talked about the "I don't give a f*ck" ethic. This is the nihilistic mindset that comes about because of our desperation and hopelessness growing up in **a society where we simply aren't meant to make it.** In turn, we find ways to express our discontent with the society that doesn't want us. In effect, we are saying "F*ck the world." And we do so many in so many ways. For example...

...We wear our pants so low that we're basically saying "kiss my ass."

...We ignore social conventions like talking low, waiting in line, or not cussing in public. Why try to fit in when we won't?

...We make public displays of our manhood, no matter how exaggerated. We might even beat on our chests and sh*t.

...We spit on the streets that surround us, and piss wherever we feel. We vandalize or destroy public property. We toss our trash anywhere. This ghetto is a sh*thole anyway, right?

...We escape this f*cked-up reality by getting drunk or high. Some of us even prefer that state to being sober. As the hook to E-40's "Pain No More" goes: "I'm doin everything I can to get my buzz on/ Tryin not to feel this pain no more/ That's why I'm poppin these pills and smokin this dro and drinkin this Henny straight/ Tryin not to feel this pain no more"

...We refuse to try to speak standard American English. Let them happy white boys talk that sh*t, cause good English won't help us with most of the sh*t we deal with.

...We ignore what the school teachers are trying to tell us or we drop out of school altogether. What's the point, anyway? A diploma don't really save nobody from being poor.

...We name our kids (and rename ourselves) crazy sh*t like "Fukaniga Jones" and "Mariwanna Alize."

It's our way of saying we don't believe in the system, and we don't care about being accepted by it. Cause we won't be.

...We try to make a way for ourselves any way that is outside of the traditional routes (eg. through crime, sports, or entertainment).

...We spend our money in the informal economy that occurs in the ghetto (barter and trade, stolen goods bought at discounts).

...We stray so far from the acceptable styles in fashion that we end up continuously starting new trends. Then everyone else copies our styles and makes money without us.

...We see ourselves as "niggas." To many of us, being a "nigga" symbolized us being one group, and identifying with the masses of people who have been rejected and sh*tted on by the "American Dream." As Society raps on Trick Daddy's "America":

> You only got 2 bucks and give less than a f*ck – then you a nigga/ Got a nice home and a Lexus truck – you a nigga/ World champions and you M.V.P – you a nigga/ 4 degrees and a Ph.D – still a nigga/ You use your platinum card you need 4 ID's – then you's a nigga/ If your skin is brown just like me – then you a nigga/ Got a promotion and a fat-ass raise – you still a nigga/ You from the islands and your peoples wasn't slaves – you a nigga/ No matter how much your ass get paid – you still a nigga/ Shot by the cops at a traffic stop – cause you a nigga

...We engage in activity that other people might call anti-social. We don't care if you don't like it. We don't need your approval to survive.

...We may leave our biological families for the families we find in gangs who seem to better understand and support us...while providing the closest thing to a rebel guerrilla army we know.

...We're the first generation to have given up on hope. Some of us just don't care anymore, and we're gonna make sure everyone knows.

Can you think of any others?

Are you stressed out or miserable enough to have stopped giving a f*ck?

Are you dissatisfied or hopeless enough to say "F*ck the world"?

Either way, what can be done to change the situation?

Nobody stops "giving a f*ck" for no reason. If you understand the reasons for our hopelessness, you can work on realistic solutions.

Party Like a Rockstar

Party til the Cops Come Knockin'

Manuel was drunk off his ass. He had just worked for ten hours straight laying bricks for a new complex downtown. The specially-made bricks weighed about twenty pounds each and needed to be laid out with pinpoint accuracy along the footpath to the entrance of the main tower. Earlier, Manuel had gotten in trouble for dropping one of the expensive bricks. They docked his day's pay. Still, they paid him in cash that evening, so Manuel had money in his pocket tonight.

He'd already spent a good deal of this money with his brother on a few cases of beer, which they'd been drinking since they arrived home together. Manuel's brother also worked a manual labor job like him, as did his two cousins, who had arrived recently from Mexico without immigration papers. All of them shared a three bedroom house with their wives and children. It was cramped, but a good way to save money, which they could send back home to help out the rest of Manuel's large family.

As the night sky darkened, friends and family began filling up the house and the backyard where they ate, drank, sang songs, told jokes, and talked sh*t. Before long, a fight had broken out between two uncles, one fresh from doing a three year prison stint. No one called the police. But either because of all the cars parked in the yard, or the clamor of people laughing and yelling over loud music, one of the neighbors did. When the cops arrived, Manuel was so drunk he nearly fell over opening his front door for them. The cops decided to check Manuel's record and discovered that he had an open warrant for failing to appear in court. They took Manuel away in handcuffs as his relatives and friends protested. A few of the men were especially upset, but felt powerless to do anything about it – they either didn't have visas or had warrants as well.

Can you relate? You should. We're all related.

Examining the Mexican love for partying, Mexican Nobel laureate Octavio Paz said:

> The explosive, dramatic, sometimes even suicidal manner in which we strip ourselves, surrender ourselves, is evidence that something inhibits and suffocates us. Something impedes us from being. And since we cannot or dare not confront our own selves, we resort to the fiesta.

Deep, ain't it? Mexicans party hard cause times are harder. Makes sense. What about you? How often do you "escape" your struggle like Manuel?

Drumming for Justice

On September 9, 1739, an Angolan slave named Jemmy led 20 slaves gathered by Stono River near Charleston, South Carolina in a rebellion. His band marched to a local store and armed themselves, killing the two white shopkeepers. They then marched from house to house, killing slaveowners and their families, only skipping one man because he was said to have been "kind to his slaves."

As they continued down their path, beating a drum as they marched, their numbers swelled to 100 marchers. The rhythm of the procession was something like a cross between a FAMU marching band and a guerrilla army.

The drumming got a lot of attention. By the time they had killed about 25 whites, there was a large mob of whites trailing close behind them.

30 rebel slaves were killed in the ensuing battle, and another 30 that escaped were caught and executed within a month.

As a result of the Stono Rebellion, the Negro Act was passed, restricting Blacks from assembling in groups and reading, among other things.

But most significantly, there was a ban against Blacks having drums. After the Stono Rebellion, whites learned that drums weren't only used as a call to fight. For months before, drums had been used as a form of secret communication between slaves on far apart plantations. Through the music of the drums the message of the uprising had spread far and wide.

Music can be a very powerful tool for liberation…as long as *you're* the one controlling it. But what about the music out now? Whose messages does it spread? Will it help us get free?

Do you do music? What does your music do?

We Don't Dance No Mo'

West Africans have a very strong and rich dance culture. In fact, most of the dances we do today can be traced back to African traditions. Just visit any African dance performance and see for yourself. But over 400 years ago, white people were able to twist parts of Black culture into bullsh*t that would help keep us down, or brainwash us into forgetting the parts of Black culture that couldn't be twisted. So singing and dancing – once the favorite part of African ceremonies – became a tool that was used against us. Many Blacks were tricked into slavery by being asked to dance on European ships docked off the coast of Africa. The Europeans would even promise pay, but as soon as the Blacks boarded, the ships would pull off.

Once on the slave ships, most slaves would be forced to dance for exercise and the crew's entertainment. One doctor on a slave ship reported that, every day, "those who were in irons were ordered to stand up and make what motions they could, leaving a passage for [the slaves who were] out of irons to dance around the deck." Many danced on deck just to enjoy the brief freedom of being out of irons. The others who refused to dance were whipped until they got with the program.

And here we are today. Now tell me what's on BET. Same sh*t, huh?

"Though our hands are chained like they are, they haven't taken music from us yet. So that's how I'll fight. People tell me don't quit like everyone else. I won't have no fear."
Tupac Shakur

What's my point? Here's a riddle: What's the difference between a regular party and a political party? A regular party might get some bills paid. A political party changes the bills. I'm not knockin our love affair with music and dancing, but we can't lose sight of the bigger picture. The same way that our music helped us get free in Stono, it helped enslave us as well. Even today, our music sometimes pushes us in the right directions, but more often it pushes us towards bullsh*t.

"After the fast songs come the slow/ After the sad songs come some mo'"
Saigon, "I Believe It"

A lot of us escape into music and partying the way some of us escape into liquor and drugs. That's what rapper Saigon told *XXL*:

> After the partying and bullsh*ttin that people do in the clubs, they sober up and realize they still have these problems they tried to escape by doin drugs and drinkin to escape reality. That's all the clubs offer, is an escape from reality. Even ugly girls feel pretty around drunk, horny niggas.

He's right. Like the slaves on the boats, we're just trying to enjoy brief moments of feeling free. But tearin up 500 clubs won't get us free anytime soon. So I'm a fan of a different kind of party, and a different kind of music. If you're gonna make music, make fight music. Make rebel music. Make a change.

See, activism takes your energy and frustration and aims it…directly against your opponent. Regular-ass partying just takes all that energy and frustration and aims for nothing. And at the end of the night, we get back in our cars and return to being slaves.

There's nothing wrong with getting out your frustration. But true power is in directing your frustration back at the system of oppression that caused it. So you can live your life "White Linen Party" or "Black Panther Party." What's it gonna be?

You gonna fight or dance? Or can you conceal your fight *in* the dance?

**Unless you're putting in more work than play,
you don't have time to party every day.**

SI SE PUEDE

Back to Manuel for a minute. I included his story so that you could understand how similar we are, even with all our differences. But if we're gonna talk differences, here's the million-dollar question: What the hell, exactly, is a Hispanic? I'm not throwin stones at people who claim that category. I just want us to reconsider how we define ourselves.

I mean, I'm pretty clear on what it means to be Black. (See *Part One*, "Black is Beautiful") I also know what it means to be Chinese or Nigerian. Those are countries, and I know Hispanic ain't a country. Hispanic means "a Spanish-speaking people." Spanish comes from where, though? Europe.

Maybe it's me, but Daddy Yankee and Tego Calderon and all these other Black and brown Hispanic folks just don't look like Europeans.

So "Hispanic" can't be a "race" - it's just a language group. So what race are the people who claim it? Looking at the various groups of people who consider themselves Hispanic, they're obviously different shades of brown. But on the last Census, 42% of them reported themselves as white. Another 40% chose "some other race." In fact, 97% of the people in this country who picked "some other race" (and nothing else) were Hispanic. So Hispanic is its own race? How?

Sounds like an identity crisis to me. If you're "Hispanic," don't feel bad. We're all pretty screwed up on who we are, and what we should be. We should be. It's part of the program. You're not alone.

And when I say you're not alone, I want you to understand how deep I that goes. You see, Blacks and "Hispanics" have a lot in common.

I mean, sure, we've all been enslaved, exploited, discriminated against, imprisoned, and brainwashed beyond recognition...and we both get followed around when we go to the "nice" stores...but to truly understand our commonality, you've

Did You Know?

Just like in America, class lines in Latin America are drawn along color lines. Except in Latin America, there are more lines. In Brazil, there are In 1976, the Brazilian Institute of Geography and Statistics (IBGE) conducted a study to ask people to identify their own skin color. They came up with 134 self-classifications. Still, whites were the wealthiest and most educated. It's the same in nearly every Latin country. In present day Venezuelan society, notes Gregory Wilpert, "The correspondence between skin color and class membership is quite stunning at times. To confirm this observation, all one has to do is compare middle to upper class neighborhoods, where predominantly lighter colored folks live, with the barrios, which are clearly predominantly inhabited by darker skinned Venezuelans." Journalist Greg Palast noted that rich whites had "command of the oil wealth, the best jobs, the English-language lessons, the imported clothes, the vacations in Miami, the plantations." Researcher Luisa Schwartzmann found that, in Brazil, middle-class educated non-whites were more likely to classify their children as white. Why? According to Schwartzmann, the idea that "money whitens." Really? Is that what we all aspire to? To be like the ones who robbed and raped us into poverty and degradation?

got to go back at how it all started.

The impact of slavery in places like Puerto Rico, the Dominican Republic, Cuba, and South America is pretty obvious. In these places, there is a clear difference in the population. Some are very light, and near-white. Some are as Black as the people of West Africa. Most of the population falls somewhere in the middle range. It's easy to tell what happened.

In the islands, millions of African slaves were brought in to work while the native Indians died from disease or were killed by the whites. Hundreds of years later, only the elite Cubans, Puerto Ricans, Argentinians, etc. are as white now as the Europeans in Spain. The rest are brown and Black. This is due to varying degrees of mixture between the slaves, the native Indians, and the white masters. How? Rape. Duh.

Let's not forget that most of the Indians were dark brown themselves, and some of the earliest people here were Black explorers. If you don't believe me, read *They Came Before Columbus* by Ivan Van Sertima or *African Presence in Early America* by Runoko Rashidi.

Back to the present. In every one of these places, there are large pockets of desperately poor Black people. The only way you'd know they ain't from Mississippi is because they can't speak English and they eat chicken feet. Then again, that sounds like Mississippi.

Did You Know?

Revolutionary President Vicente Guerrero abolished slavery in the republic of Mexico in 1822. Federal shakiness concerning the abolition of slavery resulted in the Constitution of 1857 which conclusively abolished African slavery in the republic and, in a clause specifically directed to slavery in the U.S., granted freedom and protection to any slave that set foot on Mexican territory. Many Texans feared Mexican complicity in inciting slave revolts and runaways in Texas. These suspicions often led to increased repression against blacks and the Tejano and Indian populations who were thought to harbor runaways or incite rebellions. There were many reports of fleeing slaves seeking the protection of the Mexican army as it campaigned through Texas during the Texas Revolution. By 1836, a small colony of escaped slaves had emerged in Matamoros. The matter was important enough that the Texans demanded the return of runaways as a point in the treaty which ended the rebellion. The Mexicans didn't give anybody up.

In those places where the people with strong Black and Indian blood are the lowest class, the highest class is almost always the people with the purest white ancestry. In fact, in some Latin American countries, there are white communities that have never mixed with other people. Considering how some white people are, it's not surprising. There are communities of Germans, Spaniards, and even European Jews living in protected communities everywhere from Peru to Costa Rica.

But what about the Mexicans? You may have met a Black-ass Cuban or Puerto Rican, and probably plenty of Black Dominicans, but how many Black Mexicans do you know? Well, there's a story behind that, and every Black and Mexican should know it. In fact, every so-called "Hispanic" should know it, because if you see yourself as a "Hispanic," this story is perfect for you too.

Most Mexicans don't realize that a significant fraction of the Mexican population once looked markedly African. At least 200,000 black slaves were imported into Mexico from Africa. By 1810, Mexicans who were considered at least part-African numbered around a half million, or more than 10 percent of the population. According to Steve Sailer's "Race Now" series, everything from Mexican food to Mexican music has deep roots in West Africa. Even that damn song "La Bamba" has been traced back to the Bamba district of Angola.

How could Mexicans forget that during Mexico's first century of independence, more than a few of its most famous leaders were visibly part Black?

> "Seek justice from tyrants not with your hat in your hand, but with a rifle in your fist."
> Emiliano Zapata

Emiliano Zapata was probably the realest OG in 20th century Mexican politics, a poor revolutionary, still loved today as a martyr of the people. Something like a Mexican Jesus. And like Jesus, he is usually played by white men in movies. But even the best-known photograph of him shows him having clear African features and hair. It makes sense, considering that his village had been home to many descendents of freed slaves.

Did You Know?

In the early 1960s, the Five Percenters (now known as the Nation of Gods and Earths) were one of the few social movements that taught specifically about the shared heritage and unity of Black and brown people, and actually put it into practice. In fact, some of the first Five Percenters (like the first school of HipHop) were Hispanic. By the 1970s, Puerto Rican Five Percenters were spreading 'Knowledge of Self' in Puerto Rico, and by the 1990s, Five Percenters were teaching in Mexico. You can get an idea of what the Five Percent teach in another book from Supreme Design Publishing, *Knowledge of Self: A Collection of Wisdom on the Science of Everything in Life.*

Another revolutionary, Vicente Guerrero, or "El Negro Guerrero," a leading general in the Mexican War of Independence and the new nation's second president, was almost surely part Black as well.

Luis Echeverria, president of Mexico from 1970-1976, saw himself as the natural leader of the nonwhite Third World. The problem was that he, like most Mexican presidents, appeared to be pure white. So, he spent hours under sun lamps, trying to tan himself into Blackness!

When scientists examined the DNA of Mexican-Americans in Texas, they saw that everyone was at least 6 percent African genetically. But even though that proved that every Mexican had a Black person for at least one out of twenty of his or her ancestors, it didn't convince the Mexican people that they were, in fact, Black. After all, the "one-drop" rule (which states that one drop of Black blood makes you Black) was a big deal in the U.S., but ignored in many other places. Today, Mexicans and many other "Hispanic" groups see themselves as a combination of white (Spaniard) and Indian, ignoring their Black heritage.

"An ignorant people is the blind instrument of its own destruction."
Simon Bolivar

By "mixing up" the Mexicans, whites were able to turn the Mexicans against their own brothers. Mexicans immigrants to the U.S. often identify themselves as "white" when asked to choose a racial group, and politically, they often vote like Republicans – unless the issue is immigration. In California and Texas, the two states with the highest Mexican populations, many Mexican gangs are at war with Black gang members...and in some cases, even civilians. In many cases, the Black gangs and Asian gangs must unite to fight the more numerous Mexican gangs. These Mexican gangs, however, often take sides with white gangs, including racist and skinhead organizations.

Meanwhile, the Mexican is known in America as the "new nigger." He works for less than what he should be paid, for the "privilege" of being in the "land of opportunity." Unfortunately, this land doesn't offer equal opportunity. Even President George W. Bush once told an audience of Mexicans that America needed them so we could have janitors, street-sweepers, and construction workers. That's the American Dream for the "new nigger." And like the "old nigger," they've been brainwashed so thoroughly, they think it's all good. While Uncle Sam is using Mexicans to fight his war, do his cheap labor, and fill up his prisons, most of the rest remain asleep.

"If you tremble with indignation every time an injustice is committed in the world, we are comrades."
Che Guevara

There are a few Zapatas and Guerreros out there though. And I hope one of you is reading this book. And if you do get it, I hope you ain't too scared to tell it. As Zapata challenged, "Los que no tengan miedo que pasen a firmar." (Those who have no fear should step forward to cosign this.)

"El conocimiento nos hace responsables."
Che Guevara

Even if you ain't claimin your Blackness, I hope at least you're claimin our common struggle. *Viva la revolucion.* Now that's something I can say "Si Se Puede" to.

De noche todos los gatos son negros.

18 Words that Keep Us Down

I know you probably think I'm going to complain about people using non-words like "conversate" and "irregardless." Or maybe you think I'll revisit "The Names We Call Ourselves" and talk about how we call ourselves all kinds of insulting names. Nah. In fact, I understand the beauty of how original people create from an empty void. "Conversate" may not be a word in the dictionary but it's not what's keeping us down. If you think it is, you're a bit out of touch with our *real* problems, buddy.

There are about 18 words that psychologically affect us on levels we may not understand, and they do much more damage than a snob laughing at you for saying "irregardless." **These words position our self-image, and condition our minds for unhealthy states of existence.** Here they are, in no particular order.

Broke – Something is only "broke" if something's wrong with it. Is something wrong with you? Or are you just low on finances?

Hate – You can only "hate" something when you dedicate thought and energy to it. You can't hate something you don't care about. "Hating" consumes you with negative emotions, which affect you negatively, while changing nothing about whatever it is that you dislike.

Worry – Another unhealthy emotion. Are you "worried" (scared), or are you concerned?

Wish – Is there a Genie in a lamp somewhere? Are you at a magic wishing well? In real life, "wishes" don't come true. Work does. Plans do. Wishes are for people who don't work, don't plan, or don't work their plans. (Also see "Want")

Can't – Saying you "can't" automatically weakens you. But you've been trained to think of life in terms of what you can and can't do. Try to avoid saying "can't" for a day, and see how hard it is to think differently. In reality, because of the infinite potential of the human mind, there's nothing you actually "can't" do. (Also see "But")

Believe – To "believe" something implies that you don't have the evidence to "know" it for a fact. You don't "believe" you have two nipples. You know it (unless you have three). So why "believe" things will work out? Easy! You didn't plan enough to *know* if they will!

Maybe – "Maybe" is one of the favorite words of people who either hate thinking or hate making decisions. Either way, make up your mind and live in the affirmative. (Also see "Whatever")

Ugly – Words like ugly aren't so bad as long as you remember they're only your opinion. Unfortunately, people think descriptors like "ugly," "stupid," or "fat" are absolute values based on facts. Nothing is actually ugly. Some people simply choose to see things that way, while others may see those same things as beautiful. It's your choice, but always finding fault with things makes it a lot harder to stay positive.

Made – I chose the word "made" (as in "She made me crash my car"), but I'm referring to *any* example of people using the passive voice. "Passive voice" means when people say that something "happened" to them, or "caused" them to do something. Doing this gives away all your power. People who talk like this don't see themselves in control of their own lives. Don't say "He made me so mad when he kept farting." Say, "I became angry about his farting." There's a difference. First example – someone else is running your show. Second example – you're responsible for your show.

Could've – Ah, what a guilty word. But in life, there are no do-overs, so just get over it, learn from it, and move on. That's all you "can" do. (Also see "Should")

Want – When you say you "want" something, you automatically tell yourself that you are lacking something. That's the definition of "want" (to lack). So saying "I want…" subconsciously creates a hole in you that you now must fill. When you can't fill that hole, you feel like less of a person. When you do fill it, you realize there's never a way to satisfy ALL of your wants. This is how people end up with addictions! (Also see "Need")

Need – Besides food, clothing, and shelter, what do you REALLY need? Not much. You can survive without the new sunglasses, homey. Instead of using words like "want" and "need," be honest and say "I'd like…" or "I plan to…"

Should – "Should" isn't always a bad word, unless your life is full of "shoulds" without the actions that are supposed to follow. If you're constantly saying, "I should work on my credit," "I should wake up earlier," "I should stop takin that Promethezine," and you DON'T follow through…then you "should" stop talking and start doin. On the other hand, if you're the one always telling people what they should do, please make sure that: (a) You've got your own sh*t together, and (b) they want your advice in the first place.

Whatever – "Whatever" is what people say when they don't care. Half of the time, they actually DO care, but try to act indifferent so no one will know how they really feel. That's unhealthy. But not AS unhealthy as REALLY not caring! If you have a "whatever" attitude to life, one day in the future you'll be looking back, asking yourself, "Man, what ever happened to everything that mattered?" It's good to be able to let stress and problems roll off you, but it's another thing entirely to be completely apathetic.

Try – Whenever people fail at doing something, they love telling you that they "tried." Well, if you "tried" to pay the rent, does that mean you paid it? And when you tell your landlord you "tried," will he let you stay? Trying is a word for people who give up, because to "try" something usually means you gave it a shot and that was it. People who continue to work at something til they get it, they "strive."

But – "But" is another weak word. Example: I'm qualified for the job, BUT they probably won't like me cause I'm in a wheelchair. "But" weakens the strength of any positive statement you make, and sometimes it's strong enough to cancel it out altogether. Example: "My girlfriend would make a great wife, BUT she's leaving me in two weeks." Or "I want to make more money, BUT I don't want to work more." Watch how many times you contradict yourself with "but" and work harder on being consistent.

Assume – I'm sure you've heard that "When you assume, you make an ASS of U and ME." Um, ok. All I know is that assumptions can be based off facts, but usually aren't. People usually assume based on preconceived notions, or ideas they have before they've even gathered any information. And when you assume, you're usually only making an ass of yourself. Rather than assuming, ask.

Sorry – This one is a double-edged sword. "Sorry" is a state of existence, as in saying "I'm sorry" suggests something about you as a person. But what's more significant is that a bunch of "sorries" don't solve any problems. People tend to think that simply saying "sorry" is as good as resolving whatever is wrong. I always tell people, don't say "sorry," just make it right. On the other hand, our communities go through a lot of conflict because of the fact that us men have too much false pride to apologize to each other, even when we know we're wrong. "I apologize" goes a long way. "It's my fault, so I'm going to…" goes even longer.

Your choice of words expresses the way you think. The way you think shapes your reality. So don't pull yourself down with your words.

The spoken word is empowering. Speak up.

TRICKS OF THE TRADE

"Powerful people never educate the victims of their power in how to take their power away from them ...the ideology of our former slave masters cannot save us."
John Henrik Clarke

The first Christian missionaries to come into Africa were sent by the Portuguese to Benin (in what is now Nigeria) in 1485. Between slavery and Christiany, it's been all downhill since then.

For most European missionaries, their number one goal wasn't "teaching civilization" or healing the sick (as they'd later claim), but the spreading of Christianity. It's been written that "no missionary came to Africa to learn languages or uplift and educate the African, but only to make him Christian." Damn. Why?

Understanding the reasons for this goal will help you see why European missionaries were involved in Africa in the first place. And it will help you understand how to see people who come offering *you* "something for nothing."

I bet you thought the missionaries were over there to help. Nah. Their ultimate goal: The takeover by European political forces in Africa so that whites could control the people, the land, and the natural resources.

For most Africans, they saw Europeans coming among them as a way to learn how to build wealth, as Europe obviously had. (If only they'd known that Europe had gotten rich by exploiting folks!) Bishop Samuel Crowther admitted that the Niger Delta trading chiefs didn't want the missionaries to teach religion to their children since they already had a God of their own. What they *did* want was to be taught how to do business like the Europeans. This was the only reason some Africans supported the missionaries in Africa.

But most European powers had something else in mind. One writer reported, "Prominent British leaders and missionaries felt that the regeneration of Africa, which had sunk to such depths as a result of the slave trade and unfavorable environmental conditions, could be combined with **commercial advantage** to British businessmen." *Always* an ulterior motive. Keep that in mind.

It turned out that the land and economy of Europe made slavery much less profitable in Britain than the new factory system (like the North during the American Civil War). Because of the Industrial Revolution, Britain, with the rest of Europe soon to follow, lost interest in the slave trade and now wanted to "commercialize" Africa. And I bet you thought Europeans fought slavery and went into Africa because it was the "right" thing to do.

So Britain went from being the biggest slave-trader in the world to being the biggest opponent of the slave trade. Ain't they clever? By pretending to care about Africans, they convinced people that Christianity could "help" Africa. Once again, it was really all about money and power.

David Livingstone, one of the most famous missionaries ever, declared that – through his work – he'd begun "opening the way for commerce and Christianity" in Africa. Livingstone said the motive of his mission was to "lay a Christian foundation for anything that may follow," and that the "ulterior objects" of his exploration included building an English colony in Central Africa. There's that ulterior motive again! According to one author, Livingstone "set in motion events sparking an era of mission expansion which didn't end until the nations of Western Europe effectively spread their colonial nets, often with active missionary support, at century's end." Basically, he set 'em up for the takedown.

In every way, the spread of European Christianity was fundamental in the colonization of Africa. According to Ado Tiberondwa's *Missionary Teachers as Agents of Colonialism*:

> The European missionaries who went to Uganda and other African countries did much more than the mere spreading of Christianity. They also introduced Western education and **assisted their home governments in carrying out their colonial policies**. Both the Roman Catholic and the Protestant missionaries became deeply involved in the country's political and economic rivalries, **using religion as a tool**.

These European missionaries, armed with the gospel of European Christianity were – from the beginning – instrumental in the spread of more European settlers, European culture, and European government throughout Africa. Meanwhile, they actually *escalated* our problems!

In his *History of the Colonization of Africa by Alien Races*, Harry Johnston says that almost every white explorer to come into Africa brought with him priests and chaplains who began preaching Christianity as soon as the Europeans planted their flags in the African soil. But why was their presence so important? Tiberondwa concludes:

> The missionary teachers were agents of cultural imperialism because they suppressed African culture and replaced it with European culture. Similarly, we can conclude that since **the European missionaries helped to place the economy and the administration of Uganda in the hands of their brothers from Europe**, these missionaries were agents of British colonialism and economic exploitation in Uganda.

This wasn't just in Uganda, homey. This happened everywhere.

It was said about Cardinal Lavigerie of the White Fathers of Tunisia (a group of missionaries in North Africa) that "his presence is worth that of an army to France." Basically, the work of spreading Christianity did more to get power for white people than any army could.

So what kind of Africans would believe a pasty-face foreigner? Well, we weren't *all* kings and queens, you know. Some of us were losers, lames, and disgruntled f*cks back then, too. And that's who they targeted. The missionaries worked best with the "outer fringes" of African societies. Recaptives (slaves who'd been captured and later set free) and social outcasts were among the first to convert. It's always the losers and rejects that get with the "other side" first.

But among the common people, reactions varied. Some hoped to learn the business skills they believed would help them "make it" and get rich (under Western standards), while others simply came looking for a good time (complete with singing, dancing, and story telling). Hmm...people coming to Christianity in pursuit of prosperity...or simply looking for entertainment and enjoyment? Sound familiar?

However as time progressed, many Africans began to realize what a few outspoken members of their communities had been saying all along.

During the 1870s and 1880s, Niger Delta ruler Jaja of Opobo was certain that the missionaries were part of a bigger plan for Europeans to eventually take over his land. So Jaja openly and consistently opposed the spread of missionary work in the Delta. He refused to show them the routes to the hidden areas that housed their valuable palm-oil. But meanwhile, other Africans jumped at the chance to provide them with maps and free escorts. Once the missionaries found their way in, they quickly denounced Jaja's government and, as Jaja feared, encouraged the lower classes to revolt and overthrow him. Guess who was in charge after that? The Europeans. I know, it's sadder than an episode of BET's *American Gangster.*

Again, this happened everywhere. Cetewayo, a Zulu leader in the 1870s said, "First a missionary, then a consul, and then come army." In time, more and more Africans realized they were being scammed.

> "First they had the Bible, and we had the land. Now we have the Bible, and they have the land."
>
> South African saying

In the words of Richard Gray, "African reactions began to be marked by disappointment and delusions...The Gospel might proclaim that God was no respecter of persons, but His European servants were deeply conscious of racial and class differentials." Meaning, white folks may *preach* equality and democracy, but only as long as they're on top!

Kenyan nationalist leader Oginga Odinga noted that the European missionaries preached unity and love, "yet lived [apart] from the people to whom they preached." Sounds like those damn white boys from the suburbs who go around preaching to the hood.

Such double-talk and double-standards, along with the onset of European military and political domination, finally opened up the eyes of many Africans to what was *really* going on in Africa.

But by then, it was too late.

Do you question the intentions of people who offer you things for free?

How can you tell when someone wants to take advantage of you?

Beware those who propose to help and want nothing in return. Especially when they may have ulterior motives.

Rappers Ain't Role Models

"The great debaters debate about who's the greatest MCs
Subject matter don't matter because the verse is empty
No food for thought, nothing for the brain to digest
So I guess it'd be about who can jive talk the best...
I'd be a liar if I wasn't sick and tired of this mess"
Big Boi, "Something's Gotta Give"

Rappers ain't been saying much for years now. Occasionally someone will surprise you by stepping out of the norm and saying something that makes you think about our world, but it's rare...and it's not consistent. Every mainstream album has about one positive or socially-relevant track, and the rest of the album is promoting bullsh*t. The rappers who *are* consistent with socially conscious material, however, ain't exactly what's hot in the streets. And maybe it's cause a lot of them are plain corny. But what happens to artists who *can* relate well to what the streets like, and *want* to deliver music that is actually REAL?

Why is it that popular artists almost never say anything that will help better the streets? It's almost like they're being held back from saying what needs to be said.

Even Russell Simmons was worried about the state of hip hop when he said: "I do wonder if there's enough diversity, 'cause I pulled the top 10 [hiphop] records for the year, and they're all f*ckin' dance records. Nobody's saying nothing. 'Put Some D's on It'? What's that?"

It's ironic then, that even the rapper behind "Throw Some D's" felt the same way. In a recent interview, Rich Boy said:

> It's in an era where songs that are playing aren't head-banging. It's more of a certain feel-good party song revolving around a dance move, where

> artists like Tupac used to talk about deep topics, world issues, racial profiling and things of that nature.

But is it that rappers are just too ignorant to do things differently? Or do they have their reasons? Maybe it's what happened to political-minded thugs like Tupac (see page "Tupac Lives") and Soulja Slim (see "Soulja 4 Life"). Then there's all the artists that just can't make it big until they make a bullsh*t pop song. Both David Banner and Jim Jones have spoken about the fact that they really want to rap about reality, but they have to make songs about nonsense to make money and keep people listening! As Jay-Z says on "Ignorant Sh*t":

> Y'all niggas got me really confused out there. I make "Big Pimpin" or "Give It 2 Me" – one of those – y'all hail me as the greatest writer of the 21st Century. I make some thought-provoking sh*t – y'all question whether he falling off…

So Jay continues, rapping, "C'mon, I got that ignorant sh*t you need/ Nigga, f*ck, sh*t, ass, bitch, trick plus weed/ I'm only trying to give you what you want/ Nigga, f*ck, sh*t, ass, bitch, you like it don't front" Young Jeezy says the same thing on "Crazy World," where he raps, "They want that young sh*t, that dumb sh*t/ That 'Where you from?' sh*t/ That ride-around-your-hood-all-day-with-your-gun sh*t."

Even T.I. – who describes himself as a "living revolutionary" – told *Vibe* magazine about his attitude towards making socially-conscious music:

> If I knew that there was more of a demand for songs like these, then that's what I would do. I'm only gonna make songs that the market supports…I can rap simple, I can be complex. I can do whatever I want to do. The thing is, to sell records you have to reach everybody…This is a business, brah. I'm not gonna cut off my nose to spite my face. Some of my best songs most of my fans have never even heard. For your own self-gratification, you make the songs you want to make around those other songs. You get them in where you can, but I'm not fixing to block my blessings.

T.I. is not alone with this attitude. Rappers don't want to held up as role models or educators. They usually run from that responsibility like a 17-year-old babydaddy. But can we really be mad at them? They're just speaking on what's real for them, right? Well, maybe not. Or haven't you learned anything from 50 Cent and all the other well-known imposters?

"Music is supposed to inspire…so how come we ain't gettin' no higher?"
Lauryn Hill

There's a rapper comin out of New York – who I won't name – who has entire songs encouraging young brothers to start hustling, and all the benefits the lifestyle will get you…but his music never mentions anything about the risks it involves, or what it takes to avoid getting caught. There's no message in any of his sh*t. The irony is that someone like him should be the first person to speak on risks, considering that he had a hit out on his head over $40,000 worth of weed that he never delivered to a Pennsylvania crew. Worst of all, I hear he's broke anyway.

So if the popular rappers are fakes, and the real gangsters are broke…when's the truth gonna be popular again?

The good thing is, everyone isn't fooled. Rap game vet Pimp C gave an interview to Hot 107.9 on July 26, clarifying some very strong comments he made about the industry in *Ozone Magazine*:

> You know why I'm mad? Let me tell you why I'm mad. I'm mad because everybody on these records lyin.' Everybody lyin…C'mon mayn, at the end of these records we listenin to, we don't get nothin out of em no more. We don't get no social commentary, we ain't getting no kind of knowledge out these records. Everybody just talkin bout how many chains they got on and how much dope they sold. But the truth of the matter is this: I don't believe you! Cause I know you, dude, and I know you didn't sell no dope.

In addition to the fake drug dealers and the lack of social commentary in our music, Pimp C also addressed what the game, heavy on dope and bling, was missing:

> Cause these kids listenin to us and lookin up to us – cause a lot of em don't have no father figure in they house – and every record you get on, you lyin bout some dope…If you gon talk about some squares, and talk about the drug game, then you need to talk about the bad side of it too. What about when you get busted and you go to jail? What about when your mama and your wife and your kids is cryin cause they at home and you in prison in a cell? What about that part of the dope game? Everybody talkin bout how many cars and how many jewels they gon buy, and how many squares comin off…but ain't nobody talkin bout the other side of it. So if you gon talk about that, you gotta talk about both sides.

"God, I know that we wrong
God, I know I shouldn't talk about Moet in all of my songs
I know these kids are listening, I know I'm here for a mission
But it's so hard to get 'em when 22 rims all glistenin"
David Banner, "Cadillacs on 22s"

Pimp even dug into one of the dirtiest sides of the industry – the side Terrance Dean would later reveal in *Hiding in Hip Hop*. If you didn't know, many of the most powerful people in hip hop, Black and white, are gay or bisexual. The author of *Why do Black Men Date White Women?* even relates the following:

> One well-known member of the hip-hop elite was overheard saying that he has sex with guys not because he is gay and likes it, but because as long as the person lives, "he will always know he was f*cked in the ass;

> no matter how big he gets, I will always have that over him, I own that motherf*cker forever.

After talking with a few industy heads, I've learned that there are at least *eight to ten* major players who could have made this exact comment, as it describes *exactly* how they get down. And that's not including Chris Stokes! Pimp C, an industry veteran, knew much more than he told:

> It was a bunch of things I could have said about a bunch of people, and I could have really, really digged and hurt some feelings. Now, don't you know that? Cause I know who the gay rappers is! I know who let them models stick them dildos in em, and I know who did what, where, when, and why!

But rather than naming names, Pimp C finished the interview by promising to spark a movement that would change the course of hip hop – for the sake of all Black people:

> Somebody gotta do it. But guess what, you think anybody that [told the truth] thought that [the people] was gon like it? Don't nobody like medicine. It don't taste good. They just want a whole bunch of the same old sh*t, everybody lickin each other booty and bein cowards. But guess what, I'm taking a stance against the cowards. I'm takin a stance against the liars, and I'm tellin you we need to stop doin all this negative sh*t. And anybody got somethin to say bout me...you can come see me. I'll give you my address. We can box it out, pop it out, stab it out, or talk it out.

Pimp C promised that he would change the game if no one else would. Less than five months after this interview, the great Pimp C was found expired in a hotel bed in California. He was found dead due to complications from a sleeping sickness. Yeah, right. And Johnnie Cochrane *suddenly* got cancer...while preparing a fight for reparations.

What really happened to Pimp C?

Why would it be *that* dangerous to reveal the truth about the music industry?

Now who's going to tell the truth?

Did You Know?

While we're on the topic of entertainers with messages, it's only right we recognize Michael Jackson. Sure, he had serious issues with his appearance, but so does Lil Kim, Sammy Sosa, and probably a few of your cousins too. But unlike them, Mike was about something. People don't know he gave millions to Africa, millions to fund Black scholarships, and millions to Black organizations. He might have looked white, but all of his closest friends know he "thought" Black. And that was the problem. Mike owned the rights to half of Sony's catalog, including the Beatles, some Elvis and even Eminem. And he wouldn't give it up. But he was giving Black artists their rights back! This was too much. They tried to break him with those bogus charges most of us believed. (Google it...all of it was fake. Even the main kid who accused him admitted he was lying...and then his pops killed himself.) But Mike still didn't relent. And he started speaking on it. When he started studying Islam...well, we know what happened next.

Rappers ain't here to teach you sh*t. Find your inspiration somewhere real.

MIXTAPE MESSIAH

"If I am not for myself, who will be for me? If I am not for others, what am I? And if not now, when?"
Rabbi Hillel (30 BC – 9 AD)

"Messiah" is the title given to one who can save the world. In Jesus' times, many believed he was that one. In the 1960's the FBI believed that a "Black messiah" would rise up out of the ghetto and lead the people to revolution. They even created the CoIntelPro program to try to prevent that from happening. The way I see it, anyone can be a messiah, just as anyone can be a savior. First, you save yourself. Then you can save everyone else. However, many of us, once we've saved ourselves, forget about anyone else. In the high-paid industries of sports and entertainment, there's a lot of rich people who don't use their power to "save." A few are different.

"Still tryin to find a way to accept
That ain't a way I can help nobody till I save myself
Technically, I'm still a slave myself
I gotta climb out the grave myself"
T.I., "Prayin for Help"

Houston rapper Chamillionaire made so much money off the ringtones for "Ridin Dirty" alone (over 4 million sales), his new album didn't even need to sell. So he went out on a limb. He decided to keep the *Ultimate Victory* album absolutely clean (no cursing, no sexual references, no violence and free of the "n-word"). That's why his album became the first mainstream "hardcore rap" album not to wear a "Parental Advisory" label. In fact, even children's radio stations like *Radio Disney* began playing his new singles off this album.

Why did he do it? He says he looked at the trends in hiphop and decided it was time to make a change. He made the decision to cut the "n-word" after hearing too many white fans rap along (with *every* word) during the concerts for his last album. *Ultimate Victory* received good reviews across the board. It wasn't soft, and it wasn't pop. The beats were hard, the lyrics were sharp, and instead of wasting time on the "same ol, same ol," Cham addressed some real social issues. But with today's industry, that's almost a form of suicide. As David Banner said in "So Special," "Damn…and I sure miss Pac/ Ever since that boy died, all the rappers done stopped/ talkin bout real sh*t, but if they don't, their records flop."

Chamillionaire, the "Mixtape Messiah" was trying to "save" hiphop, and was willing to give his life (record sales) to do it. So what if he didn't go platinum? He didn't have to. According to *Forbes* magazine, he was the 18th highest paid rapper in 2007, worth at least $11 million.

"Determined to be the best, not lookin back at regrets
How many people you blessed is how you measure success"
Rick Ross, "Shot to the Heart"

It's really not that hard to do what you know is right. We just make it seem harder than it is. We fill ourselves with doubts, and we fail to be who we could. We're more worried about falling back in that hole than helping other people out of it. I give a lot of credit to people like Chamillionaire, who ain't scared to do what needs to be done.

What are you doing to help people who need it?

How can you help yourself into a position that makes doing so easier?

Save yourself. Then save others.

SUPREME THE ASSHOLE ON "SELFISH-ASS MOTHAF*CKAS"

Some of y'all mothaf*ckas only care about yourselves. If you were given the choice to save your own life by pushing a little red button that killed a million Chinese babies, you'd probably push that button. Then you'd die a few years later anyway, probably over some dumb sh*t.

In a world where all of our lives are connected, you're that mothaf*cka that's f*ckin sh*t up for everybody. You were that kid that never felt sorry for anybody. You probably stuck firecrackers up cats' butts and molested your little sister. There's a word for that sh*t: Sociopath.

White sociopaths grow up to be serial killers, but Black ones become drug kingpins and serial rapists. If you're the type of person who only cares about yourself, you've got two choices: (1) Change how you look at people and life, and start caring, giving, and doing for others, or (2) Stick your dick in a light socket and do us all a favor.

13 TIPS ON MONEY MANAGEMENT

Are You Bad with Money?

"And niggas buying sh*t now they can't even pronounce
Done f*cked up so much money, sh*t, can't even count"
Plies, "Worth Goin Fed Fo"

- ❑ Do you go to the mall/shopping every weekend?
- ❑ Do your friends influence your spending?
- ❑ Do you buy things that you want, but really don't need?
- ❑ Do you always seem to need more stuff than you can afford?
- ❑ Do you have a million better things to do than to plan what you are going to be doing ten years from now?
- ❑ Do you sometimes find yourself wishing you hadn't spent money on something?
- ❑ Do you find yourself wishing you'd saved more money?
- ❑ Do you borrow money often?
- ❑ Do you lend money to unreliable people?

❑ Are there some loans or accounts you just don't plan on paying?
❑ Do you often scrape by "from check to check"?

If you checked off two or more of these questions, you have money problems. What can you do about it? Well there's several books you can read in addition to this one, but the most important rule is this: You have to MANAGE your money wisely. That means you need to plan, budget, and save.

How to Start Managing your Money

"I hate to have to be the one to say, 'I told ya'
Lord knows I can't wait 'til this recession's over…
It was all good a week ago – Young, the big tipper
Grindin all week and threw it all at the strippers
Got me lookin at my stash like, 'Where the f*ck is the rest at?'
Lookin at my watch like it's a bad investment
Speakin of investments, we talkin investments
My re-up money, yeah, I'm tryin to invest it"
Young Jeezy, "Circulate"

I wish somebody would've given me this list ten years ago:

1. Create a budget. Calculate how much you MUST spend every month on bills, transportation, food (that's big), and other expenses. Factor in unexpected expenses, and a small set-aside for entertainment and clothes. But keep purchases like new clothes down to a minimum. Use your budget to figure out how much you need to make per month to live comfortably. Be realistic.

Did You Know?

There are alternatives to greed and exploitation in business? Supreme Design Publishing is one example of how a business can be successful, ethical, and socioeconomically responsible at the same time. Our business structure is a profit-sharing web instead of a capitalist pyramid. Every one of our stakeholders, from our street hustlers to our online promoters, has the same profit-earning potential. We replace all the paper we consume by planting trees. We use open source software like Ubuntu and OpenOffice. We partner extensively with nonprofits serving at-risk youth. We make sure the Black bookstores eat first. And we make money doing it.

2. Stick to your budget. Don't spend more than you have allocated. If you do, make sure you are spending money you already have, not money you PLAN to have.

3. Never spend what you don't have. Nothing is guaranteed. And life gets rough when you're in debt.

4. Avoid being L.O.C.ed out. (Living On Credit). You don't need more than one credit card, and if you have one, don't abuse it. Bad credit sticks with you for years like an STD. And the same way, it runs a lot of people off. So be careful, and only spend what you can afford to pay THAT month.

5. Date smart. All them dates and late nights cost a lot of money when you add it all up. If you're constantly taking women out, you're probably a trick. If you're just trying to *get some*, step your conversation game up and do the "Blockbuster night" more often.

6. Save. Whatever money you have, don't believe it's always gonna be there. Money comes and goes like the weather, and it's unpredictable. I've seen major hustlers become murderers when droughts hit, and it's bad business. Set aside a savings, and don't dip in for silly sh*t.

7. Stop paying retail. That means start hitting outlets instead of malls. Don't buy a car new; buy it used. Get your jewelry from a pawn shop and your furniture from a storage auction. Count every dollar saved as a dollar earned. Anyway, the first "brand name" your family wore was the slavemaster's name branded in their flesh with a hot iron. So get over that sh*t. Go to Marshall's, Ross, or T.J. Maxx or something. Or at the very least wait til an after-holiday sale!

8. Don't lend money to friends. Don't borrow it either. Family and money don't mix, so don't even try it.

9. Eat out less. Buy groceries. Learn how to cook. Any woman will be impressed, plus you'll save hundreds every month. And buy in bulk.

10. Learn you some math. Calculate everything in advance. Don't get caught by surprise when the bill comes, or worse yet, gypped out of money you didn't even notice missing.

11. Invest. "Save" and "invest" are two key words to long-term financial success. If you can't figure out how to have your money *make more money*, you'll forever be a slave to the pursuit of the Almighty dollar.

12. Learn from others. Find people who are successful at managing or investing their money and spend a good deal of time observing them before you attempt to do the same.

13. Finally, be responsible. Money don't grow on trees, and jewelry can't feed your seeds. So spend wisely. Ask yourself how any purchase you make is helping your or hurting you, or whether it's even necessary. A lot of the time, thinking about it a few times before buying will save you from "buyer's remorse."

No matter how you get your money,
you're powerless until you know how to KEEP it.

F*CK THANKSGIVING

"Intellectuals out to study the past, not for the pleasure they find in so doing, but to derive lessons from it."
Historian Cheikh Anta Diop

I don't hate everything. I just don't like bullsh*t. And unfortunately, our position as oppressed people requires for us to be lied to about 90% of the time. But here's a lie that EVERYONE gets told: The Myth of Thanksgiving. I normally fast on Thanksgiving Day, in memory of the millions of Indians killed since the first one. You can eat your turkey with your family, but I want you to know the true history of this holiday, because there are lessons throughout. Hopefully, those lessons will help you avoid the same costly mistakes in your own dealings.

The Lie

The Pilgrims left England seeking religious freedom. When they landed here, the righteous Pilgrims met wild, half-naked Indians, who – impressed with hardy resolve of the newcomers – became their friends. They learned to work together even though they had different languages and cultures. In October of 1621, the Pilgrim settlers and the Indians of Plymouth Plantation in Massachusetts celebrated their good harvest and had a feast together. They each brought foods, which they shared with each other, in the first Thanksgiving, a celebration thanking God for taking care of all of them. Now Thanksgiving is a wonderful way to remember all that we should be thankful for, and a reminder that white people and people of color can unite and be happy together.

The Truth

Before they left for the "New World," the Pilgrims were already in the Netherlands, where they were free to do whatever they hell they wanted with their religion. The truth is that they wanted more. And there was a Dutch trading company that was very interested in the money it could make if it sent a group out to settle this "new land." So let's be clear: The Pilgrims went with their mind on other things besides religion.

In a stretch along the east coast of what would one day become the United States, the Pawtuxet people had lived in peace for thousands of years. That is, until the English settlers began arriving. In 1614, an English soldier named John Smith had arrived and began taking Indians to sell into slavery in Europe. Another common European practice was to give blankets to the Indians as "gifts," secretly knowing what would soon happen to their new "friends," since these blankets were infected with smallpox. Since smallpox was unknown on this continent before the arrival of the Europeans, Indians didn't have any immunity to the deadly disease. In a short time, smallpox would wipe out entire villages with very little effort required by the Europeans.

The Europeans thanked their God for the Indians' demise. A colony founder remarked in a letter back to England:

> But for the natives in these parts, God hath so pursued them, as for 300 miles space the greatest part of them are swept away by smallpox which still continues among them. So...God hath thereby cleared our title to this place.

In 1620, the Pilgrims arrived. They were pleased to find the ruins of a former village of the Pawtuxet Nation. They settled here and built a colony which they called the "Plymouth Plantation." Only one Pawtuxet had survived, a man named Squanto, who had spent time as a slave to the English.

When the Pilgrims met Squanto, they were already sick and near starving. Since Squanto understood the language and customs of the Pilgrims, he taught them to use the corn growing wild from the abandoned fields of the village, taught them how to fish, and taught them about the foods, herbs and fruits of the land. Basically, Squanto saved their lives. Without his help, Plymouth Plantation would not have survived its first winter.

Squanto also negotiated a peace treaty between the Pilgrims and the Wampanoag Nation, a very large Native nation which totally surrounded the new Plymouth Plantation. Because of Squanto's help, the Pilgrims enjoyed almost 15 years of peaceful harmony with the surrounding Indians, and the Pilgrims prospered.

Did You Know?

Native Americans and other people of color have - for thousands of years - used natural herbs and vitamins to treat and cure most sicknesses and health problems, without the negative side effects of prescription drugs? For example, chamomile relieves insomnia, horsetail herb helps stop hair loss, St. John's wort fights depression, anamu relieves pain and helps with arthritis, and even garlic normalizes blood pressure and fights colds.

At the end of their first year, the Pilgrims (who also called themselves Puritans) held a great feast following the harvest of the food that Squanto had taught them how to farm. The feast honored Squanto and their friends, the Wampanoags. The first Thanksgiving was a day of the Pilgrims giving thanks for the Indians who helped them and took care of them.

However, the Indians who were there were not even invited! Actually, a few days before this feast took place, a squad of Puritans were after the head of a local Indian chief, and an 11 foot high wall was erected around the entire Plymouth settlement for the very purpose of keeping Indians out!

The feast was followed by three days of "Thanksgiving" celebrating their good fortune. Each Pilgrim drank even more than the daily custom of half a gallon of beer, and engaged in drunken acts of violence and sodomy. They were having a good old-fashioned European party.

Soon after this first "Thanksgiving," in 1629, the Puritans began a march inland from the shore. Using Bible passages to justify their every move, they seized land, took the strong and young Indians as slaves to work their land, and killed the rest.

They destroyed their "friends" the Wampanoag pretty easily. Their chief was beheaded, and his head placed on a pole in Plymouth, Massachusetts – where it remained for 24 years.

Do you offer your help to people who wouldn't do the same for you?

Are there people who don't deserve your help? Why?

You can't help everybody. If you try, you'll only hurt yourself.

The Pequot weren't no Pussies

But when the Puritan forces reached the Connecticut Valley around 1633, they met a different type of force. The Pequot Nation, very large and equally powerful, had never entered into the peace treaty negotiated by Squanto, as had the Wampanoag and the Narragansett. They were not interested in helping or befriending the white settlers. The elders of the Pequot had warned them not to trust these people.

When resisting Pequot Natives killed two slave raiders, the Pilgrims demanded that the killers be turned over to them. The Pequot refused. This act of resistance led to the Pequot War, the bloodiest of the Indian wars in the northeast.

An army of over 200 white settlers was formed. They also convinced over 1,000 Narragansett warriors to join them by using lies and deceit. Although they would later destroy the Narragansett as well, the Narragansett Indians believed that they were helping the right group of people. Dummies!

Commander John Mason decided not to fight a head-on battle. Instead, the Pequot were attacked, one village at a time, in the early hours of the morning. Each village was set on fire with its sleeping Natives burned alive. Women and children over 14 were raped and captured to be sold as slaves. Other survivors were brutally tortured and murdered.

"Assassinations, diplomatic relations
Killed indigenous peoples, built a new nation"
Nas, "America"

Indians were sold into slavery in the islands of the West Indies, Spain, Algiers, and England; everywhere the Pilgrim traders went. The slave trade was so profitable that boatloads of 500 at a time left the harbors of New England. Of course, all this helped lay the foundations for the African slave trade. As Ras Kass rapped on "Nature of the Threat":

> Stealin land from the indigenous natives/ Gave them alcohol to keep the Red Man intoxicated/ Whites claim they had to civilize these pagan animals/ But up until 1848, there's documented cases/ of whites bein the savage cannibals, eatin Indians/ In 1992, it's Jeffery Dahmer/ They slaughtered a whole race with guns/ Drugs, priests, and nuns/ 1763, the first demonic tactic of biological warfare/ As tokens of peace, Sir Jeffery Amherst/ passed out clothin and blankets to the Indian community/ Infested with small pox, knowin they had no immunity/ Today it's AIDS, you best believe it's man made/ Cause ain't a damn thing changed

The destruction of Indians in the Pequot War soon led to King Philip's war. And in 1641, the Dutch governor of Manhattan offered the first scalp bounty. I bet you thought that the Indians were the ones scalping white people. The truth was that it began with whites scalping Indians, and other Indians being paid or tricked into scalping their brothers and sisters.

The Dutch and Pilgrims joined forces to exterminate all Natives from New England, and village after village fell. Following an especially successful raid against the Pequot in what is now Connecticut, the churches of Manhattan announced a day of "Thanksgiving" to celebrate victory over the "heathen savages."

One colonist in Manhattan wrote, "There is now but few Indians upon the island and those few no ways hurtful. It is to be admired how strangely they have decreased by the hand of God, since the English first settled in these parts." Strange, indeed.

This was the Second Thanksgiving. Since that day, Thanksgiving has been a celebration of the destruction of Native people in the name of white supremacy.

During the feasting that followed this second Thanksgiving, the hacked off heads of Natives were kicked through the streets of Manhattan like soccer balls. This is the origin of the football tradition on Thanksgiving.

From then on, a Thanksgiving feast was held after each successful massacre. Each town held days of Thanksgiving to celebrate their own victories over the Natives until it became clear that there needed to be an order for these special occasions. It was George Washington who finally brought a system and a schedule to Thanksgiving when he named one day to be celebrated across the nation as Thanksgiving Day.

Years later, Abraham Lincoln decreed Thanksgiving Day a legal national holiday during the Civil War – on the same day and at the same time he was ordering troops to march against the Sioux Indians in Minnesota. (Check out Glen Ford's "The American Thanksgiving: Rejoicing in Genocide and White Supremacy" or Dr. Tinga Apidta's *Black Folks' Guide to Understanding Thanksgiving*)

In 1492, there were over 80 million Indians. A century later there were only ten million. Today, there are less than two million left. The native people felt like they were doing the right thing by helping these foreigners, beginning with helping them survive when the first arrived. Without Squanto and the others, the first European settlers would have starved and died.

Without the Narragansett, the Europeans would have had a very hard time defeating the Pequot. Imagine if only the Narragansett had checked the Europeans' history before committing to help. Imagine if they'd learned whatever became of the Wampanaog. But they had helped the wrong people. They learned that lesson the hard way. The Pequot were nearly destroyed...and so were the Narragansett. And so were over 70 million others.

How can you tell if helping someone will end up hurting you?

Would you help someone who offers to reward you, but who also intends to hurt your brother?

Make sure you check someone's background before you offer your assistance.

The "Help" They Received in Return

First, the Europeans gave those "smallpox blankets" to the Indians as token of "friendship." The Indians wouldn't be cold during the winter, thanks to the generous white people, right? Then oops, you're dead.

Then, the Europeans offered alcohol to help the Indians cope with the cold winters (especially since many of them had lost their homes), and also to help celebrate their...um, well they ain't have sh*t to celebrate, did they? And now alcoholism is a major addiction in what's left of the Indian community.

Finally, some tribes learned that casinos could be built legally on Indian land. This seemed great. After all, the Pequot Indians, who were almost destroyed in the Pequot War, now make about $9 billion a year off a casino built on the land where they once fought. But guess what?

Now, the Indians have two more problems. First, they're losing their traditional values and wisdom about man and nature. Instead, the new generation is becoming shallow and materialistic in the pursuit of more money. Not to mention that a bunch of white folks are now claiming Indian heritage to get in on the hustle. And now the Indians have another addiction after alcohol: gambling.

How can you tell when a blessing is a curse in disguise?

Be careful whose "help" you accept. Everyone offering isn't sincere.

One Night at the Bar

A drunk is in a bar, lying on the floor, and looking pretty bad. Some of the other guys at the bar decide to be good Samaritans and take him home.

They pick him up off the floor, and drag him out the door. On the way to the car, he falls down three times.

When they get to his house, they help him out of the car and he falls down four more times. Mission accomplished, they prop him against the door jamb and ring the doorbell.

"Here's your husband!" they exclaim proudly.

"Where's his wheelchair?" asks his puzzled wife.

You get it? It's a joke. The point is:

Everyone doesn't NEED your help. Sometimes, when you think you're "helping" someone, you're only helping to cripple them.

10 Reasons We Can't Come Up

1. "That's not my department" (Apathy)

An early supporter of Hitler during his rise to power, Martin Niemöller later came to oppose the Nazi regime. Niemoller's status in the world of the wealthy and powerful saved him until 1937, when he too was imprisoned by the Nazis. His poem "First They Came" can teach *us* a lot about the consequences of apathy:

> First they came for the Communists – but I was not a communist so I did not speak out.
>
> Then they came for the Socialists and the Trade Unionists – but I was neither, so I did not speak out.
>
> Then they came for the Jews – but I was not a Jew so I did not speak out.
>
> And when they came for me, there was no one left to speak out for me.

If you're not doing anything to help save the rest of us, who will be left to save you? Well, Dr. King said, "Injustice anywhere is a threat to justice everywhere." So why is it so hard for us to pick up a fight that we feel is not ours? Sure thousands of people came out for Jena 6, but how often does that happen? And how many of those people were willing to go to jail to fight for those boys? But think about it on a personal level. When is the last time that YOU stopped a crime or injustice from happening? I don't mean sicking the cops on someone either. Do you fight on behalf of others, or do you sit by idly while people are done wrong? I know a lot of tough guys who wouldn't think to stop someone from snatching an old lady's purse, and much less to give up their seat on the bus for her. The Jews today teach their children "Help another Jew," but do we teach the same for our own?

Or do we teach our children that it's every man for themselves?

Here's two quotes that make a lot of sense to me. Properly applied, the "golden rule" could change a lot of our lives.

If you're concerned about others, it makes immediate sense. Just don't underestimate the importance of even the smallest gestures of consideration. As inspirational author Leo Buscaglia has said:

> Too often we underestimate the power of a touch, a smile, a kind word, a listening ear, an honest compliment, or the smallest act of caring, all of which have the potential to turn a life around.

But even if you're only thinking about yourself, don't forget that there are studies proving how acts of kindness and generosity actually improve the mental and physical well-being of the people doing them. Tenzin Gyatso, the 14th Dalai Lama, has said:

> The greatest degree of inner tranquility comes from the development of love and compassion. The more we care for the happiness of others, the greater is our own sense of well-being.

So, the next time you see someone needing a hand, or simply an ear, what are you gonna do?

Take responsibility for yourself AND others. "We" instead of "I"

---

2. "I'll get to it later" (Procrastination)

I guess if you're the type of person who's used to getting a check a certain time every month, you won't have too much of an independent hustler grind in you. No, you're on their clock, and you've been conditioned to wait on them. So the idea of being a "go-getter" may be foreign to you. Ambition drives people to wake up with work on their mind. Unfortunately, most of us wake up with sleep on our mind. So when given the chance, we'd rather sleep than work. We'd rather lie in wait than pursue opportunity. And rather than seize the day, we let the shot clock run out without attempting a single basket. Think about it. What's on your to do list? How much of it did you get done TODAY?

Don't put off til tomorrow what can be done today.

3. "I'm mad enough to..." (Emotionalism)

In kwami k. kwami's *The Tables Have Turned: A Street Guide to Guerrilla Lawfare*, former special agent Dr. Tyrone Powers explains:

> During the time I was in the FBI, working intelligence issues, a report came across my desk. And it was in regards to going out and talking to African-Americans, interviewing them about intelligence issues, or crimes, and things of that sort, and a document came out of the Behavioral Science Unit at Quantico, Virginia, and **it said that African-Americans, or blacks in America, were an emotional people, but not an intellectual people.** And there's nothing wrong being emotional. We should be emotional. But what they were saying is this. That **an issue will come up. They may get angry about it, they may protest, they might hold vigils, they may hold marches, but then they will go away, without there being any logical conclusion to it.** But based on this analysis, you have to understand this report that comes out goes to almost all the intelligence agencies, to the police intelligence agencies. This is the way you deal with African-Americans, this is the way you deal with them, whether you're conducting an interview, or any other kind of investigation. Or if they're holding a protest, or if there's a police brutality shooting. Sure, they'll protest for a while, but let them have their protest, and they'll go away.

Like David Banner says on "So Long":

> Mrs. Catherine Johnson was murdered by police/ In north-west Atlanta but I don't hear it in the streets/ Where the anger in the hood for this old lady dying?/...And I got a damn question, why the city ain't pissed off? When I know yall heard shots and little lady got hauled off?/...Y'all gonna march? March to the motherf*cking cops' house, my nigga! Make these motherf*ckers fear something, cause they got US scared. They got niggas scared to go strip clubs, nigga!"

Banner's not talking crazy. In fact, our inability to enact prolonged political action, particularly in the field of active resistance, is a major reason why we rarely get the changes we need. Instead of educating each other on what's wrong and what needs to be done, we rally around empty movements, phony leaders, parades and marches, and the idea that we can sing, scream, or vote our way to freedom.

When's the last time you participated in a march, protest, or other political event?

When's the last time you educated someone who wasn't into politics?

Stop screaming, crying, and marching. Start working and teaching.

4. "Me too!" (The Follower Mindset)

Do you really think celebrities spend thousands of dollars on clothes? Only the stupid ones do. Most of the rappers talking bout thousand dollar jeans are getting those jeans FREE. Celebrities get free stuff so often that they don't have to buy clothes, cars, or alcohol if they don't want it. The companies send it to them for promotion. Even Lil Kim, who was notorious for bragging about her Versace and Fendi sh*t, admitted a while back that she hadn't actually bought an outfit in years.

But what about you? It's not like Bentleys are the most attractive – or high-performing – cars. And platinum isn't really the best looking material for jewelry. And most of that high-end designer sh*t is really ugly or gay. And you know it! But you're willing to follow along. Why?

And this syndrome applies to all kinds of trends. We see others doing something, and feel like it makes sense to do it too. But just because your rich white boss is voting Republican and smoking a Cuban cigar doesn't mean you'll enjoy those things. Especially since he's probably also propositioning gay sex in public restrooms. You gonna do that too?

Followers aren't good for much except being used by leaders.

5. "On top of the world" (Capitalism)

This one is related to the Follower Mindset. But what makes this problem unique is that people who are consumed by capitalism aren't always concerned with fitting in. They're just concerned with having as much as they can…whether it's tangible and material, or whether it's just a gang of money hoarded away somewhere. But whether our desire for wealth and power comes from growing up poor or being raised by rich parents, it never gets us anywhere. We typically don't use the money to help our communities, and we normally can't even pass the money down to our next generation. Meanwhile, we're exploiting and backstabbing others to get to the top of the dogpile. Not a system that works for former slaves, especially since YOU were the original down payment for the system!

Anyway, if it's all about you now, how did it feel when someone else was thinking that way…and YOU were the one who needed the help?

As T.I. says on "Live Your Life":

> Seems as though you lost sight of what's important when depositin/ Them checks into your bank account now that you up out of poverty/ Your values is in disarray, prioritizing horribly/ Unhappy with your riches cause you're piss-poor morally/ Ignoring all prior advice and forewarning/ And we mighty full of ourselves all of a sudden aren't we?

Selfish people lose what they get anyway, so share the wealth.

6. "Anything you want" (Overcompensating)

I remember when Baby and Slim first came out onto the mainstream with Cash Money Records. They were on MTV burning hundred dollar bills. And not in the way that Dead Prez was burning money on MTV to make a statement about materialism. Baby was saying he was burning it "because he could." Then he went on to talk about his solid gold teeth, and how he could eat something that was 400 degrees because his mouth was coated in gold. But listen. This isn't just a Black thing, as the media would have you believe. Recently, there was a news report about how poor people in India, upon becoming wealthy, immediately buy expensive items to show off their wealth. That's what you do when you're overcompensating. You make up for what you lack, or have lacked in the past, by going to excesses. But that's how we "burn out," so to speak. Whether it's someone from the hood blowing through money, a guy with a little dick trying to get super-muscular, or a single mother spoiling her child because daddy's gone…we're all shortchanging ourselves and others. Because we can't be satisfied with what we have, we do things we don't need to…and once again we lose. No spoiled child turns out good. Most super-muscle-men are still super insecure. And the newly rich are usually soon broke.

Do you *give* your children everything you couldn't have? How do you think that affects them?

Do you spend most of your money on things that make you *look* successful? Do you spend more than that look pays in return?

Stop trying so damn hard. Success doesn't mean excess.

7. "Whatever you say" (Blind Faith)

"Believe nothing, no matter where you read it, or who said it, no matter if I have said it, unless it agrees with your own reason and your own common sense."
The Buddha

Dr. King once said, "Faithfulness is walking up the stairs even when you don't know how far it is to the top." But that's not the kind of faith most of us have. We have what's called blind faith, where we don't CARE where the stairs go (up or down)…or if they go anywhere at all. We'll just go, as long as we're led. And that's one of the major problem with all of movements. They're

Did You Know?

Confirmation bias (or "myside bias") is a tendency for people to prefer information that confirms their preconceptions or beliefs, whether or not they are true. People can reinforce their existing attitudes by selectively collecting new evidence, by interpreting evidence in a biased way or by selectively recalling information from memory. This psychological flaw has been shown to explain "belief perseverance" (when beliefs remain after the evidence for them is taken away) and "illusory correlation" (in which people falsely perceive an association between two unrelated events).

mostly comprised of a gang of people blindly following leadership, without ever thinking critically for themselves. Critical thinking leads to questioning, and questioning leads to change. And most of these groups are not REALLY about change. They're about feeding the people's appetite for being a part of something bigger than them. Whether it's your fraternity, church, or civil rights organization, you should ask yourself: "When is the last time I questioned a decision? And when is the last time my questioning made a difference?"

Think critically and independently.

8. "One day soon!" (Salvation-Seeking)

"Quit waiting for people to come and do things for you. Nobody is showing any initiative!...Jesus is not coming to do this because Jesus is in you and God's in you. Am I right? Then why are you letting them lie dormant?"
Bill Cosby

You don't have to be waiting on Jesus for this one to apply. In fact, many Christians – thankfully – are not salvation-seekers. They use Jesus and the Bible as models for the good they do in the real world. Similarly, many other religious people are not sitting at home waiting for God to transport them to a better life. On the other hand, I know atheists, agnostics, and humanists who are constantly waiting on some sort of magical transformation to occur. They gave up on Jesus coming, but they're waiting for their lottery number to hit. Or they're not looking in the clouds, but they're looking online for that "perfect job" to pop up.

Did You Know?

If you're reading this book after 2012, you already know nothing special happened. Just like Y2K, 1984, and every other "magical" date when everything is supposed to change. While some are expecting salvation and others doom in 2012, the Mayans themselves have been clear that the year simply represents the end of a cycle, with no fantastic event expected. Yet the media and the so-called experts have gotten rich selling gullible people dreams and nightmares, as usual.

"The whole secret of existence is to have no fear. Never fear what will become of you, depend on no one. Only the moment you reject all help are you freed."
The Buddha

We were taught hundreds of years ago to wait on salvation outside of ourselves. In 1964, a brother named Allah started teaching young people to stop that sh*t. Since then, more and more people have started seeing God in the mirror. But there are still millions of people waiting on a magic day, a magic wish, or a magic being. It ain't happening. You do it.

Don't expect someone/something else to save the day.

9. "I'm straight" (Wearing the Mask)

When is the last time someone asked you "How are you?" and you said "Fine" even though you felt like sh*t? That's common for most of us. It's a programmed response. But it's deeper than how we respond to small-talk. We really do brush over our mixed feelings with a patina of ambivalence and nonchalance. Simply put, we act like sh*t ain't fazing us. Of course, some of us are emotional basketcases, but that's a disorder that needs years of therapy. On the other hand, our inability to talk about our problems is something we can fix quickly. First, we need to admit when something is wrong. Second, we need to be able to identify which parts of that problem we're responsible for. Those are the parts we can change. We can only change how we feel about the rest of it. But if every insecure woman could be strong enough to admit her insecurities, she'd have better relationships. If every Black man in corporate America could be authentic, less of us would have to be fake to be acceptable. And if we could tell our children what's REALLY going on in the world, they might actually be prepared for it.

How often do you tell the truth about how things really are?

Be real with yourself and others.

---

10. "But it felt right!" (Instant Gratification)

Instant soup. TV dinners. On Demand Cable. Strip Club VIP Rooms. Yeah them too. All of them are ways to satisfy our craving for instant gratification. We don't just want things fast, we want them immediately. We don't think long-term, so we have sex without rubbers, eat whatever's available, and say anything that comes to mind. Then we deal with the negative consequences, but we rarely learn our lesson. I think I understand the reason why so few of us can see beyond our noses. The way I look at it, if you've been conditioned to live without a vision for the future, or a realistic plan for how to get there, then of course you'll only think about the present moment. I mean, it's not like we've been taught how to plan our lives. We were never instructed on how to ensure long-term success for ourselves. The most we ever got was a set of useless clichés like "Believe and achieve," "Dream big," or "You can do it too!" And that sh*t is emptier than OJ's bank account.

> **Did You Know?**
>
> The marshmallow experiment is a well known test regarding instant/delayed gratification, conducted by Walter Mischel at Stanford University and discussed by Goleman in his popular work. In the 1960s, a group of four-year-olds were given a marshmallow and promised another, only if they could wait 20 minutes before eating the first one. Some children could wait and others could not. The researchers then followed the progress of each child into adolescence and demonstrated that those with the ability to wait were better adjusted and more dependable (determined via surveys of their parents and teachers), and scored significantly higher on the Scholastic Aptitude Test years later.

As Young Jeezy told *XXL:*

> Nobody ever won this sh*t. Nobody ever won life. You not gonna win

> nothing [thinking] like that. You gotta play the game to the best of your ability. You don't bring dice to the chess game. You don't play fast money. You gotta take your time and move your pieces.

But if you consider the effects our history has on us…oppression doesn't condition people to think about the future. Suffering people are just trying to make it through the damn day. So let's stop bashing our people when they can't think long-term. But at the same time, let's be real about how that's one of the main reasons we can't come up. It's gotta change. Hopefully this book provides some training on how we can begin thinking outside of the box, beyond our nose, and towards a future of realistic success. At the very least, think before you make that next move. Whether it's a purchase, an encounter, a statement, or decision, every moment has power depending on how you play it.

How often do you choose *quick* over *quality*, or "now" over "need"?

Stop rushing to satisfy your base urges, and work towards a bigger (long-term) goal.

Review

The principle for this chapter was **"Identify your Strengths"** This means: Find your power within, in life, and in the world…and focus on developing it.

Here are the principles and lessons we covered in this half of the chapter:

Critical Thinking
Be careful whose "help" you accept. Everyone offering isn't sincere.
Make sure you check someone's background before you offer your assistance.
Followers aren't good for much except being used by leaders.
Beware those who propose to help and want nothing in return. Especially when they may have ulterior motives.
Discipline
No matter how you get your money, you're powerless until you know how to KEEP it.
Stop rushing to satisfy your base urges, and work towards a bigger (long-term) goal.
Don't put off til tomorrow what can be done today.
Unless you're putting in more work than play, you don't have time to party every day.
Reality
Stop trying so damn hard. Success doesn't mean excess.
Don't expect someone/something else to save the day.
Think critically and independently.
Be real with yourself and others.
Rappers ain't here to teach you sh*t. Find your inspiration somewhere real.
The Power of Giving
Without guidance and opportunities, we're all bound to fail.

Save yourself. Then save others.
Take responsibility for yourself AND others. “We” instead of “I”
Selfish people lose what they get anyway, so share the wealth.
You can’t help everybody. If you try, you’ll only hurt yourself.
Everyone doesn’t NEED your help. Sometimes, when you think you’re “helping” someone, you’re only helping to cripple them.
True Power
The spoken word is empowering. Speak up.
Stop screaming, crying, and marching. Start working and teaching.
De noche todos los gatos son negros.
Nobody stops “giving a f*ck” for no reason. If you understand the reasons for our hopelessness, you can work on realistic solutions.
If you’re going to risk your life, do it for hope, not hopelessness.
The spoken word is empowering. Speak up.

J G I W V P E O P L E S P T F U I A K L
C B N M H X H T W O R G D Z G R I R G F
P H S I H H P E R S U A S I O N P G O M
I N A M D T G T L I S T E N I N G E C W
H Y U R F L G E W N N Y E P L X V Y E L
S D H Y A J I T H G I S E R O F Y F Q T
D O U Q V C K U K W M N H F O A B W Z J
R K V J H C T U B Z V O I Z F R R D X O
A R H R G E N E R O S I T Y S Z I I O B
W Y H T A P M E R G E T J U V S L O Q O
E Y R N M R Y O Y C Q A J O C U T Y G Y
T W Q E F D Q B N H J C M E X C E Q T F
S A W M T H U E M U V I R N T O D I O C
J L W T S V T W F G S N D S P F N Q O O
U B A I H E D L N C M U K T H U T U X J
C W B M P R G I B E V M X H M O R D D O
I N T M E W L U N G S M T M F A V Q A E
G S O O U A A T O F A O O Q G V O J M S
T C C C E K Q P X E H C K E D P G I G J
L I K H O I N I T I A T I V E C W W H X

6

The World Is Yours

EXPANSION AND DISTRIBUTION

"Learn to embrace change, and you'll begin to recognize that life is in constant motion, and every change happens for a reason. When you see boundaries as opportunities, the world becomes a limitless place, and your life becomes a journey of change that always finds its way."

Are you well-rounded? Can you function equally well in the business world and in the streets? Can you switch from speaking proper English to the current slang, or vice versa? Can you relate to children as well as you do to adults, or vice versa? Do you have enough talents and skills to change jobs or hustles without a serious setback? What about your money? Is it diversified? What about your friends? Are they?

Confucius taught that the best course for the righteous man was the middle path. He called it the "golden mean." In mathematics, the "mean" is the average. This doesn't mean you should live an average life. In fact, what most people consider average is closer to the bottom of the barrel than you'd think. The middle path is a perfect average because it not only requires moderation and balance, but you must step up your game in most cases to get there.

You don't have to be a jack of all trades (and a master at none). You simply have to be well-rounded. That type of distribution requires expansion. For example, if your goal is to visit every continent, you either have to cut down on the money you put aside for the club, OR you have to increase your income by working harder. You either spread it out evenly or raise the bar on everything. Either way, you become a better man.

QUIZ SIX: ARE YOU WELL-ROUNDED?

It's so important to be a well-rounded individual that I seriously I hope I'm not the first person telling you so. One-dimensional people go NOWHERE in life. So if you want to move up, you'll first need to spread out. Rate yourself on how well the following criteria describes you. Don't lie! Circle 1 for "Not at All," 2 for "Not Really," 3 for "I Don't Know," 4 for "Somewhat," and 5 for "Very Much." Get it?

	NA	NR	?	SW	VM
1. I am athletically capable	1	2	3	4	5
2. I am well-read on a variety of subjects	1	2	3	4	5
3. I am artistic, or I enjoy the fine arts	1	2	3	4	5
4. I am comfortable in the ghetto	1	2	3	4	5
5. I am comfortable in high society	1	2	3	4	5
6. I am comfortable around small children	1	2	3	4	5
7. I am comfortable around elders	1	2	3	4	5
8. I am comfortable around other races	1	2	3	4	5
9. I can fight well	1	2	3	4	5
10. I can dance well	1	2	3	4	5
11. I can speak well	1	2	3	4	5
12. I can write well	1	2	3	4	5
13. I can cook well	1	2	3	4	5
14. I can conduct business well	1	2	3	4	5
15. I can fix things around the house	1	2	3	4	5
16. I am good at math	1	2	3	4	5
17. I cheer people up when they're down	1	2	3	4	5
18. I give good advice	1	2	3	4	5
19. I can follow directions well	1	2	3	4	5
20. I can give orders well	1	2	3	4	5
21. I've been outside my country	1	2	3	4	5
22. I understand how people think	1	2	3	4	5
23. I understand proper etiquette	1	2	3	4	5
24. I understand street slang	1	2	3	4	5
25. I understand economics	1	2	3	4	5
26. I understand politics	1	2	3	4	5
27. I understand sports	1	2	3	4	5
28. I understand different religions	1	2	3	4	5
29. I understand the streets	1	2	3	4	5
30. I understand the opposite sex	1	2	3	4	5
31. I am good at relationships	1	2	3	4	5
32. I am open-minded	1	2	3	4	5
33. I have many different types of friends	1	2	3	4	5

Explanation

Now grab a sheet of paper and add up your total score. **Total:** _______

Now take that number and divide it by 33, the number of questions you answered. This will give you your average (it's okay, use a calculator if you need to). It should be between 1 and 5. **Average Score:** _________

Average 1.0 - 2.4 Either you just suck at a lot of things, or you haven't even given most of those things a shot yet. So unless you want to live the rest of your life like you're stuck in a box, it's time to try some new things...and get better at the things you're already trying. The closer you are to 1, the less well-rounded you are. Oh, and if your score was somehow lower than 1, your math sucks too, because that's impossible.

Average 2.5 - 3.9 Your average says that you're, well...you're average. You're a regular Joe. And some people are happy with halfway. But life has a lot more to offer you if you go that next step and embrace all those areas where you just "don't get it." Worlds will open up to you, as well as new relationships (both business and personal) that were previously out of your grasp.

Average 4.0 - 5.0 I'm impressed. The closer you are to 5, the more well-rounded you are. If your average score is anywhere in this range, you're practically a modern-day Renaissance man (or woman). Now all you have to do is put all that ability to use. And not all at the same time, because you don't want to spread yourself thin (though you probably already are). But really, what *are* you doing with your many skills, talents, and gifts? Is it working?

The Sixth Principle

"Expansion and Distribution" means: Broaden your horizons, spread your reach, and find balance in all you do.

What You'll Learn

- What we can learn about distribution from T.I. (no, not *that* kind)
- How the Native Americans *almost* stopped the European takeover.
- How African martial arts made it to American prisons.
- How certain common chemicals can affect - or change - our *sexuality*.
- What men and women *must* know to understand each other.
- Why the world is waiting on *our* revolution.
- Why so much of what we've learned about Dr. King is untrue.
- How to tell if the people around you are actually *against* you.

✦ Why men ain't men anymore, and what can be done about it.

KING OF EVERYTHING

T.I. is a hell of a distributor...of his time and energy. Meaning he knows how to spread it out. From being a teenage dopeboy in Atlanta, "running fast, going nowhere," he's come a long way.

After a series of best-selling classic albums and singles, T.I. has – like many other rappers – gone on to appearing in major films like *ATL* and *American Gangster*. The Grammy-award winning T.I. has also executive-produced film soundtracks like that of *Hustle and Flow* and started a movie production company with two films in development with major distributor New Line Cinema. Not to mention that T.I. also owns Atlanta's Club Crucial, and is working on the release of a print publication called *Dapper Magazine* and a clothing line called AKOO (A King of Oneself). T.I. has also stepped outside of the entertainment industry with his other business ventures.

"I'm the number one customer at my own car lot
You wanna know how much I'm makin, just imagine a lot
You know I'm probably gettin more than you'd imagined I got"
T.I. "You Know What It Is"

In addition to a high-end car concierge company, T.I. also runs New Finish Construction, which is building sub-divisions and an Atlanta shopping mall.

"Jail, I don' done this, rap I'm just havin' fun with
I could be a local joker, never have one hit
Nigga, New Finish alone'll get me dumb rich
While these rappers sellin' records gettin' pennies
If Grand Hustle sell any, I'ma get plenty"
T.I. "Motivation"

Of course, there are also the nonprofit charities that T.I. has contributed to, like the Make-A-Wish Foundation, the Boys and Girls Club, and single parent initiatives, as well as his own K.I.N.G. Foundation. In August 2007, when *Vibe* magazine asked T.I. about his many ventures, he stated confidently:

> Everybody knows when they're at their best. I can do better – but how much better can I do? Once you've been the best you can be [in one field], it's time to move on and start the growth again. Get in another field, another arena, and acquire the skills and broaden your spectrum. I'm eager to do that, but that don't mean I like rapping any less.

Am I saying that you should start a dozen business ventures this year? Of course not. The fastest way to go broke is to do too much of something you're not that good at to begin with. So start a business if you can, but make sure it's profitable and self-sustaining before you consider starting another. What I AM saying is not limited to business, however. I'm saying you have to expand your horizons. It'll take more than a one-hustle hustler to stay alive in a dying economy. Similarly, it'll take more than a one-dimensional man to have a successful life in today's world.

How many different things are you currently studying?

How many different activities are you currently involved in?

How many ways do you have to make money or secure your necessities?

Expand your horizons.

Checks and Balances

Finding Equilibrium

Every natural system on earth seeks balance. "Homeostasis" refers to this tendency (as opposed to any other homo tendencies). Homeostasis means that when there is an imbalance in any natural system, that system will try to correct it bring bringing balance, or equilibrium, back. Human beings are just about the only ones who don't give a f*ck about being balanced. We don't even eat a balanced diet! And I don't even want to get into how chemically imbalanced some of our brains are (see "Gay Bomb"). Human life is pretty imbalanced all the way around. Everywhere you look, the negative side of life seems to be overtaking the positive side of life. That's where you come in, buddy.

According to Mwalimu Baruti in his book *Mentacide*:

> We cannot make the mistake of assuming that all life, all of Creation is good. At least half is not. This is necessarily so in order to maintain balance in the Universe. Every person, every community, every living entity, continuously strives to realize equilibrium. When equilibrium is not sought, imbalance sets in resulting in stagnation and illness. Prolonged illness brings death to any life. If the good is chronically inundated and overpowered by the evil then it is the responsibility of the good to wage war against the evil to correct the imbalance.

While you try to find balance in your own mind, and become a well-balanced person in your personal life, make it your mission to balance out the negativity in the world. It's not like one man can't make a difference. All through this book, you see examples than one can.

The Numbers Game

Casper Holstein was a Black man born on the island of St. Croix in 1876. With his mother, he moved to New York City in 1894 and soon joined the Navy. After serving in World War I, Holstein could only find work as a janitor and doorman. However, he eventually became a messenger, and then worked his way up to head messenger for a stock brokerage on Wall Street.

Although he was only a messenger, he began to become familiar with the stock market and began studying the system and numbers. He was eventually able to devise a lottery system based on those principles.

Shortly before World War I, he devised a "numbers game" based on the Spanish game bolito. Players placed bets on a three-digit number in hopes of a large reward. The odds of winning were 1 in 900, and Holstein paid off at a rate of 600 to 1, which left him a sizeable profit. As Prohibition began, Holstein's lottery system became very popular and soon Holstein became known as the "Bolito King" earning an estimated $2 million from his lotteries.

Even with Madame St. Clair as his main rival, Holstein's income may have been as high as $12,000 a day at its peak (by today's standard, around $250,000 daily), and he was generous with his wealth. According to the *New York Times*, he was "Harlem's favorite hero, because of his wealth, his sporting proclivities and his philanthropies among the people of his race." Sure, he owned some of the finest buildings in Harlem, a slew of expensive cars, a beautiful home on Long Island, and even thousands of acres of land in Virginia.

"If a stick is bent in one direction, it must be bent even further in the other direction to again become right."
Ancient African proverb

But more importantly, Holstein donated much of his income to good causes like building dorms at Black colleges and giving scholarships, from his own pocket, to many of the neighborhood's artists, writers, and poets during the Harlem Renaissance. He even helped establish a school in Liberia, a home for delinquent girls in India, and a hurricane relief fund for his native Virgin Islands, as well as a dairy farm on St. Croix that distributed free milk to needy children.

Many other prominent philanthropists and community members didn't like the idea of Holstein's dirty money. They believed that great works like the writings and art of the Harlem Renaissance should not be bankrolled by gambling money, much of which was also tied to other crimes throughout the city. But others ignored Holstein's criminal side, and loved and respected him for the good he did.

What will they say about you when it's all said and done? Good? Bad? Nothing? Add up all the good you do (for others). Now add up all the bad you do. Subtract the bad from the good, and see where you stand. Oh, by the way, all the time and money you waste counts as bad.

**Even if you're doing wrong,
find a way to balance it out by doing more right.**

Why the Indians Lost

The Indians of the Ohio Nations were stressed out. It was August of 1794, and they'd just suffered the defeat of their Native American Alliance at the battle of Fallen Timbers. The crushing defeat devastated their hopes of stopping the advance of invading white settlers, who were claiming land further and further west with each passing day. After the British stopped helping the Indians and signed treaties with the Americans, the once strong Native American Alliance disintegrated. It was soon obvious that an alliance of just the Ohio Nations alone could not block the U.S. advance. It would take an alliance of Indian Nations both North and South to present any kind of real resistance against white expansion.

Tecumseh (meaning "Shooting Star") was born on Mad River, in Clark County, Ohio in 1768. A full-blooded Native American by birth, he was raised by his older brother amongst the Shawnee, where he excelled in the use of the bow and arrow, and "exerted a great influence over the youth of his tribe." After spending two years living among the Cherokee Nations of the South, he returned home to Ohio in 1790.

As a young adult, Tecumseh was known for his "remarkable coolness and good judgement in the command of his men," a reputation he earned during several small battles with whites. Tecumseh boycotted the treaty that gave Ohio to the Americans and refused to accept its terms. Tecumseh would later explain that such deals were invalid and corrupt. Whites were buying land from Indians who had no right to sell the land in the first place. One group of Indians was being tricked into selling another group's land, and these conflicts were being used to make the two gangs - I mean tribes - go to war.

Around this time, Tecumseh began to see the big picture of the American onslaught. He saw that it could not be fought by any alliance that wasn't made up of all Indian Nations. He realized that all Indian Nations were one by blood, were one in the ownership of the land, and that they would have unite as one to keep it. From 1795 until May of 1808, Tecumseh joined with a number of neighboring Nations, earning their loyalty and respect, as he developed his plan to create a collective Native confederacy.

Tecumseh's younger brother Lalawethika (Loud Voice) was not the calm, respectable leader Tecumseh was. He was known for his bad reputation, and often brought shame to his people with his drunkenness and promiscuity. At age 30, he had a near-death experience and told his people that he had seen the punishments to come for those same vices he was so well-known for, and for the vices of his people as a whole. He renamed himself Tenskwatawa (He who opens the Door), and declared that he had been "sent back" from the Creator with great power and a message:

> In the Beginning, we were full of thisshining power, strong because we were pure. We moved silently through the woods… That was our state of true happiness. We did not have to beg for anything. Thus were we created. Thus we lived for a long time, proud and happy.
>
> We had never eaten pig meat, nor tasted the poison called whiskey… nor hunted and fought with loud guns, nor ever had diseases which soured our blood or rotted our organs. We were pure, so we were strong and happy.
>
> But, beyond the Great Sunrise Water, there lived a people who had iron, and those dirty and unnatural things, who seethed with diseases, who fought to death over the names of their gods! They had so crowded and befouled their own island that they fled from it, because excrement and carrion were up to their knees.
>
> They came to our island. Our Singers had warned us that a pale people would come across the Great Water and try to destroy us, but we forgot. We did not know they were evil, so we welcomed them and fed them. We taught them much of what Our Grandmother had taught us, how to hunt, grow corn and tobacco, find good things in the forest.
>
> They saw how much room we had, and wanted it. They brought iron and pigs and wool and rum and disease. They came farther and drove us over the mountains. Then when they had filled up and dirtied our old lands by the sea, they looked over the mountains and saw this Middle Ground, and we are old enough to remember when they started rushing into

Did You Know?

Indian leader John Horse and the Black Seminoles created the largest haven for runaway slaves in the American South, led the biggest slave revolt in U.S. history, won the only emancipation of rebellious North American slaves before the Civil War, and formed the largest mass exodus of slaves in U.S. history. In the 1830s, Horse's people journeyed from the Florida Everglades to what is now Oklahoma and then across the border to Mexico, where they ultimately secured title to their own land.

> it. We remember our villages on fire every year and the crops slashed every fall and the children hungry every winter. All this you know.

Man, that speech was so gangster, I still can't believe that dude was saying this in the 1700s. Tenskwatawa, or "The Prophet," as he became known, went on to demand that his people give up the white man's liquor, his "filthy swine," the teachings of his "Jesus missionaries," and all other European customs. Like an Indian Malcolm X! With the oratorical skill of a preacher, he illustrated how the Indians' use of, and dependence upon, the white man's goods was a setback to traditional Native American society and had caused them to lose their ability to take care of themselves.

> "We used to root for the Indians against the cavalry, because we didn't think it was fair in the history books that when the cavalry won it was a great victory, and when the Indians won it was a massacre."
>
> Dick Gregory

He shouted to his audience, "We learned to need the white men's goods, and so now a People who never had to beg for anything must beg for everything!" His message was felt by many who heard him and his followers grew in number. Thousands more accepted him as a spiritual leader when, in 1806, he correctly predicted a solar eclipse. His followers came from the Senecas, Wyandottes, Ottawas, and Shawnees. According to Reed Beard, who wrote about the Prophet in 1911:

> He insisted upon temperance, preaching total abstinence from intoxicants. He taught reverence for old age and sympathy for the weak and infirm. He condemned the intermarriage of different races and believed that Indians should adhere to their own customs of living, especially in dress.

But although the Prophet's new

Did You Know?

Native Americans, after more than two centuries, are still being cheated by the government and U.S. companies. Oil companies operate at Montezuma Creek in Utah, which lies on a Navajo Reservation. The companies have under-paid the Native Americans for the right to their natural resources since the 1950s. Meanwhile, court-appointed investigator Alan Balaran discovered that non-Native Americans in the same area received royalties that amounted to more than 20 times the amount given to Native Americans on the reservation. These reservations are filled with natural resources, but the government allows energy companies to short-change the tribes. In Balaran's findings it shows that the government owes Native Americans as much as $137.5 billion in back royalties. Many Native Americans depend on these royalty checks for the bare necessities. The Navajo Nation has more than 140,000 members and is the country's largest tribe, but it is also one of the poorest. More than 40 percent of its people live in poverty while the median household annual income is $20,000, less than half of the national median. Navajo tribe members who live in trailers or one-room houses, sporadically receive royalty checks for less than 5 dollars.

religion was able to change the Indians' values and attitudes, he had "failed to arouse them to action." But where the Prophet was lacking in organizational skills, his brother Tecumseh took up the slack.

While the Prophet organized the spiritual unity of the Indian Nations with his speeches, Tecumseh was building a political and military leadership like never seen before, in both size and effectiveness. Other Indian leaders like Pontiac and Little Turtle had tried to unite the many Nations before, but Tecumseh was outstanding. General Harrison once wrote of Tecumseh in a letter to the War Department:

> The implicit obedience and respect which the followers of Tecumseh pay to him... [identifies] him as one of those uncommon geniuses, which spring up occasionally to produce revolutions and overturn the established order of things.
>
> If it were not for the vicinity of the United States, he would be the founder of an empire that would rival in glory Mexico or Peru. No difficulties deter him. For four years he has been in constant motion. You see him today on the Wabash, and in a short time hear of him on the shores of Lake Erie or Michigan, or on the banks of the Mississippi; and wherever he goes he makes an impression favorable to his purpose.

If The Prophet was Malcolm X, Tecumseh would have been Huey P. Newton. Tecumseh and the Prophet together built a confederation of Native American Nations that numbered in the thousands. But while Tecumseh was known as serious and sober, the Prophet was still known to be boastful, untrustworthy and unpredictable. Tecumseh learned to use the Prophet's magnetism to the best of his advantage, and continued to build his confederation. Similarly, the Prophet knew he had better speaking skills than Tecumseh, but would never speak in Tecumseh's presence at councils and meetings.

Tecumseh has been called "daring and far-seeing – a sagacious and able orator, a remarkable military chief and a successful negotiator." In a speech to General Harrison, he spoke as if he, too, saw the future:

> It is you, the Americans, by such bad deeds, who push the red men to do mischief. You do not want unity among the tribes, and you destroy it. You try to make differences between them. We, their leaders, wish them to unite and consider their land the common property of all, but you try to keep them from this. You separate the tribes and deal with them that way, one by one, and advise them not to come into this union...You never see an Indian come, do you, and endeavor to make the white people divide up?
>
> You are always driving the Red people this way! At last you will drive them into the Great Lake...The only way to stop this evil is for all the red men to unite in claiming an equal right in the land. That is how it was at first, and should be still, for the land never was divided, but was for the use of everyone. Any tribe could go to an empty land and make

> a home there. And if they left, another tribe could come there and make a home. No groups among us have a right to sell, even to one another, and surely not to outsiders who want all, and will not do with less.

Once again, this is how these dudes were gettin at white leaders 200 years ago! Some of y'all busters nowadays are scared to even look a judge in the eye before he flushes your life down the drain!

In the following year, on November 6, 1811, General Harrison and the Prophet, mutually agreed that there would be no fighting between their forces until a meeting could be held on the following day. But Harrison didn't trust the unpredictable Prophet. And he had good reason. Historian Carl Waldman writes:

> Although Tecumseh had warned his brother not to attack the white men until the confederation was strong and completely unified, the incensed Prophet lashed his men with fiery oratory. Claiming the white man's bullets could not harm them, the Prophet led his men near the army campsite. From a high rock ledge west of the camp, he gave an order to attack just before daybreak on the following day.

Of course, as with most religious rah-rah, it was a lot of empty hoopla. **The men obviously *weren't* invincible to bullets**. The battle was disastrous. The Prophet's fiery words were of little use on the battlefield, where strategy and numbers counted most. Thousands died. Tecumseh returned three months later to find his dream in ashes. Can you imagine the look on The Prophet's face? How would you explain that?

Do you know when to lead and when to follow?

Do you know when to take charge, and when to take orders?

Or do you constantly confuse your proper position?

Know your role. Play your position, and play it well.

Whippin' Ass and Feminine Ways

Black Martial Arts

There are literally hundreds of martial arts styles practiced across the world today. Many are traditional styles that are native to different regions on the Earth, like Escrima (the Phillipines) and Pankraton (Russia), while others are variations on already existing traditions. For example, the samurai fighting art of Japan produced the fighting style of judo, which led to the development of juijitsu. After being brought to Brazil, Japanese juijitsu was improved upon further to result in Brazilian juijitsu, the fighting style that the Gracie family used to win several of the Ultimate Fighting Championship competitions.

Lesser known than the Asian-derived martial arts are the martial arts of Africa. This is ironic, considering that the cradle of civilization most likely also birthed the first systems of military defense. Even the ancient Asian tradition of Kung Fu was brought to China by a Black Buddhist monk named Bodhidharma. Bodhidharma was born in the year 440 A.D. in southern India. According to Wayne Chandler in *African Presence in Early Asia*, he was a Dravidian, a member of the native Black people that dominated much of Asia at that time. (See *Part One*, "Outcasts")

Bodhidharma brought Buddhism to China, and founded the Zen school of Buddhism. He also taught the Shaolin monks meditation and strength and breathing exercises to help them cultivate their "chi" (life force). He also instituted the now famous Shaolin "temple boxing" that birthed modern-day Kung Fu and its many styles. The Shaolin Temple, with its Buddhist teaching and warrior training, taught manhood to young men from all walks of life in China. These monks would later become world famous after only 13 of them defeated the *entire* Sui army during one of the battles for control of early China. Now *those* were some *bad* dudes.

Further examination of the historical record reveals no shortage of traditional African martial arts. One of the earliest papyrus scrolls from Egypt shows a system of attacks and takedowns that has yet to be further explored.

Then there's Brazilian Capoeira, the acrobatic martial art used by Eddie Gordo in the Tekken video game series. Brazilian Capoeira was the fighting style used by runaway Brazilian slaves to defend their hidden communities. These maroons would teach the art to other slaves, who could secretly practice their skills by disguising the deadly fighting style as a dance. With all the spinning, flipping, handstands, and high kicks, the Europeans had no idea what was being taught until the slaves were one day jumping out of trees, kicking at their necks with razors between their toes.

Brazilian Capoeira's origins can be traced back the Kikongo of Central Africa, Angola, the Dahomey, the Fon, and the Yoruba of West Africa. All of those groups of people were taken to Brazil.. Few people have heard of Capoeira Angola, the original art, in comparison with its more popular Brazilian counterpart. However, many schools and centers now offer training in both styles.

Jailhouse Rock

But there is one martial art that remains ignored. It is called the first and only martial art originated by Black people in the United States. As a whole, the style has been called "Jailhouse Rock."

Jailhouse rock (or JHR) is a name which is used to describe a collection of different fighting styles that developed within the street gangs and prisons of the U.S. The different regional "styles" of JHR seem to vary greatly, with a common emphasis on improvisation governed by a specific set of underlying principles. According to Dennis Newsome, an expert on JHR, JHR began to adapt as prisoners were taken across the country into prisons that were designed differently. Some examples of the many styles of JHR are Comstock Style, San Quentin style, Mount Meg, 42nd and Closing Gates. Many of these styles of JHR evolved regionally in different penal institutions. Some experts think JHR developed from much older Black fighting styles, such as the "knocking-and-kicking" tradition of the South, or other African martial arts like Capoeira, Cuban Mani, Martiniquese Ladja, and Eritrean Testa.

But the most famous form of the style is undoubtedly the 52 Handblocks. 52 has been referenced in dozens of rappers' lyrics, and even Mike Tyson and Zab Judah have incorporated its techniques into their boxing styles. 52 was even shown in an issue of the *Punisher* comic book in the 1980s. Man, even Mel Gibson used some in his fighting sequences in *Lethal Weapon*. Said Dennis Newsome, who taught Gibson for the movie, "As a Black man, it makes me super proud, because 52 Blocks is one of the most sophisticated of the martials arts to ever come through this planet."

The Best "Man"

Perhaps the most skilled and dangerous practitioner of the 52 Handblocks ever, **Mother Dear** struck fear into his competitors. But Mother Dear was an effeminate, lightweight dude, and this was Riker's Island in the 70s! It didn't matter. Fellow inmate Tom Roof reported:

> The faggot would come down the tier shouting, "Dicks on the gate! I wanna see all dicks on the gate!" And if you didn't actually have your dick on the gate, he was knockin your ass out, takin that sh*t by force.

According to Roof, Mother Dear went after the most massive "thugged-out niggas and murderers," though he "really acted like a bitch. But there was a man inside, and when you made him mad, that's when the man came out."

According to Dennis Newsome in the August 2001 issue of *Details*:

> Mother Dear had a fight one time that was so famous, we heard about it out here in San Diego. He whipped eight [inmates] at the same time. And this ain't like kung-fu in the movies, where they all stand around in a circle and run in one at a time. They all had 52 skills, and Mother Dear knocked em all out. Man, the cat was ill. He made some people do some hard time – made em suffer.

Mother Dear, it appears, was of the "new" brand of Black males that we are seeing more and more of these days. These individuals blend their masculine "thuggishness" with feminine tendencies. Many are secretly gay, while keeping manly fronts, while others – like Mother Dear – are aggressive to the point of making their femininity seem like manhood.

Are wild emotions masculine? Is jealousy and envy masculine?

Is gossiping and backbiting masculine?

Does "manhood" involve fighting over petty things?

Does a man avoid dealing with problems and solving them?

Does a man care more about what others think than what he knows is true?

All of these are traits that we pick up by watching the many women we grow up under, many who didn't have *themselves* together to begin with. The only difference is that most women can get past these issues without bloodshed. On the other hand, we men may squabble like women, but we'll end up killing each other over words, while a woman will forget what her best friend said about her by tomorrow.

"I hope they mamas raised em, cuz they got bitch ways"
Lil Wayne, "Time to Give Me Mine"

In Mother Dear's world (prison) "taking" another man's manhood aggressively is still seen as "being a man." In the world outside, as long as a man doesn't cry or ask for help, he is seen as a man. Just as sodomy is often overlooked in prison, we overlook how feminine most men are in their reactions to life. As Ice-T said, "some of y'all niggas is bitches, too." Examine yourself. If you fit the description, it's time to start "straightening" yourself out.

Man up. Literally.

24 Things Real Men Don't Do

Now that we're on subject of manhood, I think it's important to clarify what a "real man" is or, better yet, what he ISN'T. Especially since 30 is the new 20, dumb is the new cool, pink is the new black, and gay is the new straight. Enough said. Let's go. Real men don't…

…base their manhood off how many times they've been shot or stabbed. Being shot a lot of times doesn't mean you're a tough guy. It means you're a victim…actually a repeat victim.

…base their manhood off how many times they've been locked up. Going to jail over and over doesn't mean you're a gangster. It means you're not good at what you do, cause you keep getting caught.

…drink anything with an umbrella in it. No explanation necessary.

...bitch and moan or gripe and complain. When things aren't right, either they make a change or they soldier up and deal with it like men.

...talk about other men when they're not around. If it's not big enough to step to him about, it's not worth discussing. If it is big enough to step to him about, then do so, or you're spineless.

...steal and "sneak-thief" from each other. If you're going to take something from someone, take it in their face.

...betray each other. When a "friend" goes to jail, you help support his family, not f*ck his wife.

...obsess over their clothes and shoes. Being fresh is one thing. Being a metrosexual in a muscle shirt is another. **Real men don't check each other's tags.**

...get their salad tossed. If I've got to explain that to you, you're so lost that I can't help you.

...neglect their families and communities. Especially if you're neglecting your family to get your salad tossed somewhere.

...gossip and spread rumors. Real men talk about business and ideas, not other people.

...do the dutty wine...or any other female dance. You should not be bouncing your ass in the club because *you think* the girls find it cute.

...talk tough and then back down. If you don't want to fight or shoot it out, don't try to be a tough guy. There's nothing worse than when a fake thug shows his true coward colors.

...hurt innocent people. Killing women and children is still some sick and weak emotional sh*t to do. So is shooting into crowds or homes and hoping you get your guy.

...stalk or harass women. If she doesn't want you, find somebody who does. If nobody does, fix whatever the f*ck is wrong with you and worry about pussy later.

...beat on women. Cause no matter what it is that you're mad about – it's your fault. Even if it's only for one simple reason: you chose her. Don't like it? Pissed off? Then man up or leave.

...arch their eyebrows. This pretty-boy sh*t has gone too far.

...cry in public...unless someone close to you just died, your woman just gave

Did You Know?

Sugar is just one molecule away from the chemical composition of heroin. One teaspoon of sugar reduces your immune function for 8 hours. Caffeine affects your body's chemistry and often does much more than simply give you a headache. In fact, 10 grams of caffeine is considered enough to kill a human being. Imagine what drinking a whole can of Mountain Dew (46 grams of sugar, 54 mg of caffeine) does to you!

birth, or you just dropped something really heavy on your big toe.

...bow down or kiss anyone's ass. I don't care how much money or power is involved. Real men have dignity.

...compromise their principles. The number one person you've got to be true to is yourself.

...die over pride, jealousy, envy, wrath, greed, lust, or any other weak emotional vice. In fact, real men work overtime to kill them demons.

...hug another man for longer than 6 seconds. After that point, it becomes inappropriate and you must let go.

...disrespect decent women. And 50% of women are decent, another 30% could be decent if someone treated them right, and 20% are too f*cked up to fix.

...share pussy. At least not at the same time. That's just nasty.

Hold yourself and others to standards that don't change with trends.

Gay Bomb

Hold up. Let me start this off with a disclaimer. I sincerely don't think gay people are twisted or sick. I know plenty of gay dudes and lesbians who are a *lot* more mature and responsible than many of the "no homo" advocates I know. So let me be clear: I'm not *against* gay people. I *am* against the proliferation of *homosexuality*.

Now I know some of you are thinking, "Supreme, you just said you wasn't against gay people. Now you say you're against being gay?" Look...before you try to put me in a box, I want you to read this and understand what I'm saying. Put simply, you can be opposed to a situation *without* hating the people in the situation. And you have to understand *why* I'm opposed to *our* situation. So let's move on.

I've heard a lot of people say it's not natural. I agree with them.

I've also heard people say part of it is natural. I agree with them too.

How? Because there's truth in everything. If you've ever read about human genes and hormones, then you know a man can be born with an XXY chromosome instead of the normal XY that makes a man a man (and a woman can be born with a similar defect). Everyone is also born with a certain amount of estrogen and testosterone. If you are born with the wrong amount (happens all the time), you'll *naturally* be imbalanced.

So yes, a male could *naturally* be a little more feminine than most, just as a female could naturally be more masculine. But there's no dick-in-the-booty gene. They've found plenty of chemicals that can screw people up in thousands of ways, but has science found a biological imperative for a creature of any species to mate with its own sex? No. Even if nature gave a child a hormonal imbalance, it's not "nature" that makes a man decide to physically *be* with other men. That's something *else.*

Many years ago, a psychologist named Alfred Adler came up with the idea of "Nature vs. Nurture." He said that some of what we do is a result of things we were born with, and those are things we can't change. But there's also a lot more that is caused by how we've been raised and things that have happened to us in life.

Just consider this: When did **people of color** start to embrace homosexuality? Recently. Even in places like Jamaica, Haiti, and parts of Africa where authentic Black culture has been preserved, how many gay people are there? Very few. Why?

Sure you can say, "Well, in Jamaica, they'll set a man on fire if he acts gay. That's why there's less gay people there." But isn't that true for anything out of the ordinary *anywhere*? If society didn't frown on people having beating their children in public, wouldn't more people do it? If we didn't lock up pedophiles, wouldn't there be more R. Kelly's and Chester the Molestor's? If society didn't say having sex with your cousin is nasty, wouldn't a lot more people would be okay with doing it?

Be honest. If it's all about what two consenting adults want to do, then what's wrong with incest? What's wrong with a brother and sister gettin it on? You can't knock it. What can you say? Nothing that can't also be said about homosexuality. If the white man told y'all that it was cool to f*ck your cousin, and put that message in all your music, TV, and movies, some of you would probably be f*cking your cousin right now. If not, all it would take is a few celebrities you respect coming out and saying, "Yes, I too am a cousin-sexual. And we need to stop these ignorant attacks on the millions of other cousin-sexuals. This incestophobia must stop! God loves us too!"

Let's be real. If you're 30 or older, even *you* probably didn't think being gay was okay until white people started making you think it was. But it makes complete sense *for them.* They've had homosexuality in their culture for thousands of years. It goes back to even the earliest days. The ancient Greeks and Romans were gays and lesbians. **Even the men with wives also f*cked each other.** It was the cool thing to do. Europeans even created celebrations around it! (see "Holiday Madness") It was one of the ways white people expressed the freedom bestowed by their wealth or status (eg. "I have the power to f*ck whoever I choose"). Out of the first 15 Roman emperors, only one, Claudius, was a strict heterosexual. To this day, most of the powerful white people in America and Europe are secretly gay. Just check out all the recent news about politicians getting caught having sex with men in public bathrooms or molesting little boys. I won't even get started with the church. Indigenous people of color don't even *think* like that. Europeans, on the other hand, make *holidays* out of it.

There isn't even an indigenous African word (in any language) for "gay." The last time I heard about any large number of Africans being gay, it was when white people were forcing them to work the mines in South Africa. They kept them away from their wives and only let them live with other men. Not to mention that these strong Black men were beaten and humiliated daily. Over time, these men broke down and began sleeping with each other. What does that remind me of? Jail. As Beanie Sigel said on "What Ya Life Like":

> You got 5 years in, neva been flown a kite/ You hearin' grown men moan at night/ They got you stuck in the can/ White man got you f*ckin' your hand/ Your wife on land f*ckin' your man/ What you know about no parole? Life in the hole?/ Life's cold, you be eatin' them SWAGs/ Guards on the nightshift, they be beatin' you bad/ The hardest nigga turned bitch, be sleepin' wit fags

It's called being stripped of your manhood. But nowadays, many of *our* young boys don't even develop a manhood to be stripped of. Just makes it easier, huh? Think about it. Most of our children don't know what a two-parent family is like…as they almost never get to see a strong Black man being a strong Black man…unless he's a criminal. So our boys end up tough enough to die or go to jail…or soft enough to be a "sissy." Why not? Psychologist Francis Cress Welsing argued in *The Isis Papers* that being gay was a Black man's unconscious response to living in a society that was ought to destroy strong Black men. It's a way to escape being a Black man in this white man's world *without committing suicide.*

On the other hand, there are many of us dying for acceptance, and the ones who can't find it in traditional support networks (like schools, cultural groups, and families), find that sense of belonging *elsewhere.* The hard ones get into the gang life. The soft ones get into the gay clique. And they find a sense of belonging…at a cost. In both scenes, our young men lacking guidance and direction turn to older men who *turn them out*, one way or the other. And the cycle continues. But most gay men don't see themselves as victims. They adopt the European message of empowerment through "sexual preference," and many actually find themselves inducted into a secret allegiance of closet homosexuals having wealth, status, and even a crusade to believe in. The cost? It's simple. Do you. Just don't threaten the power structure. And it works for a lot of people. Since white men and Black women see gay Black men as "unthreatening," they are often given more job opportunities and promotions than their heterosexual peers. If you work in corporate America, you know I'm not making this up.

Everywhere you go in this country, you'll get the message that it's good to "experiment" and have the "freedom" to make your own "choices"...as long as you're not questioning white America. You can do "whatever and whoever the f*ck you want" (literally), as long as you're not on no militant sh*t. You can fight for being gay, but you better not fight the U.S. of A. Because of this conditioning, gay Blacks identify more with gay whites, and identify more with the fight for "gay rights" than our collective fight for freedom – thinking that other Black people are the problem. We're not the problem. White supremacy is. What y'all forget is that most of the white people in power are actually closet homosexuals themselves. So who and what are y'all *really* fighting?

The truth is that white supremacy is against *all* of us. It just treats us differently, depending on where we fall in their program. If you're gay, you're being used too. Just think about how the women's liberation movement swept up so many of our strong Black women and turned them against their men, only for them to find out that white women didn't give a sh*t about them...our men will have to learn too. So much of the damage is done. Our women let the people in power push them to be "independent" and look at our men with general disdain, just as all the jobs started getting pulled from the Black community. Men went broke. Women went to work. The men gave up on trying to be fathers because they couldn't pay the bills. And the women gave up on the men because they didn't see them as having anything else to offer. The Black family has since fallen apart. We should have known better. Then again, we should see this gay thing for what it is. But as Houston's Scarface has said, "Niggas keep missing the point."

Did You Know?

Many popular "movements," such as the "peace movement" of the 60s, are actually designed to work against us? Nicholas Rockefeller once told filmmaker Aaron Russo how his family had bankrolled the women's liberation movement in order to "destroy the family unit" and make individuals more vulnerable to manipulate. One example he used: Once women left home to work in order to feel "equal," there would now be more taxpayers AND their children would now be taught by the school system instead of the parents.

I don't want you to miss *my* point. I'm not encouraging anything ignorant. I think if someone is *really* concerned about slowing down the explosive growth of homosexuality among young people, you first need to start looking at all the social factors that contribute to this development. And then you go out and combat the root causes, such as (a) the lack of fathers in the home, (b) the lack of male role models in the community, (c) hypersexualization in popular culture, (d) sexual abuse or rape, and of course (e) the American phenomenon of finding a false sense of power through the illusion of "choice"). Meanwhile, the media (TV, film, radio, etc.) constantly pushes homosexuality on our boys just as hard as it pushes misogyny (ill treatment of women). So we end up with an unhealthy perspective on relationships with Black women either way. In the end, we're *all* being programmed.

I know you may have heard people "venting" on homosexuality before. That's not what this is. Sure, there are those who want to demonize gay people...but there are also those who want to demonize anyone who's not a supporter of homosexuality. I don't want to demonize anyone except the real demons. But we need to address this issue, because it affects the continuance of our community as a whole – even though it may seem that an individual's personal preference doesn't decide the fate of the community. Even if you believe that homosexuality is a natural impulse, you can't possibly believe that the explosive growth of homosexuality among young poor people (especially people of color) is natural by any means. How did all the teenagers suddenly start going gay? Is it just a coincidence that of the 5,000 young people (aged 13-24) who are infected with HIV *every year,* 70% are Black? While we're on that topic, another study revealed that 55% of young gay men (aged 15–22) don't reveal that they're having sex with other men. 14% of these young men were HIV positive, and most of them also had at least one female sex partner in the last 12 months...who didn't know sh*t.

So why are Black women stronger supporters for Black male homosexuality than any other group of people? Aren't Black women the same ones complaining about all the "good-for-nothing niggas" out there? What exactly are gay men doing for these women to avoid being grouped with the other "niggas"? Aren't Black women 64% of the 126,000 American women with AIDS/HIV, mostly because of sleeping with men "on the DL"? Isn't that something to complain about? Is it all by coincidence? Is this part of "God's plan" too? Or is it just okay so long as white people say it is?

Now, I know a feminine-ass man won't be happy with a feminine woman. But in places like Jamaica, Haiti, Africa, China, and so on, a feminine dude usually ends up marrying a butch-ass woman. And they're cool, because they fit each other's needs. They stay together, have children, and society keeps working. But here, a feminine man ends up getting with...a masculine man? Huh? And do those relationships last longer than the ones in Jamaica, Haiti, Africa, or China? Be honest.

But I'm not trying to attack anyone *personally*. The point is, we've been MADE to turn out this way. It's even deeper than the influence of the media (which is their tool, you know). It's deeper than sending thousands of Black men to prison. It's actually even deeper than your daddy not being there, or being molested by a relative when you were six. In order to crush the development of the Black population, America is effeminizing the Black male in any and every way they can, and you probably have no idea how deep the rabbit hole goes. If you know that Black people were once having more babies than white people everywhere in the world...you have to think about how they planned to stop that trend. In many countries, the gay movement just wouldn't catch on (but they're still working on it), so AIDS is doing the trick. Here in America, we get a triple-dose of population control: AIDS, Prison, and Black Male Homosexuality. And guess what? They're all tied together in a big freaky ménage a trios of genocide. Think about it. While you're deciding whether to love me or hate me, there's more.

The Chemicals

I told you it gets deeper. You may still believe that what's happening is all a product of nature. If only our world was so innocent. Did you know that there are chemicals that can affect your hormones and sexuality? How about if I told you that you were probably exposed to at least one of them today?

You know those little Hugs? The 25 cent drinks that every corner store sells in the hood? Guess what? They reduce sperm count. There's more. The plastic in those bottles, as well as many other cheaply-made bottles contains a chemical that ends up in our system. These chemicals, called phthalates, can activate the same receptors in the body as the female hormone estrogen. Gender-bending phthalates are found in many plastics, including cheap children's toys, Saran Wrap and PVC pipes, and can seep into food and water. Phthlates, which also contribute to asthma and cancer, can even be found in the milk we feed our babies. Guess where you find the most? In a recent study of 246 Black and Hispanic pregnant women, phthlates were present in 85-100% of the samples.

Another chemical is even more common. Bisphenol A (BPA) is an endocrine disruptor and hormone-mimicking agent found in hard plastic. Biologist Frederick vom Saal's research suggests that BPA can lead to ADHD, prostate cancer, decreased sperm count, sex-hormone imbalances, and "behavior changes." Hmm. How does it get into our systems? Easy. You just have to be born into the type of family that reheats plastic baby bottles or other plastic containers. So guess what? Over 90% of people in the inner city are born with traces of BPA in their systems.

And there's more. In fact, a scientist named Theo Colborn has been building a large database of chemicals she believes are "hijacking" our hormone systems. These chemicals don't just damage men's fertility – even increasing the risk of testicular cancer – they change our sexuality. While they increase femininity in males, they push young girls to reach puberty earlier. Not only that, but these chemicals are on the increase.

There are other chemicals, known as NPEs (Nonylphenol ethoxylates), which are found in cosmetic products. Usually they are in those fruity-ass shampoos and hair products some of you pretty boys wear. Those NPEs are also endocrine disruptors, and they have been shown to change the sex of fish in affected water. It also increases estrogen, and has been shown to cause the growth of breasts in boys. According to an article in *New Scientist Magazine*, "Slight anatomical oddities in infant boys are being heralded as the first evidence that gender-bending chemicals are affecting humans."

There are other chemicals in the food we eat. We now use about 10 lbs. of pesticides per year for every man, woman and child in the U.S. Many of these chemicals are affecting us to the point where we are in danger of not being able to reproduce within 50 years. Many cheaply produced foods average over 10 different pesticides in one sample. Depending on where you live, there are even herbicides and insecticides in your glass of water. These chemicals are not removed by water treatment such as chlorination. Endocrine interrupting pesticides can alter the sex of a child during the first 6 weeks of pregnancy, and in some cases, cause a person to have traits of the opposite sex.

Phthlates. BPA. NPEs. And dozens of others. And studies show that poor communities, especially Black and Hispanic ones, get most of this sh*t sent *straight* to them. That sh*t is in you *right now*. And if you have a child, your child has 20 times more in their system than you do. What does that tell you? Do you still think it's *all* natural?

While we're debating who's f*cking who, there's a war being waged on us...and we have no idea. But some of y'all are gonna be so busy trying to attack *me* for sharing this, that you'll miss my actual point. You'll think *I'm* the f*cking enemy. And that's why *they* keep winning. We'll be fighting each other instead of fighting the people f*cking us *both* over (no pun intended).

If you're *still* not convinced that there's something going on...and think none of this is on purpose...or that what I'm saying is the problem, I've got one last piece of proof to share. What do you know about the "Gay Bomb" the U.S. was going to drop on Iraq?

> Pentagon officials on Friday confirmed to CBS 5 that military leaders had considered, and then subsequently rejected, building the so-called "Gay Bomb." Edward Hammond, of Berkeley's Sunshine Project, had used the Freedom of Information Act to obtain a copy of the proposal from the Air Force's Wright Laboratory in Dayton, Ohio…The documents show the Air Force lab asked for $7.5 million to develop such a chemical weapon. "**The Ohio Air Force lab proposed that a bomb be developed that contained a chemical that would cause enemy soldiers to become gay**, and to have their units break down because all their soldiers became irresistibly attractive to one another," Hammond said after reviewing the documents.

Now tell me I'm making this sh*t up.

(I intentionally don't bog this book down with the hundreds of sources I use, but I figured I'd *have* to name a few for *this* section. So here's 3 out of the 18 I used: Andy Coghlan, "Infant males affected by 'gender-bending' chemicals" *New Scientist Magazine*, Issue 2502, June 4, 2005; Julie Wakefield, "Boys won't be boys" *New Scientist Magazine*, Issue 2349, June 29, 2002; Hank Plante, "Pentagon Confirms It Sought To Build A 'Gay Bomb'" *CBS 5 News*, June 8, 2007)

SUPREME THE ASSHOLE ON "NO HOMO"

Some of you dudes be tryin so hard NOT to be gay that it makes me wonder. Now, I wouldn't let a broad toss my salad, nor would I let another man flirt with me, but some dudes be goin overboard. Unless you're feelin real self-conscious that you MIGHT be gay, there's no need to keep telling people you're not! Anyway…The people who hate gay people the hardest are usually the same dudes with the secret sh*t goin on behind closed doors. And let me add this as well: The way I see it, putting your money first is one thing, but if you go about life like you HATE women, you pretty much on some gay sh*t. How you gonna be 30 or 40 with no woman, no family? THAT'S gay, homey.

SMUTTING 101

Let's talk some more about women. Not beautiful, intelligent women with careers and their own cars, but the kind of women that are an absolute waste of time and energy. The kind of women you simply want to smut. I'm going to identify the women in this picture as Type A, B, and C.

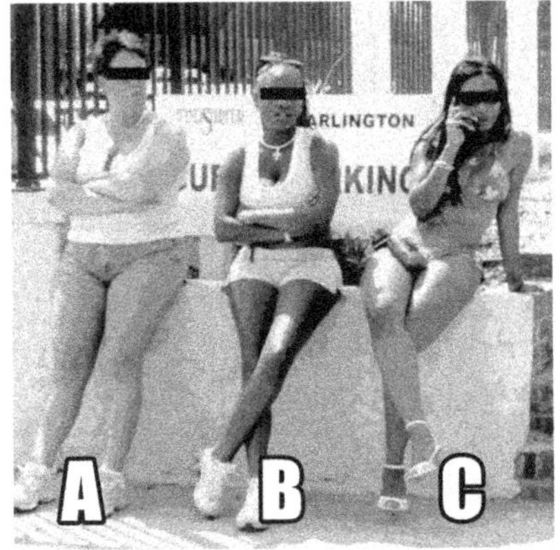

Type A: Type A is the chick you have to lower your standards for. You don't want to be seen in public with her, but you'll go for it if you're really lonely or desperate one day. To make things worse, you're sick with yourself once you actually get it, cause it smells like straight poochie (poop and coochie). Trust me, it's not worth it. It says a lot about you that you gotta mess with a girl who you're ashamed of. Man up.

Type B: Type B is a step up from Type A. But she thinks she's a supermodel because her ass is big. So she's the one who cusses you out, who gives you a gang of drama, who might try to fight you over nothing, and who will break every window on your car if you ever cheat on her. Oh, and trust me, she is watching, snooping, and spying on your ass. Type B has a hell of a body, but sometimes her face is hell too. She doesn't know it though, because all her suitors have given her nothing but compliments. **You'd probably go out with her too, because you think her body makes up for her face**. But what about her terrible attitude? This girl couldn't have an intelligent conversation with you if you held her at gunpoint. And her babydaddy's more liable to hold you at gunpoint one day, anyway. Why are you playing with fire? Oh, did I mention getting burned? That's probably going to happen, too.

Type C: Type C has the stripper body AND the model face. You've hit the jackpot, huh? Well, get ready to hand over all your winnings, buddy. You'll be broke in no time messing with this girl. And just like a parasite, she'll move on to someone else when you're through. She might tell you she loves you, but her game is so tight that she could tell you anything with a straight face. Her cousin on the phone? That's not her cousin, that's one of her other sponsors. If you've got one of these girls, you ain't pimpin, you're getting broke by a *real* pimp.

How many Type As are currently in your life? Type Bs? Type Cs? What about Type D: The sensible, decent female who certainly has flaws, but who isn't a complete waste of time, energy, and money. You got any of those? Then why are you killing yourself with the first three?

Know what you're dealing with, and what you expect to get out of it. Have some standards and don't compromise them often.

How to Get the Cookies

If you were offended by the last essay, you'll definitely want to skip this one. But I've got to address it. For us men, the pursuit of sex is a major preoccupation. So how can I not talk about it?

Okay, let's be real. As much as we chase it, the truth is that 'pussy' is actually pretty plentiful. Especially with the growing ratio of single women to available, straight, free men. You can close your eyes, take 10 paces in any direction, and you'll inevitably fall into some sex.

It's *love* that's hard to get.

So when it comes to sex, you have to be more selective. Just like with food, if you ain't starvin, then you should be selective with what you eat. And speaking of what you eat, that's a good way to start being selective. If you wouldn't eat it, then you shouldn't beat it. This applies to those of you that eat coochie and those who don't. It means if you don't think it's clean enough to put your face in, you definitely shouldn't have your dick there. I mean, how do you enjoy nervous sex?

I figured it'd be easier to show you than tell you, so I've included a few of my own personal experiences. Every one of those times, I thought I had learned something important. But I hadn't. I'd keep doing more dumb sh*t until I learned the REAL lesson I had missed each time.

Smut Story 29

She wasn't very cute. She also wasn't very smart. Even her personality kinda sucked.

BUT the pussy was pretty damn good.

And I was going to make the sex worth every minute I'd had to endure her wack company. I was really getting into my rhythm when I realized everything was feeling a little warmer and more "real." I pulled out quickly. The condom had broken. My mind didn't jump immediately to STDs. Instead I thought about the infamous "pre-cum." I'd heard stories of girls getting pregnant just from the one-drop rule.

Oh my.

What if I got this girl pregnant? How long have I been in there unprotected? She started moaning and pushing herself against my hips like a cat in heat. I felt sick. I couldn't shake the thought of this sorry woman becoming my babymama. The idea consumed me. I pictured us fighting daily, during and after the pregnancy, over the most trivial of issues. I pictured her feeding my child pickled pigs' feet, and calling the police on me when I complained about her having ugly dudes over to the house while I was at work. I could see myself engaged in a custody battle for a child who'd probably have half my IQ anyway.

Returning to reality, I walked out of the room and told her I wasn't feeling well. She got pregnant a short time later. But, thankfully she was a slut, and the little bastard wasn't mine.

Lesson I thought I learned: Wear a condom, and check it regularly.

And that's what I thought the lesson was. Until I kept going through similar situations with only slightly different factors involved. That's when I figure out the real lesson I was meant to learn that day:

Lesson I should have learned: A piece of trashy pussy usually ain't worth the possible pain and punishment that may come with it.

Consider how stupid you'll feel when you get diagnosed with leprosy just because you couldn't resist the skank with the purple hair. Or worse, when that skank not only gives you a terminal illness, but demands child support for your newborn cross-eyed daughter Aquafina, who is gonna learn to booty-shake before she can walk.

Watch where you stick that thing.

Smut Story 67

This girl wasn't a prostitute, but she damn sure acted like one. I was wary about taking her home with me after having just met her, but I think my dick was doing a lot of my thinking for me at this particular phase in my life. After it was clear that she wasn't expecting a financial reward (at least not that day), we headed to my place. Once there, things transpired as they normally do, according to my "2 Hour Instant Pussy Plan." Yes, I had **an instant gratification routine.** I won't get into the details here, but it generally involved a stimulating environment, some stimulating conversation, a stimulating massage, and in less than an hour, I was receiving some oral stimulation.

Yeah, those were my triple-X years. You may not like it. But if you don't understand why almost ALL of us need to experience a time of "sowing our wild oats," you're probably not very good at relating to young people. And you'll probably have a ton of regrets as you get older. Just look at what happened to R. Kelly, who probably got no action in high school. And you see how he made up for it, right?

At any rate, I was doing my regular routine, except halfway through the massage, she just comes out of nowhere.

Girl: I don't really need a massage. Can you just f*ck me?

Me: (looking like I just won a bag full of doodoo) Uh, okay.

Girl: (walks toward bathroom) Hold on, I need to call somebody.

Me: Uh, okay.

Girl: (shouting from bathroom) You know you out of washcloths? How's a bitch supposed to get the pussy clean for you?

Me: Shouldn't the pussy already be clean?

Girl: What?

Me: Nothing.

Girl: (returning to bedroom) Lay on the bed. I'ma suck your dick.

Me: Uh, okay.

So she starts sucking my dick, which doesn't last as long as I'd usually like (2-8 hours if you let me tell it), because then she tells me she's ready to get f*cked. Uh, okay. I threw on a condom and laid back, hoping she'd realize I wanted her to climb on top of me. She did. Yes! Laziness pays off once again! I was just getting ready to enjoy Easy Street, when – Wow! She was riding me like her hips were possessed by the spirit of a Brazilian carnival. It was actually a lot better than what I'd expected.

Suddenly, I heard a crash at my door – like someone was kicking it in. Ka-d-doom! I jumped up, tossing her off me like she was a hot potato, and dove for the .380 under my pillow. I knew she was unarmed (unless there was a .22 in her booty), but I had no idea what kind of firepower she'd called in on me. I figured it would be smarter to shoot from behind something solid as they entered my second-floor bedroom. I ran towards the far end of the room, around my desk, and took my position. From there, I was able to peer out the window to see a black sedan in my driveway...It was my roommate's car. Peeking out of my bedroom doorway, I saw him picking up the groceries he'd dropped when he came in.

Lesson I thought I learned: Everyone should announce themselves when they come in the house.

But as smart as I thought I was, that wasn't it.

Lesson I should have learned: When you're doing some bullsh*t you know you shouldn't be doing, you should expect for bad things to happen. If you want to stop worrying about bad things happening, you have to stop doing that bullsh*t.

The guilty have reason to walk in fear.

The Lesson about the Lessons that Weren't the Real Lessons

Unfortunately, it took me several bad experiences before I finally learned to raise my standards for who I pursue and lay down with. In fact, it wasn't until I had a near-death experience until I finally saw the lessons I'd been missing.

When you go through life experiences, do you pick up small, trivial lessons, or do you get the big picture right away? Look back at your life and think about what you have learned the most from. Are there any events from which you didn't pull a bigger, more meaningful lesson?

Do the lessons you normally learn only apply to special situations or are they important messages about the bigger picture? How can you tell?

Don't miss the major life lessons for the minor ones.

Have Some Damn Standards

Before I got with my present queen, I decided to come up with a list of some standards, which I turned into a "plus or minus" point system. It was mostly for me to get an idea of what was really important to me in a partner. I posted it on Myspace, and before long, girls were sending me their "scores." This is how it went. It may be funny, but I was serious.

Trait	Points
1. Has natural hair	+5
2. Doesn't eat pork	+5
3. Is a vegetarian	+10
4. Knows how to cook	+10
5. Knows how to catch a flight to come see me	+20
6. Only knows how to catch the "holy ghost" at church	-30
7. No hang-ups, lingering issues, or ongoing conflicts	+20
8. Hangs up the phone any time there's an issue or conflict	-10
9. Honest and open	+30
10. Not particularly religious	+10
11. Watches BET religiously	-10
12. Not married, engaged, or involved	+20
13. "Married" to Jesus	-20
14. Likes goin to botanical parks AND theme parks	+30
15. Likes goin to clubs and only MORE clubs	-10
16. Has a booty	+15
17. Smells like booty	-20
18. Takes it in the booty	-5
19. Is supportive and considerate	+15
20. Is pro-Black or something close	+20
21. Is involved in her community	+10
22. Is involved in her community as the neighborhood whore	-40
23. Has a great sense of humor	+10
24. Laughs at my jokes even when they're not funny	+20
25. Has an oral fetish	+15
26. Satisfies it by smoking Newports	-15
27. Is highly literate and educated	+40
28. Is just plain high	-40
29. Plays games with my head	-50
30. Plays games in the bed	+20
31. Thinks "reparations" are something a mechanic does	-20
32. Knows that with a real man, his woman comes first	+10
33. Doesn't care if the man comes at all	-20
34. Reads books	+20
35. Reads books, but only the scandalous smutty ones	-20

Most of it may have seemed like a joke, but at least I was clear on what my expectations were. Too many times, I'd shortchanged myself by accepting less than what I deserved. Maybe I just didn't know what I deserved. Maybe you don't. The thing is, you really have to stop, sit down, and think about it. You have to say, "What can I accept, what won't I accept, and what are the things that I don't necessarily need, but I'd like?" It's only after that point that you start getting more of what you really want.

Do you have a set of standards for the people you accept into your life?

Do you constantly encounter the type of meet who don't meet your standards? Is it because of where and how you meet them?

Do you have a set of standards and expectations for yourself? Do you consistently rise to meet them or do you lower them to do so?

Which expectations are flexible and which are set in stone? Why?

Have a high set of standards for yourself, and whoever you bring close to you.

SUPREME THE ASSHOLE SAYS "F*CK A HOE"

Hoes come in a hundred different flavors. And all of them leave a sh*tty taste in your mouth. So don't eat em. Actually, don't waste your time period. Whether it's the young hoe who's willing to try anything because her uncle raped her, or the kinky hoe who wants to f*ck a man in the ass, or the old hoe who always needs some desperate dude to pay her rent, you need to leave them hoes the hell alone. Hoes bring nothing but headaches. Not to mention all kind of worms and bugs that soap won't wash off.

20 SIGNS SHE'S INSECURE

It's funny how the most insecure women scream "I'm not insecure" the loudest. Here are my observations about insecurity, and if the shoe fits, fix your feet. To be fair, I may not be insecure, but I can be impulsive, insensitive, inappropriate, indecisive, and a ton of other words that start with "I" (but not impotent). But I'm *me*...so *I* just can't be insecure.

T F	She says she's NOT insecure about ANYTHING, very loudly (reassuring herself so she'll believe it)
T F	She attempts to control what you do and where you go (a control mechanism intended so you only answer to her)
T F	She attempts to change your friends, or puts them down (another control mechanism)
T F	She won't leave the house without makeup on or a jazzy outfit (not comfortable with herself as she is)
T F	She uses makeup to make herself look COMPLETELY different from her natural appearance
T F	She's attempting to redecorate herself as a white woman (blonde hair, light makeup, blue contacts, self-hating attitude)
T F	She's scared to have feelings for you, or has other walls up
T F	She's always putting down other women (being comfortable with yourself allows you to not feel like you're competing with every other woman)
T F	She spends a lot of time drunk or high (staying in haze to escape her reality)
T F	Shes been abused, traumatized, or victimized and NEVER dealt with it (and thus never healed)
T F	She needs the lights off to have sex (insecure about her body)
T F	Shes a germaphobe, hypochondriac...or paranoid schizophrenic

T F	She constantly needs attention, of any kind, negative or positive
T F	She can't spend quiet time alone enjoying herself
T F	She needs to be on her cell phone throughout the day (her way of never being alone)
T F	She uses material things (clothes, cars, money, etc) to make her feel valuable and confident
T F	She draws attentions to what she feels are her BEST features, but they are all physical (but what's under the surface?)
T F	She makes assumptions about who you've been with or what you've been doing (jealous paranoia is hell!)
T F	She argues about everything (another unhealthy way for her to feel some sense of power)
T F	She checks your phone, reads your email, attempts to kill your ex, or cuts off your penis

If the shoe fits, it must be legit. But don't look at this list as a means to condemn women. The truth is that almost all women of color are insecure to some extent. It's natural. Just as our men are bashed into running from responsible manhood, our women have been scrutinized, dehumanized, objectified, and hypersexualized to the point where they worry about the most minute details as if they can determine how much of a woman she is. A woman ain't a woman because of how skinny she is, how pretty she is, or how much other people love or like her...but our women have been led to believe that. So of course they're insecure. So work with em. And tell em to work with you. Cause a lot of the items on this list can apply to men too! We're all f*cked up. Let's fix us.

Our women are just as messed up as our men.
We've all got to grow up together.

---

22 Guidelines for Women

I had no idea how many women would read my book. Turns out that a lot of the men reading *How to Hustle and Win* found out about it because their women pushed them to read it! That's a beautiful thing, ladies. And I hope y'all men can do the same and push some of these young dudes to read this revolutionary sh*t as well. But I don't just want to write ABOUT women. Many of the lessons in both books can apply to any gender (or race, or class, or whatever), but I wanted to dedicate some space specifically to the ladies. I hope this helps you on your journey. I know it's a tough road for you too.

1. **Don't get "a-dick-ted."** This is the #1 reason why y'all stay in bad, even abusive, relationships. You know the pussy has power, but stop letting it overpower your damn *mind.* Use the pussy, don't let it use you.

2. **Don't become a high-class hoe.** When I say "use" the pussy, I'm not saying that you offer it in exchange for goods or services. That's

really called prostitution. You don't need an escort service or a pimp to hoe yourself. So let sex only result from love and passion, not the pursuit of what you want from a man.

3. **Passion can be a problem.** A passionate woman is a thrill to spend time with, but your passion can lead you down a road to your own destruction. Before you let your feelings determine what choices you make, always consult your logical mind first. If it don't make sense for the long run, leave it alone. It'll suck, but it's better than the bullsh*t.

4. **Enjoy the XXX years.** I'm talking about the years from 18-24, where you should eXplore, eXperience, and eXperiment to your heart's content. That's your time to find yourself, including what you really enjoy, what you don't, and what you just want to try once to get it out of your damn system.

5. **Test drive a few cars before you buy one.** Especially during those XXX years. Date someone from each sign of the Zodiac. See what fits you best. Or date different types of men (businessman, hustler, nerd, country boy, athlete, etc.). Try different jobs, consider different approaches to life. You may have not found your perfect path yet!

6. **But don't make any life-changing decisions.** If you're in those XXX years and you do decide to date a hustler, don't carry his dope. If you date an athlete, don't have his kids (even if you want that six-digit child support). Even if you meet a real good dude (you hope), don't marry him until you've been with him long enough to have survived some real drama. Above all, think things through.

7. **Don't put money over happiness.** I know a lot of corporate women who love telling me how "liberated" and "independent" they are. But they're also miserable. They can't help but keep coming back to the idea that they'll die alone. And who wants that? Don't put aside having a family and children to pursue a million-dollar dream. In fact, the *right* kind of family will HELP you get to your dreams.

8. **Stop accepting less than you deserve.** Yes, I know there's a man shortage out there. But when you date someone who doesn't deserve you, it just makes the rest of us mad as hell. There are good men out there. They may not drive fancy cars or wear expensive suits, but they'll make sure you're happy. And what's better than that?

9. **Splurge less, save more.** Do you know why strippers and prostitutes take on pimps they don't need? Because they *do* need them. And not for protection. They'll all tell you that they needed someone to "manage" their money for them. You can say it's brainwashing, but I

know far too many "regular" girls who can't control their spending habits enough to set aside a decent college fund for their kids.

10. **Don't let the media influence you.** Don't let Reality TV and talk shows tell you how a Black woman is supposed to carry herself. Oh, you don't? Listen…If you watch it, it's affecting you subconsciously. Think about it. When's the last time you felt you were "having a moment" like one of the scandalous heffers on TV?

11. **You lose with game.** Don't use game or any other deceptive tactics to "trap" or manipulate a man. The outcome is never good.

12. **Potential ain't enough.** First of all, potential alone shouldn't satisfy you enough to stick around forever. And if you do plan on "changing" or "molding" him (instead of just encouraging him), guess what? No woman respects a man she "makes."

13. **Let him be a man.** Support him when he's down, and encourage him to do better. That doesn't mean nag him until he runs away. I've met a lot of women who have tried begging their man to read *Part One*, and it just doesn't work that way. If you are in love with a man who's just not "with it," you can't try to "make" him get with it. For any man with a decent pair of nuts, you've got to **let him lead**. *Ask* him what he thinks. Ask him to *teach* you about things you secretly want *him* to learn.

14. **Don't let miserable people coordinate your happiness.** Letting one of your single girlfriends (or your single mama) tell you about what to do with your relationship is like letting Britney Spears give you advice on being a responsible parent.

15. **Listen to the advice of older, successful women**. Find a mentor. A woman who has accomplished the goals you have for yourself. Make sure they're happy, though. A cushy job and 800 pairs of shoes doesn't make her a role model. But being married 30 years does.

16. **Be careful of ulterior motives.** All men want something. We're not innocent. Unless we invite you to meet our wife or girlfriend, we're probably up to something. Especially if we're offering you something with no expectations of return. So scrutinize everything and everyone.

17. **Decide on your ultimate goals.** What do you want out this life?

18. **Find yourself.** Look for a greater meaning and purpose for your existence. You're here to do more than have kids or make money. Being single for a while can help you free your mind to think about the big picture. Keep reading books that help. Women can change the world.

"Break the chains, unleash the fury of women as a mighty force for revolution!"
Slogan of the Chinese Cultural Revolution

19. **Don't exploit yourself.** Are white people the ones keeping us down, or do *we* play a big part in it? Similarly, if you claim that women are exploited by men, you take a lot of responsibility and power away from yourself. Unfortunately, *we* do y'all wrong because of how white supremacy has screwed us up, so don't *just* point the finger at us alone. We've all gotta take responsibility for our own bullsh*t. Nelly can only swipe a credit card up a girl's booty if she *chose* that part in the video.

20. **Be real.** You can't try to look like a white woman while complaining that Black men are running to white women! Even if you ain't ready to "go natural," at least kill the obsession with doing everything else the way they do it. And stop acting like you just came up with the idea to be "unique" with blonde hair, when there are 3 million other chicks doing the same thing. Call it what it is.

21. **Don't objectify yourself.** As India.Arie sings on "I Am Not my Hair," "Does the way I wear my hair make me a better person?" Don't define the quality of your existence by your weight, your hair texture, your clothes, or the size of your ass. It's whats under the surface that counts. Cultivate THAT.

22. **Finally, don't screw up the men that are trying to do right**. If you're still struggling to find yourself, take a break from the dating game while you do that. Otherwise, you'll be ruining men the same way we ruin women. And that brings us to…

17 Ways Women Mess Up Good Men

Women always tell me, "Supreme, I can't find a good man....there ain't no good men left!" Sometimes I want to fake sympathy for em...but the truth is, many of those women couldn't tell a good man from a transexual werewolf. So let's be clear: Ladies, you've probably had a chance with a FEW good men, but you may have run them away, ignored them, or just plain messed it all up. I thought I'd share 17 ways you can do it…so you can avoid it next time. Men, take notes as well.

1. **Walk all over us.** Don't think "generous" means "sugardaddy" or "tolerant" means "weak" (or anything similar), and then try your luck. When you take kindness for weakness, we either stop being kind or get used to being treated wrong. It's a simple choice for most of us.

2. **Uneven exchange.** Don't expect to be showered with gifts, praise, and lavish dates, and offer nothing but sex in exchange. Surely, you have something greater to offer than a hole between your legs. Worse yet, if you hold out on THAT too.

3. **No Call, No Show.** Don't stand people up without explanation. Sure, it's a woman's prerogative to simply not "feel" like going out even

after making a date, but it is human courtesy to give sufficient notice to the other party. It is simply spoiled to flake, go MIA, then hit someone up later with a nonchalant "What's up!"

4. **Double standards.** If you feel that something is perfectly okay when you do it, but just cause for war if *he* does it, something is wrong.

5. **Avoid awareness.** Don't find something weak or feminine in education, literacy, or activism. Promote self-education among men or you'll have nothing to date but empty shells of men.

6. **Mixed company, mixed messages.** Don't keep company with gay men while denouncing the lack of strong, real men. Your "buddies" and "shopping partners" never face any of this scrutiny, which is reserved for all the "sorry" straight men. But what can your gay friends teach you about finding or judging a good (straight) man?

7. **Date the dude on the DL.** Your metrosexual man may dress better than the next guy, but he also wears your panties. And he might give you HIV. Statistics don't lie. That's how most Black women get it.

8. **ADHD.** If you meet a decent guy, give him a chance before your attention is drawn to the guy you meet the very NEXT day (or hour), and so on. Don't get swept up in every next hot thing. But that doesn't mean commit instantly to anyone who asks! Take your time.

9. **Materialistic selection criteria.** If the qualifiers for your attention are mostly material or physical, you'll never find a man who is right for you. You'll get a few trinkets, but not a worthwhile companion.

10. **Get caught up in game.** The guy that stutters may not have any poetry or jokes for you, but he may be a better man than all the other suave players you'll choose over him. Remember, even Moses had a speech impediment. So choose substance over style.

11. **Narrow-mindedness**. Don't run from new avenues of learning and diverse perspectives. Narrow-minded people never get much out of life. If you won't talk to someone because they don't attend Reverend Jonah Chickenfoot's Congregation of Holy Spirit in Your Left Pocket Church of Donations, you may never grow.

12. **The tried and tired.** You can't keep using the same bait and then complain about the fish you catch. If you wear a hoe outfit, you will get hoe-seekers. If you can only talk in 3-letter words, you won't be snaggin the "intellectual" guy you claim you want.

13. **Presto-chango!** Want to lose a man fast? Just pretend and fake it, then change later! If you did it when you met him, and kept it up to reel him in, you better keep it up as long as you plan on keepin him.

14. Get it twisted. Don't think long talks about nothing constitute "intellectual" conversation, or that your guy is "sensitive" when he's really a sissy. Meanwhile, he's not "strong" just because he's a jail-bound fool. **It's one thing to know what you want, but it's another to actually know it when you see it.** But some of y'all *never* seen a good man, so you really have no idea what it's like. Just be careful that you don't think you got a kiwi when you're only holdin a moldy ass peach.

15. Think Sex = Relationship. We don't like that kinda pressure. Sex is just a part of things. A good man won't beg for it, nor will he leave you if you don't give it up the first night. He won't lose respect if you give it up quickly either...as long as you've got more to offer. But when you equate the act of sex with consummating a relationship, you show us the limited extent of what you offer. We all want more than a bust it baby. The jumpoff *gets* attention, but it never lasts. The woman who inspires us, supports us, and challenges our minds *keeps* our attention.

16. Transference. Don't hold some other guy's mistakes against us. We ain't break it, so we shouldn't have to pay for it.

17. Babymama drama. I know a lot of guys who "tried" to stick in there and stay for their children, but just couldn't withstand the drama of the relationship. This isn't why *all* men leave, but if you're constantly giving your baby's father hell, this may be *your* situation...and your fault.

Women, don't blame us. Work with us. We're both part of the problem, so we've gotta work together.

Mind over body?

Strong Discipline

"It is better to conquer yourself than to win a thousand battles."
The Buddha

In Saigon, Vietnam, a protest was underway. 350 Buddhist monks and nuns marched into a busy city center in two military-style columns and formed a large circle in front of the Cambodian embassy. They were there to denounce the Cambodian government and its policy towards Buddhists, demanding that it fulfill its promises of religious equality. In the center of the circle was Thích Quảng Đức, a senior monk. Thích Quảng Đức calmly seated himself in the traditional lotus position on a cushion. **Gasoline was poured over his head.** Calmly, he struck a match and dropped it on himself. Flames consumed his robes and flesh, and black oily smoke emanated from his burning body.

Police trying to stop him could not break through the circle of Buddhist clergy. One of the officers threw himself to the ground and prostrated himself in reverence. Throughout the whole ordeal, down to the point where – ten minutes later – his burnt body finally toppled dead to the ground, the only screams to be heard came from the terrified onlookers. The senior monk kept a look of calm to his last moments. David Halberstam, one of the few journalists there, reported, "As he burned he never moved a muscle, never uttered a sound, his outward composure in sharp contrast to the wailing people around him."

"He who gains victory over others is strong, but he who gains victory over himself is all powerful."
Lao Tzu

Homey, what kind of discipline do YOU got? Can you not eat for days, like Gandhi? Could you handle a prison hunger strike? Or do you get cranky when you miss lunch? Can you discipline yourself enough to burn without screaming? Or do you bitch over headaches? Do you reach for drugs (prescription or not) any time you feel just a bit "off"?

Stronger Impulses

Isaiah knew he shouldn't be this close to the boss's wife. But here she was again, in the office, long after everyone had left. She'd made a habit of coming in to look for her husband at a time when she should have known he'd be gone. It seemed she did it just to be alone with Isaiah, because as soon as she'd "somehow" run into him, she'd immediately find some excuse to engage him in small-talk. But soon, the small-talk progressed to her slapping his thigh as she laughed at his jokes, or stroking his back while he talked about his divorce.

Isaiah knew he should ignore her advances. After all, the boss wasn't a man to take lightly. "A woman like Esmerelda is up to no good," he told himself repeatedly. The last time Esmerelda had brushed her juicy little ass up against Isaiah, he nearly threw her down and f*cked her right there on his office desk. But a janitor had interrupted them at the last minute.

Isaiah didn't want to give into his impulses, but here she was, sitting on his desk, and talking about how her husband "doesn't satisfy" her. He too-short skirt made it almost unbearable for Isaiah to hide his excitement. He couldn't help but look up from his seat to see that she hadn't worn any panties today. By the time she leaned in to whisper another "secret," Isaiah couldn't take it any longer. He pulled her down into his lap and kissed her passionately. She didn't resist in the least. The sex was incredible. Possibly the best sex he'd had since his wife. But in the end, Isaiah *should* have controlled himself, because the whole episode was captured on the office's security cameras…which the boss always reviewed the next morning.

What do these two very different stories have in common? Discipline. Each story is unified by the theme of man's ability (or inability) to discipline himself.

Any man who cannot master himself does not deserve to have the freedoms of being a man. Why? **Because he's not even in charge of his own mind and body, so you damn sure shouldn't put him in charge of anything else.**

People like that, lacking self-control, end up in places where they are controlled by other people. In prison and the military, you get "External Discipline," which means other people force you to do as instructed. Otherwise you get punished. Either you get worked, or you end up in isolation, or a mothaf*cka finds a way to see to it that you're hurt. But after a few years of people forcing discipline on you, telling you when to way, how to make your bed, and things like that, you start doing it on your own.

That's why anybody who comes home from a 5 year bid is gonna wake up at the same time every day – with or without an alarm clock – for months, sometimes years. But sometimes, it's not too long before the dude starts getting lazy and sleeping in. The same way, a man who only stayed in shape for the military can either remain "Army Strong" or become a pot-bellied fat-ass five years after he's out.

Why? Because their discipline didn't come from them. They weren't the masters of themselves. They didn't have "Internal Discipline," which mean deciding – on your own and for your own reasons – that you'll do something, even when no one else is watching. Most of us don't have the internal discipline to do the kinds of things in the first story above. Instead, like Isaiah, as soon as the man in charge is gone, we're gonna slip and lose self-control.

"The best Jihad (struggle) is for one to perform Jihad against his own self and his desires."
Prophet Muhammad

That's why a man – to truly be a man – must be in complete control of his

Did You Know?

Project MKULTRA was the code name for a CIA mind-control research program that began in 1950, run by the Office of Scientific Intelligence. There is much published evidence that the project involved the use of many types of drugs to manipulate individual mental states and to alter brain function. 14-year CIA veteran Victor Marchetti has stated in various interviews that CIA mind control research continued. In 1975, it was made public that the CIA had been conducting these experiments on U.S. citizens without their knowledge.

mind and body. To do this, he has to impose discipline upon HIMSELF. The way to begin disciplining yourself is to deny your weaker desires, like:

- ❑ the desire to f*ck a skank just cause she's rubbin on your thigh
- ❑ the desire to sleep in, and waste half your day in bed
- ❑ the desire to eat anytime you see food
- ❑ the desire to do something stupid, knowing you won't get away with it
- ❑ the desire to slap your probation officer just because you're mad

So how do you deny yourself? Easy. **You fast.** You're already doing it. Every time you sleep, you're denying yourself of things you do during the day. That's why the first meal of the morning is called breakfast (break "fast"). But to discipline your mind and body, you have to **consciously** deny yourself various things. The following are a few fasts you can take to start developing that Internal Discipline. Man up.

Fasting from Food. Fasting from food is the most common kind of fast, but it's not exactly easy. Considering how most people can't stand to go hungry for more than an hour or two, you can see how strong-willed and disciplined you are by how crazy you get not having food for more than a day or two.

Juice Fast. While Muslims avoid food for half the day during the month of Ramadan, and some Christians avoid meat for Lent, you ain't REALLY fasting unless you cut it ALL off. That's right. Some of the most thugged-out dudes I know couldn't handle no food for three days. But if you can't handle a few days without food, trust me, you can't handle solitary confinement...at least not without goin crazy. Eat a good meal the day before you start, and drink natural juices (100% juice, not that Hawaiian Punch sh*t) for the next few days. Do 3 or 4 days if you can (I sometimes do 6 or 7), but you're a bitch if you can't do two. I promise, it gets easy after the second day! By the third day, you'll feel different, and your mind will be clear, but your breath will stink. After all, you're finally giving your poor stomach a break, which means your body will start expelling all that nasty sh*t you were killing it with. If you happen to throw up, that means you *really* had some poison in you, buddy! So good for you. (Google *The Master Cleanse* if you're extra serious about cleanin yourself up)

Water Fast. I don't think you're ready for this, but I'll throw it in here if you feel like testing your nuts. No juice, no smoothies. Three to nine days. Water and air. That's it.

Fasting from Meat. This one isn't really that hard, so you need to do it for a lot longer for it to count for anything. Either leave red meat alone for a month, or leave all meat alone for a week or two. C'mon, how hard is *that*? Just try it and I promise you'll notice a difference. As you do it, you'll feel better, you'll sleep better, you'll have more energy, you'll think clearer, and your health will improve if you do it long enough. I'm not tryin to force you to go vegetarian, but you should have SOME discipline about the way you eat. After all, you're supposed to control what you eat instead of letting it control you.

Fasting from TV. The average American spends between 9 to 13 years of his or her life in front of a television. In an average U.S. home, the TV is on 7 hours, 40 minutes a day. Of course, it's worse in poor communities, where the TVs are our babysitters. Studies show that 10 or more hours of TV watching per week will negatively affect a child's academic achievement. The average time per week that an American child ages 2-17 spends watching television? 19 hours, 40 minutes. How many hours per year does the average American child spend in school? 900. How many hours per year does the average American child watch television: 1,023! So who's teaching your kids? The government or the media? Damn sure ain't you, huh?

If I've gotta explain to you why it's a good idea to see if you can take a week-long break from TV, you need to read that first fact over and over until you get it. 9 to 13 years. That's how much time we waste, usually on bullsh*t like "A Shot at Love with Tila Tequila." Not only will you think clearer if you leave that idiot box alone for a minute, your thoughts will be a lot more positive as well.

Fasting from Talking. Also known as a silent fast, this ain't no joke. Even at only 3 days, this is the hardest one (in my opinion), especially if you spend a lot of time around people who won't support you. But it's one of the best ways to get into yourself, digging deep into your subconscious mind, reviewing and reconsidering your life and choices, looking at what and how you think. In a nutshell, when you actually shut your mouth, you get to know yourself better. (see *Part One*, "The Mirror Don't Lie") If you want to improve the way your mind works in just 3 days – and fasting from TV was a piece of cake – try a silent fast.

> "If they took all the drugs, nicotine, alcohol and caffeine off the market for six days, they'd have to bring out the tanks to control you."
> Dick Gregory

Fasting from any Vice. Whether it's cursing, eating junk food, or arguing with your family, you know what your unhealthy habits are. Pick one, and avoid it for a time period you can choose yourself. This isn't like a New Year's Resolution, where you promise that you'll "never" do something again, only to be back doin it in full force by January 18th. No, this is different. This is where you test your ability to avoid a behavior that is a problem for you. If you can cut it off for a week, you're strong enough to cut it off for longer. If you can put it out of your mind for 3 weeks (21 days), well, you've made that a habit, which means you're done with it. Congratulations! (see *Part One*, "21 Days")

Fasting from Sex. Even though I already hit you with Isaiah's story, I needed to save this one for last and address it in depth. In fact, I figured I'd share one of my own experiences. I decided to fast from sex for the entire month of August 2006. Now don't get me wrong, this wasn't an involuntary fast like when some of y'all dudes claim y'all are "abstaining." You ain't abstaining, homey. You're going through a DROUGHT. It ain't that you don't *want* none. You just *can't get* none.

No, this was a voluntary fast, not involuntary. That means I had plenty of opportunities, but I was turnin them down. Not only was I ignoring new prospects, all my old regulars got turned down that month, even the psychiatrists (head doctors). My mindset was: "I don't want to date you and waste money if I don't genuinely dig your personality (just being cute wasn't cutting the mustard anymore)...and I don't want to have you over and waste my precious energy either."

Now, I came up like most dudes, believing a man's greatness was somehow tied to his sexual prowess and the number of smuts he had smutted, as if getting pussy was like winning some kind of a victory in a war. Then again, to many of us who have no idea what kind of war is REALLY going on, we're soldierin for all the wrong sh*t, huh?

In my early 20s, I got into a relationship that seemed to be heading towards commitment, and I nearly went crazy. I couldn't stop thinking about all the things I hadn't done, all the things my brothers bragged about that I never did...and I knew I'd want to "indulge."

I had a choice: Either postpone the relationship, or move full steam ahead and inevitably indulge later, as most guys do. All those 40-year-old horndogs in the strip club are married men blowing their paychecks trying to reclaim whatever they missed out on in their younger years. Why you think R. Kelly's a molestor now? Have you ever seen his high school pictures? You know he ain't get no high school pussy in high school! So he's gonna get it now!

That wasn't gonna be me. So I postponed the commitment...and I went all out. Strippers, swingers' clubs, "freak parties," head in a candy store... sex, lies, AND videotape. I ain't do nothing sick or suspect, but I damn sure did everything I've wanted to do. Of course, I lost the girl (no woman wants to "wait"). But when my brothers brag about their smutfests now, I can say "been there, done that, blah blah whatever." And I don't need that anymore.

Somewhere through it all, I learned something: Sex is like pizza. No matter where you get it from, it's pretty much all the same after you've had enough. No matter how it's prepared, it still won't taste THAT different. And the hotter it is, the more you risk gettin burned.

Don't get me wrong, pussy is (usually) pretty good…but we go too hard for it. I don't have the desire to waste time and energy with someone I don't love (or even like in some cases). So if you're a man and you do spend a lot of your nights with women you don't even like, I have a question. Why?

Pick a fast you plan on doing. How long do you plan on keeping it for?

Master yourself.

Money and Power

"We have two evils to fight, capitalism and racism. We must destroy both racism and capitalism."
Huey P. Newton

This is going to be a quick lesson in world politics and economics. There are basically two major systems of handling economic relations in the world: Capitalism and Socialism. Capitalism is all about the accumulation of "capital" or personal wealth. You do what it takes to get more money, more ownership, and more power. America is one of the best examples of a capitalist country. Socialism, on the other hand, is about ensuring a fair balance for all. Instead of the huge gap between the rich and the poor, as in America, socialist communities want everyone to be able to eat, not just the wealthy. Labor is divided equally, and so are the products gained from the labor: food, goods, and property. Socialists barter and trade, while Capitalists buy and sell. Communism is one form of Socialism. Countries like China and Cuba are Communist. In those countries, few people are very poor, homeless, or unable to go to school. But here in the richest country in the world, we have as many poor and homeless as the nations where you have to sh*t in a hole. And if you think it's a fair trade because you're "free" you must be clueless. Go tell all the political prisoners we're free. Go tell all the victims of CoIntelPro that we're free. Go tell anyone who's gotten racially profiled that we're free, you dodo.

> **Did You Know?**
> Modern Capitalism was built off the destruction of people of color? Karl Marx said that what was good for Europeans was obtained at the expense of untold suffering by Africans and Native Americans. According to him, "the discovery of gold and silver in America, the extirpation, enslavement and entombment in mines of the aboriginal population, the turning of Africa into a commercial warren for the hunting of Black skins signalized the rosy dawn of the era of capitalist production."

"Something is wrong…with Capitalism…There must be a better distribution of wealth and maybe America must move toward a Democratic Socialism."
Dr. Martin Luther King, Jr.

The "American Dream" is all about getting rich by any means. White people built this land on the principles of greed and exploitation, and things aren't changing. Wait, I'm wrong, huh? White people didn't build this land, they had *others* build it for them.

Throughout the world, capital is king. Did you know that 85% of the world's wealth is held by 10% of the people, and 85% of the world's resources are controlled by 10% of the people? Matter fact, 85% of the world's PEOPLE are controlled by 10% of the people!

And those 85% follow the ways of the 10%, thinking they will one day be rich also. But the wealthy don't want new members in their good ol' boy club. They'll show you what they've got, but they'll never show you how to get it...in a way that will allow you to keep it. So we try "keeping up with the Jones" and spend our money on expensive cars and clothes...only to leave our children broke or drowning in our debts. We don't understand the business, we just want what they've got. But you have to understand that America is not about everybody "making it." In order for Capitalism to work, the rich people at the top need to have a LOT of people down at the bottom, living poor. It's how the system works. Some of us understand that, and many of them have become angry and developed a "get it by any means" mentality, as Tupac explained here:

> If you know, in this hotel room, they have food every day and I knock on the door. Every day they open the door to let me see the party, let me see that they throwin' salami, throwin' food around...telling me there's no food. Every day, I'm standing outside tryin to sing my way in: "We are weak, please let us in. We're weak, please let us in." After about a week the song is gonna change to, "We're hungry, we need some food." After two, three weeks it's like, "Give me some of the food! I'm breakin down the door." After a year it's like, "I'm pickin' the lock, comin' through the door blastin."...We asked ten years ago, we were askin' with the Panthers, we were askin' in the Civil Rights Movement. Now those who were askin' are all dead or in jail, so what are we gonna do? And we shouldn't be angry!?

Did You Know?

Since 1990, the U.S. prison population, already the world's largest, has almost doubled. In July 2003, the U.S. prison population surpassed 2 million.
There were also more than 10,000 juvenile offenders in adult prisons. The number of women in prison reached 97,491.
More than 10% of the entire Black male population aged 25-29 was incarcerated, (compared to 1% of white men in that same age group). The number of Black men in prison has grown to 500% the rate it was just 20 years ago.
In 1980, there were 463,700 Black men enrolled in college and 143,000 in prison and. In 2000, there were 603,032 enrolled in college, but 791,600 in prison. Land of the free, huh?

But most of us who develop the "rise up and take it" mentality lose focus on the fact that ALL of us need it. They lose focus on the struggle for the people, and get caught up in a struggle for themselves. Pretty soon, it's "all about me." And as Mumia said, the more we care about getting "things," the less we care about each other. And this materialism (see *Part One*, "20 Common Illusions") makes us like them. And what do we get in the end? Nothing.

Nowadays, rappers can brag about being "shopaholics," how their *bag* matches their shoes, or even their "fruity swag," and it doesn't even seem gay. 50% of any rapper's album these days is about how much they spent on their clothes, their shoes, their cars, or their jewelry. Of course, most of them are lying, but they're pushing an idea that's gonna kill us off. And one day, we're gonna see it for what it is and stop supporting that bullsh*t.

"It ain't what you don't know that gets you; it's the things you know that ain't so."
Mark Twain

Most of us, by white America's standards, are actually poor or near-poor, whether we know it or not. That doesn't stop us from impulsive spending and buying tons of things we don't need, while failing to buy things that are actually worth something. A dollar stays in the Jewish community for six months before it is spent outside. A dollar stays in the Black community for six minutes before it is spent outside. Even when we're "popping rubber bands," we're usually not spending it with each other. As I explained in *How to Hustle and Win,* most dope money goes back to white people any damn way.

How the hell did we get this way? Most traditional African societies were socialist before the slave traders came. We worked together and shared everything. But after slavery began, Africa was completely transformed by European economics. And so were we.

Since slavery, we've taken on an alien value system and hoped that it would work for us, as it did for them. But we can't function like that. We can't exploit each other and keep each other down in order to come up. The only way we can rise is together...but that's just so hard. The middle class dislikes poor Black people more than some white people! Du Bois said the "talented tenth" was supposed to take their money, education, and resources, and use it to help the poor 90% of Blacks who "didn't make it." Yeah right. Even Dr. King sadly lamented, "Middle-class negroes have forgotten their roots and are untouched by the struggles of their underprivileged brothers."

But if you think we can make it alone, on the backs of others, just remember that ***this* system wasn't made for us to benefit**. We aren't the capitalists. We are their capital. We aren't the rich slavemakers. We are their slaves. We are the CEOs. We're SOL.

As Minister Farrakhan says on Tupac's "White Man's World":

> The seal in the constitution reflects the thinking of the founding fathers that this was to be a nation by white people, and for white people. Native Americans, Blacks, and all other non-white people were to be the burden bearers for the real citizens of this nation.

Socialism is all about shared benefit and mutual cooperation. As the rap group A-Alikes say, "I eat, you eat." But we live on the premise of "I eat, you watch." Most of us can't see TEAM meaning "Together We Achieve More." The most important letter in *their* alphabet is "I."

Ujaama (cooperative economics) is a part of Kwanzaa because that's vital to the development of the Black community. But we tend to think strong economics simply means "getting rich." Yes, America is definitely about getting rich…off our labor. We aren't part of that plan. We aren't part of the American Dream. Sh*t, we shouldn't even consider ourselves Americans! As Malcolm X said in his infamous "The Ballot or the Bullet" speech:

> No, I'm not an American. I'm one of the 22 million black people who are the victims of Americanism. One of the 22 million black people who are the victims of democracy, nothing but disguised hypocrisy. So, I'm not standing here speaking to you as an American, or a patriot, or a flag-saluter, or a flag-waver – No, not I. I'm speaking as a victim of this American system. And I see America through the eyes of the victim. I don't see any American dream; I see an American nightmare...Sitting at the table doesn't make you a diner. You must be eating some of what's on that plate. Being here in America doesn't make you an American. Being born here in America doesn't make you an American.

We have to transform our focus from chasing the almighty dollar for ourselves…to pursuing freedom and prosperity for all of us. There's a ton of books you can read on this issue, but here's two to start with: *Black Liberation and Socialism* by Ahmed Shawki, and *Capitalism's World Disorder: Working-Class Politics at the Millennium* by Jack Barnes.

Getting the Game in Perspective

I didn't always think like that of course. I was well on my way to being a millionaire, actually. I was 24, and I owned about 7 houses, a couple of cars, and had a dozen side businesses and investments. One of my real estate partners said I'd be the next Trump. Then everything started going bad. *Real bad.* So bad, I was considering running away to Africa, way before Dave Chappelle made it cool to do so. It was *that* bad. I spent my last five grand to fly across the Atlantic to check out Ghana.

> "It's suicidal, how I smoke in so much la
> I saw a dead bird flyin through a broken sky
> Wish I could flap wings and fly away
> To where Black kings in Ghana stay"
> Nas, "You're the Man"

But when I arrived in Ghana, I realized I'd had the whole game twisted. I saw what I was missing. People were poor there, but they didn't act like it. They didn't look stressed and miserable. I was hopping into dollar vans and riding to nearby villages where I was treated like family. I saw a dude get hit by a car (the traffic is crazy), and a dozen people stopped what they were doing to help him. Meanwhile, Walmart shoppers in New York recently trampled a Black employee to death as they rushed into the store for the after-Thanksgiving sales. They also trampled a pregnant woman who ended up miscarrying! When they informed the shoppers they'd killed someone, they kept shopping! That's the difference between here and there. So if you don't understand why a dude like me would go off to Africa to get away, you need to get away from this sick place and see for yourself.

I saw that people who were living a simple life were happier than people who have money in America. I could eat a good meal for less than a dollar in Africa, but many days I didn't even need to because everyone ate together and shared meals. When I dropped my cellphone in a Liberian refugee camp, some brothers spent the next two days with me trying to help me find it. And they weren't looking for a handout, either.

That's when I realized I had the whole game twisted. The more I obsessed over having or not having money, the more miserable I was. I learned how to stop worrying about money. Ever since then, money ain't been a problem.

Would you rather be poor and happy or rich and miserable?

What parts of life do you think we miss in pursuit of money?

Do you think you'll be rich one day? Does it matter? Why?

Would you risk sacrificing your life in pursuit of wealth? What about your sanity? What about your friends and family?

We ain't here to get rich or die tryin.

MOVIES TO SEE

Robots; Big Brother, Big Business; Super Rich: The Greed Game; The Corporation

Robots is a flick you can watch with your kids, and both of y'all can learn something. Most of the good computer-animated movies has a deep social message, and *Robots* tells the story of the poor and their fight for socialism against the wealthy and capitalism.

The other three films are documentaries (all of which you can see free at www.supremedesignonline.com) dealing with corporations, capitalism, greed, and the problems they create.

SUPREME THE ASSHOLE ON "GET PAID AND DIE"

I'm getting sick and tired of hearin people braggin bout money. These fools got a little money and no power. White folks are still laughin at them. And I don't mean the "Look at his funny outfit" kind of laughing. I mean the "That dummy just bought that ridiculous outfit from one of our stores, and we don't even respect him there!" kind of laughing. It seems like all mothaf*ckas want nowadays is to get paid and die...and it doesn't even matter when they die, as long as they get paid sometime before then. That's some simple-minded sh*t, I tell you. I'd rather be poor and powerful like Jesus (the real one), than rich and retarded any day. It wouldn't even bother me that much if these dudes would invest some of that money back into the hood. But nah, just keep throwin it in the air, right?

A GLOBAL BLACK REVOLUTION

"Our loyalties must transcend our race, our tribe, our class, and our nation. This means we must develop a world perspective."
Dr. Martin Luther King, Jr.

When people throughout the world saw the devastation Black people in America were suffering after Hurricane Katrina, over seventy countries pledged monetary donations or other assistance. Kuwait made the largest single pledge ($500 million), and other large donations were made by Qatar ($100 million), South Korea ($30 million), India, China (both $5 million), Pakistan ($1.5 million), and even poor-ass Bangladesh ($1 million). Guess what the U.S. did? They turned most of it down. What does this show us? Black people in America have a lot more friends than you'd think. But white America just ain't one of em.

The following are seven examples of different people coming together for a common cause. Maybe we could learn something from these examples. As they say, "United we stand, divided we fall."

Did You Know?

Some hurricanes and natural disasters are man-made?

There was even a special about this on TV, called "Weather Wars." According to *The CIA's Secret Weapons Systems* by Andrew Stark:

"Perhaps the most frightening weapon of all is the one that can be used to alter weather and climate. It was used with considerable success in Vietnam. It slowed troop movements with heavy rains, and it destroyed the rice crop, as well. The danger is that these climatological changes may become permanent, affecting not only enemies of the United States, but also the entire planet."

The Nation of Islam

Many people think the Nation of Islam is a Blacks-only group. In a sense, they're right, but the teachings of the Nation of Islam state that any "Original" (meaning non-white) person is part of the Black family. While the NOI today has Hispanic, Asian, and even Native American members, the NOI of the 1930s and 1940s was almost entirely "Black" in the traditional sense of the word.

But, as World War II began, Elijah Muhammad learned that the Black man in America had allies no one else would have believed. When Japanese General Takahashi showed up in the States and began meeting with NOI leaders, he explained to them that Japan was committed to the Black man's struggle. He said that Japan wanted to destroy America for all the crimes it had committed against people of color throughout the world. He said he believed in the unity of the Black and yellow peoples, and if Black people would rise up and support Japan, then surely the U.S. could be destroyed.

When the American government found out about General Takahashi, they immediately snatched him up. He was never to be seen again. Soon after America learned that Japan was trying to join with the Black people of America, they decided to end that threat immediately. In 1945, the United States dropped two nuclear bombs on Japan. This was the first and only time a nuclear weapon has ever been used by any country. The damage that was done was so severe that people in Japan still wear masks so they don't breathe too much of the air. Shortly after our country nuked Japan, they promised to help rebuild it...but according to *their* rules. Over the next few years, Japan became the U.S.'s personal pet. The Japanese national sport changed from sumo wrestling to baseball, American businesses started taking over, and racism began to spread. Only sixty years after the bombing, today most Japanese love white America.

Marcus Garvey

When Marcus Garvey was developing the UNIA and his Black Star Line, he had no idea of the different kinds of support he would get. Gangsters like Casper Holstein gave money to the cause, but so did Ho Chi Minh, future leader of Communist Vietnam. In fact, according to Yuri Kochiyama, who knew Minh personally and hung out with him in Harlem during that time, tt was Garvey's speeches that inspired Minh., who would later lead Vietnam to independence. Even Mao Tse Tung, leader of Communist China, voiced his support for Garvey and his agenda for Black Power. (Yuri Kochiyama, by the way, was a Japanese human rights activist who had joined Malcolm X's OAAU. She was the woman who held Malcolm as he died at the Audobon Ballroom. In 1977, Kochiyama joined the group of Puerto Ricans that took over the

Statue of Liberty to draw attention to the struggle for Puerto Rican independence.)

The Black Panthers

The Black Panther Party didn't work alone. They gathered community support from the common people, but they also formed coalitions and alliances with other groups that wanted to accomplish the same things. In the Asian communities, the Black Panther Party joined with Asian militant groups like the Red Guard Party and the I Wor Kuen.

The Young Lords were the Hispanic group who shared the revolutionary platform of the BPP, while white radical groups like the Student Democratic Society (SDS) and the Weather Underground turned out to be down for the cause as well. These white groups surprised everyone, because they were willing to fight and even die in support of Black revolutionaries like the Panthers.

Today, there is a New Black Panther Party, but there is also a New Red Guard Party, as well as a few white groups who actively fight white supremacy (Unfortunately, there are more of these white anti-racist groups in Europe than in America, the home of white supremacy). Elsewhere in the world, other groups model their revolutionary platform after the original Black Panthers. In India, the Dalit Panthers seek serious changes for the conditions of the Black people of India. The Aboriginal Panthers of Australia have fought a similar battle. It's not just you, homey.

Hugo Chavez

> "Sticks in a bundle are unbreakable."
> Bondei (African) proverb

Hugo Chavez, president of Venezuela, understands the idea of finding allies very well. First, he controls a large supply of oil, which gives him **economic power**. He also is sincerely committed to the elimination of white supremacy and the empowerment of people of color and the poor, so he also has **ideological power** (power of ideas or knowledge). Finally, he is aligned with leaders and governments who share these ideas. Chavez is tight with Castro in Cuba, Ahmenijad in Iran, and many of the other countries in South America who are starting to join his side. Not only that, but he has relations with the leaders of North Korea and Zimbabwe, folks who stay in the news for standing strong against white people. But Chavez had more than one Black friend. Chavez held a conference in West Africa with several African leaders to declare that Black and brown people must unite and fight together. He said that America owes a debt to both Africa and Latin America for slavery, and that Black and brown people share "a common heritage." When he came to America, Black people, including dozens of Black celebrities, came out to show their support for his revolution. (see "Watch What you Say") **Note:** This was written in 2008. If you're reading this years later, many of these leaders may have already been killed or removed from power by that time. F*cked up, ain't it? Do something bout it.

Black Indians

When Blacks fled slavery, they ran off into jungles and mountains where they encountered Native American communities. These Africans were experts in tropical agriculture, so they shared and combined their knowledge about indigenous farming with the Native Americans. Meanwhile, the Native Americans thought that Africans had some sort of divine "medicine" in their bodies because they didn't get sick from the European diseases that were killing off the Indians. According to Nomad Winterhawk, this seemed like a very good reason for the two groups joining together, so they could create stronger, healthier children from the unions. Their slave experience also qualified Africans as experts on whites – their motives, ideas, weapons, strengths, weaknesses, languages, defenses and plans.

Based on having a common enemy, Africans and Native Americans found the first link of friendship and earliest motivation for an alliance. They discovered they shared some vital life views and strategies that they could combine to ensure their survival together. **Today, most Blacks have an average of 5-10% Indian blood.**

David Walker's Appeal

When David Walker wrote his *Appeal* in 1829, he called for slaves to rise up and revolt. But he made it clear that it wouldn't be good enough for just the Blacks in America to get free:

> Your full glory and happiness…shall never be fully consummated, but with the entire emancipation of your universal brethren all over the world…For I believe it is the will of the Lord that our greatest happiness shall consist in working for the salvation of the whole body. When this is accomplished a burst of glory will shine upon you, which will indeed astonish you and the world.

Non-Aligned Movement

This is pretty big, so big that I can't cover it all here. You can look it up on Wikipedia.org, but I'll just give you the basics. The Non-Aligned Movement is an international organization of nations that are against white supremacist rule. It currently has 118 members. That's two-thirds of the United Nations and more than 55% of the world population. I bet you had no idea.

That's right, 118 nations standing up to the bullsh*t. More specifically, they have declared that they are united in the "struggle against imperialism, colonialism, neo-colonialism, racism, Zionism, and all forms of foreign aggression, occupation, domination, interference or hegemony as well as against great power and bloc politics."

The five principles governing members are: (1) Mutual respect for each other's territorial integrity and sovereignty; (2) Mutual non-aggression; (3) Mutual non-interference in domestic affairs; (4) Equality and mutual benefit; and (5) Peaceful co-existence.

If only we could do the same sh*t. Ain't it time we stopped fighting each other and united based on something we all have in common?

Have you been able to set aside differences with others to work towards a common goal? Did you reach it? Why or why not?

Do you regularly build with people of different backgrounds? What do you learn from each other?

Do you have a platform or an agenda that you stand for? Do you use it to unite people or divide them?

Find allies in your struggle. We can't win it alone.

Movie to See

The Fourth World War

It's a visual version of much of what I'm talking about above. Like anything else, however, it doesn't *fully* address the role of white supremacy and the global oppression of people of color...but until *I* make a movie (one day), it's worth seeing. Check it out free at www.supremedesignonline.com

You Want to Be Colorblind?

Who wants to be colorblind? That means something's wrong with you. Who wouldn't want to see the diversity of life? Who would want to ignore all the different people and cultures on this planet, and ignore all their unique accomplishments? Why would someone believe that ignoring color was a way to respect people?

The crazy thing is, we wouldn't have to try so hard to be colorblind if the world wasn't so racist. I didn't say America either...I said the world. The only people who need to be colorblind are the people who do the hiring at jobs and the enrollment at schools. That way, we can all have an equal opportunity. Beyond that, it's bullsh*t. First of all, the white people in power will never be colorblind. And they're the ones that matter. But you know who says they're colorblind the loudest? Black people! They want to forget about all the sh*t white people have done, and ignore it, because they're in such a rush to get back to loving them…hoping that white folks will love them back. If you believe that, I've got some jewelry to sell you too.

Being colorblind means that, when you talk to a Chinese person, you act like them being Chinese is not important. But being Chinese is important. They have a history, a culture, a legacy that they should be proud of…not IGNORED, because "somebody" wants a colorblind society. A "colorblind" society won't do anything but make us ignore the greatness of our people, while dying to fit in and be accepted by people who don't like us anyway.

As my brother I Majestic Allah writes in the book *Knowledge of Self: A Collection of Wisdom on the Science of Everything in Life*:

> The Nation of Gods and Earths is not anti-white, nor pro-Black, yet it doesn't mean that with a "magical eraser" we erase the tide of history that includes colonialism, slavery, Jim Crow laws, racism, the Maafa, segregation, genocide, etc…The REAL effects of the tides of history are still being played out. There are those who BENEFIT from that tide of history. It is RIDICULOUS for anyone to advocate "not pointing it out" or "the past is past."
>
> What we don't do though is DWELL in the past. I manufacture the future by teaching the youth about the past AND who they are NOW. Thus they become the architects of the future.
>
> Ironically Original [Black] peoples are often the ones whom are most often asked to "let bygones be bygones." You never hear anyone asking the Jews to "forget the Holocaust." You never hear anyone asking the U.S. to "forget 9/11." (nor the Alamo or Pearl Harbor) You never hear anyone asking Christians to "forget the Crucifixion."
>
> I could go on and on. Being color blind is a disease and deficiency.

Isn't it interesting that people of

Did You Know?

Black was once seen as good? The people of Kemet and many other ancient civilizations believed that black or dark-blue skin was a divine attribute. In Rastafari culture, among others, black is seen as beautiful. In early India, black skin was highly regarded, and babies were coated in sesame oil to make them darker. In Japanese culture, kuro (black) is a symbol of nobility, age, and experience. This has resulted in many martial arts as the black belt being one of the first senior ranks.

In the Maasai tribes of Kenya and Tanzania, the color black is associated with rain clouds, becoming a symbol of life and prosperity. Black was also the color of the Arab dynasty of Abbasid caliphs, so black is frequently used in flags of Arab-Muslim countries. Blackness was regarded by ancient people as the source of all existence. The first gods of all the ancient civilizations were Black, including Osiris, Buddha, Krishna, and even Jesus H. Christ.

color are the only ones expected to relinquish their heritage and forget the past in order to be an "American"? Why do we have to lose ourselves?

Does treating everyone "equally" meaning seeing everyone as the same?

Want to get deeper into the issue? Try reading *Whitewashing Race: The Myth of a Color-Blind Society* by Michael K. Brown, or *Racism without Racists: Color-Blind Racism* and the *Persistence of Racial Inequality in the United States* by Eduardo Bonilla-Silva.

Don't ignore what's right in front of your face.

THE KEYS TO THE COLORS

When members of Detroit's Young Boys Incorporated were arrested in the crackhouses they ran, the police confused them with the addicts and released everyone, including high-level leaders. While working, YBI members were low-key and dressed down, often bummy, so as to avoid attention and suspicion. But these guys were making hundreds of thousands of dollars.

I remember a time when the thugs and dopeboys wore black. I remember a time when we bummed it out in faded-ass jeans and t-shirts with little holes in em. I remember when the boss of a strip where my friends hustled would come through every week and nobody else could tell who he was because he was so low-key. I remember when only the pretty boys and faggots wore bright pink and purple. I remember when a man wouldn't wear straight-leg jeans and a muscle shirt unless he was a transvestite. I also remember when all that changed.

If wearing twenty bright-ass colors is your thing, I ain't knockin you. But you can't do dirt dressed like that, so don't pretend you're really puttin in work in the streets. **How the hell you gonna avoid the police lookin like a damn fruit salad?**

Really, there's nothing wrong with wearing flashy sh*t…*if* you want attention. If you want to avoid getting profiled, photographed, and possibly indicted, you may want to do things differently and avoid being the "man on the scene." Either way, keep in mind that everything counts. From your outfit to your fingernails, people are paying attention.

I started understanding that the day a female told me that what I was wearing made her think about sex. I wasn't wearing silk pajamas or anything, either. I was just wearing red. She pulled out a book that explained the significance of colors and what emotions they affect. What do you think I did?

Okay, besides the sex. That's right, I borrowed the book.

I learned just how deep the science of colors goes. I learned that companies and organizations put a lot of thought into the meanings and effects of the colors they use. I learned that politicians wear red ties with dark suits because the colors make voters believe in your integrity I learned that, in many prisons, the walls are painted pastel colors like pink and sky blue to decrease angry feelings and violence among prisoners… while promoting homosexuality. I started thinking about more symbolic things. I heard RZA rap:

> Inside my lab, I'm going mad/ Took two drags off the blunt, and started breaking down the flag/ The blue is for the Crips, the red is for the Bloods/ The white is for the cops, and the stars come from the clubs/ or the slugs that ignite, through the night, by the dawn's early light, while the suns fight for the stripes

That's around the time when I learned that the Pan-African/RBG flag was red, black, and green because "the Black is for the people, the Green is for the land, and the Red is for the blood we've shed fighting for both."

From there, I started paying attention to the symbolic meanings of everything we're surrounded by. Turns out that damn near everything means something else. For example, our paper currency is LOADED with symbolism. On an American one-dollar bill, there is an owl in the upper left-hand corner of the "1," and a spider hidden in the upper right-hand corner. The owl and spider are occult symbols, often used by Masons and other secret societies. The number 13 is also an important occult number that occurs all over the dollar. Then there's the meaning behind the eye on the pyramid. The Latin below it means "New World Order."

You play pool? That's one very symbolic game. Think about it. White ball knocking all the balls of color off the green table. What's the green table? The Earth. Who's the last one to take down? The Black one.

Did You Know?

White was once seen as bad? According to Chancellor Williams' *The Destruction of Black Civilization*, early Africans regarded white as evil in itself. Across much of modern Africa, white is still a color of mourning and is worn during funerals. In Japanese culture, shiro (white) symbolizes serfdom, youth, and naiveté. This is why the white belt is one of the lowest belts in the martial arts. In Chinese, Japanese, and Indian tradition, white is the color of mourning, and death. In Africa and some parts of Asia, when they saw white people for the first time, they were thought they were demons or very sick people. Those orientations didn't change until Europeans went all over the world brainwashing everyone. Like the title of another book worth checkin out, we were *Blacked Out by Whitewash* (Google it, it's free). Dr. Cress Welsing's book *The Isis Papers: The Keys to the Colors* explains the significance of our color complex in much greater depth.

Do you know the symbolic meanings behind: The Washington Monument? The 6-pointed star? The CBS logo? The game of football? The movie *Planet of the Apes*? The Shell logo? Valentine's Day hearts? The Christmas tree? Hanging a bandana from your pocket?

There's always more to life than what meets the eye.

---

18 People who Need to be Slapped

Journal Entry: November 17, 2007

I almost slapped a couple folks today, until I realized there are way *too many* people who could use a good backhand to the face. These are just the ones I thought of today:

1. People who put rims on old Hyundais and Subarus
2. People who *want* you to hear their stupid cell phone conversations
3. People who *still* eat chitlins or hogmaws
4. Metrosexuals and the women who love them
5. Preachers who lie, steal, and cheat, and the believers who love them
6. People with stanky breath who want to whisper in your ear
7. 14-year-old girls booty-shakin in they SpongeBob PJs on YouTube
8. 34-year-old men sittin at home, waitin on the next booty shake video
9. People who steal the squeegees from the pump at the gas station
10. Women with fake hair, fake nails, fake eyes, etc. complaining that they can't find a "real man"
11. Losers who pretend to be non-losers online
12. People older than seven who forward chain letters and other stupid sh*t about ghosts and devils coming to kill you or rape your dog
13. The millions of idiots who fall for email scams, encouraging scammers to keep sending them out...to non-idiots like me
14. Old people who know their blind asses shouldn't be driving anymore
15. Girls with tire-track stretchmarks wearin shirts that show their belly
16. People who pretend to be bums so they can beg for money
17. Finally, O.J. Simpson and Tiger Woods. For obvious reasons.

Watch Out for the Sellouts

Slaves fought back daily in many ways, many of which they did alone. Some would find ways to con or outsmart the slaveholder, while others would engage in acts of theft, poisoning, sneaking away, or even arson. These ways of "getting back" or "getting out" didn't take much planning, but they only helped a few people at a time.

When a group of slaves felt they were ready to take things to the next level, they planned an insurrection, or slave rebellion. A slave rebellion demanded a great degree of planning, as well as the participation of as many of the enslaved as possible. That's where the problems came up: Every time you involved more people, you raised the chances of someone f*cking up. Usually, the plans would come together just fine, but somebody always ended up telling. Either somebody spilled the beans because they were drunk or just plain stupid, or they ran and told the white folks because they thought it was the "right thing to do." **Every losing slave revolt had one thing in common:** Somebody didn't know what side they were on. (see *Part One*, "Stop Snitchin")

Denmark Vesey, Rebel Slave

One of the most famous insurrection plans was that of Denmark Vesey in 1822. Vesey had been planning this revolt for nine years. He was convinced that all slaves would want their freedom. He said "Let us assemble a sufficient number to commence the work with spirit, and [we won't be looking for more] men; they'll fall in behind us fast enough."

But when one of Vesey's co-conspirators, William Paul was captured, he testified against two other individuals. He claimed these two, Harth and Poyas, were major players in raising the insurrection. These two were released, but Black spies were sent amongst them to further monitor their dealings from thereon. Sound familiar?

Things stood still for awhile afterwards, until William Paul started fearing that his time would soon be up. Hoping to buy time, he gave a new, longer confession. This new confession claimed that the plot was "very extensive." The new details scared the hell out of the white people, and hundreds of sentinels and patrols being put on high alert.

But three or four days would pass, and things remained quiet. There was no proof of Paul's story, until one day, one of the Governor's slaves, Ned Bennett, came and "offered himself for examination."

This really confused the authorities, who didn't expect any of the slaves involved to come forth **on their own**. My, how times have changed.

Anyway, even after Bennett named names and told tons of previously unknown details, the authorities kept all their knowledge secret until further arrests could be made. Sound familiar? Today, it's called a secret indictment. On June 18th, ten slaves were arrested (including Harth and Poyas), Vesey was discovered, and the insurrection was defeated.

Nat Turner, Rebel Slave

During Nat Turner's famous rebellion, there is one highlight that stands out most. Nat Turner's rebellion was picking up steam, right up until they reached a Dr. Blunt's house. When they were about to fire on it, Blunt's slaves used his guns and fired back at them to defend his home. This act of defense was the only reason Turner's band scattered, never to reunite again. The separated, weakened forces were soon caught and killed.

And this is where we get the saying: "Watch out for a nigga that's a slave to the blunt." Okay, maybe not.

Josiah Henson, Brainwashed Negro

James M. McPherson must have been wrong in his book, *Black Rebellion*, where he said "all slaves seethed with rebellious hatred against the white oppressors..." Didn't these enslaved Blacks want to be free? Or did they desire to remain slaves? It's not that simple. Not then, and not now.

Josiah Henson was a slave so loyal and dedicated to his master, that he was trusted to transport all the other slaves over a thousand miles to Kentucky. Henson alone was left to do the task, and he traveled through a number of free territories. Not only that, but he was repeatedly offered freedom by free Blacks, if he would also free the other slaves he was transporting. Henson recalled:

> I had never dreamed of running away. I had a sentiment of honor on the subject. The duties of the slave to his master as appointed over him in the Lord, I had ever heard urged by ministers and religious men. It seemed like outright stealing...I had undertaken a great thing; my vanity had been flattered all along the road by hearing myself praised; I thought it would be a feather in my cap to carry it through thoroughly, and had often painted the scene in my imagination of the final surrender to Master Amos, and the immense admiration and respect with which he would regard me.

And so Henson continued with his task, undaunted. As you can tell, two of the main influences on Henson's twisted thinking are his religious beliefs and his empty hopes of earning some kind of privilege under his master through unquestioning allegiance. Henson didn't just want to do what he thought his master wanted, he had come to believe that what his master wanted was *best.* Before long, he could think like white folks even when white folks weren't around.

Former slave Henry Bibb expressed a popular view among slaves that the preferential treatment of house slaves weakened the slave class:

> The domestic slaves are often found to be traitors to their own people, for the purpose of gaining favor with their masters; and they are encouraged and trained up by them to report every plot they know of being formed about stealing anything, or running away, or any thing of the kind; and for which they are paid. This is one of the principal causes of the slaves being divided among themselves, and without which they could not be held in bondage one year, and perhaps not half that time.

A slave quoted in Julius Lester's *To Be a Slave*, narrated:

> They taught us to be against one another and no matter where you would go you would always find one that would tattle and have the white folks pecking on you. They would be trying to make it soft for themselves.

Austin Steward claimed that a domestic slave "will for the sake of his master and mistress, frequently betray his fellow-slave...hence it is insurrections and stampedes are so generally detected. Such slaves are always treated with more affability that others, for the slaveholder is well aware that he stands over a volcano."

What do you do when confronted by people who are against what you stand for? What do you do when you're not sure where they stand?

Do you share your plans and ideas freely with everyone you encounter?

Everyone doesn't share your values,
so be careful who you work with or share your plans with.

Other Snitches and Sellouts

When slaves throughout Virginia began planning rebellions, many slaves were arrested who were not even involved. When Martha L. Nelson's house slave Coleman was being held, she petitioned the governor for a pardon. She spoke of his devotion to her, adding that he would:

> ...inform on the negroes, **as soon as any white person would**, if he knew or suspected anything wrong was planning among them...such a servant ought not to be sent away particularly in these perilous times of insurrection.

While on a slave ship, slave William Hayden could hear into the next room. There, the other slaves, still in chains and shackles, were planning a mutiny. He was shocked to learn that he was going to be murdered with all the whites on board, because he seemed to be down with the whites, at least more than with the Blacks. He said:

> They had even provided themselves with a file from the lot of blacksmith tools on board, and that many were at that moment free from their chains. This information I carried to my master; and after ascertaining the truth of my statement, he had them again bound more firmly than ever.

In *The Peculiar Institution*, Kenneth Stampp describes the domestic slaves:

> [The house slaves are] devoted to the master and his family and alienated from the other slaves. "They are just the same as white folks," said a former slave in disgust, "Some of them will betray another to curry favor with the master." In this way...the master destroyed "the sympathy that unites...the victims of the same oppression...He has but to arm the human passions against each other."

Scholars on slavery identified Blacks who cared only about pleasing whites as "Sambos." **Samboism**, they said, produced slaves who displayed "an insensitivity to others, and a dangerous selfishness. The untroubled sambos served masters and themselves, sowing suspicion in the quarters and thus adding to the troubles of all."

Hussein Bulhan, in *Frantz Fanon and the Psychology of Oppression*, explains:

> In prolonged oppression, the oppressed group will internalize the oppressor without. They adopt his guidelines and prohibitions, they assimilate his image and his social behaviors, and they become agents of their own oppression. The oppressor without becomes an intropressor – an oppressor within.
>
> The well-known inferiority complex of the oppressed originates in this process of internalization…Intropression…is an ensemble of internalized aspects of oppression that prompts a betrayal of self and loved ones and plots of resistance.

Do you know anyone who seems to hate themselves in this way? What do you think happens when you give that kind of person power?

What do you do when confronted by this mentality?

The Willie Lynch Syndrome

One of the most eye-opening moments for me was reading the "Willie Lynch" speech when I was a teenager. This was the first time I'd ever heard that there was such a diabolical plan to keep us down. After a brief introduction, it goes:

> I caught the whiff of a dead slave hanging from a tree, a couple miles back. You are not only losing valuable stock by hangings, you are having uprisings, slaves are running away, your crops are sometimes left in the fields too long for maximum profit, You suffer occasional fires, your animals are killed. Gentlemen, you know what your problems are; I do not need to elaborate. I am not here to enumerate your problems, I am here to introduce you to a method of solving them.
>
> In my bag here, I have a fool proof method for controlling your black slaves. I guarantee every one of you that if installed correctly it will control the slaves for at least 300 years. My method is simple. Any member of your family or your overseer can use it.
>
> I have outlined a number of differences among the slaves; and I take these differences and make them bigger. I use fear, distrust and envy for control purposes. These methods have worked on my modest plantation in the West Indies and it will work throughout the South. Take this simple little list of differences and think about them. On top of my list is "age" but it's there only because it starts with an "A." The second is "color" or shade, there is intelligence, size, sex, sizes of plantations, status on plantations, attitude of owners, whether the slaves live in the valley, on a hill, east, west, north, south, have fine hair, course hair, or is tall or short. Now that you have a list of differences, I shall give you an outline of action, but before that, I shall assure you that distrust is stronger than trust and envy stronger than adulation, respect or admiration.
>
> The Black slaves after receiving this indoctrination shall carry on and will become self refueling and self generating for hundreds of years, maybe thousands.

> Don't forget you must pitch the old Black male vs. the young Black male, and the young Black male against the old Black male. You must use the dark skin slaves vs. The light skin slaves, and the light skin slaves vs. the dark skin slaves. You must use the female vs. the male. And the male vs. the female. You must also have your white servants and overseers distrust all Blacks. But it is necessary that your slaves trust and depend on us. They must love, respect and trust only us.
>
> Gentlemen, these kits are your keys to control. Use them. Have your wives and children use them, never miss an opportunity. If used intensely for one year, the slaves themselves will remain perpetually distrustful. Thank you gentlemen.

This speech was supposed to have been given in 1712. And "300 years" from then, huh? When's that? Now, I'm not so sure if Willie Lynch was a real person, or if it's just a myth, but I know that these methods are very real. Historian Larry Koger documents early uses of "Willie Lynch" tactics in his book *Black Slaveowners,* in the chapter titled "The Denmark Vesey Conspiracy: Brown Masters vs. Black Slaves":

> It is evident that the Black community was divided along a number of lines, including those between free and slave, Black and Brown (mulatto), house slave and field slave, and any number of others, though these are the most influential in the issue of insurrection.
>
> **These class lines, created ultimately by the master, provided him a position of relative security and stability in the slavery superstructure as he was neither affected nor judged by these standards, and was thus the only one free from their divisiveness and the combative inferiority and superiority complexes associated with them.**
>
> (Superiority in the slavemaster's mind was something absolute on account of his white manhood; in comparison, superiority in the enslaved Black's mind was something relative to the master's ultimate superiority. So the mulatto house slave was superior to the dark field slaves, but still had no amount of power in regards to the white master they all answered to.)

Did You Know?

Betrayal happenned everywhere white people turned us against each other. Not long after arriving in Boriken (Puerto Rico), the Spaniards enslaved the indigenous Taino people. The natives rose up to defend themselves. The Battle of Villa de Sotomayor was the first and only success the Taíno had, killing almost all of the Spanish living there and destroying the village. Soon after that battle, 16 chiefs were captured, betrayed by a fellow Taino, and extradited to Hispaniola for conspiracy. The remaining rebels retreated either to the mountainous center of the island or to the Lesser Antilles where they allied themselves with their former enemies the Caribe. Even with their strong resistance to the Spaniard's weapons, they fell victim to widespread smallpox, a disease the natives could not easily resist. The Taino population fell significantly, due to disease, warfare, enslavement, mass suicide, and exodus to other places. Yet the Taino remain...in the blood of 61% of Puerto Ricans today.

> Inferiority and superiority played a pivotal role in the self-image of Blacks, creating roles of submissiveness, servility and docility to whites, as well as creating rifts of disunity between the enslaved through each side of each class line having a negative image of the opposing side. One of the major tools used to implant such ideas both consciously and subconsciously was slave religion.

Where do you fall in the food chain? Are you a house slave, field slave, snitch, sambo, rebel, or runaway?

And what do you with people who fall into the other categories?

Though we *should* be, we're not all on the same page.
Be strategic in the way you deal with others.

ALL DOGS AIN'T LOYAL

"Every brother ain't a brother cause of color/ Just as well could be undercover
...Cause a Black hand squeezed on Malcolm X the man"
Public Enemy, "Welcome to the Terrordome"

Fred Hampton

On December 4, 1969, Chicago policed raided the home of Black Panther Party organizer Fred Hampton. The raid was conducted with the full involvement of the FBI.

Earlier that night, Fred and others had been drinking with fellow Panther William O'Neal, one of Hampton's trusted bodyguards. At the time of the raid, everyone was sound asleep.

In the raid, Hampton was shot and killed along with guard Mark Clark. The others in the home were then dragged into the street and beaten. These people, including Hampton's 8-month pregnant girlfriend, were then charged with assault and attempted murder of the police officers.

But ballistic evidence revealed that the Panthers fired only one bullet. Nearly 100 bullets came from police guns. And guess who shot first?

In 1976, the Church Committee's investigation into ColntelPro revealed that William O'Neal was actually an FBI agent. Days before the raid, he had delivered an apartment floor-plan to the FBI with an "X" marking Hampton's bed. Ballistic evidence showed that most of bullets fired were aimed at Hampton's bedroom. O'Neal didn't just set up the murder...he made it *that much* easier by drugging everyone's drinks.

Gabriel Prosser

Gabriel Prosser had big plans. He would seize Capitol Square in Richmond, Virginia and take the governor hostage before making demands for the benefit of slaves everywhere. Prosser then planned to establish a government, having already named positions for presidents, princes, governors, and counselors, once he was crowned as the King of

Virginia. If the plan failed, Plan B involved a retreat into the mountains. The plans seemed foolproof. Seemed.

Prosser's rebellion was originally set for August 30, 1800. On that day, more than a thousand slaves arrived at the designated meeting place ready to discuss their strategy, which involved **as many as 50,000 slaves ready to fight for freedom.**

However, heavy rain made it necessary to postpone until the following day. In that short lapse of time, two slaves, Tom and Pharaoh Sheppard, "entered their master's office, closed the door behind them, and related to him the well-planned insurrection of General Gabriel, which was to have taken place than night." Just goes to show that *anybody* – from a "Tom" to a "Pharaoh" – can sell out.

Within days, 30 of the slaves involved were captured. Gabriel Prosser himself avoided getting caught and remained a fugitive. With help from others, he did like Assata would almost 200 yars later – he laid low and made plans to flee the country. By offering pardons in exchange for information, the officials gained some crimestopper tips about Prosser and others' whereabouts (hmm, sounds like their style ain't changed). But they didn't get nearly as much help as they hoped. Instead, many of slaves valiantly chose their own death over giving up details on their plot for freedom (hmm, sounds like it's *our* style that changed).

Prosser was on the verge of escaping the country by boat when another slave spotted him. Immediately, the slave thought of using the reward money for himself. He hoped to buy his own freedom…at the expense of Prosser's life. What had Prosser *done for him* anyway? The slave quickly told the authorities. Prosser was caught and hanged.

Meanwhile, because he was Black, the slave who turned Prosser in was given much less than the promised reward. Dumbass!

Wu Tang Clan

"There's danger in having too much trust."
Ancient African proverb

Today, the closest thing to a rebel slave is a Black celebrity who's not kissing up to white folks. If you pay attention, people like Mike Tyson, Tupac Shakur, and even Michael Jackson were in the most trouble RIGHT after publicly talking trash about white America. Or just look at what happened to Rap-A-Lot's J. Prince, Death Row's Suge Knight, and Murder Inc.'s Irv Gotti RIGHT after the three of them started talking about forming their own distribution network (cutting out the white distributors everyone depends on now).

It's no accident that Black people in high (and low) places are still being taken down daily. And guess how? The same way they did it in the past.

T.I.'s bodyguard turned informant to get leniency on his own charge. Even Mike Vick's cousins couldn't be trusted. And the list goes on and on. But what you need to learn is that many of the crazy ideas that turned out to be life-changing mistakes, from the dog-fighting to the machine guns, didn't come from Vick or Tip themselves. A lot of times, the ideas that send people to jail come from the agents, informants, and outsiders in the first place. That's when a person isn't just telling *on* something you did. That's when a person tells you *to* do something…and THEN tells ON you for doin it!

Do you know what caused the break-up of the otherwise "invincible" Wu Tang Clan? You'd never believe it. It turns out that a white boy, a federal informant named David Caruso, already in trouble for previous drug charges, got in good with the Clan and worked his way up.

This white boy switched his style up, going from the "raver" look popular on the Ecstasy scene to dressing like a street thug and talking "street." Soon, he had worked himself into all the Clan's affairs. It wasn't long before he was startin trouble, causing members of the previously "invincible" Wu Tang Clan to distrust *each other*! All the while, *he* was gaining their trust.

> "It is the foolish sheep that makes the wolf his counselor."
> John Ray (1628-1705)

According to the *Village Voice* article that exposed the infiltration, by the time RZA found out he was a federal agent, Caruso had taken over as Ghostface and Cappadonna's manager. RZA told them to cut their ties with the snake in their midst. Ghostface refused. By now, he trusted his new "friend" Caruso more than his former friend and mentor, the RZA.

Before long, the Wu Tang Clan was falling apart. RZA and others were being investigated for gun-running and other serious crimes. Even unrelated incidents were being tied back to the Clan. Music industry

Did You Know?

Modern-day agent provocateurs are apparently spending less time gathering information (thanks to the Internet, which makes just about any information only a click away), and more time sowing the seeds of dissent, conflict, and neutralization. Instead of killing off organizational leaders, all that is needed nowadays is for a single rabble-rouser or agitator to enter a group, establish a following, incite conflicts, and cause the group to spiral into a cycle of unproductive debate and dissent. Or worse, they initiate violence and then disappear. Recently, agent provocateurs attempted to start riots during otherwise peaceful protests in Montreal, Greece, and Oakland. Many were later discovered to have been working for the police. Just like many of our favorite people will be…one day.

insider Cedric Muhammad was told that "individuals arrested on certain charges in New York City were being offered less time if they would say that they were doing what they were doing on behalf of Wu Tang Clan."

Even the music suffered, as group members could no longer agree and work together as a team. Since then, the once unstoppable shine of the Wu Tang Clan's dominance over the music industry has faded to black.

> "All domination involves invasion – at times physical and overt, at times camouflaged – with the invader assuming the role of a helping friend."
> Paulo Freire (1921-1997)

When things fall apart like this, it's almost always because of someone close to you. When you're in a position of power, it's never by accident.

Who do you trust? How have they earned it?

Have you ever stopped trusting someone, only to let them get back close to you? Why?

Are there people in your circle who seem to cause nothing but trouble and confusion? Why are they still around?

Watch who you allow into your inner circle.

F*ck Dr. King

Now I don't mean that literally. The *real* Dr. King was a good dude. But the Dr. King we learn about in school is a myth like Santa Claus. So f*ck the bullsh*t idea they *gave* us. Let's talk about what really happened.

While Dr. King is given most of the credit for the gains made by the Civil Rights Movement, it is important that we look seriously at OTHER factors that were in play at that time. After Black soldiers returned from the Korean War, many Black communities were galvanized to begin resisting oppression. As a matter of fact, several armed resistance groups sprang up between the 50's and 60's. One of the most notable early groups was that of Robert F. Williams in North Carolina (see "Negroes with Guns"). At the same time, the international community was becoming increasingly aware of America's injustices. Several other nations were identifying with the struggles of Blacks in America. As a matter of fact, as early as World War II, Japan was promising to be the savior of the dark races of the world, and was sending representatives to align forces with the Nation of Islam! (see "Global Black Revolution")

We don't read about this in history class do we? That's why there's people like me. Where were we? Oh yeah, the world was on the verge of rebellion against the wicked oppressor that is America. Meanwhile, America was in serious danger of an *internal* racial uprising. The book (and movie) *The Spook who Sat by the Door* was not all fiction, you know.

To avoid being overwhelmed by increasing international pressure, or being deluged by the increasing violence at home, America needed to appease the easily lulled massess. After all, that's how it works with "the masses." As my brother Kwami K. Kwami points out in *The Tables Have Turned: A Street Guide to Guerrilla Lawfare*:

> There is yet another reason to consider myself a guerrilla. I do not consider myself as a member of that body of people that calls itself "the general public." A federal court in the case, J.W. Collins v. F.M. Paist Co. (DC Pa) 14 F2d 614, has defined "the general public" as "that vast multitude, which includes the ignorant, the unthinking, and the credulous, who, in making a purchase, do not stop to analyze, but are governed by general appearance and general impression."

So since the government knows that the majority of us will fall for anything, what did they give us? Civil Rights. Not *revolution*, but the *revision* of a few laws. How did they sell it to us? By promoting, through the media, a single leader who became *their* posterboy because of his stance on nonviolence and passivity, while others were calling for total uprising. Worse yet, Derrick Bell, author of *Faces at the Bottom of the Well* has said that Civil Rights for Blacks wasn't exactly what we thought, and was actually intended to benefit WHITES more than Blacks.

To be fair, Dr. King made as many gains as he could, but he didn't exactly win the fight, remember? He was given what the government *felt* like giving us to *appease us*. **Dr. King was actually killed as soon as he started asking for BIGGER changes**. More on that in a minute.

Over forty years later, we see the results of these "changes." Voting rights? Yeah right! Forget whether you believe in this country's election scam – I mean process. Did you know you voting rights still have to be voted on and renewed every few years? What does that *tell* you? School integration? Well, it wasn't until *then* that Black students began doing worse than their white peers, BECAUSE of these changes. (see "Integration was a Lie") And our schools are *still* segregated, except now we're not teaching our own people our own curriculum. Integrated communities, workplaces, and businesses? All the discriminatory practices are still here, except now they are covert (hidden). At least when they were out in the open, we had to stick together and fight. Now what the hell are we fighting? Besides ourselves? And let's not forget that the 60s is when all the jobs started disappearing from the Black communities. You know what happened next. The breakdown of the Black family. Before the jobs started disappearing, more than 3/4ths of Black families had working fathers. Now that number of two-parent households is down to less than half. Why? 'Cause they said, "Okay you can work equally now" and then they took away all our daddies' jobs!

But somehow we now believe we're equal participants in this American Dream. We've really just been rocked back to sleep.

"The most odious of all oppressions are those which mask as justice."
Robert H. Jackson (1892-1854)

After Dr. King met with the Honorable Elijah Muhammad at his house and agreed that whites were of the same accord and weren't going to change, the government (who'd been listening in) began fearing that their posterboy wanted more than they were ready to offer. Dr. King began fighting for workers' rights, struggling for the poor, and rallying around causes that could have torn the very exploitative fabric of America to shreds. You see, this "American Dream" is built on oppression and exploitation. That's how it began, and that's how it will always be. To believe otherwise is to either believe in fairy tales, miracles, or *revolution.*

At any rate, when Dr. King began challenging the status quo of America, galvanizing poor people, Black and white, to buck the system, it was undermining some of the fundamental principles America is based on (exploiting the poor, poor people being voiceless and easily appeased, etc.). Well, of course, we know what happened then.

And let's be real. This country didn't like Dr. King until he was dead. Once dead, his ideas and image could be exploited like a modern-day Jesus, designed to fit the ideology that they would like us to have. Half of the ideas we associate now with Dr. King didn't even come from him.

Try the following True or False quiz and see how much you know:

		Supreme's "How Well Do You Know Dr. King?" Quiz
1	T F	King opposed the Supreme Court's ban on school prayer
2	T F	King supported reparations, hoping if Blacks received them, poor whites would realize the real enemy was rich whites
3	T F	He believed that no one should use violence against another, even in self-defense
4	T F	He supported preferential hiring and race-based quotas so more Blacks could get jobs
5	T F	He wanted to be the head of the Civil Rights movement, and voluntarily stepped up to the plate
6	T F	He praised the militancy engulfing the Black community, warning that there'd be no peace until things changed
7	T F	He believed the Declaration of Independence and the Constitution were meaningless for Blacks because they were written by slaveowners
8	T F	He thought Christian myths and doctrines were historically and logically unrealistic, and saw the ministry as a way to position his ideas on social protest
9	T F	He said America was the greatest nation in the world, a nation "born in the ideals of freedom, justice and equality"

10	T F	He said America was the greatest force of violence in the world, a nation "born in genocide"

You picked your answers yet? Don't cheat. Dr. King wouldn't do that. Or would he? Here goes: All the odd statements are false, and all the even ones are true. Don't believe me? Just look it up. Now, who do you think our false ideas came from? Dr. King's dream was not about whites and Blacks going to the same churches, people. His true dream, like many other leaders at that time (most of who were similarly assassinated) was revolution. So let's stop celebrating messiahs long gone, and let's live to fulfill their visions.

Don't let your oppressor reinvent your history.

Revisionist History

Also, another lesson I can't leave out deals with the fact that King has been reinvented by damn near every group who wants to claim him as a modern-day messiah of sorts. Maybe someone will even say I'm twisting Dr. King's message up. What I do know is that no matter how many people claim to love Dr. Martin Luther King, Jr. NOW, he wasn't so loved back then. No matter what his philosophy was, there was no way he was going to please everybody. Perhaps you think he united everyone with his "I have a dream" speech, but even in that speech, King spoke about the "bad check" America had made out to Black people, promising freedom and equality, while offering nothing. In the same speech, he also said, "The whirlwinds of revolt will continue to shake the foundations of our nation until the bright day of justice emerges." Does that sound revolutionary enough for you? That speech made a lot of folks mad back then. But that's not the part you hear NOW. You hear about white kids holding hands with Black kids on some mountaintop. The truth is, King's message back then made some people excited while it made others raving mad. And no matter what you do or say, there's no way everyone will take your side. So as

Did You Know?

If you think about, Malcolm X is being reinvented in the same way. We already know Alex Haley left tons of information out of the autobiography, and that Haley was accused of "editing" Malcolm's views towards the end of his life. Malcolm, even after returning from Mecca, advocated that whites could contribute to the struggle in some way, but denied them membership in his Organization of Afro-American Unity (OAAU). However, he let Asians like Yuri Kochiyama join. What does this tell you? Yet, the media celebrates Malcolm X, not because he championed Black identity, but because he "accepted whites." This is what they sell us about even Malcolm X. That he is great because he learned to love white people too!

Bill Cosby once said, "I can't tell you the path to success, but I can tell you the easiest path to failure: Trying to please everyone."

You can't please everybody. So don't even worry about it!

SUPREME THE ASSHOLE ON: "BLACK HISTORY MONTH"

28 days for us to celebrate who and what we are? That's some bullsh*t. I don't care if they gave us the longest month in the year, it would still end up being some bullsh*t. It would be a bunch of sh*t about Rosa Parks, Martin Luther King, and maybe George Washington Carver and his peanuts. I bet none of the Black revolutionaries in this book will ever get mentioned. Anytime they talk about anyone Black, it's always "the first Black astronaut" or "the first Black man in major league baseball" or "the first Black man to shake hands with a white man." Don't you get it? It's never about the Black people who changed the world. It's about which Black people were accepted by white people first. Like the best thing we can do is go somewhere they didn't want us to go. One day soon, they're going to celebrate Condoskeeza Rice and 50 Snitch on Black History Month too. Keep believing in sh*t like that, and you'll think you ain't sh*t until white people accept you. If you want to tell me about the "first Black," tell me about the first Black man to backhand slap the sh*t out of a slave trader.

INTEGRATION WAS A LIE

Malcolm X, in his "Message to the Grassroots," on integration:

> It's just like when you've got some coffee that's too black, which means it's too strong. What do you do? You integrate it with cream, you make it weak. But if you pour too much cream in it, you won't even know you ever had coffee. It used to be hot, it becomes cool. It used to be strong, it becomes weak. It used to wake you up, now it puts you to sleep.

If you weren't alive to see the difference, you may not get it.

So let's do a quick review of how things were BEFORE and AFTER integration.

BEFORE	AFTER
BEFORE integration, Black students went to shabby Black schools where they were taught by Black teachers who really cared.	AFTER integration, Black students either went to shabby Black schools where they were taught by white teachers who didn't give a f*ck OR nice white schools where they grew up being treated like SH*T.
BEFORE integration, Blacks couldn't eat with them, party with them, or live with them, so you created a sense of family with your own people.	AFTER integration, Blacks could go hang around whoever they wanted, so you started liking that better than doing it with your own kind (even though they still didn't like you!)
BEFORE integration, Black students had raggedy books, but they finished school.	AFTER integration, Black students still had raggedy books, and now they didn't even finish the damn book.
BEFORE integration, money stayed in the Black community because you shopped with each other.	AFTER integration, money leaves the Black community in six minutes because you can buy white sh*t now.
BEFORE integration, Black men married Black women and raised Black families.	AFTER integration, Black men chased white women, vice versa, and what happened to the Black family?

BEFORE integration, Black people didn't get paid as much as white people, and had worse jobs.	AFTER integration, ain't sh*t changed.
BEFORE integration, Black people couldn't live in white neighborhoods, so they had to make the best out of the hood.	AFTER integration, Black people could move into white neighborhoods, but all the white folks would move out right after, so it *turned into* a hood.
BEFORE integration, Black people thought white people were pretty f*cked up.	AFTER integration, Black people think white people are pretty f*cking great.
BEFORE integration, Black women looked like Black women.	AFTER integration, Black women look like white women.
BEFORE integration, there were about 8 gay Black men out of every 1,000.	AFTER integration, it's more like 80 out of 100. And of the 20 left, 10 are in jail and 5 are crackheads.

Joining the ones who beat you won't make your life better.

REVIEW

The principle for this chapter was **"Expansion and Distribution"** This means: Broaden your horizons, spread your reach, and find balance in all you do.

Here are the principles and lessons we covered:

Balance
Expand your horizons.
Even if you're doing wrong, find a way to balance it out by doing more right.
Relationships
Our women are just as messed up as our men. We've all got to grow up together.
Women, don't blame us. Work with us. We're both part of the problem, so we've gotta work together.
Insecurity is a security threat. Stay away from it.
You can't please everybody. So don't worry about it.
Self-Mastery
Man up.
Master yourself.
Watch where you stick that thing.
The guilty have reason to walk in fear.
Sensibility
There's always more to life than what meets the eye.
Don't ignore what's right in front of your face.
Don't miss the major life lessons for the minor ones.
We ain't here to get rich or die tryin.
Don't let your oppressor reinvent your history.
Standards
Have a high set of standards for yourself, and whoever you bring close to you.
Hold yourself and others to standards that don't change with trends.
Know what you're dealing with, and what you expect to get out of it.
Have some standards and don't compromise them often.

Strategy
Know your role. Play your position, and play it well.
Though we should be, we're not all on the same page. Be strategic in the way you deal with others.
Watch who you allow into your inner circle.
Everyone doesn't share your values, so be careful who you work with or share your plans with.
Find allies in your struggle. We can't win it alone.
Joining the ones who beat you won't make your life better.

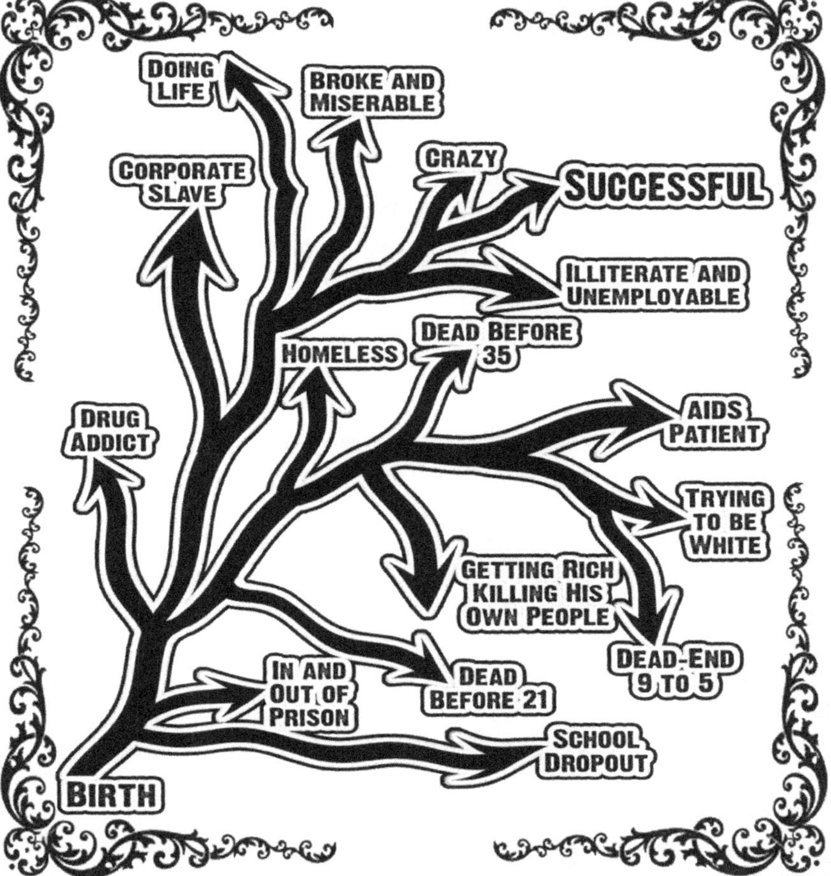

SUCCESS AIN'T EASY...

Top of the Food Chain?

LEADERSHIP AND GREATNESS

"A true leader has the confidence to stand alone, the courage to make tough decisions, and the compassion to listen to the needs of others. He does not set out to be a leader, but becomes one by the quality of his actions and the integrity of his intent. In the end, leaders are much like eagles...they don't flock, you find them one at a time."

Before you read anything else on this page, write your name seven times on this line: ______________________________

Now honestly answer this question: Are you a leader? Really?

Well, what does leadership mean to you? Is being a leader a 24/7 kinda gig? If you wrote your name on the line as directed, are you truly a leader? Seems kinda followish if you ask me. I mean, you didn't even know why you were doing it, yet you did it. It didn't even seem to have a purpose. And how would it all even fit on that little line? Or did you read ahead to see what was up first?

If you didn't do it, don't pat yourself on the back just yet. You may be following someone's lead in many other ways. In fact, you may have refused to do it because you subconsciously figured that's what *someone else would have done.* Lame. But the truth is that everyone's a follower at times. That's cool. You should know when to let whoever knows best do his or her thing. When I get in the airplane, I don't run up on the cockpit, trying to take control. (Especially since I look like an Arab)

I know when to take orders, and when to give them. But I also know that when change is necessary, you have to stand up and speak for it. I know that when you're surrounded by losers, you either lead, or you end up like them. So what are you doing?

Quiz Seven: Leadership Style

1. How important is status to you?

A. Very important: I like to feel like I'm on the top of the food chain.
B. Quite important: It's good to be in with the in-crowd.
C. It's more about the quality of relationships than where you fall within those relationships.
D. Not very important: I just want to get in where I fit in.

2. In your early childhood what was your 'gang rank' among the other children?

A. The leader: feared by all.
B. The funny one: adored by all.
C. The thinking one: listened to by all.
D. The shy one: noticed by few.

3. How often do you come up with new ideas and suggestions?

A. All the time: I really let everyone know what I think.
B. Quite often: But not at all if it would mean upsetting anyone.
C. Often: But being careful of creating other problems or taking away from what others have done.
D. Rarely: What if it's the wrong thing?

4. A partner has been caught slipping on a business matter and reprimanded as a result. What do you do?

A. Tell them why they should have known better.
B. Take them out for a drink to get over it.
C. Offer to help review their plans next time.
D. Avoid them. You've got too much to do as it is.

5. You have just been criticized for how you handled a matter. How do you respond?

A. Get angry and defensive.
B. Listen carefully but come away feeling disappointed.
C. Consider what you could change and how you could improve.
D. Sigh and think, "Yeah, that's me."

6. Faced with a problem to solve, what do you do?

A. Come up with one solution and declare it "THE way."
B. Generate a few possible solutions and ask others what they think.
C. Brainstorm with a couple of nearby colleagues.
D. Seek your manager's advice.

7. Your boss has asked you to do something that is beyond your abilities. Do you?

A. Take it on with confidence: You're up to anything.
B. Give it your best shot: Joking not to blame you if it all goes wrong.
C. Agree to do the task: But ask for further direction and assistance.

D. Stress out, keep quiet, then finally confess that you just don't think you can manage it.

8. "Change" to you means...

A. Something you need to be in control of.
B. An opportunity where anything could happen.
C. A chance to make progress.
D. Something to go along with.

Explanation

Okay, different series of questions, different sets of answers. That means different results, of course. Again, you're looking at which answer you picked more than the others. This chapter deals with behaviors. So if you don't like what you find, it's not impossible to change it.

Mostly As: The Dictators You're a natural born leader just waiting for the right job to come along. You're strong, decisive, and authoritarian. Everyone around you respects you. At least that's what you'd like to think. In reality, things may be a little different. You're probably arrogant, narrow-minded, and can only see what you think and what you want. As a result, people may obey you, but they don't believe in you. It would be wise to be less forceful and more interested in what others have to offer.

Mostly Bs: The Good Guys You've got good potential. You support people. You listen to others. You don't like taking sides. Those are mostly good qualities. But you've got to get past wanting to be liked. There's nothing wrong with wanting the approval of others, but as Bill Cosby said, "I can't tell you the key to success, but the key to failure is trying to please everybody." Don't try to be everyone's best friend. When it's time for difficult and direct words you probably try to be nice instead. Instead, you have to learn to confront conflicts, but with the sensitivity and honesty you already have. People will respect you more for being straight-up than for beating around the bush.

Mostly Cs: The Naturals Leadership is in you. You're creative, assertive and empathetic. You can bring people together for a common cause and build them up to make things happen. But the best part is that you value the abilities of others. You have high expectations of people, sometimes higher than they have of themselves. You may even be prepared to do what you can to help them see their own potential. That's one of the most valuable skills for a leader. Beware, however, not to let people of the first type bully in and take over your position.

Mostly Ds: The Team Players You've figured out by now that your place isn't at the head of the team. You'd rather listen to ideas than voice them yourself. You'd rather put in the work than decide what work needs to be put in. That's not necessarily a bad thing. There are way too many chiefs and not enough Indians, after all. You're – hopefully – a solid, reliable team player. But be careful that you don't end up somebody's puppet, pawn, or stepping stool. At times, you need to be ready to do things your own way. Stand firm when it's time to stand firm.

The Seventh Principle

"Leadership and Greatness" means: Be yourself, lead yourself, and put the weight of the world on your shoulders.

What You'll Learn

★ What Lil Wayne could teach us about self-actualization.
★ How hiphop has been used against us without our knowing.
★ The difference between weak and strong-minded people.
★ How a car crash can change your religion.
★ Why your mind is the most powerful weapon in existence.
★ Who the world's best hustlers are, and why you can't beat them.
★ Why racism is all about a fear you can't fix.
★ The disturbing origins of our myths, superstitions, and holidays.
★ What we can learn about survival from roaches.

God of War

He is considered one of the greatest military commanders and tacticians in history. He has been called the "father of strategy" and even his greatest enemy, Rome, ended up adopting his military tactics in its own strategic arsenal. He has been credited with the famous quote "We will either find a way, or make one." Who was he? He was a Black man named **Hannibal**, born in 247 B.C., during the ancient Roman Empire.

When the Roman army hoped to extend the Roman Empire by taking over Carthage, in what is now North Africa, **the Africans weren't havin it.** They took up arms and went to war

Hannibal led his army, traveling on horses, elephants, and on foot, over the mountains of the Alps. It was a treacherous journey, and many died along the way, but by coming into Rome from the north instead of south, Hannibal would catch his enemies by surprise. Gangster!

When Hannibal's army finally neared a Roman base, they stopped at a hillside in the darkness of night. They knew they were outnumbered by far, due to the heavy losses from the mountain journey. But Hannibal had a plan. Seeing a large herd of cattle, he had his soldiers tie a lit torch to each horn and send them stampeding down the hillside. In the dark, all the Roman soldiers could see were thousands of torches making their way down the hillside, accompanied by terrible screams. They damn near sh*tted on themselves and retreated.

As Hannibal's army approached his next target, the Roman soldiers were again shocked to see that Hannibal's soldiers had explosives. At this time, no one had knowledge of bombs and missiles, but it seemed like Hannibal, an African, had. In fact, Hannibal had simply told his men to light rags tied to bottles of alcohol and throw them ahead of their path as they marched. This was the first "Molotov cocktail." The scare tactic worked. The once-brave Romans weren't ready for war anymore.

So when it finally came time to actually battle, the Roman soldiers were terrified, especially when they saw Hannibal's soldiers riding in on African elephants. They had never seen beasts so big, and they believed that they were up against the Gods themselves. They were right. But the elephants weren't just a scare tactic. After stampeding into the enemy's army, he commanded his soldiers to cut the tendons of the elephants' legs. Entire troops of Roman soldiers were crushed alive as the elephants fell on top of them.

Hannibal led his troops to victory using these tactics as well as other military strategies that the Romans had never thought of. He had his soldiers maneuver and fight their battles in ways that are still being studied and used today. Hannibal successfully defended Africa from European conquest through the First AND Second Punic Wars.

> **Did You Know?**
>
> In 202 BC, after one of Carthage's old allies switched sides because the Romans offered them more land, a Roman general named Scipio was finally able to overpower Carthage's army. His army destroyed Carthage, killed everyone they found, and poured salt over all the land so that nothing could grow there again. Scipio earned the name *Africanus* for conquering Carthage, the capital of Africa Province (the Roman name for that area). The name Africa, a Greek name, was eventually used by Europeans to refer to the whole continent.

Resourcefulness. Innovation. Drive and Determination. These are the keys to success when one is born with less.

SLAVE NAMES

Riddle: Everybody says this to you, but you probably never say it to anyone else. What is it?

Answer: Your name, you big dummy.

They say a man goes through two births: one when he is physically born from his mama's belly, and the other when he is born into manhood. When we become men – our own men – sometimes we rename ourselves to stake out our own identities. But the sh*t we come up with shows a lot about how screwed up we really are.

I'll explain. A good place to look for examples is in the world of rap, where Black men are busy establishing their identities and their reputations. Let's look at two popular names in hiphop, and try to figure out what these dudes were thinking when they named themselves.

Jim Jones. Would you name yourself after a white cult leader who – with CIA help – ordered the mass suicide of almost a thousand followers, most of whom were Black? (see *Part One*, "Outcasts")

Rick Ross. Why would you name yourself after someone just because they created a plague that has destroyed millions of lives, and continues to take millions more? (see "The Real Rick Ross") The REAL Rick Ross (who is now a serious ANTI-drug advocate), ain't even okay with it:

> After seeing all the stuff that has been going on with the Correctional Officer that stole my name, makes me think back to a year and a half ago when we spoke. I tried to talk to him like a big brother and let him know to be you, and that he couldn't be me. And that if he wanted to rap the lifestyle that he couldn't frame it based on my life.

There's a ton of others. There's even a rapper named Big Koon. Really.

A lot of us are just confused. We're naming ourselves after people who became famous for exploiting other Black people! I've heard rappers name themselves after African dictators, famous drug dealers, and even comic book characters, but I bet you'll never hear of a rapper named Huey P. or David Walker…it's sad and ironic that "Souljah" Boy is the closest you'll get to some militant sh*t.

So if a good name is better than gold, why are we naming ourselves after people who didn't give a f*ck about us? No Black man should be callin himself "Gotti" or *anything* Italian. The Mafia does NOT respect Black people to begin with, especially if you're hangin off their nuts, naming yourselves after them like you're their illegitimate bastard children. Spike Lee actually addresses that in a great movie titled *She Hate Me.*

Moving along, we want a good name, right? We want our own name, right? Then why is everybody either reusing someone else's name, or named "Lil" this or "Young" that? And sh*t, there's 30 and 40-year-old men rapping, callin themselves "Young" or "Lil." Makes me think dudes is still livin in their mama's basements! (see *Part One*, "The Names We Call Ourselves")

So...what's in a name? Well, if your mama named you "Stupid Retard Jenkins," then guess what? You'd probably turn out pretty stupid. Even if you were born smart, you'd get programmed by hearing yourself get called a dummy every day. If you were named "Nobody" or "Nothing," it would be the same kind of effect. You'd feel like a nobody, think like a nobody, and you'd become a nobody. And no one would be surprised, because, well, just look at your name.

Well, what the hell does your name mean? Do you know? If you do know, does it fit you? Do you live it out? If you don't know, how does it feel answering to some sh*t that doesn't mean anything? Did you know that EVERY other culture in the world names their children using words in their language that refer to special qualities in the child? Even white people name their kids using white names that mean some sh*t when you trace them back to their white origins, like Greek, German, or Latin. Your name probably isn't so lucky. If your name is Jeremy or Kevin, your name means nothing to you being a Black or brown person. That's why most Black kids with white names go by nicknames for as long as they can.

But you might be special. You might have a Black name for your first name. Hopefully, it's not just a made up word and it really means some sh*t. But what about your last name? Where did that come from? Ah...you know the answer to that, don't you? I'll give you a hint: George Washington is the first and last white man I've heard of who had the name Washington. But I know a whole LOTTA Black people named Washington. That means our first President probably had a lot of slaves, and they all got his name!

So what am I saying here? I'm saying two things: First, while you are reclaiming your mind and your identity, you probably need to come up with a good name for the new you. Second, when you do that, don't name yourself some silly meaningless bullsh*t like "Young Pimpin" or "Tony Soprano."

So what's your name? What does it mean? Does it fit who you really are? Where did it come from? And does it tell where you're going?

A good name is better than gold.

Poor Righteous Teachers

Allah the Father

On February 22, 1928, Clarence Smith was born in the small, segregated town of

Danville, Virginia. As a teenager, he came with his mother to New York City where she hoped to find work. After struggling through a series of odd jobs, Clarence decided to join the Army. He ended up on the frontlines of the Korean War, where he earned several medals for bravery and combat.

After his return home, he learned about the Nation of Islam and joined. His speaking ability and expertise in the martial arts helped him move up quickly. Observing his leadership skills, the NOI leadership gave Clarence the opportunity to teach classes.

But Clarence, now named Clarence 13X, didn't always stick to the script. As the lessons of the NOI clearly say that the Black man is the original man and God of the universe, Clarence 13X began teaching the Muslims that they were God, and shouldn't look outside themselves for answers. This didn't sit well with the NOI leadership. Rather than create a rift, Clarence left the mosque. He changed his name to Allah, and began teaching street youths in his Harlem neighborhood.

Almost instantly, Allah was the man to see. Every thug and hustler from each of the five boroughs wanted to know more about this new teaching. When they came to Allah, thinking he was some kind of new God, he told them they could see God in themselves as well. Instead of a sermon about salvation from outside forces, Allah taught them a different concept of God: one combining manhood and divinity. Although he required them to study and memorize the NOI lessons which had opened his own eyes, he required them to use critical thinking in applying the teachings to their own lives. Allah also gave them a simple way to analyze and understand the complexities of the universe. These teachings were known as the Supreme Mathematics and Supreme Alphabets. As Lord Jamar raps on "Greatest Story Never Told:

> Allah made Supreme Mathematics, Supreme Alphabets/ A profound way to break it down/ He took it to the poor and the hardcore/ Young thugs and niggas on drugs.../ They called Allah 'the Father,' they were from broken homes/ And this man was the only father they had known

Allah didn't preach to them about abstaining from drinking or smoking, because he knew that would only run away his most promising students. Instead he pushed them to pursue an understanding of everything they did, which naturally led them to rethink their habits. As the youth spread word of this new teaching, Allah taught in more and more depth.

> "No one saves us but ourselves, no one can and no one may."
> Siddhartha Gautama, one of many Buddhas

His students called themselves "Five Percenters," for the five percent of the population who are not followers, who – instead of believing what they are told – know the truth and share it with those who don't. Allah didn't teach them to pray to or wait on a savior from above. He taught them to save themselves…and then to save others. Starting with the first nine he taught, Allah had required each Five Percenter to teach nine others. By 1967, the Five Percenters had grown to the thousands.

Although Allah was constantly criticized by other Black leaders, many of whom said he wasn't militant enough, Allah was content knowing that he was helping troubled youth take control of their lives. Many of them were now in school or working. Now there were young Gods and Earths everywhere. But this was the 1960s, and this "Black God" teaching was considered to be explosive. In three years since he had begun working with youth, Allah had attracted the attention of everyone from the Mayor of New York to J. Edgar Hoover, director of the FBI. Allah was soon under constant surveillance. The FBI's CoIntelPro documents described a top priority of theirs as "preventing the rise of a messiah in the ghetto." Allah was high on the hitlist. In 1965, he was thrown in a mental institution for claiming to be God in court. While there, he continued teaching. Twice, he had been shot and critically wounded in failed murder attempts. One of those times, Allah had charged the shooter, yelling in his Southern accent, "Bring it on, lollipop!" before being blasted with an elephant gun, one of the most powerful rifles on the streets at the time.

Still, Allah was undeterred. He knew that no one else would teach young people of color how to save themselves; many times, it seemed no one even cared. But Allah cared enough to risk his own life. Even as people made death threats against both him and many of the young Five Percenters, they continued to teach. When they were thrown in jails, they continued to teach. When they were offered incentives to join other organizations, they refused and continued to teach Allah's lessons.

By 1968, Allah would often remark that he knew something would happen to him. A young Five Percenter named Kalim told him, "Tell me who it is, Allah. I'll take care of them! Just tell me!" But Allah laughed, and explained that it *had* to be this way.

On June 13, 1969, Allah was entering the building where his wife lived. He stepped onto the elevator, and was ambushed by gunmen. Knowing Allah's strength and survival skills, they shot him several times from behind. The forces behind the assassination obviously believed that by killing Allah, they could stop the growth of the Five Percenters. But the Five Percent's teaching continued to spread, reaching across the entire country over the next forty years.

Today, there are Gods and Earths in nearly every major city and state in America (even Alaska and Hawaii), Canada, Mexico, Puerto Rico,

Jamaica, England, Germany, Ghana, Zimbabwe, Kenya, Japan, and probably other places you'd never even think to look. And they continue to teach. So was Allah really killed? Or did he live on through his works?

> "You could have a million dollars and a white collar
> Liberation costs more than a damn dollar
> It costs what Christ gave, King gave, X gave
> A billion dollars don't make you an ex-slave"
> Killer Mike, "Pressure"

That's a pretty easy question. One that requires more thought is: What did he get out of what he did? He never took an offering, tithe, donation, or handout, unlike many other leaders. He knew he would be killed, and did not quit. He knew many hated him for what he taught, and did not change. Why did he do it?

It's called altruism. Altruism is defined as giving or doing for others without expecting anything in return. In the 1700s, Dr. Samuel Johnson observed, "To act with pure benevolence is not possible for finite beings. Human benevolence is mingled with vanity, interest, or some other motive." Maybe that was true for Europeans like Johnson. But *we* are greater than that. And culturally, taking care of others is what we naturally do. But we're a long way from home, and we don't think like we once did. So yes, obviously, true altruism is rare now. How many people do you know that do good…and expect no benefit? Are you sure? If you can't come up with anyone, make it *your* agenda, and name yourself. How often do you "do good" just for the sake of doing good?

Did You Know?

Like many other African kingdoms BEFORE European conquest, the south African kingdom of Monomotapa had a social welfare system up until the 1700s. A Portuguese explorer reported that the Emperor "shows great charity to the blind and maimed, for these are called the king's poor, and have land and revenues for their subsistence, and when they wish to pass through the kingdoms, wherever they come food and drinks are given to them at the public cost as long as they remain there, and when they leave that place to go to another they are provided with what is necessary for their journey, and a guide, and some one to carry their wallet to the next village. In every place where they come there is the same obligation." In several societies where people of color dominated, taking care of others was an important obligation. Those who could were required to take care of those who could not. As Prophet Muhammad instructed his followers: "Especially if you are well-to-do, see that no one goes hungry or naked."

Ol' Dirty Bastard

Allah's teaching made it to thousands of people over the past four decades. One of those people was Russell Jones, who many of us knew as the Ol' Dirty Bastard. When I met him, I didn't meet someone who fit the description of a dirty bastard. I met the sincere, intelligent brother known to the Gods and Earths as Unique Ason Allah. When I heard the following story, it struck me as true to Allah's teaching:

One weekend in February of 1998, Ol' Dirty Bastard was in the studio recording with a Wu Tang label group in Brooklyn. Dirty heard the screech of tires on the street outside. He rushed outside to see that a four-year-old girl had been hit by a car near the studio. The child was trapped underneath the vehicle when Dirty and some other Gods rushed to her aid.

Incredibly, they **lifted the burning car off of her**. Dirty actually crawled under the suspended vehicle - risking his life - to rescue the little girl.

She was taken to the hospital and treated for first and second degree burns from the car's engine. Dirty visited the hospital to check on the girl's condition, but the normally anything-but-low key ODB never identified himself to her family. However, they recognized him and alerted the media. Even after she recovered, Dirty continued to check on her periodically.

Does it take a superhero to exhibit superhuman consideration for others? When's the last time you did something along those lines?

Other Old Dirty Bastards

Perhaps, when I asked you to think of someone who was altruistic, before you named your grandma or the teacher who bust their ass to wake you up, you thought of a preacher. I don't think all preachers are bad, but I don't think it's the Church's agenda that encourages the good ones to do good.

Even Dr. King only got involved with the ministry because he saw it as a platform where he could push for social change. Didn't know that? Man, you should read some of Dr. King's college papers on Christian theology! I'll tell you one thing: He wasn't no blind faith believer!

But preachers like Dr. King, Reverend Jeremiah Wright, and Minister James H. Cone are rare nowadays. The majority can be lumped with our politicians: out for their own interests, though they claim to represent our needs. Instead, they give us a philosophy that actually works *against* us! Because they live so well doing so, it inspires a lot of us to do the same. As Black historian J.A. Rogers said in *From Superman to Man*:

> Another fact — there are far too many Negro preachers. Religion is the most fruitful medium for exploiting this already exploited group. As I said, the majority of the sharpers, who among the whites would go into other fields, go, in this case, to the ministry.

Even Carter G. Woodson, author of *The Miseducation of the Negro*, observed: "Practically all of the incompetents and undesirables who have been barred from other walks of life have rushed into the ministry for the exploitation of the people…Almost anybody of the lowest type may go into the Negro ministry." Wow. Don't look at me! I didn't say it!

While I don't think we *all* need leaders, I know some of us can't find our own way without them. **But if you must follow someone**, you should be concerned with what they are *really* about. So how can you tell if your "spiritual leader" is living *for* the people, or simply living *off of* the people? Here's a few questions you can ask yourself:

Do they practice what they preach? Even in secret?

Does what they preach have practical significance, and is that clear to the audience?

Do they rely on facts and reason or blind faith and emotion?

Do they address social ills in a realistic manner that actively addresses and transforms those social ills?

Do they challenge the status quo without fear or hesitation?

Is there a proportionate amount of social change occurring for the number of followers and supporters?

Do they suffer or sacrifice in order to take on their position, or do they benefit more than their followers?

Are they under attack from the people in power, or are they supported by the people in power?

Are liberation and resistance to oppression central themes in their message?

It is only the greatest of people who give of themselves without wanting anything in return.

"We need workers, not leaders. Such workers will solve the problems which leaders just talk about."
Carter G. Woodson

Allah was unique in other respects as well. He met the youth on their terms, and came off as someone they could relate to. Considering that most of these youth were what others considered "street thugs" and "juvenile delinquents," Allah couldn't have accomplished this task if he'd been "stuck up" in any way. While the preachers scolded their flocks and warned that they were headed to hell, and the Muslim leaders forbade their recruits from smoking, drinking, clubbing, and dating.

Meanwhile, Allah allowed his youths to smoke and drink so long as they were still cleaning themselves up. Allah himself was one of the best gamblers in Harlem, and met many of the first Five Percenters in the basements and corners where young men were playing dice. And he was playing dice with them. However, while others rolled their dice only hoping for "good luck," Allah spoke of the mathematical properties inherent in the universe, and how he could *predict* his outcomes that way. *Anything* would become a lesson. Now you know where *I* got it from.

When Allah spoke, people listened. Not simply because he was wise, because there were many leaders who were wise, but because he came to them as if he was one of them. Allah didn't talk down to them, or act as if he was better than them. He understood self-development is a continuous process, and the struggle can take many years. He came to the people as the people, but offered them so much more.

Do you speak FOR the people, AT the people, TO the people, WITH the people, or WITHOUT the people?

What about in terms of young people? How well do you relate to teenagers? How often do you connect with them?

A true leader is of the people, with the people, and for the people.

Movies to See

Pay It Forward; Seven Pounds

I know I'll seem like a cornball for recommending this cheesy movie…but if you can watch some bullsh*t like *Napoleon Dynamite* or *Superbad*, you can watch this. I'm not saying it's funny, I'm just saying it's completely white too. But the idea of this movie is that we can change the world by looking out for other people. Basically, you'll get back what you put out. Now I know we'd have to overthrow the mothaf*ckas in power TOO, but I still felt good after watching it, and being reminded that "Karma" doesn't have to be a bitch.

Seven Pounds starts out slow, but really makes sense by the end. It also deals with the idea of how you can "give back" even if you ain't Oprah.

Blood and Guts

The typical waiting time for a white person in need of a kidney for transplant is 553 days. Meanwhile, the typical waiting time for a Black person is nearly double that, at 1,082 days! Why?

I was recently taking a test where – as a security measure – everyone had to put their driver's licenses out on the table in front of them. All the white people had "organ donor" stamped on theirs, but I didn't see *any* Black people with that mark. That made me think about facts like the numbers above. I thought about how Black people's bodies aren't compatible with everything in white people's bodies, so Black people usually need Black organs (and blood). I thought about all the Black people I know who need a kidney or a liver or a brain and can't get one. I thought about Alonzo Mourning *and* Walter Payton (ask somebody).

So here's my simple advice. When you get your state ID or driver's license, go ahead and check off the box for "organ donor." It's that simple. It don't cost you nothing. All it means is that when you die, your organs can go to someone else who needs them. It's not like your dead ass is gonna need them for anything. Even if you believe in heaven, I'm sure you won't miss your kidney there. But that kidney from you could save another Black man's life.

Now that I think about it, what about blood? There's a lot of Black people who need Type O blood, but can't get it because Black people don't like giving blood. So after you get your ID, go donate some blood. Oh, and while they're at it, they'll give you a blood test. Uh oh, y'all were with me right up until then, huh?

Every one of us can give of ourselves.

Supreme the Asshole on "Out of Touch" Folks

Over the past few months, I've read three recently-published self-empowerment books by prominent Black authors, and they all sucked. Every single one of them has said something like, "Most importantly [preachy voice], we've got to stop saying 'the white man is holding me down.' Blah blah blah." Are they for real? Who the f*ck still says that? Have they been to the hood lately? Nobody's talked like that since the 90s. Maybe I missed the memo, but most people nowadays are so brainwashed that they don't even know the white man is *involved* in their misery! So maybe they're all out of touch. Middle-class motherf*ckers who have no idea of the current conditions of people in poverty...and people in poverty who have no awareness of the politics that create their conditions. Makes me want to assign partners like we're in school or something. At least the poor folks can blame ignorance. What's the excuse for a Harvard-educated clown who thinks white supremacy isn't still alive and well? What about you? Are *you* out of touch?

Niggaz With Attitude

After N.W.A. released the 1988 album *Straight Outta Compton* with the infamous single "F*ck the Police," the media went into a frenzy. Radio stations and MTV refused to air it, and the resulting controversy catapulted the record to gold status. But even with half a million records sold, there were problems brewing for N.W.A.

Members of the group had been questioning Eazy-E about their share of royalties and gate receipts, concerned that Eazy was benefiting unfairly from his close relationship with manager Jerry Heller. In Phoenix in 1989, halfway through a nationwide tour, the internal feuding had come to a head. Eazy decided to call Heller in to help settle the matter.

When Heller arrived, he brought with him a set of questionable contracts for all the members to sign, promising a $75,000 signing bonus. He stated, "If you sign the contract, you get the check." Immediately, Dr. Dre, Eazy-E, and MC Ren were signing their names.

The one holdout was Ice Cube. He wanted to bring in his lawyer. Heller almost fell out of his chair. Cube explained bluntly, "I want to make sure my sh*t right first." The other members mocked him, saying, **"Yo! $75,000! If that sh*t ain't right, ain't nothin' right!"**

Since Cube – ghostwriter for both Eazy-E and Dr. Dre – had written the lyrics to half of both *Straight Outta Compton* and Eazy-E's solo album *Eazy-Duz-It*, Cube was advised by his lawyer of the amounts he was truly owed by Heller. Cube then proceeded to take legal action, soon after leaving N.W.A. In response, the remaining members attacked Cube on the EP *100 Miles and Runnin'*, as well as their next and final album, *Efil4zaggin*. On *Efil4zaggin* ("Niggaz 4 Life" backwards), Ice Cube is first referred to as "Benedict Arnold" (after the infamous traitor of the American Revolution) before being named outright in a torrent of abuse from both the group and its fans: "When we see yo' ass, we gon' cut yo' hair off and f*ck you with a broomstick," promised MC Ren.

After remaining quiet for some time, Ice Cube finally responded on his 1991 album *Death Certificate* with the dis record "No Vaseline":

> Cut my hair and I'll cut them balls/ cuz I heard you're, like, givin' up the draws/ Gang-banged by your manager, fella/ gettin' money out your ass, like a mothaf*ckin' Ready Teller/ Givin' up the dollar bills/ now they got the Villain with a purse and high-heels/ So don't believe what Ren say/ cuz he's goin' out like Kunte Kinte/ but I got a whip for ya Toby/ used to be my homey, now you act like you don't know me/ It's a case of divide-and-conquer/ cuz you let a Jew break up my crew...

Did You Know?

Rico Todriquez Wright recently joined the ranks of over a dozen dummies who have incriminated themselves with their rap lyrics. He shot a man twice and felt *so* good about it, police said, that he wrote a song describing the shooting and calling out his victim by name. A judge sentenced the 25-year-old to spend the next 20 years in prison and another 20 years on probation. All because his victim, Chad Blue, recognized Rico rapping, "Chad Blue knows how I shoot," on what was probably a wack song anyway.

By the time the song was released, N.W.A, for all intents and purposes, was fading from the limelight. But its mark in history had been made. Without Ice Cube writing the lyrics, N.W.A.'s music had become empty of social commentary and full of increasingly ridiculous amounts of violence and ignorance. They had transitioned from "reality rap" to "gangsta rap," and the millions of young, suburban white kids who bought into the image pushed them quickly to gold and platinum status. Of course, the rest of the music world followed as a result. Gangsta rap soon established itself as the single most popular form of hip hop for the decade of the '90s. Millions of youth across the world, Black and white, began imitating the gangsterisms they saw on TV and heard on the radio. This led to a new surge in the gang and drug epidemic, often in towns where the young gang members and drug dealers were coming from middle-class, two-parent households.

What happened? Gansgter rap went from being the "CNN of the streets" to an overdone, cartoonish version of a world envisioned by white suburbanites. Just as Reality TV is now a showcase for the super-ghetto, the people in power use mainstream music to brainwash and program us. Does life reflect art, or does art reflect life now? When you consider how many of these rappers are faker than George W. Bush's college degree, you start to wonder: Who's coming up with this sh*t?

Easy. They are. Meanwhile, our "entertainment" isn't just dumbing *us* down. It's desensitizing OTHER communities to the plight of our condition. Whereas hiphop once used to broadcast the misery of Black America to the rest of the world, now you'd think we're just smoking, drinking, partying, f*cking, and balling out of control…and that we love it…we love it enough to rub it in everyone else's faces!

First, hiphop was our voice. Now we're just ventriloquist dummies. We say what they program us to. It's no accident that when the violent ethic of gangsta rap led to a revolutionary movement of politically aware hiphop in the late 80s, that trend was somehow replaced with a new one by the 90s. The last phase of hiphop was all about materialism and our obsession with consumerism…we were literally doing free commercials for other people's companies. "Pass the Courvoisier"? You serious?

But there's always a flaw to their design (the glitch in the Matrix). The spread of gangsta led to new violence among suburban white kids, which is when lawmakers and activists started complaining. The spread of "consumer rap" actually led to the development of a number of successful Black businesses. That's when things changed again. What did they give us now?

Turn on the radio. What are all the songs about? You figure it out.

They did the same thing with Black programming on TV. Most of the earliest Black TV shows were very clear on how Blacks felt about race and politics. But as the fanbases grew, the people in power gradually changed the content of the programming. It was slow enough not to notice, but deep enough to change the way we think. For example, the show *Good Times* began with a positive Black family, complete with a strong Black father and a militantly pro-Black son. In a few years, the father was gone, and Michael, the former revolutionary, was now dating a white girl. And the star of the show was now J.J., a full-time "coon," illiterate, unemployed, and ignorant as hell, yet celebrated as the new definition of "cool." This ain't by accident. **This is how they do it.** They did the same thing to *Sanford and Son*, as well as *The Jeffersons*. Pretty soon, all the Black shows on TV were just like white shows except with Black faces. No social commentary. No racial or political content. Anything different gets canceled...or co-opted, like they tried to do the *Chappelle Show*. Just like any rapper with something to say. Oh, and then there's Reality TV, celebrating the worst of us, promoting disfunction and equating love with manipulation and financial gain. And you'll see twelve gay blowjobs before you see a married couple kiss on TV nowadays. What effect is *that* producing?

Are you programmed? Does what you see and hear affect you?

Have your views gradually been watered down by an outside influence?

Has you ever gotten into something that seemed strong, only for it to gradually change into something much weaker?

Pay attention to your programming, or be a pawn in the game.

BLACK INVENTORS

There is a pretty interesting story I read once about a group of white people who were fed up with Black Americans, so they joined together and wished themselves away.

> They passed through a deep dark tunnel and emerged in sort of a twilight zone where there is an America without Black people. At first these white people breathed a sigh of relief. "At last," they said, "No more crime, drugs, and violence. All of the Blacks have gone!" Then suddenly, reality set in. The "NEW AMERICA" is not America at all - only a barren land.
>
> There are very few crops that have flourished because the nation was built on a slave-supported system. One of the pioneers of agriculture was a Black man, George Washington Carver.
>
> There are no cities with tall skyscrapers because Alexander Mills, a Black man, invented the elevator, and without it, one finds great difficulty reaching higher floors.
>
> There are few, if any, cars because

Did You Know?

Blacks brought Europe out of the Dark Ages? The Moors were a Black population from North Africa who crossed into Europe through Spain in the early 700s. After a number of amazing military victories, these Black Moors were in control of most of Europe for more than 700 years (from 711 to 1492). During this time, the Moors, with their advanced knowledge of science, mathematics, and medicine, reintroduced civilization to Europe. At that time, most Europeans did not even bathe. (Check out the scene in movie Robin Hood). It was in fact the Moors who taught science and culture to the Europeans before they came out of the Dark Ages and began the Renaissance. Some authors propose that it was the spread of the Moors that caused some Europeans to want to find a way out of Europe in the 1400s. Check Ivan Van Sertima's *Golden Age of the Moor* for more.

Richard Spikes, a Black man, invented the automatic gearshift, Joseph Gambol, also Black, invented the Super Charge System for Internal Combustion Engines, and Garrett A. Morgan, a Black man, invented the traffic signals.

Furthermore, one could not use the rapid transit system because its predecessor was the electric trolley, which was invented by another black man, Albert R. Robinson.

Even if there were streets on which cars and a rapid transit system could operate, they were cluttered with paper because an African American, Charles Brooks, invented the street sweeper.

There were few if any newspapers, magazines and books because John Love invented the pencil sharpener, William Purveys invented the fountain pen, and Lee Barrage invented the Type Writing Machine and W. A. Love invented the Advanced Printing Press. They were all, you guessed it, Black.

Even if Americans could write their letters, articles and books, they would not have been transported by mail because William Barry invented the Postmarking and Canceling Machine, William Purveys invented the Hand Stamp, and Philip Downing invented the Letter Drop.

The lawns were brown and wilted because Joseph Smith invented the Lawn Sprinkler and John Burr the Lawn Mower.

When they entered their homes, they found them to be poorly ventilated and poorly heated. You see, Frederick Jones invented the Air Conditioner and Alice Parker the Heating Furnace.

Their homes were also dim. But of course, Lewis Lattimer invented the Electric Lamp, Michael Harvey invented the lantern, and Granville T. Woods invented the Automatic Cut off Switch.

Their homes were also filthy because Thomas W. Steward invented the Mop & Lloyd P. Ray the Dust Pan.

Their children met them at the door-barefooted, shabby, motley and unkempt. But what could one expect? Jan E. Matzelinger invented the Shoe Lasting Machine, Walter Sammons invented the Comb,

Did You Know?

Black people pioneered basic arithmetic (Evidence includes the 25,000 year old Ishango bone found in Zaire). We were also the first to engage in mining (eg. a 43,000 year old hematite mine found in Swaziland at Bomvu Ridge). We were the first to develop agriculture (eg. 12,000 year old tools and evidence of crop cultivation in Egypt's Western Desert). We even pioneered fishing and sailing (eg. 90,000 year old harpoons and other tools found at Katanda, a region in northeastern Zaïre).

In fact, several thousand years ago, Black civilizations pioneered the production of steel, medicine and surgery (including brain surgery and C-sections, accurate astronomy, city planning (including paved roads, multi-story buildings, and sewers and plumbing), education (including large universities and libraries), fabric-weaving and export, and dozens of other industries for which we receive no credit. And that's why we have to study. "Until the lion has his own historian, the hunter gets all the glory."

> Sarah Boone invented the Ironing Board and George T. Samon invented the Clothes Dryer.
>
> Finally, they were resigned to at least have dinner amidst all of this turmoil. But here again, the food had spoiled because another Black man, John Standard invented the refrigerator.

I liked it, but whoever wrote it missed a few things (probably because most people don't know we had a history *before* America):

First, without Black people, there wouldn't be any houses or buildings *at all*, because Blacks were the originators of architecture!

Without Black people, these white people wouldn't have been in America either, since a Black Moor was the one who showed Columbus how to get here!

Finally...without Black people, there wouldn't even *BE* white people any damn way! Think about it. **Now back to you.** What can *you* offer this world? I'm sure you see a need that can be filled. It doesn't have to be an invention. It just has to be an *innovation.*

Find a need and fill it.

SUPREME THE ASSHOLE ON "STUPID NIGGAS"

Some of y'all are stupid. Retarded. Dumb. Foolish. And fruity too. I ain't talking sh*t, I'm just repeatin the sh*t y'all sing along to on the radio. Back in the 80s, it mighta been slang to say "your jacket is dumb fresh" but we weren't calling *ourselves* dumb. Now, not only do I hear rappers say "I'm fruity," it turns out that saying "I'm stupid," "I'm foolish," "I'm dumb," or "I'm retarded" is the same as saying I'm cool. So dumb is the new cool? Just like gay is the new straight, huh? Do you get what they doin to us? Or are you too dumb?

5 LESSONS ON LEADERSHIP

Leopold Senghor, first president of Senegal, said the slave trade "ravaged Black Africa like a brush fire, wiping out images and values in one vast carnage." The majority of the human destruction occurred in West Africa, where civilization on the continent had reached its highest point outside of Egypt. The removal of the best of the population deprived the continent of its most valuable resource: young men and women. To make matters worse, not only did Europeans provoke and intensify conflicts between African groups, they supplied the rivals with deadly guns and explosives to take the destruction to the highest level.

Africa was culturally on equal footing with Europe and Asia at the beginning of the fifteenth century, not counting the European tradition of exploiting people economically, which wasn't a part of socialist African culture. But by the time the damage of the slave trade had really set in, and Europeans had begun taking over, Africa was in terrible shape. But weren't our Black leaders wise enough to see this coming?

Why didn't they do something? Why didn't they avoid such an evil business? Why didn't they fight to stop it?

They did. And here's what happened then, and what will happen to you if you don't avoid the mistakes of our ancestors:

1. Kongo

At the beginning of the 16th century, the king of Kongo asked the Europeans for masons, physicians, and people who could offer technical expertise. (see *Part One*, "Tricks of the Trade") Instead, he was overwhelmed by Portuguese slave ships.

Today, we go to school and hope to receive a good education. Instead, we learn how to slave at work for other people, and often aren't prepared to get a good job at all.

Today, we go to religious institutions, looking for help to improve our lives. Instead, we become slaves to blind faith and waiting on salvation.

Don't ask for something you need, expecting the giver to want the best for you. Instead, find a way to get it yourself, on your terms.

2. Nzingha

In Angola, the state of Matamba was founded in 1630 in direct response to the threat of the Portuguese. Queen Nzinga, acting as its head, attempted to garner widespread support in resisting the Portuguese in Angola. So by 1648, Portugal had not only blocked Queen Nzinga's efforts to assemble a coalition against them, but had effectively isolated the state of Matamba from its Angolan neighbors.

As long as Matamba stood in opposition to trade with the Europeans, it suffered hostility from the neighboring African states that had already succumbed to the pressures of being involved with the slave trade. Backed into a corner with no allies, Nzinga was forced to resume business with the Portuguese.

Today, a man can "try" to leave his gang, only to learn that there's no way out, because – in addition to his old enemies – everyone who was once with him will now be against him. Today, you can try to embrace a different way of thinking, only for everyone to turn on you until you go back to your old ways.

Make sure you have a team who'll support you before you step out on your own against a stronger force.

3. Toomba

In what is now Guinea, the Baga people were once organized in small states. In 1720, Toomba, one of their leaders, wanted to build an alliance to stop the slave traffic in the region. Toomba was crushed by a mix of local white traders, slave trading Africans, and proud mulattos.

Today, when you "do what's right," many of your own people will be the main ones against you. Worse yet, these opponents can come from all walks of life, so long as they are opposed to your vision.

Be prepared to find yourself at odds with people who you may "think" are your people.

4. Agaja Trudo

In the 1720s, the kingdom of Dahomey stood firm against the European slave traders. As a result, Dahomey was denied European imports. By this time, African societies were dependent on goods from Europe. Dahomey's king, Agaja Trudo, realized that the slave trade was detrimental to Dahomey's development.

From 1724 to 1726, Trudo worked tirelessly to destroy the business, looting and burning European forts and slave camps, and blocking the paths into the country, where slaves were obtained. Within two years, he had reduced the slave trade in his region to "a mere trickle." Of course, the whites were enraged.

At first, they attempted to sponsor African collaborators against Trudo, but couldn't unseat him or crush his state. However, Trudo was also unable to steer the other African leaders to develop new means of economic productivity.

For example, with the profitable slave trade in place, few leaders wanted to return to growing crops. Also, the growing threat of his now unfriendly neighbors created a need for European firearms in Dahomey. In 1730, Agaja Trudo agreed to resume participation in the slave trade in exchange for European guns and goods.

Today, it's hard for many of us to step away from "doing wrong" because of the easy money and the luxuries we've gotten used to having. It also becomes a lot harder to let those things go when we see that other people have them. Plus our desire for material things creates an environment where we're either killing other people to get them, or defending ourselves from those who are. Who/what comes first?

Remember, the people come first. Material sh*t is worth nothing if your people are dying around you.

Who Wants to be a Puppet?

Phyllis Wheatley

Phyllis Wheatley is considered the first Black female poet to get published in America. She is celebrated because, in 1773, no one would expect a Black woman, especially a slave, to have people like George Washington as her audience! Now let me tell you why this sorry broad is important.

Wheatley became famous for her poetry on religious and "moral" themes. She very rarely spoke about her own condition as a slave. One of her few poems that refers to slavery, "On being brought from Africa to America," begins:

> Twas mercy brought me from my Pagan land,
> Taught my benighted soul to understand
> That there's a God, that there's a Saviour too:
> Once I redemption neither sought nor knew.

Mercy huh? Sounds kinda like Soulja Boy, being thankful for slavery and being "rescued" from Africa and whatnot! Although whites appreciated this attitude (and that's why they enjoyed her poetry), **they still didn't believe a Black woman was intelligent enough to write it**. So they had a group come together to examine her. Once they were satisfied, they gave her a stamp of approval, which she included in the beginning of her book. Pathetic, huh? Wait, ain't some of us waitin for recognition from white folks?

For a while, everywhere she went, whites aided her and offered her financial support. In return, she kept producing the kind of poetry they adored. Her popularity as a poet both in the United States and England ultimately brought her freedom from slavery on October 18, 1773.

But then Wheatley married a free Black grocer named John Peters. Yes, a Black man…with his own business. Their marriage produced three children, two of which soon died. Makes you wonder if that's what happens to people who hate themselves enough. Of course, her husband soon left her…and Wheatley was back to working as a f*ckin servant! Damn!

By 1784, she was living in a boarding house. In December of that year, she and her remaining child died within hours of each other, and were both buried in an unmarked grave. Once-famous Black poetess Phillis Wheatley died in poverty at the age of 31.

And this is the fate awaiting all of you uppity Negros who think being a a "race traitor" comes with a retirement plan. Maybe that's just what the folks in power do with you when they're done using you (see "Toilet Paper Hustlers"). Or maybe they dissed Wheatley because she married a Black man instead of doin the Condoleeza. Or maybe she experienced a "change of heart" and shared it in her second volume of poetry, which was completed shortly before her death, and which – to this day – has never been seen.

Lamar and the Carmichaels

Lamar was born to a single mother on welfare in South Central Los Angeles. Somehow, he had scraped by through early childhood into his teenage years without getting involved with the gangs or getting into too much trouble. At least his record was clean, and that's all that mattered. In high school, Lamar proved to be a strong student and was soon enrolled in a magnet program. Once he got into his school's Young Ambassadors program, he wasn't exactly getting all the girls, but he *was* getting offers from local colleges. But the schools offering full scholarships weren't exactly the top of the line, and Lamar's mother couldn't afford Ivy League tuition, so things didn't look too promising. Somehow, as a result of making a good name for himself in the Young Ambassadors program, a benevolent family took interest in Lamar and asked to meet with him.

The Carmichaels were a wealthy white family that operated a large philanthropic foundation in California. Basically, they funded "worthy causes," and they felt Lamar may have been the kind of worthy cause they had in mind.

"If we don't stand for something, we may fall for anything."
Malcolm X

Upon meeting with Lamar, they saw that he was polite, humble, ambitious, and eager to please. They noted his views were not strongly conservative or liberal…he really didn't have ANY "views." Not only was he a "blank slate," he didn't share the anger and frustration of so many of the other young Black men who grew up in the ghetto like him.

After their meeting, the Carmichaels officially became Lamar's sponsors. In exchange for Lamar's hard work and participation in advanced-track courses, the Carmichaels pledged full financial support. They sent Lamar to Morehouse College to pursue a degree in political science.

They also encouraged Lamar to become involved with a local political organization and paid for his flights and accommodations whenever they held a conference. They found other charities and families who would contribute financially, and Lamar found himself whisked away from poverty and all its problems in no time. Lamar found himself writing political essays, making speeches, and eventually acting as a spokesperson for the Carmichaels' political hedge group, a highly conservative wing of the Republican party. By pushing him into their circles of friends and making him self-conscious and even ashamed of his troubled background, the Carmichaels had gradually worked Lamar into adopting their often extreme political perspective. Lamar, at this point, still disagreed at times, but he kept those thoughts to himself.

He'd voiced some "alternative" views in the past, and his benefactors quickly warned him that he was making them "uncomfortable" and "disappointed." He quickly learned to retract his words.

He couldn't afford to lose his sponsors and be sent reeling back into the pits of poverty back in L.A., nor did he want to lose all of the support he was getting from his new political buddies. He desperately wanted to get into office, and was sure that this political platform was the way to get there.

Over the years that followed, Lamar advanced at a breakneck pace. He went from position to position, always moving upwards, always with the financial sponsorship it takes to stay busy doing nothing but talking politics. Ten years after he graduated from Morehouse, Dr. Lamar Crawford was elected governor of the state of California. Under his leadership, California enacted the harshest drug laws ever proposed, banned abortion, imposed stricter regulations on immigration, dismantled welfare, and sentenced 35 Black and Hispanic men to death row, all while increasing tax cuts for the rich.

At 56, Lamar was one of the most successful Black men in America. His political platform didn't win him many friends in the Black community, of course, but he was loved by wealthy whites as "everything a Black American should be." When Lamar published his autobiography that year, he attacked Black communities like the one where he grew up for failing to produce more success stories like himself. He argued that, if *he* could do it, then *everyone* could do it, and that Black families were too concerned with rap music and getting high to put their kids into college. Lamar's mother was shocked. She tried to call her prodigal son, but her message to his answering service was never returned.

Don't allow yourself to be manipulated by the interests of others.

Do What You're Told

The above scenario has played itself out in the lives of so many famous people of color. From Clarence Thomas to Condoleeza Rice to dozens of others I won't name, wealthy white people are almost always somehow behind the rise of the "Good Negros." Those "Good Negros" (or Uncle Toms, mammies, house niggers, sellouts, etc.) are the ones who say exactly what white people wish every Black person would believe. They are the ones who are the first to attack hiphop culture, to bash the young "thugs" who are "ruining" America, and to criticize any Black leader that says or does anything about Black people's problems. Some of them defend racist policies. Some of them attack Black movements. Some just play the "token" role when an agreeing Black face is needed. They have different agendas, but there's always one thing in common: They will never speak out against white people.

These white people select only the best and brightest of Black people. They take the smartest of us, and by pushing them to fame and fortune, convince them that the ghetto is an equal-opportunity kind of place where everyone can make it on their own – like they did. These people really begin to believe in the stuff they're saying. When they start to have moments of doubt, their sponsors always have some dirt or dark secret as blackmail to keep them in check.

All of the stories in *How to Hustle and Win* and *Rap, Race and Revolution* are based on fact. The story above, however, is only *half* true. It starts with the true story of a brother who attended Morehouse College with me. From there, it's "what could have been."

But one year, he was telling me about his white girlfriend and his sponsors and we got into a pretty deep conversation. A while after this "talk," he started having more and more disagreements with his "sponsors." Finally, he dropped them (or maybe they dropped him?) and he got serious about being a real "brother in the struggle." He couldn't finish Morehouse without their money, but he never became a big-ass puppet either. Recently, I heard Lamar came back to school with a new agenda. He finished with flying colors, and I hear he's putting in serious political work for the Black community now.

Keep in mind, the people that pay your way control what you do and say. Basically, they own you like a pimp owns his hoes. So who are you hoin for? And how long is your leash? Unless you're self-employed AND you have all of your own mind back, those questions apply to you!

Don't always do whatever you're told. Do what's right.

COINTELPRO and the BPP

Here's a perfect example of someone who can't be his own man because of the path he chose:

In 1969, the FBI special agent in San Francisco reported back to FBI director J. Edgar Hoover about his investigation of the Black Panther Party in his city. His investigation had found that the Black Panthers were primarily feeding breakfast to Black children. Hoover fired back a memo implying the agent's job depended directly on him supplying evidence that the BPP was "a violence prone organization seeking to overthrow the Government by revolutionary means." The agent, a Black man, complied and came up with the bogus evidence. This same evidence was used as justification for CoIntelPro's violent attacks on the Party, including the night raid that killed Fred Hampton while he slept, not far from pregnant fiancé.

What's Worse?

A Black farmer is driving his pickup truck down a country road when he crashes into a huge deer. Bleeding but alive, he's barely crawled out from the driver's seat when a passing car brakes hard and pulls over on the other side of the road. The door of the blue Toyota Prius slams open and a startled white woman jumps out. Obviously concerned, she runs over. "Oh my God!" she yells, "You poor thing! Are you okay?" The Black farmer can barely see in front of him, but responds, "I think I'll make it." The white woman – with a look of disgust – yells back, "You asshole! I was talking to the deer!"

Get it?

A rich white lawyer is driving his Black girlfriend around in his brand new BMW when he crashes into a telephone pole, leaving the car wrapped around the pole in a twisted heap of metal and glass. The lawyer isn't hurt badly, but his girlfriend is bleeding and unconscious. Just then, a rich *Black* businessman pulls over and jumps out of his brand new Benz, screaming, "Oh no! She was so beautiful! Do you think she can be saved?!" Dazed, the white lawyer responds, "I'm not sure, can you call an ambulance?" The rich Black businessman looks at him – completely confused – and shoots back, "Ambulance? For what? I was talking about saving that beautiful car!"

Get it? Now, who's worse? The white person who cares about an animal more than a Black person's life? Or the Black person who cares about material things more than another Black person's life?

Movies to See

Drop Squad; Bamboozled

There needs to be a real "drop squad" out here for some people. Just watch the film and you'll understand. *Bamboozled* deals with the same kind of people as well, but from a different perspective.

I Pledge Allegiance

This is a story I told Lamar during one of our many talks about his white girlfriend and his "sponsors":

There was once a young man named Ijjut who lived near a forest. One day, driving along the highway, he found an injured bear cub on the side of the road. He took interest in the cub and decided to bring it home and nurse it back to health. When the cub was healthy again, Ijjut continued to keep the cub around him as a pet. Although his family was scared at first, they eventually grew fond of the bear cub.

The bear became like a member of the family over time. But the cub grew bigger quickly, and Ijjut decided to bring it back. He brought the young bear with him into the woods where he first found him. Finally, he found the cave where the young bear's family lived. The bear's family, seeing Ijjut, immediately attacked him. And guess what? The young bear did nothing to stop them. After all, this was *his* family. In fact, after Ijjut was dead, the young bear shared in eating his flesh with his family. After all, this was *his* family. Ijjut may have been confused about the fact, but the bear had never forgotten who he was.

Think about that a minute. Who do you pledge allegiance to? Do they pledge allegiance to you?

If you still don't get it, maybe I can help you with Tony Norman's *Pittsburgh Post-Gazette* article from June 16, 1998:

> Last week, a Black man was found all over Jasper, Texas, decapitated and missing an arm. James Byrd Jr.'s skid-charred torso greeted travelers along an East Texas road just as the sun was rising in a hazy Sunday morning sky...James Byrd Jr., 49, was dragged two miles down the road sometime after midnight, his body thumping along paved and unpaved streets like a string of cans tied to the bumper of a newlywed's pickup truck...Three young suspects, self-professed white supremacists, were arrested for the killing less than 48 hours later...After going through all the trouble of covering themselves with racist tattoos, Shawn Berry, 23, John King, 23 and Larry Brewer, 31, will have a hard time refuting the evidence amassed against them at trial...The East Jasper native **may have assumed he was among friends**, or at least acquaintances who wouldn't lynch him at the first opportunity.

Did You Know?

Bayer, makers of Aspirin, are responsible for introducing heroin to the world? The American Medical Association offered its stamp of approval to heroin in 1907. After the problems caused by all the addictions that occurred, they got out of the heroin business in 1913. But that didn't stop them from making other drugs from the same poppy plants that produce heroin. Today, most pain relievers, from hospital-grade morphine and codeine to over-the-counter Advil, are made from the same opiates as heroin.

If you still ain't feelin me, see "Friends That Hate You" further along.

Don't think people with pressing outside alliances will always be in your corner.

SELLING COKE

"From the home of Coca-Cola,
I'm not referrin' to soda"
Killer Mike, "Re-Akshon"

Want to sell coke? You'll never compete with the world's biggest supplier.

As many of us already know, the "coca" in Coca-Cola comes from a time when the soft drink contained cocaine as part of the "secret formula. Coke was originally formulated in 1886 by John Styth Pemberton, an Atlanta chemist and former Confederate army officer. Among other things, it contained three parts coca leaves to one part kola nut (a bitter African nut also having narcotic properties).

Coca-Cola was promoted as a medicine that would cure any ailment, from headache to depression. For years, Southerners called the drink "dope" or "a shot in the arm," and Coke delivery trucks were known as "dope wagons."

In the 1890s, however, public opinion began to turn against cocaine. This was because the government and media claimed that cocaine caused racial violence by drug-crazed Blacks. Cocaine, it was said, made Blacks "stronger, wilder, and more lustful for white women." In 1903, the *New York Tribune* published an article linking cocaine with Black crime and calling for legal action against Coca-Cola. Soon enough, cocaine went from acceptable to illegal.

> **Did You Know?**
> Creating false scares, like "cocaine-crazed Negroes," is a clever way for the people in power to get more money and control? By creating widespread fear and panic, they are able to push through government measures designed to stop the new threat. These expensive new measures help line the pockets of the same people who created the false scare, lied to the public, and proposed the expensive solution. In fact, this "Problem-Reaction-Solution" model is still used nowadays. 9/11 is one example.

Shortly after, Coca-Cola quietly changed its formula, now using coca leaves that were drained of cocaine, with only cocaine trace levels left over at a molecular level. I wonder what they do with all that unused cocaine from those half-used coca leaves?

In Bolivia today, the U.S. is working to destroy the native coca crops, which are vital to the livelihoods of the local people. David Herrera, a state government supervisor there, complained of how unfair the situation is. He said, "They export coca as a raw material for Coca-Cola, and we can't even freely sell it in Bolivia." Crazy, right?

Today, the Coca-Cola Company boasts a roster of 300 different products, ranging from Dasani water (filtered tap water with added salt) to Minute Maid juice drinks ("fruit" juices with almost no fruit juice). These products are sold in over 200 countries.

These products reap enormous profits for a corporation with such a foul record of human rights abuses and environmental pollution, that in 2004 the Multinational Monitor named Coke one of the world's "14 Most Evil Corporations." (Google it) According to the "War on Want" articles on Coke's offenses around the world (at www.cokewatch.org), the charges against the corporation include:

- Using high fructose corn syrup, to reduce costs, with the corn coming from genetically altered plants.
- Marketing soft drinks to children which cause obesity, diabetes, chemical dependency on caffeine, and lower vitamin intake
- Contaminating local ecosystems worldwide through the dumping of toxic waste from its plants; pollution of agricultural land, rivers and groundwater
- Exhausting community water reserves in India and other third-world countries by drilling deep into underground reservoirs, drying up local wells and leaving farmers unable to irrigate their crops.
- Using paramilitaries to crush union organizing at Coca-Cola bottling plants in Colombia. Eight union leaders have been murdered and at least 100 others have been detained and beaten
- Supporting and working with corrupt governments in Africa, like the military regime in Nigeria
- Adopting union-busting tactics in Pakistan, Turkey, Russia, Indonesia, Peru, Chile, Guatemala, Nicaragua and other countries
- Poisoning workers through exposure to toxic waste and pesticides
- Poisoning consumers by allowing unsafe levels of pesticide residues such as lindane, heptachlor (carcinogens), malathion, chlorpyrifos & DDT (neurotoxins) in their products, sometimes more than 30 times the legal levels

Did You Know?

Many of the foods we eat are genetically modified organisms, or GMOs? Research from 2005 found that more than half of the offspring of rats fed GMOs died within the first 3 weeks of life (6 times as many as those born to mothers fed on non-modified food). They were also 6 times as likely to be severely underweight. GMOs were also found to cause an immune response, misshapen liver cells, and other cellular anomalies. Personally, I just hate the fact that now there's tomatoes with fish DNA (true story).

In the Indian state of Kerala, the sale and production of Coca-Cola, along with other soft drinks, was initially banned. This was decided after the people of Kerala, a poor Black region in southern India, learned about how the Coke factories were poisoning their land and their people. However, the High Court in Kerala overturned the ban. The Court ruled that only the federal government of India can ban food products. So Coke stayed. Gangster!

I dare you to compete with that. Coca-Cola can sell trillions, kill millions, and make billions… while you can sell one ounce of coke and do five years.

Do you think you can outhustle the ultimate hustlers on this planet? What gives you the nerve to think you'll be better than the devil at doing devilishment? Or better than the slavemakers at making slaves? You must think you can out-torture the CIA too!

My point here is not about how foul Coca-Cola is, because it's addictive too, so you're probably not gonna switch. If you do switch, you're only gonna switch to some other company with a foul history as well. My point is about the fact that we can't do what they do, and hope to win. As ex-druglord Larry White advised upcoming hustlers in *Street Elements* magazine:

> There will come a day when the government will get enough evidence to convict you. When you read the indictments they always say, "The United States versus _______. Just put your name in the blank. You tell me how a person or persons can win against the world's superpower? And how can you win against their most powerful weapon: conpiracy?

This lesson ain't just about coke, and it ain't just for hustlers. No matter what game you're playing, if it's one that white guys made for white guys to win, *you're* not meant to win! So you can try, but you'll learn exactly how the system works. When white CEOs mismanage their business affairs and the corporations go bankrupt, *they* get million dollar bonuses. If *you* try that sh*t, homey, *you're* going to federal prison! So stop trying to win at their games…all of em.

You can't win at their game.

Lil Wayne and Self-Actualization

Lil Wayne is one cocky dude. He ain't go after the title of King of New Orleans, or even King of the South. No, he stuck his chest out and declared, "I'm the best rapper alive, since the best rapper [Jay-Z] retired." Now, he just says he's the best rapper alive. Period.

He's got reason to be cocky. He's been in the game since he was a kid, making noise in the industry for 11 years or so, which is more than most rappers can say. And he records damn near as much as Tupac. In just 2007 alone, he was featured on 77 songs! And like Pac, Wayne ain't no dummy. He'll make a song about getting his dick sucked one minute, but he can do something like "Georgia Bush" or "Hollywood Divorce" just as easily. I'm not saying he's *the truth*. I'm just saying he *could* do it.

Wayne proclaims he's the greatest so consistently, it's like listening to Muhammad Ali. And fans, magazines, and media are starting to buy in, saying it may be true. Wayne goes hard when it comes to speaking on himself. You might even hear him call himself God. (eg, "Weezy, F ya reverend, preach about me/ I'm the God, 1-7 Apple and E" or "I'm the God, I should ride with the Pope/ But the boy so hood, I just ride with my hoe") Ignorant as hell, but I understand his self-concept.

And what's wrong with it? What's wrong with seeing yourself as infinitely great?

I think some of us are just scared to see ourselves that way, so it sounds wrong when someone else does. As Marianne Williamson once wrote:

> Our deepest fear is not that we are inadequate.
> Our deepest fear is that we are powerful beyond measure.
> It is our light, not our darkness, that most frightens us.
> We ask ourselves, "Who am *I* to be brilliant, gorgeous, talented, fabulous?"
> Actually, who are you not to be?
> You are a child of God.
> Your playing small doesn't serve the world.
> There is nothing enlightened about shrinking so that other people won't feel insecure around you.
> We are all meant to shine, as children do.
> We were born to make manifest the glory of God that is within us.
> It's not just in some of us; it's in everyone.
> And as we let our own light shine, we subconsciously give other people permission to do the same.
> As we're liberated from our own fear, our presence automatically liberates others.

Lil Wayne may or may not really be the best rapper alive, but he lives out the words above. Here's how he explained his comments about being "God" and "the best" on his *Dedication II* mixtape with DJ Drama:

> Let me let y'all know what I mean by that 'best rapper alive' sh*t. I don't think I'm better than anybody personally. I don't think I'm better than anybody spiritually. I don't think I'm better than anybody in any way, form, or fashion.

But as far as this rap thing, I think I am better than everybody. I'm a competitor, I hope everybody else feel the same way about their craft. If you do, it makes it better for the people. It makes it better for the listeners. And that's how I feel about mine, so if you a listener and you wanna hear somebody that's dedicated to what they do, I'm so dedicated that I feel I'm the best, and that's that.

> **Did You Know?**
>
> All of the earliest gods, female divinities, and founders of world religions were Black. A partial list of these ancient Black figures includes: Buddha (India), Fu-Shi (China), Zaha (Japan), Zeus, Apollo, Athena, etc. (Greece), Krishna (India), Tyr (Scandinavia), Lao-tse (China), Scotia (Scotland), Caillech (Ireland), Quetzalcoatl (Mexico), Osiris, Isis, Horus, etc. (Egypt), Ixliton (Mexico), Kali (India), and of course Jesus (Palestine). There is even evidence that Muhammad and Moses were Black. Even (white) historian Godfrey Higgens wrote in his 1836 text *Anacalypis*:
>
> "We have found the Black complexion or something relating to it whenever we have approached the origin of nations. The Alma Mater, the Goddess Multimammia, the founders of the Oracles, the Memnon of first idols, were always Black. Venus, Jupiter,
> Apollo, Bacchus, Hercules, Asteroth, Adonis, Horus, Apis, Osiris, and Amen: in short all the...deities were black. They remained as they were first...in very ancient times."

Whether or not you like Lil Wayne, his self-confidence isn't a new idea. What he has said about himself is what learned scholars have been writing about for hundreds of years. Most of these men were members of secret societies, so their knowledge was much deeper level than most folks at the time.

In *The Secret Teaching of All Ages* (1928), Manly P. Hall says:

> All that man is or can ever hope to be depends upon his concept of God. No Individual is greater than the God he worships, nor is he capable of worshiping a concept of God greater than himself.

According to Albert Pike, author of the *Morals and Dogma* (1871):

> ...every man's conception of God must be proportioned to his mental cultivation, and intellectual powers, and moral excellence. God is, as man conceives him, the reflected image of man himself.

James Allen, author of *As a Man Thinketh* (1902), had the same idea, saying:

> A noble and Godlike character is not a thing of favor or chance, but is the natural result of continued effort in right thinking, the effect of long-cherished association with Godlike thoughts.

Even poet Henry David Thoreau (1854) explained in *The Walden*:

> If you advance confidently in the direction of your dreams, and endeavor to live the life you have imagined, you will meet with a success unexpected in common hours. You will pass an invisible boundary: new, universal and more liberal laws will begin to establish themselves

> around and within you and you will live with the license of a higher order of beings.

What did these white folks know over a hundred years ago that we just can't get into our heads now?

See yourself for the greatness you were meant to be.

MOVIE TO SEE

Children of Men

What if all of the problems on Earth kept getting worse? This movie tells that future. Nuclear war has made the environment so foul that no one can have babies. America has fallen apart. The last surviving country is keeping its people in a prison state, and keeping all immigrants and refugees out by force. Oh, and the government is corrupt.

THE GREATNESS IN MAN

> "He who experiences the unity of life sees his own Self in all beings, and all beings in his own Self, and looks on everything with an impartial eye."
> The Buddha

Do you realize there is a conscious intelligence that is running every system in your body right now? As you read this, this innate intelligence is ensuring the smooth operation of your body's 11 systems:

Circulatory system	Reproductive system	Muscular system
Digestive system	Endocrine system	Respiratory System
Nervous system	Immune system	Urinary System
Skeletal system	Lymphatic system	

On Ghostface Killah's *Ironman* album, Popa Wu explains:

> See, some people don't have no directions God, because they don't know the science of they self. See, the science of life is the science of you – all the elements that it took to create you. Cause everything in the universe God, that created the universe God, exists within you. You see what I'm saying? And that's the mind that you can't see. Don't you know that if a man could take and flip himself inside out God, he'll fall out and die, if he sees the sh*t that goes on, inside?

This "mind that you can't see," this innate intelligence keeps your heart beating and your lungs breathing without you even having to think about it. How else could all those processes go on inside of you without a glitch? But there's nothing spooky about it. This intelligence is definitely within you. It's even within your control. You simply don't know about it. You see, there are actually five "stages" to the mind:

1. Conscious
2. Subconscious
3. Superconscious
4. Magnetic Conscious
5. Infinite Conscious

Most people are only aware of their conscious thoughts. They are reminded of their subconscious thoughts when they dream at night or have fantasies, but even then they don't realize that their mind is functioning on more than one level. A computer works the same way. There are processes that happen on the desktop screen (like the program I used to type this book), and processes that happen in the background (like the computer managing its memory so it doesn't slow down while I type).

If you were to start investigating your subconscious thoughts, you could learn a lot about yourself. You could learn "what makes you tick" as they say. You could understand what you're REALLY thinking about or why you REALLY did something you did.

It's not that hard to do: It begins with looking past the basics, and asking questions like "Why?" about everything. If you ask yourself what everything means, even the little things you do, you'll begin to see clearly in no time. Unfortunately, most of us function solely on the conscious level: satisfying our most basic needs (food, clothing, shelter, sleep, and sex). We don't know why people (including us) do what they do, nor do we try to learn and find out. I'm hoping you're not like that, because I'm about to take you deep into the rabbithole.

Remember that conscious intelligence that runs every system in your body without pause? Remember how I said that intelligence is within you?

Think about the following:

Every one of the 92 naturally occurring elements on Earth also occurs within your body. Even gold is found in small proportions in the human body, whether you have eaten it or not. This makes you a "microcosm" of the universe, which means that the universe is within you. Just the same way, a seed is a "microcosm" of the adult tree, as it contains all the potential within it for that giant tree, even as a tiny seed.

Just as the Earth's surface is 3/4ths water, the human body is 3/4ths water, and so is the human brain (See "Science of the Brain"). And just as the most powerful natural forces on the Earth (and in the universe) involve electricity and magnetism, your body has its own magnetic field and your brain operates using electricity.

It takes the same amount of time for blood to circulate from your heart throughout your body as it does for light to travel from the Sun to the Earth (8 minutes, 20 seconds). Coincidence?

Light will actually change its course *and nature* based simply on the presence of an intelligent observer. (Why? How?)

In a woman's body, the egg can be found in only one fallopian tube at a time. A man's sperm, upon reaching the woman's uterus, consciously decides which way to turn, and picks the correct path 90% of the time. This sperm has almost nothing in it, except DNA. That's your mind *still* at work. Why do you think *you* get tired when she's the one pregnant?

A human fetus progresses through several stages, which resemble all the different points in human evolution.

Melanin, the chemical substance that gives you your skin color is present in the brain as neuromelanin, and throughout the blackness of space. Carbon, a black element, is fundamental to all life…and your melanin.

The Ancient Egyptians understood all this, which is why they reached the highest level of development any civilization had seen at the time. While the Europeans were still living in caves, these Black men and women were building pyramids that folks still can't build today! In fact, the three pyramids of Giza are arranged in the exact same orientation as the stars in Orion's belt, and the Great pyramid lies in the exact center of the earth's landmass. The height of the Great pyramid is almost exactly one-billionth of the distance from the earth to the sun. The perimeter of the Great pyramid divided by two times its height equals Pi up to the fourteenth digit. In Europe, Pi was not calculated accurately to the fourth digit until the sixth century A.D. In the ancient Egyptian "mystery schools," the students were taught that man was God on Earth, and trained in methods to unlock this great potential.

In fact, every god, in every ancient religion's scripture, has been described as a great *man*, and often specifically as a Black man. As it reads in a 1981 issue of the 5% periodical titled *The Black Family*:

> God is the highest extent of the mind. And energy and matter is the medium through which he expresses his ideas. And the black physical body of the Original man (the first) is the SUPREME medium. In other words, the amassment of elements…which comprise the physical body of the Original man, is the only vehicle in the universe through which (in all its essence) the great mind in the universe, in any and all ramifications and manifestations, manifested in the character or nature of the Original man.

What is my point in telling you all of this? I want you to look deeper within. Because if you can fathom that there is more to your mind and body than what happens

Did You Know?

Your stomach secretes corrosive acid? There's one dangerous liquid no airport security can confiscate from you: It's in your gut. Your stomach cells secrete hydrochloric acid, a corrosive compound used to treat metals in the industrial world. It can pickle steel, but mucous lining the stomach wall keeps this poisonous liquid safely in the digestive system, breaking down those hot Cheetos.

on a conscious level, you can fathom that the same intelligence running your body is also running the planets. That same intelligence, again, is within you.

Get it yet?

Think of the mind that designed the universe as an infinite, timeless consciousness. Think of that consciousness as a sea of water. If you take a cup of that water, the water in the cup has all of the properties of that vast sea. Nothing is missing. It's not about quantity. It's about quality. You have all the qualities of that supreme intelligence in your mind. Whether you tap into it is up to you. As I said, most of us function at the lowest level of consciousness for most of our lives. Some of us step up to a higher level. It begins with making the conscious decision to look deeper and see things from a higher plane.

Can you get there?

(I won't get any deeper than that…but you can find more jewels like this in *Knowledge of Self: A Collection of Wisdom on the Science of Everything in Life*)

See life through the All-Seeing-Eye. Find the greatness within.

Movies to See

What the Bleep Do We Know?; Pi; The Wizard of Oz

The first one may be tough to understand, but I think the people who made it did their best at keeping it simple. Basically: We made this universe, and there is no mystery God watching over us. This film is more of a documentary than anything, but it's great if you get it. If this movie doesn't make your brain do backflips, try watching this movie called *Pi.* If you don't get either one, just watch *The Wizard of Oz* again. I'm serious This old-ass movie was meant to be symbolic…and deep. That's why it's all so damn weird. Watch it again…Just keep in mind that the Wizard represents the made-up God we think is in charge. And everything else was meant to mean something too, even those damn flying monkeys.

God and Car Crashes

Things were tough for Twista in the 90s, even after his debut album dropped in 92. After getting off public assistance upon signing his first record deal, he figured he'd have it made. Instead, he was soon watching himself rapping on TV while washing tires at the car wash where he'd had to start working to make ends meet. Damn.

After over ten years of struggling with extortionists, shady record label practices, and twisted contracts, Twista finally made it big with the success of major hits like 2004's "Slow Jamz" and "Overnight Celebrity." Since then, Twista's been doin pretty good for himself.

On September 6, 2004, Twista and his crew were rolling home in their tour van from a show in upstate New York. The Chicago-bred rapper, known for his notoriously fast flow, was slowly falling asleep, unaware of how fast they were traveling on the dark night road. His bodyguard Butch and his cousin, the driver, occupied the front seats of the van, while Twista and his boys occupied the back. Then something happened. Everything went black for Twista. The next thing he recalled was lying in a grassy yard looking at a twisted van with its top torn off.

After the initial shock and amnesia wore off, Twista recalled that, in the accident, everyone had been thrown out of the van. Butch had been the only one not to survive the crash. Describing his painful memories, Twista explained to *XXL Magazine*:

> At one point, I believed that there wasn't a God. People say there ain't a God. But I feel like it was meant for me to be here. Because one thing that we [the people who were in the van] agreed was, how the f*ck are we still here? I couldn't believe how the top came off and all the bodies flew out and landed and we're still here.

Can you spot the flaw in Twista's logic?

Ask anybody you know who's survived a terrible car crash about what happened. At some point in most of their stories, they'll get to the part where they survived because God saved them. God has a purpose for them, and He wanted them to know that he was real, so he saved them.

Right. Almost every car crash victim I've ever met has credited God with their survival. Even pimp Don Magic Juan found religion and became "Bishop" Don Magic Juan after surviving a near-fatal accident.

But what about the people that don't survive? This kind of logic would lead you to believe that God picks and chooses who he saves and kills off. What is it that Twista's bodyguard deserved to die for, while one of his homeboys lived? Why did Left Eye and Aaliyah die in crashes, but rapists and serial killers have survived?

> "My man Bobo just lost his baby in a house fire
> And when I got on my knees that day to pray
> I asked God, 'Why you let these killers live
> And take my homeboy's son away?'"
> Pimp C on UGK's "One Day"

I've been in a bunch of car crashes, and not once did my survival result from divine intervention. The circumstances and the laws of physics put me in a position where I wasn't fatally wounded. If I'd been going ten miles faster, or sat three inches to the left, maybe my fate would have been different.

But maybe that whole "near death epiphany" thing isn't just a coincidence. Did you know the hospital almost always send a priest or chaplain up to your room when you are hospitalized for a car accident, life-threatening illness, or other traumatic event? Good time to preach to somebody, huh? Kinda like selling home insurance to somebody when they think tornadoes are coming!

In Ice T's book *The Ice Opinion*, he relates a story different from Twista's:

> A car accident twelve years ago really changed my outlook on spirituality. I woke up in a hospital with a priest sitting beside me. He was going through some religious rites, and I yelled, "Get him away from me!" It's not that I didn't want his help, but at that point I didn't feel like I wanted to pray for anything...They told me I'd never walk again, so I went into myself and pulled myself together the only way I knew how. Alone. I didn't want to rely on prayer and think that it alone was gonna make me get better. I didn't trust it. "I *have* to get better," I told myself. I refused to pray. I just went right into myself. I learned that no religion is more powerful than your own spirit and determination.

See how a priest was already sittin there? I *told* you that's how they get you. But there's more than one way to respond to a situation like that. You can see things like Twista or Ice T or Don Magic Juan for all I care. But which one is based on *reason*? It's not like life and logic naturally point you to looking at the heavens. Someone *else* has to do that. Doesn't mean it makes sense. And if you wanna do as many churchgoers do, and judge the strength of a faith by the quality of someone's life...then um, Ice T ain't even *close* to broke. So who's right?

Life and logic will point you in one direction, but other influences can point you in the other. Use common sense.

Movie to See

The Matrix Trilogy

This is one of my favorite movies series ever, and my enthusiasm for them has nothing to do with the special-effects. What you may not know is that film was plagiarized from a manuscript submitted by a Black woman named Sophia Stewart. The Wachowski brothers stole her idea and turned it into one of the most fantastic movies ever...but in the process they scared a lot of white folks.

Did you know that Will Smith was the original actor they had in mind to play the role of Neo, but he turned it down? They were also looking for a Black Trinity, and tried casting Jada Pinkett-Smith, but that didn't work out either. I sure would have rather seen Jada layin half-naked than that old white lady they had playing Neo's girl.

But why the Black leads? Well, the whole premise of Ms. Stewart's story was the rise of a Black Messiah from among the masses. It's the story of God at its best. Neo represents a common man who awakens from the lies he's being told, and finds the knowledge of himself. At first he doubts his potential, but once he accepts it, nothing is impossible. Still, he continues to remind people that he is no different from them, and that they must save themselves.

Watch it again and pay attention. I bet you never noticed where (in the very beginning), right after a guest calls Neo "Jesus Christ" and his "Savior," he says, "You look a lot whiter than usual." Chew on that one.

In order to produce an effective screenplay, the Wachowski brothers consulted a lot of sources, even Cornell West and other Black scholars, many of who appeared as the council of Zion in the last two films. Speaking of Zion, did you notice how Black those people were? That represents the hereafter...that is who and what will be here after the last World War. And all those Black people dancing around half-naked with their dreads swingin made a lot of white audiences uncomfortable.

Almost everything in the first flick has a serious meaning to it. Even the names: Neo means "new" in Greek, but Neo is also a rearrangement of the letters in "one," as in The One. His birth name is Mr. Anderson, which the agents insist on calling him. "Ander" + "son" literally translates to "Son of Man." So Neo goes through the transformation of the Christ, from "Son of Man," to "Sun of Man," and demands that he be called by his chosen name, "Neo." This is a transformation we go through once we gain the knowledge of ourselves.

Not only do all the names and numbers have symbolic meanings, all the characters represent something as well. The agents are agents of the oppressive system of the machines. The machines represent many things, including the systems that keep us down, but they clearly represent white people, something we "made," but which eventually wanted to rule over us. One thing you learn in the film is that ANYONE who is not awake can be an agent of the machines. That's deep when you think about our people. As Stokely Carmichael said, "When you're in the struggle, don't trust anybody. Even your own mother can sell you out."

Unfortunately, the following two movies didn't hit home like the first, at least not message-wise. Why? No more of Sophia Stewart's ideas to rely on. So the Wachowski brothers made it up as they went along. Neo went from a symbol for Black Godhood to a weird halfway-Christ, crucifixion and all. Ah, what can you do? At least the special effects were good.

Science of the Brain

Your brain is split into halves called the left and right hemispheres.

The left hemisphere governs logical thought and the right side of the body.	The right hemisphere governs creative thought and the left side of the body.

You can tell if someone is lying by looking at which way their eyes turn just as they are about to answer a question. If left, they are using the left hemisphere to be creative and make something up. If right, they are using the right hemisphere to be logical and remember something the way it happened. Different parts of the brain also have different functions. For extra credit, look up the functions of (a) the Cerebrum, (b) the Cerebellum, (c) the Medulla Oblongata, and (d) the Pineal Gland.

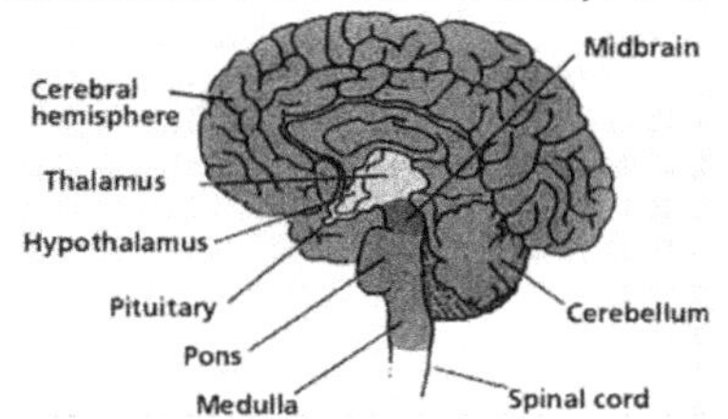

Your brain operates through electrical impulses fired between neurons and synapses. When you learn or memorize, you build and strengthen the connections between these neurons and synapses. If you could harness the electricity used by your brain, you could continuously power a 10-watt light bulb. Mine, however, can power a nuclear reactor.

Your brain consists of about 100 billion neurons! That's about 166 times the number of people on the planet!

The brain represents about 2% of your total body weight. But your brain is major, using approximately 20% of your total oxygen, as well as 20% of your blood. In fact, there are about 100,000 miles of blood vessels in the brain. If they were stretched out they would circle the Earth more than 4 times. But that would be gross, so don't do it.

Your brain grows the most from birth to early childhood, and then slows down. For many people, it stops growing at age 18. However, in many cases, the brain continues to produce new neurons throughout adult life, especially in response to intellectual stimulation. Put away the lotion. I said *intellectual* stimulation.

Information travels at different speeds within different types of neurons. Transmission can be as fast as 120 meters/sec (or 268 mph). Or much slower, like the people who can't get your order right at Taco Bell.

The number of internal thought pathways that your brain is capable of producing is: One followed by 6.5 million miles of standard typewritten zeros! Your brain is capable of having more ideas than the number of atoms in the known universe! Can a computer beat that?

Various studies say that the average human only uses about 5% of their brain at any given time. I don't know bout y'all. I'm up to at least 32%.

The average estimate of the number of brain cells lost per day is between 10,000 and 1,000,000, but the number lost when you drink alcohol is another 10,000 to 1,000,000 brain cells PER DRINK. Makes you think, huh? But not enough to drink less, huh?

Parts of the brain of a severely abused and neglected child can be substantially smaller than that of a healthy child. We won't even waste time talking about the brains of weed-heads and pill-poppers.

However, there's hope. Even among severely alcoholic individuals who have been brainscanned with "small brains" at the height of their addiction, later scans - after rehabilitation - show their brains back to *normal size*. How bout that: a supercomputer that fixes *itself*!

But are you making full use of yours? Or are you just playing Solitaire and chatting online?

The best computer ever made sits between your ears.

Are You Strong or Weak?

"Strength" is not all about how much you can bench-press, or how many people you've bullied into compliance. Not that there's anything wrong with physical force, because physical force is what makes the world go round. It's just that most people who rely on their physical strength can't apply it the right way, because their minds aren't in the right place. That's why true strength begins in the mind. Check the list and see for yourself how weak or strong you really are.

The Weak Mind Thinks	The Strong Mind Thinks
Weakness	Power
Conforming	Questioning
Comfort	Risk
Fear	Analysis
Hesitation	Determination
Status Quo	Change
Belief	Reason
Have the Answers	Look for Solutions
I Know	I Learn
Do Same Thing	Experiment
Habit	Creativity
Stuck	Fluid
Complacency	Continuous Improvement
Emotion	Thought
Self-Deceptions	Self-Examination
Confusion	Focus
Law	Consciousness
Hope	Effective Action
Give Me Liberty	I Take My Freedom
Prayer	Action
Victim	Survivor
Respect for "Authority"	Self-Respect
Helplessness	Action
Surrender	Persistence
Theoretical	Practical
Appeal to my Pocket	Appeal to my Mind
Being Right	Producing Results
Beat the System	Change the System

Apathy	Enthusiasm
Pessimism	Optimism
Obedience	Self-Determination
Symbolic Behavior	Substantive Action
Self-Interest	Big Cause
Egoism	Altruism
Profit	Sacrifice
Begging	Creating Value
Preach	Demonstrate
Escapism	Challenge
Mediocrity	Excellence
Poverty	Wealth
Laziness	Ambition
Living to Die	Immortality
External Authority	Individual Sovereignty

What a Woman Wants

They say you can't live with 'em, can't live without 'em. Just as crazy as any woman has made me, I've gone just as crazy being single and looking for that "one good girl" who I figured would make my life "complete." But a woman can't do that for you. A man or woman has to be complete in and of themselves before joining into a partnership with someone else. Unless you WANT drama, of course.

Now you can't do it like Mel Gibson in that movie *What a Woman Wants* and read a woman's mind to understand her needs and desires. You can, however, get close by understanding the psychology of the opposite sex by reading a book like Dr. Richard Gray's *Men are from Mars, Women are from Venus*. But even without psychology, there are some basics to what any woman wants. A major part of securing the right kind of woman requires that you have secured *yourself*. Secured what exactly?

Again the 12 Jewels I introduced you to in *Part One*:

1. Knowledge
2. Wisdom
3. Understanding
4. Freedom
5. Justice
6. Equality
7. Food
8. Clothing
9. Shelter
10. Love
11. Peace
12. Happiness

After all, what self-respecting woman would respect a dude who can't secure his own food and clothing? I know a father who imparted upon his sons the following wisdom, "Worry about women later; become successful first, and coochie will come to you." I don't know if he used the word coochie, but "vagina" didn't sound right either. Anyway, his sons did as he said, stayed in their books, studied to become engineers, graduated, made great money, had stable lifestyles, and – sure enough – they then had their choice of plenty of beautiful women…who were now approachin *them*. To top it off, these women were usually financially secure themselves! Meanwhile, their old buddies were still scrapin by with the skeezers. You decide.

"The men must be men, or the boys will continue to rule."
National Shrine of Afrikans in America

Short of success in life, you can shoot for one of the basic levels of security: maturity. Once you know what you want, it becomes a lot easier to get it. It also becomes a lot easier to avoid the traps that keep other dudes from attaining their goals. Of course, there probably aren't too many examples of maturity and security around you. If you've watched the movie *Baby Boy*, you understand the syndrome. A lot of us never grow up.

"Involuntary labor, took a knife, split a woman's navel
Took her premature baby, let her man see you rape her
If I could travel to the 1700's/ I'd push a wheelbarrow fulla dynamite through ya covenant"
Nas, "America"

White supremacy implanted this fear in us since childhood, and we've been "boys" in the hood ever since. During slavery, masculine men were murdered publicly, instilling fear in the other men, who grew more and more like boy...until here we are. Today, our women lead. That's what our women had to do during slavery. We never stepped back up. The Black and Brown men who have been strong since then have either been killed, sent to jail, turned against us, or went overboard in their machoism and began beating and dominating their own women and families, as well as each other.

The truth is that some of us believe that we are strong when we are truly weak. Growing up in a society where your people are taught that they are nothing creates adults who don't know how to be adults. We didn't even plan to make it to adulthood! And we didn't have too many examples of responsible adult males to begin with. Michael Jordan? Please, that dude might as well have been a cartoon. He never established himself as a real person because he never stood for anything. He just played ball and made popular kicks. Bill Cosby? He was positive, but he never struck me as being in tune with what was really going on in the hood. What about the preachers and politicians? Well, the ones who were really down for us either get killed or blackballed into obscurity, and the rest aren't really here for our interests, are they? (see "Who Wants to Be a Puppet?") As Killer Mike raps on "Pressure":

> Black politicians, stop bullsh*ttin/ And you funky Black preachers with your pulpittin/ Our kings had dreams and a big vision/ All you give us is government and religion/ Are you a freedom fighter or a stool pigeon?/ Is you down for your people in the big mission?/ Or you a dirty nigga workin for a f*ckin Clinton?/ Or a dirty nigga workin for a f*ckin Bush?

That about sums up the state of our "leadership," don't it? And I don't even want to keep talking about the "brothers on the down low" who the media parades around like they are the new examples of Black manhood.

What's left? Us, huh? So here we are. Some of us weak. Some of us strong. Most of us with no examples. No guidelines. No guidance. Some of us don't even know how insecure we are. And it shows in how we treat our women. We want to be strong, but we just don't know how to do it. What can you do? Man up, that's what. And make sure everyone you come in touch with does the same. Make sure everwhere you go recognizes you as a supreme example of Black manhood. Do enough of that, and the women will come to you.

Do what's right, and what's right for you will come to you.

Supreme the Asshole on "These Bitches"

When you're talking about a woman, callin her "bitch" means one of two things. Either it's a female in particular whose attitude sucks OR you just think all women are bitches. Now, unless you're a sociopath, you know every woman can't be a bitch, so here's my advice for the first definition. When a female falls into the bitch category, she's usually there because somebody f*cked her over in the past and she's bitter, or somebody f*cked her over in the past and she's got a wall up (Ever heard of "defense mechanisms"?). Either that, or her mama didn't raise her. In that case, it was her mama that f*cked her over by not doin her job. You have two choices now. You could either (A) try to change her mind and show her that you're a good dude, or (B) tell her that her pussy probably stinks like her attitude, and walk away.

20 Signs a Man is Insecure

Some of you dudes are raging cases of testosterone overdoses, but that doesn't mean you're a real man either. One of the biggest hurdles to true manhood is overcoming your insecurities. And unfortunately, many of our men are far more insecure than our women. Here's a way to check yourself, or the brothers you know, for defects.

1. Control Issues – He seeks to control his woman by making her think, say, and do, what he wants. What he wants is a pet, not a partner. And even a pet won't do what you tell it most of the time.

2. Overcompensating – He compensates for his shortcomings by dealing with several women at one time, none of whom know about each other. He does a lot of lying to keep himself "looking" sincere.

3. Materialism – He tries to make himself into a more impressive person by surrounding himself with material things that he can show off. Although this dude may not own a house, he WILL need the newest, hottest car to drive.

4. Appearance – He's worried about appearances more than anything. His woman has to act and look a certain way. He can't leave the house unless he is looking a certain way. There's nothing wrong with some pride and hygiene, but dudes like this are missing the important things (like a bank account) while trying to show off.

5. Support Group – Not only is he extremely concerned about what other people think of him, he needs to constantly be surrounded by other people who reinforce and support what he already thinks.

Did You Know?

You can "determine" the sex of your child? The day of conception makes a difference, as does temperature, diet, and sexual position. Since male-producing sperm are faster but weaker than female-producing sperm, you're more likely to have a girl if you don't conceive near the time of ovulation, or in a cold environment, or in a position that doesn't put you as close as possible to the cervix.

6. Takes It Personal – He thinks someone disagreeing with or criticizing him means that they have a personal problem with him...and he takes it personally.

7. Petty Boy – He gets emotional about the pettiest of things, but argues that he's right for the way he responds.

8. Baby Boy – He finds a woman who will treat him like she's his mother.

9. Big Daddy – He treats that same woman like she's his daughter.

10. Avoidance – He's actually scared to try new experiences, but lies and says that he's just not interested in things like that. He avoids any situation where he might not feel comfortable. He also runs from conflicts he can't control. And he refuses to be open about what's REALLY going on with him.

11. Contradiction – He uses his words to tell who he is and what he is about, and not his actions. Actually, his actions usually contradict what he believes about himself.

12. Loud – He talks real loud, for no reason, as if he needs attention.

13. Insecure Woman – He finds a woman who is insecure enough for him to control, and the only time they get along is during sex. Sex is the insecure woman's safety net.

14. Overdoes It – He drives in tiny nails with a sledgehammer. And he usually misses. In other words, he tries to overdo everything to make himself seem more important, more powerful, more whatever than he really is. If he can't hack it in the white man's world, he'll exaggerate his presence in a world of his own.

15. Dick Issues – He's honestly worried about whose dick is bigger or smaller than his. But he swears he's not gay, either.

16. Jealousy – Even if he has a 2008 BMW, he's still jealous of people driving a 2009 BMW. He tends to "hate" more than motivate.

17. Trendy – He waits until other people think something is hot before he feels the same way.

18. Low Standards – He often goes after unattractive women because he subconsciously believes that they have lower standards and will thus accept him. He avoids women and other situations that require someone to be sure of himself. He acts like its all about sex, but it's deeper.

20. Lies – He lies about things that don't even matter, just to reinforce the positive (false) image of himself that he's trying to put out.

Sound familiar? This may describe one of your partners (or many of them), or (if you're a woman) the man in your life. What can you do? Sadly, not much. You can point it out, and hopefully they'll change. But most of the time, a man's insecurity will keep him from even seeing your point. Your best bet is simply to find new company.

Insecurity is a dangerous weakness. Eliminate it or avoid it.

Holiday Madness

Holidays are like corn dogs. They're a mix of foul leftovers packaged up in a sweet shell. They say Christmas is all about family and the spirit of giving, Thankgiving is all about being grateful, and Halloween is all about having fun. What they really mean is: "Here's one day to do the sh*t you should be doing EVERY day, but on this one day you're going to spend a gang of money to do it."

Didn't you know that American holidays are spaced apart for a reason? There's one for every season, and each holiday sends people rushing to the stores. This is what keeps our economy going. Companies that are nearly bankrupt throughout the rest of the year get that boost they need every Thanksgiving, Christmas, Easter, and Fourth of July. If all Black people boycotted Christmas, this whole country would shut down.

The worst part is that we celebrate and spend money on days that have nothing to do with us. Either they came from some sick European tradition of eating people or molesting horses, or they're a celebration of something that only benefited white people, like St. Patrick's Day (and I'ma call you a stupid sh*thead if you try to pinch me for not wearing green). In fact, the holidays have been used to keep us down…for a long time. We get happy on these days, waste our money, and forget all about what's really going on. Here's what Frederick Douglass had to say:

> It was deemed a disgrace not to get drunk at Christmas; and he was regarded as lazy indeed, who had not provided himself with the necessary means, during the year, to get whiskey enough to last him through Christmas. From what I know of the effects of these holidays upon the slave, I believe them to be the most effective means in the hands of the slaveholder in keeping down the spirit of insurrection. Were the slaveholders at once to abandon this practice, I have not the slightest doubt it would lead to an immediate insurrection among the slaves…. The holidays are part and parcel of the gross fraud, wrong, and inhumanity of slavery.

Think about it…people who are f*cked up all year long get happy every holiday season (except Christmas when the suicide rate goes through the roof). Talk about an escape! How bout we start *dealing* with our problems instead?

Valentine's Day

The story of Valentine's Day starts out pretty sick too. The name probably comes from St. Valentine, a priest in ancient Rome. When Emperor Claudius II decided that single men made better soldiers than those with wives and families, he outlawed marriage for young men. St. Valentine continued marrying young men against the Emperor's orders. When he was caught, he was sentenced to death. Rumor has it that his heart was cut out and delivered in a box. Just like that $100 heart-shaped box of chocolates you're gonna buy. But the actual date of the celebration (and the customs that come with it) comes from Lupercalia, a festival of ancient Rome that predated the Church. Lupercalia was a purification and fertility rite where a bunch of half-naked priests sacrificed goats and dogs and ran around smearing blood on boys' foreheads and lashing women with strips of goat skin so they'd be more fertile. I couldn't make this sh*t up if I wanted to. Anyway, it was so popular the Church couldn't get rid of it, so they just renamed it…like they did Halloween, Christmas, and all your other "Christian" holidays.

Beyond the sicko factor, here's my problem with this day. Men want sex. Women want gifts and attention. And if somebody don't get what they want on this day, the relationship hits a rocky patch QUICK. Especially if your girl feels like someone else's man outdid you. So couples are in danger, single people are feelin extra lonely and miserable, and as Kanye said, "the white man gets paid offa alla dat."

Halloween

"What they have implanted here, which is really a 'gringo' custom, is terrorism. They disguise children as witches and wizards, that is contrary to our culture."
Hugo Chávez on Halloween

The Celts were a people who lived in Europe about 2,000 years ago. On the night of October 31, they celebrated Samhain, when it was believed that the ghosts of the dead returned to earth. During the celebration, the Celts wore costumes, usually made from animal heads and skins. The Celtic priests built huge bonfires, where the people offered crops and animals as sacrifices to the Celtic gods.

Later, the Christian Church adopted these rituals (along with many other "pagan" practices), and reinvented the celebration as All Hallow's Eve. The Christian people could continue wearing costumes, but this time the imagery was centered on dead saints, angels, and devils.

Today, we send our kids out masquerading as devils, demons, fairies and trolls, all in the name of "fun." Don't you think Halloween is part of the reason why there's people who grow up still believing in sh*t like ghosts, aliens, and demons?

So whether you (A) spend a bunch of money on costumes and candy and let them participate, or (B) you keep em out and have em mad as hell at you, you're damned if you do and damned if you don't.

April Fool's Day

In the old Julian calendar, the new year began on April 1st, which makes sense because that's around the beginning of Spring. That would naturally be when a year should begin, since life kinda begins then. In fact, most of the world's calendars marked the new year around the same time. But in the 1500s, Europeans switched over to a new calendar, the Gregorian calendar. January 1st, in the dead of winter, became the European New Year. Those Europeans who forgot the change and attempted to celebrate New Years on the old date were teased as "April fools." They were ridiculed and tricked and blah, blah, blah. Now, what's this day got to do with me again?

St. Patrick's Day

I swear, if anybody dares to pinch me because I'm not wearing green, I'm gonna beat them with a sock filled with baby powder. Most people who aren't white don't even know who St. Patrick was, so why the hell are you celebrating him? St. Patrick's Day is an Irish holiday. That means "not for you." There's always some genius who thinks that we should celebrate all holidays, but I bet you that joker doesn't celebrate any days for Black or brown people besides MLK Day. Sh*t, I'll bet he can't even name any others. Unless you're wearin a Mexican flag as a cape on Cinco de Mayo, don't tell me sh*t about wearin some damn green.

Thanksgiving

"The Indians saved the Pilgrim
And in return the Pilgrim killed em
They call it it Thanksgiving, I call your holiday "hellday"
Cause I'm from poverty, neglected by the wealthy"
Nas, "What Goes Around"

I've already said plenty about Thanksgiving. (see "F*ck Thanksgiving") West Coast rapper Ras Kass, in his song "Nature of the Threat," adds some more to my soundtrack:

> In the eight century Muslims conquered/ Spain, Portugal, and France and controlled it for 700 years/ They never mention this in history class/ cause O'fays are threatened when you get the real lesson/ Moors from Baghdad, Turkey threatened European Christians/ meaning – the white way of life; hence the Crusades for Christ/ On November 25th, 1491/ Santiago defeats the last Muslim stronghold, Grenada/ King Ferdinand gave thanks to God for victory/ and the Pope of Rome and declared this date to forever be/ a day of "Thanksgiving" for all European Christians

Christmas

"The descendants of those who crucified Christ... have taken ownership of the riches of the world, a minority has taken ownership of the gold of the world, the silver, the minerals, water, the good lands, petrol, well, the riches, and they have concentrated the riches in a small number of hands."
Hugo Chavez, Christmas Speech, 2005

In "Nature of the Threat" Ras Kass continues:

> December 25th, the birth of Saturn/ A homosexual god, now check the historical pattern/ December 25, now thought the birth of Christ/ was Saturnalia, when men got drunk, f*cked each other then beat their wife/ Fact is, it was still practiced, til they called it Christmas

There's a million things I could say about Christmas. I could get into the twisted origins Ras Kass spoke on. Or I could get into the way the slavemasters used it to screw us up even more, as Frederick Douglass said above. Or I could tell you how much money Black people wasted (mostly on white businesses) last year at Christmas time. But why bother? At the end of the day, you either love Christmas or you hate it. And if you love it, you won't care that it takes almost a whole year for a Black family to recover financially from the debts they rack up at Christmas (which is why Kwanzaa was designed around

Did You Know?

Biologists at the University of California at San Francisco have found that male fruit flies exposed to high levels of alcohol become hypersexual and try to court practically anything with wings, including other male fruit flies. Eventually the revelry turns into a dysfunctional orgy, with "a chain of males chasing each other," said one insect expert. Be careful how much you drink!

homemade gifts, but who does that?). And you won't care if there's more robberies around Christmastime than any other time because of the pressure to buy our kids sh*t they don't need. You won't care about the fact that Christmas ain't got nothing to do with the historical Jesus Christ. If you're one of those people who are "dreaming of a white Christmas," you won't give a f*ck about none of that sh*t. You won't even care that every Christmas, parents start a tradition of lying to children by telling them about a jolly white man giving them the gifts they busted their asses to buy.

> **Did You Know?**
> The Bible never mentions angels having wings. The angelic image of a person with wings resulted from painters and sculptors taking it upon themselves to use their imagination and creativity. The Bible also doesn't say that no one can see God. Moses saw him face to face, and Jacob even wrestled with him.

"I never believed in Santa Claus because I knew no white dude would come into my neighborhood after dark."
Dick Gregory

But damn…I still don't get *that* part! My parents bust their ass to buy me sh*t and then they gave the credit to a white man! Not even a REAL white man, but an IMAGINARY one! How sick is that? When I found out Santa wasn't real, I looked at my parents like they were either compulsive liars or completely retarded. I wonder if you felt that way too. But if you love Christmas, you won't care. So I'll move on.

The Fourth of July

When it's "Independence Day" in my hood, we don't light fireworks and wave flags around. **We bust our guns**. Last year, about twenty dudes from my street got together and we must've let off about 30 rifles, shotguns, handguns, and revolvers in all, leaving at least five hundred rounds in the yard. At the end of the night, I thought about it. We weren't celebrating. We weren't screaming "Yeehaw, America!"

Actually, these dudes were doing the same thing the American settlers did when they bust their guns back in 1776. Through their actions, they were saying, "We're a f*ckin army, we ain't scared, and one day, we're takin back what's ours!" At least that's what I got out of it.

I've never felt "independent" or "free" or even "American" on the Fourth of July. Why should I? In 1852, Frederick Douglass gave a "Fourth of July" speech at an event commemorating the signing of the Declaration of Independence. Of course, at this time, Blacks were still in slavery. You know *he* was pissed. And he didn't hold his tongue at all, and told his audience, "This Fourth of July is yours, not mine. You may rejoice, I must mourn." He asked them, "Do you mean, citizens, to mock me, by asking me to speak to-day?"

Freestylin from the top of his head, he continued:

> What, to the American slave, is your 4th of July? I answer; a day that reveals to him, more than all other days in the year, the gross injustice and cruelty to which he is the constant victim. To him, your celebration is a sham; your boasted liberty, an unholy license; your national greatness, swelling vanity; your sound of rejoicing are empty and heartless; your denunciation of tyrants brass-fronted impudence; your shout of liberty and equality, hollow mockery; your prayers and hymns, your sermons and thanks-givings, with all your religious parade and solemnity, are to Him, mere bombast, fraud, deception, impiety, and hypocrisy – a thin veil to cover up crimes which would disgrace a nation of savages. There is not a nation on the earth guilty of practices more shocking and bloody than are the people of the United States, at this very hour.

It's sad that even Dr. Martin Luther King, Jr. would say nearly the same thing over 100 years later, when he reported that there was no country more violent, corrupt, or hypocritical than his own. It's been almost fifty years since then. How much has changed? Are you free yet? You ready to put on your flag underwear and light up those red, white, and blue sparklers?

Martin Luther King Day

Yup, this day too. Forget the fact that Arizona and a few other places wouldn't even recognize this day as a holiday (because it honored a Black man). All I've got to say is that this day involves people telling just about as many lies as on Christmas. MLK didn't teach half of the silly sh*t people say in his name (Reminds me of someone else…I think his name started with a "J").

But every MLK Day, we hear white America's version of Dr. King, complete with "turn the other cheek" and "let's all get along." We never hear the revolutionary words that got Dr. King killed (see "F*ck Dr. King"). And guess what? Nobody cares, because it's a day off work. Another day to party and bullsh*t…while the bullsh*t consumes us and – year after year – leaves our people just as f*cked up as we were last season – or worse.

Myths and Silliness

> "I had doubts that religion was intellectually respectable."
> Dr. Martin Luther King, Jr.

I was talking to a young Christian about Jesus, explaining to him that he was no different from us, because he was a Black man trying to get people to see the greatness in themselves. Jesus was one of the first Black revolutionaries, I explained. He didn't want us to turn the other cheek and be passive and weak with the people who held us down.

In fact, one of the first things he told his disciples to do was to go and buy swords. He even said: "Think not that I am come to send peace on earth: I came not to send peace, but a sword."

But the Christian dude was stuck on his preacher's version of Jesus, which is very different ("Turn the other cheek," "Be a happy slave," "Wait on me to come save you," etc.). In fact, the average church's version of Jesus is nothing like the Jesus in the Bible. Kind of like how Christianity is nothing like what Jesus was teaching.

When I was telling this story, one of my brothers jumped in and said: "Man, we don't even know if dude was *real*." I'd never thought about that. I never questioned it. Even though I'm always telling people about how Jesus was really Black, how his name wasn't even really "Jesus Christ," what his real mission was about, and why he really died...I never considered whether he himself was a real historical person.

After some research, I'm not sure anymore.

Did you know that there are at least 16 "savior" gods who were crucified before the time of Jesus? There's even a book about it, titled *The World's Sixteen Crucified Saviors* by Kersey Graves.

Then there's all the contradictions about Jesus in the Bible. It seems like everybody wants to spin his image their way, so it's hard to tell who he really was at all. In fact, there's hundreds of contradictions all throughout the Bible. You can look that up online. Just Google "101 Bible Contradictions." See if you can figure out why one person said Jesus was crucified, but another one said he was hung from a tree.

"Any idiot can believe in Jesus H. Christ.
To truly understand all that confusion in the gospels takes a real contortionist scholar."
Franz Bibfeldt, German theologian

I know part of it has something to do with the fact that almost all of the people who wrote about Jesus in the Bible never met him. In fact, Paul – who wrote about 14 books of the New Testament – never even *quotes* Jesus. He just tells people what *he* thinks. Don't believe me? Just look it up. (Google: Paul "never met" Jesus)

What really takes the cake is that there are no historical records of Jesus from his time period. There's records about a ruler named Pontius Pilate, but nothing about any Hebrew revolutionaries named Yeshuah (aka the homey Jesus).

So I thought about it some more. After all, Jesus was supposed to "come back." Elijah Muhammad said that the Jesus in the Bible is 90% prophecy, meaning the story is mostly about something that would happen much later. Even the Jews believe that.

So here we are now. Still waiting on the "Son of Man." But think about that…maybe Jesus is "Just us"? Aren't you the "son of man"? After all, the Jesus of the Bible keeps telling people that they should be equally great (or better). Like in the book of Luke, where he says, "Great works I have done, but greater works you shall do." He never even says he's the Son of God. Check the Bible. You won't find it. Instead, he keeps saying he's the Son of Man. Like us.

In the Gospel of John, Chapter 10, where the people are about to stone him for having too much of a God-like swagger, he tells them he's not the one running around saying he's God. *They* are. And if they want to criticize him, they should look at his works and compare it with his words. Then he drops the bomb on what he's really trying to show them anyway, saying: "Is it not written in your law that you are Gods? And the word of God cannot be broken." (referring to the *law* of Psalms 82)

The people didn't even know what to do at this point. So Jesus avoids a beat down, but the people never got a clue. Even his disciples never figure out what he was trying to tell them about themselves. So the white folks kill him for startin a movement, and the Black folks keep the movement going with him as their new God.

They'll do the same thing with MLK in 500 years. If only our people could think critically instead of just "believing." If only we could think for ourselves instead of looking for leadership and direction.

But that's hard for the average person. What about you?

Do you think critically about things you do, or do you "just do it?"

Are there any popular conventions or practices that you don't participate in? Why?

Do you explain "why" to others who do?

Think critically…about everything.

Movies to See

Zeitgeist; The Hidden Story of Jesus; The Da Vinci Code; Religulous; The Root of All Evil?

You can see *Zeitgeist* and *The Hidden History of Jesus* free, online, at www.supremedesignonline.com. They both go over a lot of what I'm talking about in the essay above, as well other things I talk about elsewhere.

The Da Vinci Code is a fictional approach to desmystifying Jesus. The story uses historical evidence to piece together a picture where Jesus was very much human, and in fact had a child. Oh, and the Church is a bunch of liars and phonies, working overtime to keep that stuff under wraps. The only part they

The Da Vinci Code left out was that the REALLY big secret the Church was hiding wasn't that he had a child, but that he was a Black man.

Religulous just puts religious silliness on blast as only Bill Maher could do.

The Root of All Evil? Episode 1: The God Delusion, and *Episode 2: The Virus of Faith*, are also available free online at the same site.

Carnophobia

Girl: You want to go to this club with me? They have free drinks til 2 and a live band.

Me: I don't know. What kind of a club is it?

Girl: Does it matter? Did you hear me? Free drinks til 2!

Me: Why don't you want to tell me about the club?

Girl: Cause I know how you are! Look, it's not the crowd you're used to. There will be a lot of "different" people there.

Me: Different? Different how? These people gon be dancing all weird with them little light sticks or drinkin goat's blood and sh*t?

Girl: No, they're just gay.

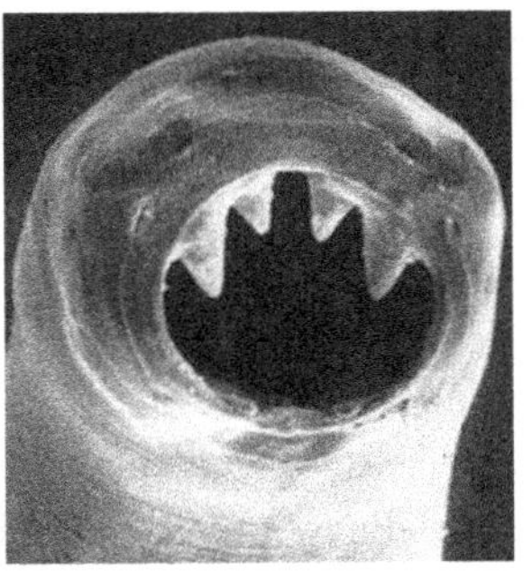

Me: Oh! Just gay! So you're JUST tryin to trick me into going to a gay club and getting pissy drunk? That's cool!

Girl: See, I knew you'd react this way. I shouldn't have asked.

Me: Look, you can go, but I'm just not interested in hangin out with a bunch of men dressed like women. That's not my thing. If somebody tries to dance on me, I'm goin to jail.

Girl: See how you are? You need to be more open-minded!

Me: I *am* open-minded. Just not open-bootied.

Girl: You are so homophobic!

Me: Who said I was scared? If they can be free to not be into women, can't I be free to not be into gayness? Why I gotta approve of some sh*t to prove I ain't scared of it?

Girl: Huh?

Me: Look, I don't eat meat. I don't support that sh*t. I think it makes people sick. But am I scared of meat-eaters? Lot's of people eat meat, and think it's natural. I don't think being a carnivore is natural to humans though. You eat meat, right? But am I *scared* of you? Am I carnophobic?

Girl: Huh? I don't get it. I said you're homophobic.

Me: Argh! You big dummy!

You Put WHAT in your Mouth?

I'd known of the health benefits of not eating meat since I began reading up on how disgusting pork was at 14. By 17, I'd given up all red meat, but a vegetarian diet still seemed too much like starving. No matter how seriously he argued his position, I laughed when one of my mentors, Reasun Allah, would heap a huge salad onto his plate in the college cafeteria, accompanied only by some bread and pasta. I thought he was possessed by a f*ckin rabbit.

But Reasun, who was a vegan, would bring me around other gods, who were the first health-conscious gangsters I'd ever met. I didn't know there were people like this. I thought all vegetarians were skinny, soft, and wore bright-colored daishikis. But not these guys. These guys could whup your ass, maybe shoot you, change clothes, and then go cook some stir-fry tofu later that night.

And the more I enjoyed those vegetarian dinners with gods like Dominant and I Atomic, the more vegetarianism started looking like it could work. I mean, these guys actually *ate*. It was anything a meat eater would like, except with vegetarian substitutes. If you wanted fried shrimp, there was veggie fried shrimp. If you wanted curry goat, there was veggie curry goat. There's even veggie octopus and sh*t like that for you weirdos.

To be real, as a meat-eater, my diet was far more limited than when I started trying new things as a vegetarian. After all, how many different meats are there to eat? Well, how many types of grains, beans, and vegetables are on the planet? You do the math.

So after a few good vegetarian meals, I decided to dig deep into whether it made sense to become a vegetarian. I wasn't trying to save animals. I was more interested in saving myself, so I was shocked I'd never learned some of what I found out. Here's some highlights. See if you can figure out which ones are true or false.

1	T F	Millions of people get sick each year from eating contaminated meat and fish, and thousands die. For example, 98% of all broiler chicken carcasses have levels of E. coli bacteria that indicate fecal contamination (meaning there's sh*t in your chicken).
2	T F	Meat-eaters are more likely to have parasites, worms, and bacterial infections resulting from the many disgusting critters that can survive in even well-cooked meat. For example, the downright scary hookworm, in an extreme close-up above.
3	T F	Every product that is put into the animal's system becomes a part of the meat-eater's system, which leads to diseases, chemical imbalances, and

		hormonal problems, such as how girls are beginning puberty younger and younger each year.
4	T F	Well-planned vegetarian diets provide us with all the nutrients that we need, minus all the saturated fat, cholesterol, pesticides, dioxins, hormones, antibiotics, bacteria, and other contaminants found in animal flesh and by-products.
5	T F	Meat-eaters are 9 times more likely to be obese than vegans.
6	T F	Vegetarians are 50% less likely to develop heart disease than meat-eaters.
7	T F	Vegetarians have a cancer rate 60% lower than meat-eaters, even if they're smokers.
8	T F	Scientists haven't yet proven that animal fat and cholesterol cause heart disease, or that animal protein causes cancer.
9	T F	Consumption of meat, eggs, and dairy products has not been strongly linked to osteoporosis, Alzheimer's, asthma, and male impotence.
10	T F	Vegetarians have stronger immune systems than meat-eaters, which further reduces their risk of disease.
11	T F	Vegetarian children grow taller and have higher IQs than their meat-eating classmates.
12	T F	Older people who switch to a vegetarian or vegan diet cannot prevent and even reverse many chronic ailments.
13	T F	Experts agree that healthy vegetarian diets support a lifetime of good health and provide protection against numerous diseases, including our country's three biggest killers: heart disease, cancer, and strokes.
14	T F	Meat-eaters are typically stronger than vegetarians, and better fighters and athletes.
15	T F	Vegetarians and vegans live, on average, 6 to 10 years longer than meat-eaters. (Answers next page)

The Connection

Makes you think huh? Now…What the hell does homophobia have to do with vegetarianism? Sounds completely unrelated, right? I'll explain.

Humans are not naturally meat eaters. We aren't physiologically suitable to be carnivores. Sure, we can *survive* eating meat. But if you examine our body's design, as well as the physical consequences of carnivorous lifestyles, it becomes pretty clear that eating dead flesh is not meant for us. Our bodies simply can't handle it. They weren't designed to – from our dull teeth to our too-long intestinal tract – and our bodies bear the burden of the results.

Did you know that nearly every one of the diseases that significantly impacts the Black community can be traced back to diet? From heart disease and high-blood pressure to all the different cancers to diabetes and arthritis – it all goes back to our love affair with dead animal flesh.

But am I against carnivores? No. I'm opposed to the *behavior*...because it is unnatural and typically detrimental to our long-term outcomes. Often, it's not something you'll notice in each and every individual (though with some folks you can just *tell* their diet is killing them), but the widespread effect on the community is easily diagnosed. Just look around. *Collectively,* we're sick because of the sh*t we eat.

Did You Know?

Answers to the True-False quiz: All true, except numbers 8, 9, 10 and 12. Random information you don't need: 23% of all photocopier breakdowns worldwide are caused by people sitting on them and copying their butts. Wearing headphones for just an hour will increase the bacteria in your ear by 700 times. In the course of an average lifetime you will, while sleeping, eat 70 assorted insects and 10 spiders. 35% of the people who use personal ads for dating are already married.

But millions of people (and scientists) believe that being a "carnivore" is natural. They believe that people are born to eat meat, ignoring the physiological evidence that man's body isn't made for that type of activity. If it was natural for us, wouldn't our bodies handle it better? (You see the connection I'm making yet?)

Like meat-eating, I don't think homosexuality is natural – just because it's accepted (and promoted). If homosexuality was a natural impulse, there'd be a natural way to do it. But there isn't. I ain't tryin to be mean, but you know it ain't natural if your booty is bleedin, and you can't control your bowels, so you're literally sh*ttin on yourself. There's no natural way to enjoy homosexual sex, and there's no popular relationship style that isn't just an attempt to duplicate male-female relationships.

Now, if you're gay, let me repeat that I ain't out to get you. The only ones who're *really* out to get you are the white people in power, running this deathcamp known as the Western World. Everyone else is just a fellow prisoner giving you a hard time. I don't have a *personal* problem with gay people. I just disagree with the "lifestyle." Just like I do with people who eat meat. And just like I do with people who believe they are "naturally" inclined to do things that our people never did until seeing white folks do it. And I understand that living in a white man's world makes it easy for any of that madness to seem pretty reasonable. Especially considering that white folks have had over 400 years to program you into their way of thinking. And one of the main programs is: "Do whatever feels good, whenever you want to, without ever considering why you do it, or the consequences that will result." That kind of thinking has us doing a bunch of sh*t that don't make sense. Our only justification? "It's what I like." But it's *your* life, so live it. But I can't cosign *every* damn thing. I'm a revolutionary, not an I'm-okay-with-everything-ary.

The best lifestyle is a natural way of life, because whatever goes against human nature only destroys the people who live that way. Still, freedom of choice means everyone is entitled to live how they please, so long as it doesn't harm others. In this sick society, however, even harmful lifestyles and influences are not just accepted, but promoted, to our people. And at a cost! We are the only group of people who pay for our own destruction!

But like Christmas day, pork, and white women, there are issues some people just don't want to debate, because nothing – absolutely nothing short of an epiphany – can change their minds. Sh*t, even if Jesus himself appeared today and said, "Stop putting up this damn tree in my name and eating that swine. Both of those are condemned in the Bible"...some of y'all would probably kill him *again*...probably with the same knife you'd use to cut your porkchop afterward. And then you'd tear those pages out of the Bible and act like nothing happened.

Maybe you're not like that. Or maye you are. Doesn't matter. If I can wake up just some of y'all, *one* of y'all may change the entire world. And your task will be to dismantle ALL of our negative programming. Including the two issues we're dealing with here.

The more we're exposed to unnatural concepts, the more they seem acceptable. Just like when we all thought Coogi sweaters were butt-ugly. Then everyone had one and they gradually stopped looking so bad. It's up to you to do your own thinking and decide whether something is okay for *you*. Just as people should be free to live how they please, you are free to disagree. In fact, without disagreement, society would never improve. The "status quo" (the way things are) is NOT always the best way for everyone, *especially* in the case of Black people in white America.

Don't allow what everyone else is doing to influence your decisions on what makes sense to you.

Movies to See

Supersize Me; Thank You for Smoking; Meet your Meat

The first is an exposé of the world of fast food marketing and how overconsumption of the wrong foods is slowly killing us off. The second is a similar take on the world of cigarette marketing. The third is a documentary that will almost definitely make you rethink a carnivorous diet. And you can see them free at www.supremedesignonline.com

EAT SH*T

Derrick Simons was escorted into court by two armed guards. Simons was to stand trial for an attack on a Neo-Nazi gang. As the judge read the charges, Simons fidgeted around and appeared not to be listening. When the judge asked him if he understood the charges against him, Simons finally looked the judge in the eyes. He smiled, reached into the back of his pants, retrieved a handful of brown goo, and promptly ate it. Smearing his face, he licked his hand clean of the leftovers.

Completely disgusted, the judge took a while to recover from the shock of seeing this happen. He declared Simons mentally incompetent and admitted him to a psychiatric prison. Simons only spent the next two years receiving therapy and medication for his obvious insanity, and was then released when he was deemed to be sane again.

If anyone ever figures out how Simons did it, they'll never serve peanut butter in jail again.

You get it? Okay. But do you get the lesson? Here it is: depending on your environment, you WILL appear crazy at some point. Especially if you start doing something smart around people who are dumb, or something positive around people who are negative...or simply trying something that no one else thinks will work...when you know it will. Can't live with those funny looks? You'll never get free.

Sometimes, the smartest one in the room will appear to be the craziest.

---

11 WAYS OUT OF THE HOOD

As Trick Daddy said on "America" (one of his best songs):

> When it's time to be a man/ Do all you can/ See other lands/ And don't be livin' for the other man/ Take time out and settle in/ Be the better man/ ...But on the other hand/ You so goddamned stubbor-ran!

Here's 11 ways to get out of wherever you're at and do just that...in order of their effectiveness and practicality.

1. Do Music. Hah! You musta been watching too much BET. For every 2,000 artists with some decent talent, only about 5 will turn their talent into their career. Out of those 5, 3 will be what they call "starving artists," meaning they'll do music for a living, but they'll stay pretty broke. Out of the two that are left, one will do real well, and the other will think they're doing well, though they're really getting scammed and shorted until they're bankrupt.

"Either you're slingin crack rock or you got a wicked jumpshot"
Notorious B.I.G., "Things Done Changed"

2. Sell Dope. Right. You might move your mama out the hood (though most don't), but when the Feds indict, **it ain't bout what you got, but what you can keep**. Most drug dealers never make it too far out of their neighborhoods anyway. Either they stay at the bottom levels of the game, or they become so caught up in their hustle they can never take a vacation from the streets. Either way, you're stuck in hell til you're stuck in the cell.

3. Play Ball. The odds of making it to the pro leagues from a high school position are 7,600 to 1. Playing ball is yet another pipe dream that we're sold, and it's not realistic to plan on playing ball and nothing else. Even the athletes who *do* make it often don't have back-up plans in case of injury, or a game plan to invest their earnings. That's why you can find former players pawning their championship rings on eBay.

4. Win the Lottery. If you just read the last three, and you think the odds are better for you to win the million-dollar jackpot, I can't help you. You're pretty f*cked up. Sell this book to someone who can use it. You can use the cash to buy 10 magic scratch-off tickets out the hood.

5. Get Discovered. There are *other* talents besides rappin, singin, and playin ball. You might be the best undiscovered artist in your city. Or you may be a champion bowler. Who knows? If you keep developing your talent, and putting yourself in the right people's faces, it will eventually pay off. Keep in mind that some of the most famous painters, poets, computer programmers, and skateboarders actually came from the hood. (see "If Einstein was Black")

6. Marry Up. Of course, I don't literally mean that you should marry a rich girl and "move on up" like the Jeffersons. But hey. What I really mean, though, is that you can change your surroundings just by changing your social group. Keep the right company and eventually you'll be right where you want to be. Just keep in mind to keep your own mind.

7. Join the Military. Ice Cube's song, "I Wanna Kill Sam" begins:

> The army is the only way out for a young Black teenager. We'll provide you with housing. We'll provide you with education. We'll provide you with everything you need to survive in life. We'll help you to be the best soldier in the U.S. of A. Because we do more before 7 AM than most niggers do in their whole lifetime.

Of course, I don't support the U.S. in their plot to take over the world through military force, but I'm somebody who says you should use whatever resources you can, as long as you use them wisely. If you are hard pressed for what you're going to do with your life, and you need an "out," the military is one way. You'll gain discipline, learn how to do all kinds of things the average person can't, and see the world...BUT you better join the right branch.

If you want to be a tough guy and join the Army or the Marines, just kill yourself now. Because you're going to get put on the front lines, fighting people who don't have a problem with you, risking your life for a country who won't give a f*ck if you live or die. Even if you make it out of that hell, you're gonna be all screwed up mentally once you come home. Did you know that 1 out of 3 homeless men in this country is a military veteran? Right. So instead of trying to test your nuts on the battlefield, join the Navy, the Air Force, or maybe even the Coast Guard. More education, less amputation.

Just don't forget what W.E.B. Du Bois said long ago about Blacks joining the military:

> We are cowards and jackasses if...we do not marshal every ounce of our brain and brawn to fight a sterner, longer, more unbending battle against the forces of hell in our *own* land.

8. Start Your Own Business. Okay, this sounds more like reality. Being an entrepreneur is hard work, however. It requires planning, ambition, and discipline. You've also got to find a market that works for you. If you do it right, however, it will pay off. Continue to expand your business – whether it's lawncare or selling socks – and soon enough you'll be able to hire people and sit back.

9. Go to College. You know I'm a fan of this one. (see "10 Reasons to Go to College...and 6 Not To") College won't work for everybody, but if you know how to make it work for *you*, it will.

10. Get a Job. I don't mean a French fry hustle with a side order of floor-sweeping. Then again, some people have enough hustle to move up from the very bottom to the very top. My brother Born King Allah went from delivering bread in a truck to managing other drivers to damn near running the company. When he was promoted to the director position, they paid for him to relocate and covered every expense. So it can happen. Just look at Kevin Liles, who went from intern to Def Jam CEO. Short of that, you could get a job as a truck driver or for an airline and start seeing the world. Eventually, you might find a place you want to be, and something you want to do there. Short of that, you buy a Greyhound ticket and go places until your ass gets tired.

11. Read a Book. Short of doing everything else, you can always escape into a book. I know it sounds corny, but you can find a lot in a book. Not only can you take your mind to different places, times, and people's lives, you can learn the way other people have accomplished the same things you are trying to do. Anyway, if you got a problem with reading, what the hell are you doing now?

SUPREME THE ASSHOLE ON "THE 'GOLDEN TICKET'"

I'm not waitin on my golden ticket out the ghetto. I could have left the hood a long time ago if I wanted to. But until I feel like my family ain't safe where we live, or I can't trust my neighbors, I'm cool where I'm at. The way I see it, too many mothaf*ckas want to run away. They think, "One day, I'ma really get paid, and I'm gonna buy a mansion and get away from these crab niggas." There's a few problems with that kind of thinking. First, no you're not. You're not gonna just "get paid" like it's some sh*t you find in a cereal box. You gotta work for anything you get outta life. Second, what's wrong with your people? You were f*cked up once too, right? (probably still are) So stick around and help out, asshole.

RACISM IS ABOUT FEAR

> We are in the midst of a growing menace. The Black man is rapidly forging to the front ranks in athletics, especially in the field of fisticuffs. We are in the midst of a Black rise against white supremacy…There are two negroes in the ring today who can thrash any white man breathing in their respective classes…What America needs now is another John L. Sullivan…Wake up, you pugilists of the white race! Are you going to permit yourself to be passed by the Black race?

These were the words of high-ranking sports editor Charles Dana, writing for the *New York Sun* in 1889, hoping other white boxers would follow John Sullivan's example and refuse to fight Black boxers. Right this great "example" wasn't that he was whuppin some ass. He was just refusing to fight Blacks!

The Negro League was formed in 1937 after years and years of discrimination against Black players in major league baseball. White coaches would refuse to let their team play against teams with Black players, leading teams to get rid of Black players, even though they were often better than the white players.

In any sport where Black people began showing their superiority, white people began finding ways to keep them out. Nonetheless, Black athletes have been able to dominate boxing, basketball, track, and football. However, in those sports, the greatest Black athletes have been destroyed by drugs or white women, starting with Jack Johnson in 1903.

What the world of sports can teach us is this: white people haven't discriminated against Black people because of "ignorance." It wasn't because they thought we were "not good enough." It's because they were scared. Not scared in the "clench your purse and lock your car doors" sense, but scared in the "these niggers are gonna take over our world" sense. Ice T once summed up what white supremacists teach as: "We're gonna be extinct. We're gonna be gone. We have to do something before them Negroes take over. We are the superior race."

Why else do you think they put abortion clinics in the hood and sperm banks in the suburbs? Why do you think they talk so much trash about Black people having lots of children? Why do you think they hate the idea of Black men taking their white women? Why do you think they do their best to take down any Black man who becomes rich and powerful? Why do you think they shot the noses off the Sphinx and all the Egyptians statues that clearly looked like Black men? Why do you think the European missionaries burned all our ancient books and writings wherever they went? What were they trying to hide? You see, it has nothing to do with them thinking they're better. White people aren't stupid. **They may know who *you* are better than you do!**

As Tupac said on "They Don't Give a F*ck about Us":

> I'm seeing it clearer – Hating the picture in the mirror/ They claim we inferior – So why the f*ck these devils fear ya?/ I'm watching my nation die – Genocide the cause/ Expect a blood bath – The aftermath is yours/ I told ya last album, "We need help cause we dying/ Give us a chance, help us advance, cause we trying"/ Ignored my whole plea, watchin us in disgust/ And then they beg when my guns bust

What do you think movies like *Planet of the Apes, Lord of the Rings, 300,* and even *I, Robot* and *The Terminator* are about? Who do you think the apes represent? The machines? The "Dark Menace" of *Star Wars*? All of these films convey the fear whites have collectively about an uprising of all the people of color who they've dehumanized (apes), enslaved (machines), or excluded (the "foreign" aliens and barbarians). They're pissing their pants hoping you never figure out your just due.

So don't forget…this isn't a fear that you can "fix" by showing white people you don't mean them any harm. This is a different kind of fear. And you know that scared people can become the most dangerous people when they feel backed into a corner…just as weak people can become the most vicious when they get a little power.

> "I see you trying to hide, hoping that nobody don't notice
> You must always remember you still a member of the hopeless
> See ya Black like me, so you snap like me
> When these devils try to plot, trap our young Black seeds"
> Tupac Shakur, "They Don't Give a F*ck About Us"

White Supremacy is real. Not in terms of what white supremacists believe (that whites are superior), because that's obviously a myth. Otherwise, they wouldn't be so scared of us. But the fact that white people control the globe, and all eight domains of human activity, is real.

And it won't go away if we just hold hands and sing sprituals. In fact, that's part of our problem. We think they just "don't know" that we're "not so bad," and we just need to "prove ourselves" so they'll accept us. F*ck that. That's not the situation. The ones in power will never accept us fully, because a free and mixed society means the end of the white race. No war even necessary. Just the laws of genetics. Unless white folks can figure out how to change the laws of genetics (which they're working on, aren't they), they can't escape the "browning of America" *and* the world. So they're gonna do what they can to stay on top until then. And we can't beg them to feel different So what do we do?

Short of letting your "guns bust" as Pac said, there are a number of ways to combat white supremacy. For beginners, we all need to become aware of what's really going on around us. The key word in that sentence is "all." Start talking to people. Share this information. Everyday lies and myths are spread. Just to keep up, you've got to be working just as hard to spread the truth. Or you could just sit there and be another man's bitch. But hey, maybe they're not the only ones who are scared!

If you're not living in fear, tell the truth that needs to be told.

Movies to See

The X-Men, Superman, and Spiderman Trilogies; Unforgivable Blackness: The Jack Johnson Story

I know you're thinking, "one of these things is not like the other." I'll explain. Instead of stories symbolically conveying a fear of uprising (like The Matrix), the first three films are a different take on the Black man in a white man's world. The Black man, stronger, faster, and – in many ways – more advanced, has always been both an alien and an outcast to the white world. He is rejected and feared because he is different, and seen as threateningly better than the people he wants to help. Unforgivable Blackness is the same story told through actual fact. Before Muhammad Ali and Mike Tyson, Jack Johnson was *that* dude. And like Ali and Tyson, white people hated him for consistently proving Black physical dominance over whites. Except this was 1910, so they were real clear about what exactly they hated. And like Tiger Woods, they used his taste for white women to bring him down.

Project Roaches

Survival of the Fittest

October 2004. DuBois High School is on fire. Everyone in the building is rushing out of the three-story building with whatever they have in their hands. Juan Ramirez stops at his locker to get his new 59/50 hat. Stacy Finch and Nisha Wright are in the girl's bathroom smoking weed. They hear the alarm, but delay their exit so they can finish the roach. Corey Thomas and Aaron Belcher, rival gang members, run into each other in the hallway and end up fighting. Ms. Ormond, a retired substitute teacher, has heard plenty of fire scares before, so she's not rushing. Out of about 800 staff members and students, only six people died. Those six. Why?

It's natural law. Charles Darwin's famous work on evolution never said that man came from monkeys. But Darwin did say that evolution occurs because of "natural selection" resulting from "the survival of the fittest." That is, weak or ill-equipped organisms fail to thrive and die out, while the best and brightest endure. This is how a species survives and becomes strong…like man. But there's always a percentage that's just plain not meant to survive. Among humans, they're usually the ones who are too stupid for their own good. As a result, they lack the survival instinct it takes to follow the first law of nature: Self-preservation.

Did You Know?

Using roach sprays and roach traps can actually worsen your roach problem? After constant exposure to the poisons, roaches will eventually develop some immunity. Then you've got a real problem! There's two cheap and more effective ways. One is known as the Vegas roach trap. You simply put a glass jar filled with coffee grounds along a wall somewhere (like the kitchen counter). Roaches will crawl in, but they won't be able to climb out because roach feet won't stick to clean glass. The other strategy is buying boric acid from somewhere like Home Depot (it's cheap) and sprinkling it in places where roaches hide or walk. Just make sure your kids don't think it's sugar and eat it. But if you've got kids dumb enough to eat sugar out of a doorway, maybe you've got bigger problems than roaches.

Survival Instincts

If you grew up in the ghetto – any ghetto – then you've become well-acquainted with these guys. They seemed to be able to survive against any odds, and almost nothing could keep them from getting what they wanted. These little brown and black motherf*ckers would ruin lives everywhere they went. And with the way they had babies nonstop, it seemed that you'd never get away from their plague. I'm talking about roaches, you know.

Roaches are pests, of course, spreading bacteria and disease as they overtake households. Growing up with roaches may even be the reason you had childhood asthma. But there's something we can learn from roaches. After all, roaches are survivors. They've been around for over 300 million years and live all over the world, either with humans or in nature. And since adult females can have up to 3,000 babies in less than 5 months, imagine how many there are in your city alone. For this reason, I've heard the cockroach described as "a gifted teacher in the art of survival and successful adaptability, especially in environment that may seem a bit hostile." So what can roaches teach us about survival? It's not as if they're highly intelligent. After all, roaches barely have a brain. Whereas humans have a centralized nervous system controlled by the brain, roaches have a decentralized nervous system, without much of a brain at all. In fact, a cockroach can survive complete decapitation – still walking around and everything – for up to several weeks before dying of starvation or dehydration.

Roaches have survival instincts that are part of their evolutionary genetic programming. On an individual level, each roach can respond to threats and flee danger much more quickly than humans. But on a collective level, roaches engage in group-based decision-making to ensure the survival of the many. This programmed decision-making is responsible for complex behavior such as resource allocation. In a study where 50 cockroaches were placed in a dish with three shelters with a capacity for 40 insects in each, the insects arranged themselves in two shelters with 25 insects in each, leaving the third shelter empty. But when the shelters were made bigger, all of the cockroaches went into one shelter. So there's a balance between cooperation and competition that allows roaches to be collectively successful wherever they go.

However, the roach's survival instincts aren't foolproof. A research study in Brussels found that roaches can be tricked fairly easily. The research team dumped roaches into an area covered by two discs, a dark one and a lighter one. Now, cockroaches use just two pieces of information to decide where to go under those conditions: how dark it is and how many of their friends are there. So they all clustered into the dark disk, as expected. But the team then sent in robotic roaches – shaped more like black blocks on wheels than actual roaches – and covered in a sexy roach scent. The robo-roaches mingled, and then started easing their way over to the light side. Guess what happened? The real roaches followed about 60% of the time, overriding their own survival instincts to "hang with the cool kids."

Now, why the hell am I talking about roaches? Consider the short story that came right before this one.

If there had been 300 roaches in that burning building, they ALL would have made it out alive. Why? They wouldn't have wasted time. They wouldn't have worried about material things. They wouldn't be preoccupied with less important matters. They wouldn't sit still because they "thought" they knew better And they damn sure wouldn't be fighting among themselves. Without thinking, without brains even, they would have immediately did only what was necessary to survive.

In a hostile environment, roaches will cooperate to make sure the entire population survives, and do only what is necessary to immediately preserve life. But us? Sh*t, we're in a society that is literally working to destroy us, but we're too busy fighting among ourselves to fight back.

We're too busy trying to buy outfits to set aside money for our children, or even our own futures.

CHE GUEVARA

> "Whoever sides with the revolutionary people is a revolutionary ...Whoever sides with the revolutionary people in words only, but acts otherwise, is a revolutionary in speech. Whoever sides with the revolutionary people in deed as well as in word is a revolutionary in the full sense."
>
> Mao Tse Tung

French philosopher Jean-Paul Sarte called Che "the most complete human being of our age." Why? Che didn't just write and speak about his revolutionary ideas; he lived and breathed them.

Ernesto "Che" Guevara was born in Argentina in 1928. He was born in a middle-class family which sheltered him during his younger years, at least partly because of his crippling asthma. At 20, he went off to the University of Buenos Aires to study medicine. A few years into his studies, he decided to take a year off from school to embark on trip across South America. Guevara and an older friend set off on a motorcycle, planning to see as much of the world as they could.

During their journey, Guevara left his sheltered reality and saw the world for what it really was. Like the story of Buddha, Guevara saw things with his own eyes that he had never thought about before. He observed the widespread poverty and oppression faced by the masses of people throughout the Latin America (and the world) under the corrupt systems of capitalism and white supremacy. Guevara had been awakened. He began studying the writings of revolutionaries like Karl Marx and others, and began to understand that the only solution was revolution. As Guevara studied and observed, he realized that the political boundaries that separated one group of people from another were not real. He began to see Latin America, and all its Black and brown people, as one people.

Guevara finished school and traveled to Guatemala, where a new president was making changes that would actually help poor people. But the United States (mostly through the CIA) worked quickly to overthrow him and set up their own puppet government.

Che did finish his degree in medicine, but he also decided to become a part of the struggle. This is about the time he picked up the name "Che" (meaning "friend"), and became a friend to those fighting oppression.

When Che met up with a young Raul and Fidel Castro, brothers who were working to stir up a revolution in Cuba, they became instant friends. Che agreed to join the expedition as a medic, and became the only non-Cuban on board when the Cuban guerrillas began their mission. The first attempt was a disaster. Most of the guerrillas were killed. This is when Che realized how deeply he had become committed to the vision of change. As they were retreating, Che had to make a life-changing decision. He wrote:

> Perhaps this was the first time I was confronted with the real-life dilemma of having to choose between my devotion to medicine and my duty as a revolutionary soldier. Lying at my feet were a knapsack full of medicine and a box of ammunition. They were too heavy for me to carry both of them. I grabbed the box of ammunition, leaving the medicine behind.

After this day, Che was a revolutionary for life. Two years later, the Cuban Revolution was won, and Fidel Castro became the new leader of Cuba. Che became a high-ranking member of the new government, and began to represent Cuba and its revolutionary philosophy on missions to Asia and Africa.

> "Money is an interesting luxury, but nothing more"
> Che Guevara

However, Che refused to take a raise. He insisted that he only take the same low pay that he had earned as an officer in the military. He refused special treatment or expensive meals. Many times, he spent his weekends and evenings volunteering in shipyards and textile factories or cutting sugarcane with the common people. Everywhere he went, people followed Che because they recognized and respected his integrity. They knew he was true to his ideas, because he lived them. He wasn't "all talk" as so many other "leaders" had been. Che said, "La revolución no se lleva en los labios para vivir de ella, se lleva en el corazón para morir por ella." (The revolution is not carried in the lips to live on, it is carried in the heart for die for.)

Did You Know?

There is a combat training school for foreign soldiers located at Fort Benning, Georgia? Over its 59 years, the School of the Americas has trained over 60,000 Latin American soldiers in counter-insurgency techniques, sniper training, commando and psychological warfare, military intelligence and interrogation tactics. These graduates have consistently used their skills to wage a war against their own people. As a result, the School of the Americas has been nicknamed the "School of Assassins." Among those targeted by SOA graduates are educators, union organizers, religious workers, student leaders, and others who work for the rights of the poor. Hundreds of thousands of Latin Americans have been tortured, raped, assassinated, "disappeared," massacred, and forced into refugee by those trained at the School of Assassins.

After spending two years trying to build a revolution in Africa, Che cut his ties with Cuba. He felt he had to do so, in order to dedicate himself to revolutionary struggles elsewhere in the world. He continued traveling the world, inspiring people to continue fighting for freedom.

"The one who is nearest the enemy, in pursuit, is the real leader."
Ganda (African) proverb

In October of 1967, Che was fighting for revolution in Bolivia, when the Bolivian Army (with CIA help) finally caught up with him. Che refused to surrender and was only captured after being shot in both knees, and having his gun destroyed by a bullet.

Before he was executed, Che said these last words: "I know you are here to kill me. Shoot coward! You are only going to kill a man." What he meant was that he was a man fully dedicated to the revolution, but he wasn't the revolution by himself. There are thousands more, just like him, and maybe millions more who could be. As his old comrade Fidel Castro said about him, "Why did they think that by killing him, he would cease to exist as a fighter?...Today he is in every place, wherever there is a just cause to defend."

"The man who leads motivates others to catch up with him; encourages those behind up to his level much more than he who pushes from behind with just a word."
Che Guevara

Did You Know?

Many governments throughout the world are still controlled by European and American interests? When you hear about an African dictator stealing UN money and food while his people starve, he was usually put in power with CIA help. On the other hand, when you hear about poor countries who are always siding with the US or Britain, those leaders are usually being paid well to do so. Very few governments still stand on their own (see "Global Black Revolution")

In this life, you can beat a drum, or be the drum. Meaning you can lead by words or by example. Which one do you think is more successful?

Put up or shut up. Don't talk about it, be about it.

Leadership: Do You Have It?

As we near the close of this chapter, I thought I'd provide you with a quick checklist on leadership. If you got it, great. If not, work on it:

- ❑ Character
- ❑ Charisma
- ❑ Commitment
- ❑ Communication
- ❑ Competence
- ❑ Courage
- ❑ Discernment
- ❑ Focus
- ❑ Generosity
- ❑ Initiative

There's also a more advanced form of leadership, actually the kind of leadership I hope this work inspires you to pursue: Servant Leadership (as a servant of the people, not the system, of course). You see, true leadership is not about being *in charge of* people, but about taking charge *for* the people. Here are the traits that characterize servant leadership:

- ❑ Awareness
- ❑ Building community
- ❑ Commitment to the growth of people
- ❑ Conceptualization
- ❑ Empathy
- ❑ Foresight
- ❑ Healing
- ❑ Listening
- ❑ Persuasion
- ❑ Stewardship

Some of us are born leaders. Others can grow into the role.

Movies to See

The Bolivian Diary; Che; The Spook Who Sat by the Door

Both *The Bolivian Diary* and *Che* tell the story of Che's quest to empower and organize common people to make revolutionary changes. Definitely a story worth studying. Now, if you want to learn how street gangs can become the ultimate force for revolution, you *have* to see *The Spook Who Sat by the Door.* That may be my favorite film ever.

F*ck the Police

On March 3, 1991, Rodney King, a Black taxi driver, was savagely beaten by four white officers of the LAPD. The event was videotaped by a bystander, George Holliday.

The intense media coverage following the beating led to a change of venue to a predominantly white county. On April 29, 1992, the jury of ten whites, one Latino, and one Asian, decided that the four white officers were not guilty and that the Black prosecutor had not proven any wrongdoing.

The jury's verdict triggered massive rioting in Los Angeles, which lasted for 4 days, making it one of the worst civil disturbances in Los Angeles history. By the time the police, soldiers, Marines and National Guard had restored order, there was nearly $1 billion in damage; 55 deaths; 2,383 injuries; more than 7,000 fire responses; and 3,100 businesses damaged, looted, or destroyed.

The video of the incident is an example of inverse surveillance (i.e. citizens watching police). As a result of the incident, several "Copwatch" organizations were formed across the nation to monitor local police and ensure against future abuses.

After the verdict, Los Angeles's Black Mayor, Tom Bradley, responded, "The jury's verdict will not blind us to what we saw on that videotape. The men who beat Rodney King do not deserve to wear the uniform of the L.A.P.D."

But here's the million-dollar question: Didn't they see it coming?

> **Did You Know?**
> The National Security Agency can monitor millions of phone conversations simultaneously. In fact, certain words said over the phone are "red flags" calling for closer monitor and possible investigation. "Allah" is one of those words. In addition, the Patriot Act has allowed for countless wiretaps and recorded phone conversations. This monitoring is often used only for drug arrests, not terrorism.

In the aftermath of the notorious Rodney King beating, the Independent Commission on the Los Angeles Police Department reviewed the messages transmitted between police mobile digital terminals (MDT) from November 1, 1989 to March 4, 1991. The messages, which are transmitted and recorded on the police computers used by dispatchers and patrol cars, reveal what many residents of Los Angeles already knew. Out of only 180 randomly selected dates, the Commission identified over 700 objectionable messages, involving repeated racial slurs against Blacks, Hispanics, and Asians, a bloodlust for violence and attacks on minorities, and frequent mentions of involvement with the KKK and other white supremacist organizations. The most disturbing fact about this is that the people who made these comments felt so comfortable that they made such statements on their MDTs, knowing that the transmissions were being recorded. Here are some samples:

11/7/89 1:30 AM
Officer 1: Where you be?
Officer 2: In the projects.
Officer 1: Good hunting.

11/13/89 12:19 AM
Officer 1: You can see the color of the interior of vehicle, dig? You stop cars with a Black interior.
Officer 2: Bees they naugahyde?
Officer 1: Negrohide.
Officer 2: Self-tanning, no doubt.

11/20/89 7:51 PM
Officer 1: This hole is picking up. I almost got me a Mexican but he dropped the gun too damn quick, lots of witnesses.

11/23/89 12:51 AM
Officer 1: I have an NHI (No Human Involved – a term used repeatedly in reference to gang members fighting with each other). Two guys in mutual combat with bottles. Do I have to make an arrest?

6/11/90 9:22 PM
Officer 1: Must be nice.
Officer 2: It is...White Power.

6/3/90 10:25 PM
Officer 1: They're Indians, the towel head kind, not the feather kind.

6/28/90 10:10 PM
Officer 1: Mexican means a wetback with no papers and likes to give bullsh*t to the police, and doesn't speak no English, until he pulls his ID out of his ass, then and only then does he become a Hispanic with papers.

10/31/89 12:00 PM
Officer 1: Did you educate him? Take one handcuff off and slap him around.
Officer 2: He's crying too hard and there's four detectives here.
Officer 1: Well, don't seat-belt him in, and slam on the brakes a few times on the way to the station.

12/21/90 5:00 PM
Officer 1: They had another shooting here...I love it when good things happen. It clears the air and gives

me more space to breathe when one more asshole dies.
12/23/90 3:47 PM
Officer 1: Ah, so! Did he tell you he was sooo solly to bother you?
Officer 2: Orientals are the most obnoxious when they're drunk.
12/31/90 8:03 PM
Officer 1: A full moon and a full gun makes for a night of fun.
Officer 2: Everyone you kill in the line of duty becomes a slave in the afterlife.
Officer 1: Then you will have a lot of slaves.
1/19/91 6:01 AM
Officer 1: Shut up or I'll cut your pigtails off, Hop Sing.
2/24/91 10:40 AM
Officer 1: What's happening? We're hunting wabbits.
Officer 2: Actually Muslim wabbits.
Officer 1: Be careful one of those wabbits don't bite you.
Officer 2: Yeah, I know. Huntin' wabbits is dangerous.

So did no one see it coming? Did they need a commission to show em? Of course, since the early 90s, we've seen plenty more. And this is just what's been on the news:

- Amadou Diallo, an African immigrant, shot at 41 times and killed for pulling out a wallet when stopped by plainclothed NYPD officers in his apartment vestibule (1999)
- Abner Louima, a Haitian immigrant, beaten and raped with a toilet plunger by the NYPD for breaking up a fight between two women (1997)
- Kathryn Johnson, a 92 year old Black woman, was shot at 39 times and killed by Atlanta police, for pulling a gun to protect her home against plainclothes officers who kicked in the door of her home (2006)
- Robert Davis, a 64-year-old retired elementary school teacher, was beaten by two white New Orleans police officers and two white federal agents for asking a question about a curfew (2005)
- Donovan Jackson, a Black 16-year-old special education student was caught on video being repeatedly picked up and slammed down by Inglewood police officers (2002)
- Martin Anderson, a 14-year-old Black youth, died in 2006 at a Florida juvenile detention facility after being beaten, choked, and forced to inhale ammonia, by as many as eight guards, also recorded by videotape (2006)
- And let's not forget Sean Bell, shot at 50 times and killed by plainclothed NYPD while trying to leave a bachelor party, just hours before his wedding (2006)
- In recent years, there's been dozens more. List any others you know about: ____

____

"The 5-0 killed Naudy, good boy dead
Man, you woulda thought they killed Cornbread
Shot him up, face down on the lawn, not to mention he had handcuffs on
Not to mention they had plainclothes on…and the complaint goes on"
Lil Wayne, "Amen"

So what makes us think things have changed? You can tell where things are going by looking at how they've been. So I can't believe that anyone in the Los Angelos government was surprised by the findings of the Commission. The people of L.A. certainly weren't surprised. And none of us should be surprised today by police brutality and other acts of injustice perpetrated by the state. Do I really need to dedicate another 5 pages to all the Blacks and Hispanics falsely convicted and put to death? Are we really just not paying attention now?

You don't need a psychic friend. The present is a barometer for predicting the future. The past helps you determine the likelihood of your prediction. So in your personal life, you have no excuse for not seeing what's coming…and doing something about it. And guess what? You have no excuse for being clueless on the world around you as well.

Pay close enough attention and you'll see things coming in advance.

How to Deal with Police

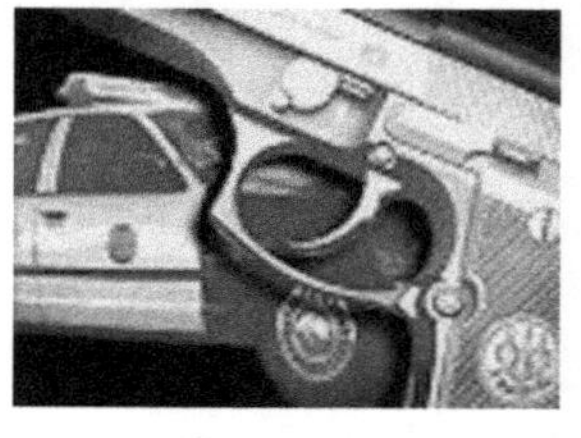

Police Officers and Correctional Officers

What do you think most police officers and correctional officers believe their job priorities are? You may think that all "pigs" are in on the plot to subjugate, or oppress, people of color. But realistically, most of these guys are not evil geniuses, or geniuses of any kind. Officers are just that: "officers." Which means - by definition - that they act as agents of the law of the land. Therefore, they serve the state, not your ass. And just like the people at any business that values results over customer service, they will do whatever they think their job expects - or allows - them to do. And until the police force, as a whole, knows it's not okay to treat us like sh*t, they'll keep doing whatever the system lets them get away with.

But if you want to have an easier time in life, you need to understand one thing above all. Beyond their personal desires to make up for getting dissed in high school, most Police Officers and C.O.s have *one* objective that overrides all others. They just want to *come home* at the end of the day. That's on *top* of the to-do-list, even above "get free sex from hookers" or "plant drugs on community organizers."

Once again, the first law of nature is self-preservation. So don't think a police officer is supposed to look at everybody like they're a friend. For all he knows, you're about to sucker-punch him and try to take his gun. So keep it cordial and keep it brief. Treat him with respect, and if he still disrespects you, take it up with his boss LATER. (see "What to Do If You're Stopped by the Police" in the Appendix of *Part One*)

I used to have a real problem with cops. Most of us growin up in the hood do. We hate em. We get nervous around em. They remind us of the fact that we are ALWAYS the enemy. I don't know how some of us end up later forgetting that we're still in a silent war. But I never forgot. For years, even into adulthood, I talked sh*t to cops whenever I could. That got me patted down, frisked, searched, roughed up, and arrested more times than I'd like to admit. Most of the time, I hadn't even done anything wrong. At least that's what I thought.

But I *had* done something wrong. In a war, enemy soldiers have a code. During times of ceasefire, soldiers from opposing armies are expected not to attack each other. They acknowledge each other if they cross paths, still knowing what side each soldier represents. But they keep it moving. It's a sense of mutual respect.

It took years before I became mature enough to let that wisdom sink in. The last time I got into it with an officer, I found myself surrounded by at least fifteen cops in the middle of downtown Atlanta. I had already been disarmed, and I was sure I was about to be shot in public. But I was *still* too damn brash to be diplomatic, *still* talking sh*t like always.

Since then, I've grown up a lot. I've learned a simple nod gains a lot more respect from an officer than a meanmug. If not, straight talk with no emotion, no arrogance, and no outright signs of "f*ck you" mentality. They show respect. I show respect. We keep it moving. And at the end of the day, we both get to go home to our families.

Also make sure to reread the ACLU's guide on "What to Do if You Are Stopped by the Police" (in the appendix of Part One) and see *BUSTED: The Citizen's Guide to Surviving Police Encounters*, which is free online at www.supremedesignonline.com

Parole Officers and Probation Officers

While I'm on the subject of law enforcement, I figure I should mention these guys as well. Since they worry less about coming home at the end of the day, Parole Officers and Probation Officers worry more about looking good to their bosses. If their cases keep f*ckin up and doing the opposite of what they're supposed to, it makes the P.O. look bad.

So their idea is: "You had your chance, and you blew it. I gave you another chance, and you knew that if you blew it, it was your last chance. You still blew it. It's on you. It ain't my fault. Now I HAVE to violate you." That's how they see it.

Even the ones who *like* you will see it that way after they've given you enough chances. So stop bullsh*ttin and making excuses. Do everything you're supposed to. Go in on time, SOBER, and make sure your piss is clean. Find a job…somewhere, anywhere, so you don't get on his bad side. I'd personally rather be *anywhere* than a cell.

Do you understand how to get the respect of people who normally don't respect people like you?

Do you know how to cater your approach depending on the type of people you are dealing with? Are you always successful?

Do you know how to get what you want without kissing ass?

Do you know how to handle a complaint without anger?

There's a proper protocol to successfully dealing with everyone.

Review

The principle for this chapter was **"Leadership and Greatness"** This means: Be yourself, lead yourself, and put the weight of the world on your shoulders.

Here are the principles and lessons we covered:

Thinking like a Leader
Don't allow what everyone else is doing to influence your decisions on what makes sense to you.
Life and logic will point you in one direction, but other influences can point you in the other. Use common sense.
Pay attention to your programming, or be a pawn in the game.
Pay close enough attention and you'll see things coming in advance.
Sometimes, the smartest one in the room will appear to be the craziest.
The best computer ever made sits between your ears.
Think critically...about everything.
Speaking like a Leader
A good name is better than gold.
If you're not living in fear, tell the truth that needs to be told.
Put up or shut up. Don't talk about it
Living like a Leader
A true leader is of the people, with the people, and for the people.
Remember, the people come first. Material sh*t is worth nothing if your people are dying around you.
You can't win at their game.
Giving like a Leader
Do what's right, and what's right for you will come to you.
Every one of us can give of ourselves.
It is only the greatest of people who give of themselves without wanting anything in return.

Doing Things Different
Don't always do whatever you're told. Do what's right.
Find a need and fill it.
Resourcefulness. Innovation. Drive and Determination. These are the keys to success when one is born with less.
Navigating Necessary Relationships
Be prepared to find yourself at odds with people who you may "think" are your people.
Don't ask for something you need, expecting the giver to want the best for you. Instead, find a way to get it yourself, on your terms.
Don't think people with pressing outside alliances will always be in your corner.
Insecurity is a dangerous weakness. Eliminate it or avoid it.
Make sure you have a team who'll support you before you step out on your own against a stronger force.
There's a proper protocol to successfully dealing with everyone.
Growing into Greatness
See life through the All-Seeing-Eye. Find the greatness within.
See yourself for the greatness you were meant to be.
Some of us are born leaders. Others can grow into the role.

Life and Death

KILL YOURSELF SO YOU CAN LIVE

> *"The highest courage is to dare to be yourself in the face of adversity. Choosing right over wrong, ethics over convenience, and truth over popularity...these are the choices that measure your life. Travel the path of integrity without looking back, for there is never a wrong time to do the right thing."*

In order for a man to truly live, a part of him has to die. In the months before we are born, the same umbilical cord that gives us life can also wrap itself around our throats and kill us. When we are finally born, the same umbilical cord that fed us in the womb must be cut or tied off. It is time for that part of us to die. If that never occurs, we never mature.

As we grow, life follows the same processes at every stage. There are points where we must let go of old ideas, old habits, and even old lives. When we shed those skins, we allow new ones to grow. If the caterpillar is not ready to lose her old self, she never becomes a butterfly. Having balance is an important thing, but the good must one day dominate the bad for your life to mean anything. In order to become strong, meaningful, worthy human beings, we have to eliminate what is weak within us. Many times, that process is hell, but any metal only becomes strong once it has been through fire. The fire purifies and strengthens the metal, as struggle, sacrifice, and strife do for us. After growing from weak followers to strong leaders, we are required to work for the good of others. Again, it takes a man being completely willing to lose for that man to truly win.

But many of us are scared. Are you?

Are you strong enough to eliminate your destructive habits and weaknesses? Or are you weak enough to let them destroy you?

QUIZ EIGHT: SELF-DESTRUCTIVE TENDENCIES	Never	Rarely	Sometimes	Most of the Time
1) I get angry over little things.	1	2	3	4
2) I give up when I'm having a hard time.	1	2	3	4
3) I may not cry, but I get miserable when things don't turn out right.	1	2	3	4
4) If I have nothing better to do, I smoke or drink.	1	2	3	4
5) When things get rough, I just pray God will help me.	1	2	3	4
6) When I'm mad, I do or say things I later regret.	1	2	3	4
7) I think about myself more than others.	1	2	3	4
8) When I see others doing better than me, I become frustrated or jealous.	1	2	3	4
9) I just don't give a f*ck.	1	2	3	4
10) I feel hopeless.	1	2	3	4
11) When I should be working hard, I'm hardly working.	1	2	3	4
12) Other people are the reason why things are messed up in my life.	1	2	3	4
13) The main thing holding me back is me.	1	2	3	4
14) I hate things about myself.	1	2	3	4
15) I don't worry about how risky something is before I do it.	1	2	3	4
16) I'll try something even if it went badly for everyone else who tried it.	1	2	3	4
Subtotals				
TOTAL SCORE				

Explanation

Add up your total score based on your choices and see where you stand.

16-27: Too Cool. I don't even mean that in a bad way. You've figured some things out that a lot of people haven't. You're happy with yourself for the most part, and you know how to handle your emotions. You are probably an inspiration to people around you. If so, keep doing what you're doing. On the other hand, you might be so calm and reserved that everyone thinks you're lame. If you're in a "shell," then go live a little. There's nothing wrong with going through some drama to learn about real life. Remember, ain't nothin great about a man too "holy" to relate to his own people.

28-43: About Average. Take this how you want, but you're not doing too much better, or worse, than most other people. You've got your share of issues, but you're not totally f*cked up. From here, you can go in one of two directions. Either you can become more self-destructive and screwy or you can eliminate the weaknesses you see above and become great. It's still in your hands at this point, and it's all determined by what you do from here on out.

44-55: Set to Blow. Most likely, you're a product of a f*cked-up environment. You've gotta be, cause you're pretty f*cked up. You're not f*cked up so bad that you can't get yourself right, but homey, you got a lot of work to do. Your whole approach to life needs work. Your mindset is just plain self-destructive. But if this description really fits you, you may not even be able to see what I'm saying without taking it personally. Still, I need to say this because you're another tragedy waiting to happen if you don't start doing things a little differently...today. It takes baby steps to start, but you've got to turn around first. Hopefully, at this point, you're still sensible enough to figure out how.

56-64: Go Get Therapy. You either need some medication or some counseling. You're crazier than Michael Jackson, Amy Winehouse, and Dennis Rodman trying to squeeze into a hot-dog costume together. You're the type of person who turned to this chapter because you thought it was really about how to kill somebody. I'm warning you now, if you don't find somebody to talk to, you're gonna be dead, in jail, or in the psyche ward in three years or less.

The Eighth Principle

"Kill Yourself So You Can Live" means: Eliminate the weaknesses in yourself and the world around you, while developing the strength and discipline it will take to do so.

What You'll Learn

- ✶ What the AK-47 can teach us about perseverance.
- ✶ Why the Jena 6 can teach us about more than racism.
- ✶ How to tell if your "friends" are worse for you than your enemies.
- ✶ What rebel slaves outside of America can teach us about resistance.
- ✶ How different Black and white America really are.
- ✶ What Bob Marley understood about conflict resolution.
- ✶ The relationship between race riots and gentrification.
- ✶ How to handle depression and other woes.
- ✶ How we can secure community control, without the police.
- ✶ Why the "War on Terror" is really all about me and you.
- ✶ How to tell if you're scared of white people.
- ✶ What we can learn about ourselves from African Killer Bees.

13 Ways to Destroy Yourself

I know people think I'm playing when I say "kill yourself" throughout this book. Of course I don't want anybody to really commit suicide. (Though we *would* all be better off without *some* of us). But the truth is, most of us are killing ourselves ANYWAY. If you want some sure-fire ways to destroy yourself, just check out the following. Before you begin however, decide what age you want to live to. You'll need this number, so keep it in your head.

> **Did You Know?**
> If you sneeze too hard, you can fracture a rib. But if you try too hard to suppress a sneeze, you can rupture a blood vessel in your head or neck and die. If you keep your eyes closed for too long, it becomes more difficult to open them. If you keep your eyes open by force, they will actually pop out.

1. Stay Angry. A little anger here and there isn't all bad. It's actually better for you than other emotions, like fear and doubt. But anger, like anything you can have too much of, is best in moderation. If you stay angry for long periods of time you'll end up with a gang of health issues, like blood pressure, sleep disorders and lung damage. As the Buddha said, "Holding on to anger is like grasping a hot coal with the intent of throwing it at someone else; you are the one who gets burned." (If this description applies to you in any way, take 10 years off the age you have in your head)

2. Sacrifice Sleep. Too little sleep (less than 7 or 8 hours a night) has been tied to many different health problems, including obesity, diabetes and cancer. Mental fatigue is also just as bad as alcohol when it comes to the worst risk factor for vehicular accidents. That's why you can get pulled over for driving drunk or just sleepy...and go to jail either way. (Take off 5 years)

3. Get Into the Wrong Line of Work. Want to die for your country? Get into a line of work where you're likely to be die before you should. I don't only mean joining the army or the police force. There are plenty of jobs that will overwork you and underpay you until you have nothing left to give. Oh, and let's not forget about all the illegal ways to make money, where most people never make it out successfully. (Take off 8 years)

4. Ignore the Doctor. It's almost impossible to get a man to take a physical exam. But if you want to find out anything before it's too late to fix it, you need to schedule an appointment. If you don't like doctors, see a holistic healer. If you don't want to see them either, start reading books on health, like *Afrikan Holistic Health* and *Heal Thyself*. If you don't want to listen to *anybody*, just kill yourself now. (Take off 12)

5. Dumb Down Your Brain. Reading, doing crosswords and problem-solving are good ways to prevent Alzheimer's, a degenerative brain disease that affects most people who live to be old enough. On the other hand, every 1 percent gain in your literacy increases your life expectancy by 2 years. Anyway, a dumb life is a life full of problems that never get solved. And those problems will kill you faster than losing sleep ever could. (Take off 14)

6. Have a Lot of Sex. Sex in itself isn't really bad. In fact, it's usually great. But depending on how you do it, you may be signing your death certificate. Keep avoiding those check-ups, checking out your partner's background, and forgetting to strap up. Watch what happens. Don't forget that 12 million Americans contract STDs every year, many of which can leave you unable to make or have children. (Take off 9)

7. Drink a Lot. The occasional drink of alcohol ain't so bad, as long as it ain't Thunderbird or Wild Irish Rose. Actually, a glass of red wine can be good for your heart. But more than two drinks per day, and you can plan on permanent liver damage or diabetes.

Did You Know?

When you eat too much, your hearing becomes less sharp? And when you talk too much, the smell of your breath worsens. When you sleep too much, your risk of death doubles, along with your chance for heart disease! Too much of anything is never a good thing.

Alcohol is also the root cause of nearly 100,000 deaths per year. Not to mention all the stupid, life-threatening problems you can create on "courage juice." (Take off 14)

8. Stress Out. Creating more stress in your life is a great way to invite all kinds of diseases to attack the body. When you're always stressed, your adrenal glands are forced to work overtime and will eventually wear themselves out, which seriously weakens your immune system. Next thing you know, you're stressed AND sick. Not to mention that stressed-out people are more "ready to die" than regular folks. (Take off 20)

9. Watch TV. The average American spends a full 9 years of his life watching TV. Those are years that could be spent exercising, reading, or working for social change. Unless you only watch the science and history channels, you're on your way to being an overweight, lazy, TV-addicted couch potato. And that's a recipe for early death. (Take off 9)

10. Associate with the Wrong People. Whether it's a gang where people care more about whether you pay your dues than whether you live or die, or a relationship that drains you of your last bit of sanity, there are a lot of people that will make your life shorter. If you want to live: Avoid people who don't care about their lives, because they won't care about yours, and avoid people who will suck the life out of you...even if she can suck the life out of you. (Take off 8)

11. Smoke. Tobacco-related illnesses are America's number two killer. They're also the most preventable. We all know that smoking leads to a dozen different cancers throughout the body. Smoking is also a major cause of heart disease, bronchitis, emphysema, stroke, and even contributes to the severity of pneumonia. Plus it causes asthma and cancer in the innocent people we smoke around. Just one cigarette can immediately increase your blood pressure and decrease the circulation to your head and limbs. Imagine what a pack does to you. (Take off 18)

12. Eat Junk. In 2006, at least 400,000 Americans managed to kill themselves based almost solely on what they ate. Heart disease is the country's number one killer and – although some of that comes from genetics – most of it's due to the crap we eat. Besides all the fat, and cholestorol, the chemicals, hormones, and drugs they put in our food are killing us slowly no matter how you cut it. Not to mention all the worms and parasites *already* in your meat! (Take off 18)

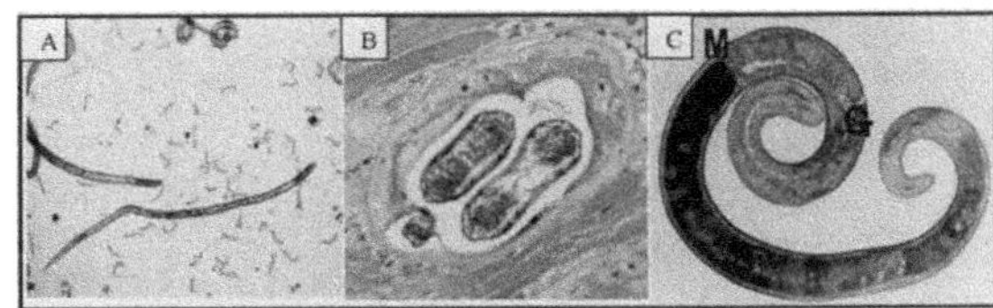

13. Hate Yourself. Here's an easy way to die faster. Live a miserable life that you hate. Hate everything about it, including yourself. Before long, you'll either create the kind of problems that will eventually destroy you, or you'll just give up and kill yourself. (Take off 15)

So…are you destroying yourself right now? What age did you end up with? I hope it's not a negative number! No matter what number you came up with, the lesson is this:

Live like you cherish life, not like you're anxious for death.

Fast-Forward the Struggle

Life is a struggle, filled with challenges and adversity. I don't know if anyone truly has an easy life. Even though rich people may seem to "have it easy," they have their own problems, some of which I know I don't want. As they say, "mo' money, mo' problems." It seems the richest people are most unhappy, so I know money can't buy happiness…or an "easy" life. Money only makes it easier to buy the things money can buy. Otherwise, we all have our struggles. Even that sheltered kid that never had to deal with real problems will one day be on his own, and that's a lot tougher when you ain't had to struggle all your life.

"Poverty sits by the cradle of all our great men and rocks all of them to manhood."
Heinrich Heine (1797-1856)

In fact, I think people who came up struggling are the best prepared. They can withstand whatever life throws at them. It's called "resilience" and it can be found in children who grew up poor, abused, or dealing with constant stress. As T.I. says on "Goodlife":

> I was born into poverty, raised in the sewage/ Streets would always be a part of me, it made me the truest/ And even when my days were the bluest/ I never ran from adversity, instead I ran to it/ Fear ain't in the heart of me, I learned just do it/ You get courage in your fears, right after you go through it

But some kids who grew up the same way never become resilient. Instead of becoming victorious, they become victims. I think one of the crucial differences between the people who can handle all of life's hell is how they handle it when it comes.

You see, there are five stages of dealing with adversity:

1. Denial
2. Anger/Resentment
3. Bargaining
4. Depression
5. Acceptance

Did You Know?

In life, losing is a part of growing. For organs to form during embryonic development, some cells must commit suicide. Without such programmed cell death, we would all be born with webbed feet like ducks.

From learning that you have 3 months to live, to finding out that you're about to be homeless, everyone goes through these stages. For example, here were my responses when I learned the bank was going to foreclose on one of my houses.

Denial: "No, not me! That can't be true!"

Anger/Resentment: "Why me? I don't deserve this! F*ck! I want to kill a motherf*cka!"

Bargaining: "Okay, what if I start paying some of it off right now? Then I have a chance, right? I won't screw up again! Please?"

Depression: "I give up. My whole life is f*cked up now. It's hopeless."

Acceptance: "Well, I'm still here, huh? It is what it is. Can't change it now. I guess I'll move on."

Keep in mind, this was over the course of several months. Some people would have taken even longer to move on.

The difference is that some people make it through these stages quickly, and some people don't. Some people can't even make it to acceptance, and waste tons of time being mad and depressed. Other people are mature enough to skip the first few stages and fast forward right to acceptance.

Here were my responses the next time I lost something, this time a fiancé who didn't want to be with me anymore:

Denial: "Really?"

Anger/Resentment: "Damn."

Fast Forward

Acceptance: "F*ck it. Holla."

This time, it took about ten minutes. Most people, as you know, would still be stuck and f*cked up.

Keeping pace with a slow crowd only makes you another loser. Think clearer, move faster, do better.

Pressure Busts Pipes

There's all kind of pressure on you right now. There's the normal peer pressure to do what everyone else is doing. Then there's the pressure to make money. Then there's of all kinds of stress, resulting from the problems that almost every man of color faces in this sick society.

In the ocean, most animals can't survive at a certain depth because of the pressure of all the water on top of them. However, the animals that must live down there will adapt and survive (see *Part One*, "Ugly Ass Fish").

In the mountains of Asia, the air pressure is low and there's much less oxygen than down here at sea level. However, mountain people like the Sherpas (the first people to climb Mt. Everest – NOT some white explorer) are able to adapt. They climb the mountains with no equipment and no oxygen masks, while the white explorers they are helping would die without them.

So, pressure can do one of two things to you. One saying is that "pressure busts pipers." However, another saying is that "pressure can make diamonds." As David Banner said about 2006 being the "worst year of his life":

> I have something call the diamond theory, if people know the origin of a diamond – a diamond is a piece of coal which is probably the most worthless element on Earth. But when pressure is applied to it, if it can stand that pressure, it totally transforms into something else.

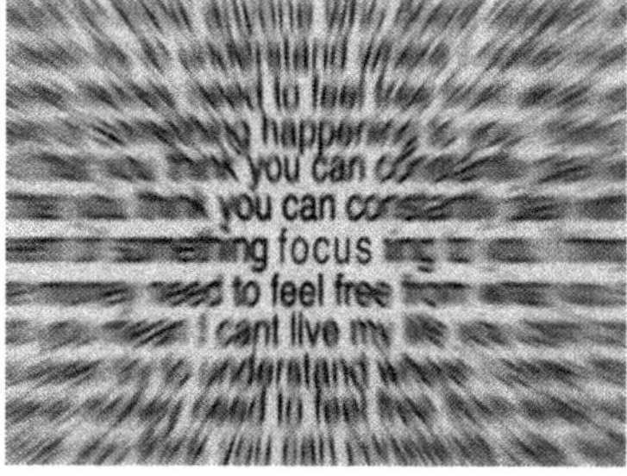

Or as Stephan Hoeller has written about another precious jewel:

> A pearl is a beautiful thing that is produced by an injured life. It is the tear from the injury of the oyster. The treasure of our being in this world is also produced by an injured life. If we had not been wounded, if we had not been injured, then we will not produce the pearl.

So how do you respond to adversity? Does it destroy you, or build you up? What will you do with the many pressures you face? Under pressure, 85% of people fold, but 5% focus. How you handle it all determines how well you'll survive in this dirty game.

Use pressure to your advantage. Focus, don't fold.

The Unstoppable AK-47

"No se vive celebrando victorias, sino superando derrotas."
(Live your life not celebrating victories, but overcoming defeats.)
Che Guevara

The AK-47 is the most popular weapon in the world – not to mention in the hood. But while we may only know them as "choppers," to millions of people, the AK-47 is known as "the gun that changed the world" or "the gun of a thousand revolutions."

In *AK-47: The Weapon that Changed the Face of War*, Larry

Kahaner details the history of the Automatic Kalashnikov – 47, named after its inventor, Soviet soldier Mikhail Kalashnikov, and the year it was made, 1947.

Since its birth, the gun has undergone very few changes. The AK-47 is essentially the same weapon it was 60 years ago. Because people still have – and use – AKs from 40 years ago, there's no way to know exactly how many are currently in service. But it's a pretty safe bet that there's as many as 100 million of these deadly weapons out there right now. **That's one AK for every 60 people**. Unfortunately, that means the AK-47 is also in the hands of corrupt militias in Africa and street gangs in America (in both cases leading to pointless and bloody civil war).

"That A-K-K-K/ In the back of the Chevrolet
Killed so many niggas it joined the KKK"
Killer Mike, "Gat Totin"

But with a gun as reliable as the AK-47, everyone wants one. In fact, U.S. soldiers are known to toss their military-issue M16s and pick up enemy AKs instead. The AK's simple design and reliability made it a favorite of rebel movements worldwide – its image can even be found on the flags of some African and Middle Eastern nations. Back when they hoped to overthrow America and Europe by supporting revolutionary movements in Asia and Africa, the Soviets sent them thousands of AK-47s, sometimes for free. Sometimes, it paid off. AK-47s were not only used by Vietcong guerrillas and Che Guevara's forces, but in nearly every revolutionary movement since the 1950s.

In 2005, Venezuelan President Hugo Chavez, one of the most vocal leaders in the fight against global white supremacy, ordered 100,000 AK-47s for his army. Since then, he announced that his country will produce AKs in its own factories, as has the government of Nigeria. I smell revolution brewing.

Why is the AK so successful? After all, there are dozens of rifles more precise *and* comfortable. But the AK-47 has two big things going for it:

1. It's cheap. In many war-torn countries, you can get one for $10 U.S.
2. It will never let you down.

I'm not exaggerating with the second reason. The AK-47 may not be very accurate, but it can fire 700 rounds a minute…without jamming.

"What does not destroy me, makes me stronger."
Friedrich Wilhelm Nietzsche (1844-1900)

You can drag it through mud, drop it in a lake, leave it buried in your backyard for a year, dig it up, kick it once, and it will fire like you just had it cleaned. The *Discovery Channel* did a special on the world's ten best weapons, and the AK-47 came in at number 2 (the human mind was number 1). In the video, which you can find on YouTube (a valuable search engine for finding *visual* information on just about *anything* you want to learn), they submerged an AK in water, buried it in sand, and even ran it over with a Humvee...and it still fired like new.

Not only that, but the AK can fire cheaply produced bullets and even bullets that have been sitting out forever in the desert sun or jungle rain.

To top it all off, the AK can be used with almost no training. Overnight, it'll turn a ragtag band of street thugs into a military force. As a result, the AK has shifted the balance of power in warfare by allowing small, determined groups, not just armies, to overthrow entire governments. Thus, the AK-47 itself symbolizes the determination of rebel groups to persist and persevere no matter what. Up against all odds, revolutionaries must become indestructible in order to succeed. They must withstand being buried under pain, pressure, poverty, and every possible problem, and still come up out the dirt *bustin.*

As Jim Jones says on the Diplomats' "Beautiful Noise"

> Sh*t, and Uncle Ricky got a month and some change/ And it feels like a garbage truck just dumping the pain/ All on my shoulders, I'm warning my soldiers/ The nights could get chilly, but the morning's much colder/ I've seen summers get cold/ And niggas do it up until the point where they done and they fold/...I gotta keep striving, I gotta keep moving, I gotta keep grinding/ If this was the road, and I was a trucker, then sh*t man, I gotta keep driving

A real man, whether revolutionary or ordinary, understands that he must be reliable as the AK-47: Put him through anything, and he will still come out fighting. Eventually, he will win.

Persistence overcomes resistance.
What doesn't kill you only makes you stronger.

Lessons on Resistance

Long before Al Sharpton, Jesse Jackson, and Oprah Winfrey, Black leaders didn't speak "for" Black people "to" white people. They fought alongside their people. It was so clear that they were "for" their people, that everyone knew they would die "for" their people. It wasn't about money then. In the times I'm speaking of, nobody had money. All we wanted was freedom. Here are some examples of true leadership in times of resistance. (For more, check out *Black Rebellion* from Two Horizons Press)

Jamaica

On many Caribbean islands the African population outnumbered the white population. This led to some very scared white slaveowners, of course. And with good reason. On almost every island there are records of serious slave revolts, and even more evidence of repeat runaways.

When these runaways fled in large numbers and formed jungle communities, they were called Maroons (from the Portuguese "cimarron," meaning "wild, untamed"). Maroon communities fought whites off for years, and played an important role in the histories of Brazil, Suriname, Puerto Rico, Haiti, Cuba, and Jamaica.

When the British took over Jamaica in 1655, most of the slaves quickly fled to the mountains. They established mountain communities, which regularly received new batches of Maroons. The Maroons harassed the nearby slaveholders by stealing, trading with slaves, and encouraging them to run away as well. Their numbers continued to increase, as did the problems they caused for the British.

In 1690, a large group of slaves, consisting mainly of Coromantees, a brave warrior class from Africa's Gold Coast, rebelled and escaped into the dense jungle. Soon they would join forces with other Maroons being led by the powerful Cudjoe. Cudjoe, described as short and "bear-like," was fearless. With the help of his two brothers and two sub-chiefs, he set off the First Maroon War.

Did You Know?

The Maroons are still around? At least 600 Maroons still live in Accompong Town. Thousands of other Maroons have spread throughout Jamaica and other countries, including the U.S. In fact, in Florida, there is a city named after them, called Cudjoe City. In the 263 years since the Peace Treaty was signed, the Accompong Maroons have had only 1 crime requiring a justice of the peace. There are no Jamaican Police in Accompong as the Maroons police themselves.

Disguised from head to foot with leaves and using the woods to their advantage, the Maroons ambushed their enemies. Not only did they know the terrain better than the British, but they were skilled in making weapons from wood. They also had legendary skill as marksman, which amazed all those sent to fight them. Long before an enemy force approached their camps, eagle-eyed lookouts would spot them and spread the warning through bugles made from cows' horns. The most skilled horn blowers could use special calls to summon everyone in their camp from miles away. The British forces suffered huge losses, both from sharp shooting Maroons as well as the tropical diseases that the Africans naturally survived.

In 1738, the King of England commissioned a Colonel to seek out Cudjoe and offer him a Peace Treaty. By its terms the Maroons were granted full freedom and liberty, given 1,500 acres of land and the right to produce their own food and govern themselves. They had won.

You may first need to get away and cut all ties in order to find and develop your true strength.

Haiti

By the 1700's Haiti's population was divided into three main groups: (1) the ruling whites, (2) the "Affranchis", a larger class of free Blacks and mulattos, and (3) the much larger masses of Black slaves. Although the mulattos of the Affanchis were born to Black mothers raped by whites, they and the free Blacks saw themselves as better than the Black slaves of Haiti. Haiti also had a large Maroon community, powerful enough to have led three major Haitian uprisings in 1679, 1691, and 1704.

In 1758, the Maroons had a fearless leader named Macandal, a native-born African who declared that he was "the Black Messiah sent to drive the whites from the island." Macandal, a highly knowledgeable herbalist, hatched an ingenious plot to poison the whites' water supply and take over the island. Unfortunately, someone sold him out, leading to the Black Messiah's prompt execution. At the time of his execution, Macandal bravely warned his enemies that the fight was not over, telling them and his fellow Maroons that one day he would return, "more terrible than before."

Then, on August 22, 1791, a great slave uprising plunged Haiti into civil war. Thousands of slaves rose up to fight for their liberty. Within ten days, slaves had taken control of the northern half of the island, leaving the whites controlling only a few isolated camps. Within two months, the rebelling slaves had killed 2,000 whites and burned or destroyed 280 sugar plantations. Within a year, all of Haiti was in revolutionary chaos.

Legions of rebel slaves were led by a number of Black commanders, but the greatest was Toussaint L'Overture. As a child, Toussaint was so frail and delicate that he wasn't expected to live. Nevertheless, he hardened his body through severe exercise. He never learned that he was the grandson of an African king, but he knew he was to be a great man. After he learned how to read, he developed a love for books, which he saw as a key to finding his greatness.

Did You Know?

There is a possibility that HAARP, a so-called "weather weapon" technology was used to create the earthquake that crippled Haiti in January of 2010. But debating that accomplishes what? Who wants to argue endlessly about how many teeth the dog has? What's of more consequence is what has happened since then. Aid workers are nowhere to be found, yet a US military presence is everywhere. Food and supplies aren't reaching people, but Black children are being kidnapped. And Venezuela forgave Haiti their oil debt, but France did nothing to relieve Haiti of the debt that had crippled its economy in the first place. And of the $255 million collected by the Red Cross as of mid-February, only $80 mil went to Haiti. Hell, the Red Cross is still holding on to Katrina and Tsunami money!

One day, he was struck by reading the prophecy of a Black chief who would free all the slaves. From that time on, Toussaint was determined to break the chains that held his people in bondage.

Once the fearless Toussaint joined the rebellion, the Haitians believed he was the second coming of Macandal. Under his military leadership, the rebel slaves were able to defeat every army they face, take full control of the country, and restore law and order to Haiti.

But Toussaint refused to surrender power back to France. He planned to rule Haiti as a free Black nation.

First, a British army came to try and stop him, and he quickly defeated them. He then led an invasion of neighboring Santo Domingo, freeing the slaves there. In 1801, Toussaint issued a constitution for Haiti which provided for its independence and decreed that he would be governor-for-life.

> "My decision to destroy the authority of the blacks in Saint Dominque (Haiti) is not so much based on considerations of commerce and money, as on the need to block for ever the march of the blacks in the world."
> Napoleon Bonaparte

In retaliation, Napoleon Bonaparte sent an army of 82,000 French soldiers to the island to restore French rule. The French soldiers were accompanied by mulatto troops led by Alexandre Pétion. These mixed-race soldiers didn't identify with Toussaint and the slaves. Petion and his troops saw themselves as better than the rebel Africans. Though the French didn't treat anyone with Black blood as equals, many mulattos believed that the French were good to them. Some of Toussaint's closest allies, including commander Jean-Jacques Dessalines, now joined the French and went against Toussaint. With their help, Toussaint was finally tricked with promises of a peace treaty, which the French then used to imprison and assassinate him.

Did You Know?

There is a possibility that HAARP, a so-called "weather weapon" technology was used to create the earthquake that crippled Haiti in January of 2010. But debating that accomplishes what? Who wants to argue endlessly about how many teeth the dog has? What's of more consequence is what has happened since then. Aid workers are nowhere to be found, yet a US military presence is everywhere. Food and supplies aren't reaching people, but Black children are being kidnapped. And Venezuela forgave Haiti their oil debt, but France did nothing to relieve Haiti of the debt that had crippled its economy in the first place. And of the $255 million collected by the Red Cross as of mid-February, only $80 mil went to Haiti. Hell, the Red Cross is still holding on to Katrina and Tsunami money!

> "Now they have felled the trunk of the Negroes' tree of liberty. However, new shoots will sprout because the roots are deep and many"
> Toussaint L'Ouverture, upon his capture

For a few months the island was quiet again under Napoleon's rule. But when the French made it clear that they planned to bring back slavery, Dessalines and Petion finally came to their senses. They realized just how Black they were. They realized that no privilege – not one of power, or class, or even half-whiteness – was real when it came from the same people who enslaved them. Those were all imaginary privileges, and they were really just to be slaves like everyone else.

So Dessalines and Petion switched sides. Raising up the old rebel troops as well as the mulattos, they went back to war against the French. Dessalines led the rebellion until its end when the French forces were finally defeated in 1803. When the Haitian rebels won their last battle, Haiti was given its independence. On January 1, 1804, Dessalines declared Haiti a free republic. On that day, Haiti became the second independent nation in the Western Hemisphere, after the United States, and the land of the only successful slave rebellion in world history.

Did You Know?

Speaking of how the French got smashed, we know it wasn't just the Black rebels who did them in. We also had a yellow ally: Yellow Fever. While some sources claim mysterious mystical forces in the defeat of the Europeans, Toussaint - although pious and religious in his personal life - didn't get down like that. Neither does the historical record. Toussaint was aware of the fact that Yellow Fever would strike when the Spring rains came...not when prayers summoned it up. In a letter to his general, Dessalines, he wrote:

"Endeavor, by all the means of force and address, to set that place on fire; it is constructed entirely of wood; you have only to send into it some faithful emissaries...Do not forget, while waiting for the rainy season which will rid us of our foes, that we have no other resource than destruction and flames. Bear in mind that the soil bathed with our sweat must not furnish our enemies with the smallest aliment. Tear up the roads with shot; throw corpses and horses into all the fountains; burn and annihilate everything, in order that those who have come to reduce us to slavery may have before their eyes the image of that hell which they deserve.

Salutation and Friendship,

TOUSSAINT L'OUVERTURE"

Gangster!

You may need to resist and refuse any and every attempt to change your vision, even as others give up around you.

South America

Slaves weren't only brought to North America and the Carribbean. Even today, South America has a large Black population because of the millions of slaves that were brought there. Like enslaved Blacks everywhere else, many of them fought and died to resist slavery.

For example, in 1550, the slaves of Santa Marta, Colombia, rose up in revolt and burned down the entire city. The revolt was finally stopped, but their spirits were not broken. Five years later, an African naming himself king led another massive slave revolt that was almost impossible to defeat. When these proud Black men and women could fight no longer, they fled to the mountains and jungles to live free.

As slaves fought back and fled, they formed Maroon communities throughout South America. One of the strongest Maroon communities was in Brazil. The Republic of Palmares was an African state established in northern Brazil in 1630. Runaway slaves from all over the area penetrated the dense forests and established village communities in the river valley. Even as the Portuguese and the Dutch attempted to take over the territory by force, the Maroons fought back fiercely and held out until 1697. It was then that Portuguese soldiers finally broke through the walled city of Palmares.

"I'll never be-have/ I'd rather be a dead man than a live slave"
Killer Mike, "Pressure"

Still refusing to surrender, the head of the Maroon community and his lieutenants flung themselves from the rocky cliff overlooking the region.

Never give in to being broken, no matter what the costs.

SUPREME THE ASSHOLE ON "THE RULE OF THE FEW"

Here's something else that always pisses me off: We take EXCEPTIONS to the rule, and think that those motherf*ckin exceptions ARE the rule. If you've had a few winning lottery tickets, you're convinced the f*cking lottery is a sure bet and one day you'll win! Never mind the 85,000 times you've lost! A few hustlers got rich...oh sh*t, that means we can all get rich sellin nickels and dimes, huh? More than anything else, though, we'll take a few white folks who treated us good and let that convince us that ALL white folks aren't so bad, and that anybody who says different must be a racist! Never mind the thousands of years of history you've gotta ignore to do that! Just go with the good feeling, right? F*ck history! F*ck global politics! F*ck economics! All that matters is that Frank from down the street helps you work on your car on Sundays! And that proves that all white people are misunderstood do-gooders! But here's the catch. We never apply the same logic to our own people. If more than 5 Black people sh*t on us, the whole race is f*cked up.

GEORGE THE FIEND

"Peace comes from within. Do not seek it without."
The Buddha

George the Fiend was a cokehead whose house we'd frequent as a group to smoke weed and watch pornos. This was one weird mothaf*cker. He lived in a small one-bedroom apartment not far from my block. He didn't have much, but he was fun to be around. At the very least, he was good to laugh at.

George would smoke the roaches of our blunts, after we were all done, using a broken off end of a car antenna. True smoker. He would offer us his little antenna-clip, but we'd impolitely decline every time. George was white, but for some reason he had a Hispanic accent, and maybe that made him a little more acceptable to us. When I finally decided I'd give sellin coke a shot, he became my best customer.

How did I get to selling coke?

If you think about it, it comes naturally given the circumstances. Living in a jungle leads to either a jungle way of life or a beast way of life, depending on just how firm you are in your prior convictions and culture. I kept the morals I'd picked up from my mother, but I didn't have much of a culture to keep. Some of my closer friends had begun hustling with the older guys on the block, and I'd started riding with them on their trips to Spanish Harlem to re-up.

At first, I was just trying to get away from Jersey City, if only momentarily, since nobody else ever wanted to go anywhere, unless it was for drugs. But, in a way I didn't anticipate, the drug trade seemed especially attractive in no time. It was immediately obvious how easy it was to not only purchase a few grams, but to pick up all the paraphernalia – baggies, vials, etc. – from the nearby bodegas. And as a kid who still had to struggle to get a pair of name-brand sneakers, it was also pretty clear how much more money I could be making than I was making with the stick-up crew.

As a matter of fact, I wasn't making ANY money robbing people. We'd go out in groups and beat the sh*t out of people. Splitting up the proceeds between a large group simply isn't lucrative. When we'd go out, we always picked the wrong victims. Broke dudes with little on them but cigarettes and pagers.

It bothered me that these tough guys I called my friends would never dare stake out a white neighborhood and rob someone with actual wealth. After I calculated the situation – we'd hurt dozens of people (often brutally) and made less than we could have workin at the fried chicken spot – I lost interest. Once the rest of crew was tired of random robberies, most of them turned to the more lucrative prospects of selling cocaine. So, eventually, I tried that too.

That stint didn't last long. In almost no time, I had become disgusted with the mothers who'd bring their children to the corner fresh from school or daycare and buy the drugs openly as if their kids weren't old enough to understand what was going on. Not to mention all the sick sh*t the addicts did to get the drugs, or that the dealers did to the addicts, or each other.

I quit. I sold the bulk of my remaining product to George the Fiend on credit – which would normally be a big mistake in the business – but I didn't care. I was done, and I wanted out. Within two weeks, I came by to see him and George paid me everything he owed me. A few days after that visit, he was found dead. I wasn't exactly consumed with grief over his death, but I wasn't all right within.

Done with hustling, I had free time to get away and think. I hopped a PATH train from Jersey City to Manhattan and headed for Central Park. I'd brought a bookbag, a Walkman, and a boxcutter. In my bookbag, I'd put a notebook where I'd write my rhymes and my thoughts, some Sharpie Magnum markers, and a bottle of Bacardi 151 Puerto Rican Rum. Drinking by myself in late night Central Park, I reflected on what was going wrong in my life. I sat ruminating for what seemed like hours. With the bottle half-gone, I grew frustrated. My vision was blurry when I wanted to see clearly. I wanted to understand what kept me from being happy.

I thought about George. I thought about his addiction to cocaine. I thought about how he craved our company, almost as much as he craved the drug. I thought about how he desperately wanted to feel accepted. I thought about how he had given his whole life to pursuing pleasures of the flesh. I thought about how he had literally given his life chasing that kind of happiness.

Did You Know?

In DC, drug distributor Cornell Jones' new concoction of PCP and marijuana was nicknamed "Butt-naked" because it was nearly guaranteed that buyers would strip naked and run through the streets once the drug hit their system. Even knowing this, people came in droves pursuing this high. This led to new levels of craziness in DC's streets, including mothers putting their children in the oven or guys pulling their own teeth out with pliers.

"No one saves us but ourselves. No one can and no one may. We ourselves must walk the path."
The Buddha

And then it dawned on me. I was looking for something outside myself to make me happy. I was always hoping for something else to save me from my own misery. I had never been into Christianity and waiting on a savior, but here I was, looking forward to the next time I see my little crew, the next time I get some money, the next time I get drunk or high…I was always looking for something to make me better. I would end up following in George the Fiend's path, pursuing pleasure and a "quick fix" instead of internal peace.

At that rate, I'd never be happy. I'd just be dead. It might be slow, it might be fast, but it was inevitable. Happiness, on the other hand, may have never come. Or it may have come as it did for George and the other fiends, in temporary moments of "getting away." But what was I really trying to get away from? I looked down at the bottle and it was clear.

Myself.

I left the bottle on the bench, gathered my belongings and headed home. I was determined to make a change.

Inner peace is one of life's greatest – and rarest – accomplishments. Find it, and you won't chase anything else.

BOB MARLEY AND WAR

Before anyone had heard of Robert Nesta Marley, he was determined to become successful in the music business. But in Jamaica, where the gangs worked for the political parties, and it cost big money to make *anything* happen, Marley just didn't have the resources. Radio stations only played what was already popular, most DJs wanted "payola" to break new music, and they certainly weren't interested in the kind of music Bob Marley and his Wailers were making.

So Marley tried something different. He gathered together a few fellow rudebwoys and barged into the local radio stations by force. They held the DJ at gunpoint, handed him their record, and demanded he play it. Naturally, no one refused.

After the first initial spins, Jamaicans were interested in the new sound, and were now requesting Marley's music. His strategy had worked.

This was the same Marley who later converted to Rastafari and used Emperor Haile Selassie's address to the United Nations as the lyrics to his song, "War":

> Until the philosophy which holds one race superior and another inferior/ is finally and permanently discredited and abandoned/ everywhere is war/ And until there are no longer first-class and second-class citizens of any nation/ until the color of a man's skin is of no more significance than the color of his eyes/ And until the basic human rights are equally guaranteed to all without regard to race, there is war/ And until that day, the dream of lasting peace, world citizenship, rule of international morality/ will remain but a fleeting illusion to be pursued/ but never attained/Now everywhere is war.

Looking at life as though "everywhere is war" allows one to approach every problem as if it is a battle. Marley would fight dozens of battles over the course of his life, some professional, some personal, but he understood that every battle requires a strategy. In this early battle, Marley prevailed because he chose the right strategy. He wasn't a gangster, a thug, or a criminal, but he understood the situation that was before him.

In a conflict, there are three approaches to resolution: **Diplomacy, Politics, and War.**

The path of least resistance is Diplomacy, where one side tries to please the other side, hoping they will agree or give in. But in Jamaica's music industry, diplomacy would get Marley nowhere. Politics were in play, and that's how most music got played, but Marley didn't have those resources. So he went for the path of highest resistance, War. And it worked.

As Marley matured and became aware of the worldwide struggle of Black people, he applied the same strategies, but to a different battle. In one of his most popular songs, "Get Up, Stand Up," he sang:

> Most people think/ Great God will come from the skies/ Take away everything/ And make everybody feel high/ But if you know what life is worth/ You will look for yours on earth/ And now you see the light/ You stand up for your rights, Jah!/...We sick and tired of-a your ism-schism game/ Dyin and goin to heaven in-a Jesus name, lord/ We know and we understand/ Almighty God is a living man/ You can fool some people sometimes/ But you can't fool all the people all the time/ So now we see the light (What you gonna do?)/ We gonna stand up for our rights! (Yeah, yeah, yeah!)

As time passed, Marley's music evolved to become more and more political. By the time he passed from cancer, in a death still considered suspicious by many, he had written and performed over 200 songs. Over two-thirds of them addressed social ills, resistance, or redemption. Marley's music and influence had spread far and wide. His wisely chosen approach had once again allowed him to effectively change the game.

Choose your strategy according to your situation.

Bumpy Johnson and the White Mob

The Boss

From the 1930s to the late 1960s, when it came to Harlem, the undisputed king of the underworld was Bumpy Johnson.

Nothing happened in Harlem without Bumpy's say-so, and crossing him was something you *didn't* want to do. From drugs to prostitution, to strong-arm enforcement, to the "numbers" racket, Bumpy's hands were in *everything.*

Even the police knew it – they came to him to negotiate peace between young street gangs. The politicians knew it – they counted on him to deliver votes on Election Day. Even the Italian and Jewish syndicates knew it, although they had to find out the hard way. When they decided to move on the Harlem numbers racket, Bumpy – only 25 at the time – sprang into action. With only a handful of loyal men behind him, Bumpy waged a successful guerilla war, forcing the white mobsters to finally come to terms with "that crazy nigger."

According to Lloyd Strayhorn:

> The legend goes that he got his nickname as a result of "bumping" the other guys around on the basketball court. He was tough, so the nickname, "Bumpy" stuck. Bumpy was known for his dapper style, wearing the latest "vines" (clothes) and always had a "knot" (a wad of money) the size of his fist. What established Bumpy Johnson, other than these outward trappings, was the fact he was fearless. He was also well known for his temper. He literally feared no man; black, white or indifferent. It was rumored he always carried both a knife and a gun, and had no problem using either one of them, depending on the occasion.

Bumpy was willing to do whatever it took to get what he wanted, but he was just as willing to use his money to help Harlemites in need. So Harlem loved him, in a way that few communities today love their gangsters. That's because, as gangster as he was, he also went out of his way to help whomever he could, in whatever manner he could.

Sure, he threw huge Christmas parties for the children in Harlem, and gave away thousands of dollars worth of presents to kids who would otherwise have none. But it was deeper than symbolic shows of generosity. If Bumpy Johnson saw a family's furniture being moved out into the street because they couldn't pay the landlord, he would reach into his pocket and peel off a few big bills from the huge wad he carried, and hand it to the evictors to pay off the back rent.

Although many claim he was the one who introduced Harlem to heroin, he was also a scholar who demanded local youth do well in school. He wasn't a dummy himself, either. Like Casper Holstein, he was known as a highly intelligent man and a published writer. According to Strayhorn:

> Despite his tough, forceful personality, and streaks of generosity, Bumpy Johnson was also a well read and cultured individual. While in prison (where he did several bids totaling over 30 years of his life), he directed his energy, time and attention to philosophy, history and poetry among other things. Interestingly enough, several of his poems were published later on in literary reviews...Bumpy loved playing chess, reading Shakespeare, and listening to the classical music of Beethoven.

So Bumpy may have been a criminal, but he was a criminal with a conscience. In a community that felt exploited and abused by both the government *and* the white criminal element, Bumpy certainly took from the people, but at least gave something back. The minister who gave his eulogy in 1968 said, "He chose his course, and he followed it with his eyes open. In a world filled with social contamination and double-talk, maybe there was no other way to be a man."

In fact, Bumpy Johnson was importing dope from Peru long before Frank Lucas lied his way into Hollywood. But at the same time, Bumpy wasn't another greasy gangster getting fat off the people. You see, during the era when when Black businesses couldn't get loans from white banks, they often had to turn to Black numbers bankers like Johnson, who had the money to support Black business initiatives…and the heart to do so. But we never hear that side of our stories, huh?

Bumpy Johnson wasn't just a supporter of Black business. He was a Black nationalist. In 1943 and 1945, he supported Benjamin J. Davis, an organizer of the United States Communist Party, to represent Harlem on the New York City Council. Only a few years later, during the Peekskill riots of 1949, he was showing his true gangster colors, going all out for Black actor and activist Paul Robeson, who had drawn the ire of white America with his revolutionary stance. As Bumpy would later tell journalist William Gardner Smith:

> Remember the Peekskill riots…when all these crackers had Paul Robeson surrounded and wanted to do him in? I heard that on the radio. So I got some of my boys together, between seventy and a hundred, and I called the chief of the state police and said, "Listen, this is Bumpy Johnson, we're coming through to get Paul out, and if anybody tries to stop us, police or civilians, there's gonna be a hell of a lot of bloodshed."
>
> Then my boys and me, we piled into a fleet of cars and we drove. We drove all the way to Peekskill, the police got out of our way; they had been warned. We had every kind of gun imaginable. And we drove right through them screaming civilian crackers, too, and they damn sure got out of the way, too. And we brought old Paul out. Brought him out in a convoy. Because Paul is black, he's my brother, and I wasn't gonna let no crackers set hand on him.

Now *THAT* is gangster. Not the bullsh*t we see on BET.

Years later, Bumpy Johnson was taking on the Italian Mafia AND the police, when a group of young members of a Black Power faction of CORE decided to picket a police station where officers had been accused of brutality against Blacks. When the picket line was formed, the youths received a warning that local Mafia intended to attack them, and possibly kill them, to make them leave.

William Gardner Smith reported what happened next:

> Bumpy was informed of the threat against the CORE pickets. He promptly sent the following message to the local Mafia leaders: "If any

> of those CORE kids are harmed, I will not guarantee the safety of any Mafia member in Harlem."

The protest continued without an incident. *Gangster.* When Smith asked him why he'd take such risks for people who had nothing to do with his operations, Bumpy told him, "Because what I really am, when the chips are down, is a Black nationalist."

Now, what is YOUR criteria for being gangster?

Whatever you do, help others enough so *that* becomes your legacy.

However…as "Revolutionary But Gangster" as Bumpy Johnson may have been, it's only in comparison to the sorry examples we have today. In truth, we have to be real about the facts. Bumpy wasn't overthrowing the system, he was getting over on the system. And he wasn't planning on retiring, he was expanding. The numbers racket may have been cool, but heroin wrecked Harlem. Some sources even say that when Bumpy offered to "protect" Malcolm X after his expulsion from the NOI, Bumpy may have been motivated at least partly by an existing beef he had with the NOI over him pushing dope in the hood. No matter how you cut it, by the end of Bumpy Johnson's career, he was doing the very opposite of what he'd set out to do.

Sure, Bumpy started his career working with the numbers boss "Madame Queen" Stephanie St. Clair. Together they went to war with Dutch Schultz, who headed both the Jewish and Italian mobs, and wanted to control Harlem. Bumpy was pro-Black, but he was also pro-dirty money. Those are two flags that are tough to salute at the same time. Though he once insisted to Amiri Baraka that "Black dudes run their own rackets and stop paying off the white boys," Bumpy couldn't maintain that stance. By the time it was all over, Bumpy had left the still-defiant Madame St. Clair…to work as an enforcer for the Genovese crime family…facilitating Mafia control of the same Black neighborhoods he once vowed to protect. The game is cold.

You can't serve two masters.

The White Tree

In Jena, Louisiana, the local high school campus has a large shade tree that is known as the "white tree," where the mostly white students of the school sit together. The small minority of Black students at the school do not sit under this tree. One day in fall of 2006, after two Black students sat beneath the "white tree," white students hung nooses from the tree.

The school superintendent ignored the nooses and called them harmless. He said, "Adolescents play pranks. I don't think it was a threat against anybody." Even though we all know that a noose is basically a symbolic death threat, saying "stay away from our sh*t, or we'll kill you, nigger," no one took any action. This led more Black students to sit under the tree in protest.

The District Attorney then came to the school with the town's police and demanded an end to the Black students' protest, telling them, "I can be your best friend or your worst enemy...I can take away your lives with a stroke of my pen."

Racial tension and Black-white fights continued over the next couple of months. One weekend, a Black student was beaten up by white students at a party. The next day, Black students at a convenience store were threatened by a young white man with a shotgun. They wrestled the gun from him and ran off. No charges were filed against the white man, but the Black students were arrested for the theft of the gun!

That following Monday at school, a white student, who was a vocal supporter of the nooses, taunted the Black student who was beaten up at the party and called him and several other Black students "nigger." After lunch, the Black students knocked him down and kicked him around. He went to the hospital but wasn't hurt badly, and even went to a social event that evening.

Six Black Jena High students, Robert Bailey (17), Theo Shaw (17), Carwin Jones (18), Bryant Purvis (17), Mychal Bell (16) and Jesse Ray Beard (14), were expelled from school, arrested and charged with second-degree attempted murder. The judge set the bail between $70,000 and $138,000 so that the boys would be stuck in prison for months while their poor families went deep into debt to get them out.

In the first trial, Mychal Bell was convicted by the white District Attorney of aggravated battery and conspiracy to commit aggravated battery (both felonies) by an all-white jury in a trial where his Black public defender didn't even bother to call any witnesses. He was facing a sentence of 22½ years. Some of the other defendants were looking at so much time they wouldn't see daylight until they were 50.

Since then, the "Jena 6" campaign received so much attention through YouTube, MySpace, and the online blogging community that Mychal Bell's original conviction was successfully challenged and overturned.

Goes to show the power we have when we say what needs to be said. So why aren't we saying more? Why aren't we demanding more? Cases like the Jena 6 are only reminders of the racism that has never gone away.

But my issue with this case isn't the racism. Nah. My issue…is us.

By now, we should not be surprised to see white people acting like this. And we need to stop getting emotional and getting our panties all in a bunch, every time they show us how they really feel about us. Why are we so surprised…every single time? We act like we can't believe this kind of stuff is happening in 2003…in 2004…in 2005…in 2006…in 2007. Wake up! This is not new! This is not out of the ordinary! If you feel like situations like the "Jena 6" case are nightmares, then you can't be awake. You're actually asleep having a stupid-ass dream that everything is all good now.

"It's impossible to awaken a man who is pretending to be asleep."
Navajo proverb

All good, huh? Since when? Since slavery ended? Since Jim Crow ended? Since segregation ended? Since lynchings ended? Since racial profiling ended? Wait. None of these things ever really ended! And if it looked like it ended, it just changed to something else…usually something sneakier! Al Sharpton and Jesse Jackson just pop up when there's something to cry about, and then they disappear again.

That's the same thing rapper Scarface said to DJ Leo G in August 2007:

> Niggas is missing the point. Niggas is f*cked up and ain't making no kinda adjustments. Being a nigga is like being in a fight. When you see how the nigga coming, you gotta make some adjustments. You see how he coming, so you can get with him.
>
> Have you seen the sh*t goin on in Louisiana? They lookin at a lifetime in prison, man. That's a f*cking federal hate crime, cuz. Why in the f*ck is these sentencing guidelines so different from a nigga and a white boy? Why in the f*ck is that so different? Why can a nigga get busted with two rocks and he lookin at fifteen years, as opposed to a white boy getting busted with ten birds and he lookin at five?

These sentencing guidelines are what Plies was talking about when he described the way our criminal justice system works on "100 Years":

> How in the f*ck can four birds get you a life sentence?/ But give a cracker seven years for money launderin' millions/ Shoot a nigga in the leg, they sentence you like you killed 'em/ Cracker catch you wit' that iron and throw you under the buildin'/ You a nigga, that mean you guilty 'til proven innocent

But we know why it's like this, don't we? So why do we keep acting all shocked when they treat us like this?

Like I said, my issue isn't the racism, it isn't the injustice, it's the attitude and mentality that led up to these events. And I don't mean the mentality of the white folks. Like I said, my issue…is you.

Did you know that the party where the Black student was beaten up was a private party. "Private" meaning for who? That's right. It was a party for the white folks. But five Black students came, asking to get in, even after the woman at the door told them they weren't invited. The five boys persisted, saying that their "friends" were already inside. Friends, I bet.

And did you know that, with all the fights between Black and white students, the only thing that kept a full-scale riot from happening was...football? That's right, Jena's high school team was doing better than they ever had, mostly due to the efforts of several star Black players (including Mychal Bell). So the students, Black and white, were trying to avoid chaos so the football team could finish the season. What great school spirit these Black students had! Go team!

Do you see what my issue is yet?

Black people are literally *dying* to be around white people. That "white tree" must have been some special tree. Or maybe it was just the "white" part. For some people of color, it could have been a "white trashcan" and they'd be fighting to eat out of it.

They should have cut that tree down instead of begging to sit under it. They should have burned the high school down instead of waiting to be treated fairly. Oh wait, someone *did* burn that school down! Now, THAT'S who I want to meet! Who I *don't* want to meet are the type of idiots who were at the Jena 6 rallies marching, holding hands with white people, in the name of "love" and "peace" and "unity." That's bullsh*t and we should know it by now. As my brother Self Kingdom Allah said:

> The problem is that too many of us break our necks to be accepted by whites. I keep reading things about how the Jena 6 wanted to sit under the DAMN tree! WHY? F*CK that tree. I am really thinking about getting some shirts made that say "Next Time, Get Your Own Damn Tree." Take it how you want. I do have sympathy for the Jena 6, but the lesson that should be learned is not being spoken on: Let the Devil have his religion, his education and his DAMN tree.
>
> Have we not learned anything from *The Mis-education of the*

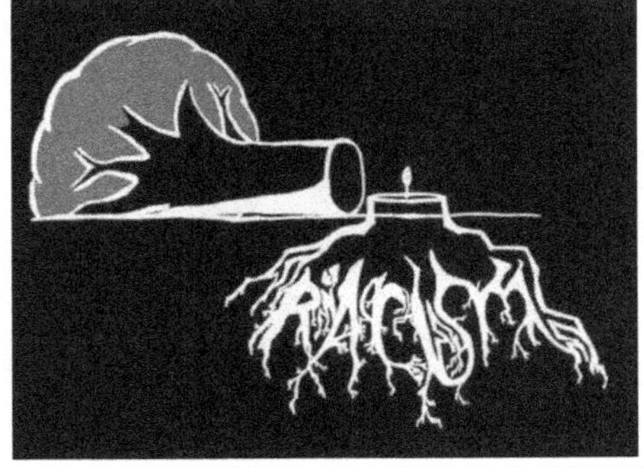

> *Negro*? This sh*t reminds me off Blacks being hit with bricks just to eat at the same diner as white folks. Why? White folk can't cook anyway. If you support the Jena 6, do it for the right reason. Because this could be the snowball that grows to Blacks forcing whites to accept us in their country clubs. DAMN IT MLK, you see what you created? Bottom line, stop crying and dying to be among people who DON'T WANT YOU.

Even Bill Cosby gets it. On a recent visit to Greenwood, Mississippi, the mayor told Cosby about the Black community's past struggle to integrate the Broad Street Pool. Cosby retorted, "Hey man, make your own pool." Even Bill Cosby gets it! And he had the balls to tell it to a Black mayor! So what about you?

> "No negro leaders have fought for civil rights. They have begged for civil rights. They have begged the white man for civil rights. They have begged the white man for freedom. Anytime you beg another man to set you free you'll never be free. Freedom is something that you have to do for yourselves."
> Malcolm X

If someone wants to exclude you, would you rather (a) beg for the chance to join them, (b) fight for the chance to join them, (c) stay separate and build up your own thing, or (d) tear down what's theirs?

Get in where you fit in, or do something about it.

Friends that Hate You

> "An insincere and evil friend is more to be feared than a wild beast. A wild beast may wound your body, but an evil friend will wound your mind."
> The Buddha

Police approached 49-year-old Frankie Brewster's trailer, where she casually sat outside on her makeshift porch. They were responding to an anonymous tip about a woman being held hostage, and asked if anyone was inside. Frankie Brewster responded with an annoyed, "No." As if on cue, a Black woman limped out the front door, crying "Help me, help me." She appeared badly beaten, with swollen black eyes, scattered stab wounds, and patches of her hair torn out.

Investigators learned that the woman, 23-year-old Megan Williams, had been raped at knifepoint in the trailer's filthy bathroom, tied with a cable cord and choked by Frankie Brewster's friend, forced to eat rat sh*t, burned with hot wax by George Messer, 27, and stabbed repeatedly by Brewster's 24-year-old son, Bobby.

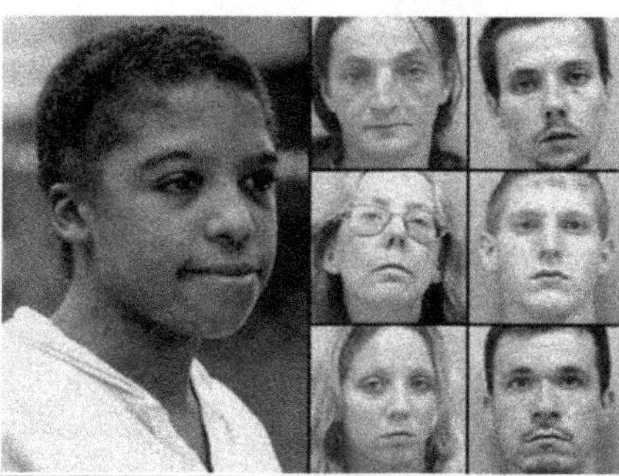

Megan's captors also forced her to lick a female captors' anus, vagina, and toes. They also forced her to lick up blood and urine, most likely her own. As they abused her, her captors told Megan, "That's what we do to niggers around here." In fact, they called her "nigger" every time they stabbed her.

The victim's mother, Carmen Williams, responded with shock and confusion: "I don't understand a human being doing another human being the way they did my daughter. I didn't know there were people like that out here."

Hold the f*ck up. Of course there are people like that out there! How do you live in America and not know that? I'm ashamed that anybody still thinks that events like this are "rare" or "unusual." They're not. But that's not my point, so let's move on.

This was one of the cruelest, sickest crimes to make the news in years. But it received very little coverage. In fact, most people have probably never heard of Megan Williams. But that's not my point either. So let's move on.

Magistrate Leonard Codispoti said, "Something like this is so horrifying it makes you want to puke...They abused her sexually, stabbed her and probably would have killed her if they had not gotten caught. I was told they planned to take her to East Lynn Lake and kill her." But unlike the Black teens charged in the Jena 6 case, there were no attempted murder charges for the 6 attackers!

For example, Bobby Brewster was only charged with kidnapping, sexual assault, malicious wounding and assault during the commission of a felony. But according to the police report, Bobbie Brewster "forced to victim to have sex with him, threatened to kill her, stabbed the victim and forced her to eat rat and dog feces and drink from a toilet bowl." Doesn't that sound more like attempted murder than some Black high schoolers beating up a racist white boy? But that's not my point either. So let's move on.

One major question was: How did she get to the home where she was held hostage and tortured?

According to Megan, a white "friend" named Christa then invited her to a "party" at the Brewsters' trailer. Christa handed her over to her captors knowing that those six people intended to torture her.

When interviewed by the *Final Call*, Megan's mother explained:

> Yes, it was a setup, she left her there. When Megan was in the hospital, Christa called and I answered the phone. Christa was asking, "How is my friend?" I told her that she wasn't a friend of Megan's because she left her. Christa then hung up the phone. We have not seen or heard from Christa since that time.

You've got to be kidding me. *This* is getting closer to my point. Next big question: Did she know the people who tortured her?

Yes. And here's the most twisted part: Police revealed that Megan Williams once had a relationship with captor Bobby Brewster. So federal authorities have decided not to prosecute this as a hate crime. Guess why? Because the victim *dated* one of her attackers in the past.

As said by the victim's father, "People don't realize that people will call themselves your friends but they are not really your friends." How true. And how foolish of us to keep thinking otherwise.

Maybe you know better than to hang around racist rednecks. But what about the company you *do* keep? How good are they for you? Do they push you to be better, or constantly bring out the worst in you?

They say you can judge a man by the company he keeps, and that "birds of a feather flock together." But, many times, one or two of the people in the crowd are just looking for somewhere to belong, and getting caught up in the bullsh*t in the process. Our fear of being alone is a major part of why we get caught up in situations almost as f*cked up as that of poor Megan Williams.

Do you know better than to hang around the kind of "friends" who will one day get you killed?

How can you predict the consequences of the company you keep?

Be careful who you consider your "friends."

MESSAGE TO THE WHITE MAN

If you're white and you're reading this, *wow*. Not because you *bought* a book like this, but *wow* because you've read *this far*. What are you thinking? Is one of these responses yours? And which ones would your white friends respond with?

A. "You're a racist prick, and shame on you for turning what a few misguided white people have done into a reason to hate *all* of us! You're worse than Hitler!"

B. "Man, I knew white people have done some rotten stuff, but I had no idea it was this *consistent*! At least I know I'm nothing like *those* people! I even have a Black girlfriend!"

C. "You're just making all this sh*t up, buddy. I don't believe a word of it. And I'm not going to look it up to prove otherwise, either!"

D. "Aw f*ck man, now I'm just ridden with guilt! I was already all screwy, and now I'm *really* ready to off myself. Thanks a *lot*, asshole!"

E. "You know, instead of focusing so much on what white people have done, why not focus on all the wrong your people are doing right now? You know, Africans started the slave trade, and even today, it's the Black gang members doing most of the killing."

F. "F*ck you!"

When faced with information that makes you uncomfortable, weak-minded people normally respond with an unhealthy response. It's either (A) Reversal, (B) Disassociation, (C) Denial, (D) Depression, (E) Condescension, or (F) Anger. But none of those are necessary. I think what I've been saying makes perfect sense. And while I wasn't expecting it, I've actually had dozens of white people tell me *How to Hustle and Win, Part One* was "life-changing" for them. I'm sure many of you will be challenged and inspired by this book as well. I'm not being dishonest or inflammatory. I'm speaking from the historical record, and there's only a few conclusions you can reasonably draw from that evidence.

Let's face it. Most white people themselves don't even benefit from the oppression enforced upon the globe by the white power structure. As Prodigy rapped, "They don't give a f*ck about they own poor white trash/ Just imagine how they feel about my Black ass." Or better yet, as the Geto Boys challenged on the phenomenal "Eye 4 an Eye":

> We ain't against all white people, but we are against all white people that's against us...You muthaf*ckas are unbelievable! Y'all talkin all that sh*t about "Go back to Africa." You weren't talkin all that sh*t when we was out there in them fields sweatin, pickin that cotton for y'all muthaf*ckin asses. We built this muthaf*cka. We deserve just as much, if not more, prosperity then you hoes do. Angry white men – who the f*ck you angry with? You should be angry with your muthaf*ckin self! Because we don't own corporate America. Y'all do!...Y'all run the muthaf*cka! Y'all took the jobs overseas. You wanna be mad at somebody? Be mad at your goddamned self!

I concur. I ain't against all white people, just the white people who are against me. But if you ain't *actively fighting* on my side, you're on the other side by default. Now, if you're reading *this*, I'm sure you're *very* different from the rest. But it takes a lot – a whole lot – to step outside the bounds of the white supremacist framework. Even many of y'all who think you're enlightened or "liberal" are still passive participants. Whiteness is a social construct rooted in the exclusion and oppression of non-whites. Ever since white folks knew they were white, that's what they've been doing. Now I'm not saying you should lie and start claiming Cherokee blood, but you need to examine the social parameters of your existence. Unless you're totally isolated from the white world and living among some Amazon tribe, you are a part of white society. You can't run from it. It's your gang, and you can't leave it. As Black radical Hubert Harrison said almost a hundred years ago, "As long as the color line exists, all the perfumed protestations of democracy on the part of the white race" are "downright lying." Any fight for "change" ain't bout sh*t if you ain't addressing the root of all social problems: Global white supremacist rule.

So if you think differently, that's also where your work lays. If you are truly against oppression, then worry less about being "down with hiphop" and concern yourself with taking down the oppressor. Where does it start? Among your own, homey. Who have you explained your ideas to lately? How many white folks have you organized? What corporation have you challenged? What charity did you contribute to? What programs have you supported? Was it really about the people? Are you honestly on the side of the oppressed and downtrodden, or are you just looking for something to do?

While you're thinking about it, try reading: Understanding and Dismantling Racism: The Twenty-First Century Challenge to White America by Joseph Barndt, Uprooting Racism: How White People Can Work for Racial Justice by Paul Kivel, The Heart of Whiteness: Confronting Race, Racism and White Privilege by Robert Jensen, and Speaking Treason Fluently: Anti-Racist Reflections from an Angry White Male by Tim Wise.

Everyone can be a part of the same struggle.
But everyone's role will different.

Give and Take

I bet you believe that sometimes we just *win*. Sometimes, we're able to convince the people in power to do right by us, and we get something we really want. Do we really? Have we really ever received anything worth having? If you study history for yourself, you'll see that everytime we were on the verge of forcing the people in power to make a "real" change, we were instead given some other sh*t to pacify us. Then we'd get happy and forget how bad we were doing, high off of hope for a better future. But these illusory blessings would always turn out to be a curse in disguise.

For example, after damn near every white comic book superhero ever made got his own movie, they decided to throw us a bone and give us our first Black superhero on the big screen. But Will Smith, as *Hancock*, had to be a drunk, good-for-nothing asshole who needed – of course – a kind-hearted white man to "fix" him. And this is how it always goes. We think we got something good but they're just pissing on us and telling us its free lemonade. Here are some more important examples:

After...	They gave us...	BUT...
After a rash of slave rebellions, uprisings, runaways, and acts of sabotage because of our resistance to slavery...	They gave us widespread church services to slaves, offering a promising message of hope	BUT this new religion taught the slaves to obey their masters, and wait for heaven after death instead of fighting for change
After a Civil War between the North and South over economic reasons in the 1860s, which threatened to tear the U.S. apart...	They gave us the abolition of slavery in states that seceded, to weaken the South	BUT free slaves soon became poor sharecroppers, while the prison system expanded as a way to reenslave Blacks
After civil disobedience, militant Blacks, and international shock brought attention to the Civil Rights movement in the 60s...	They gave us the Civil Rights Bill, along with school and neighborhood desegregation	BUT Blacks then stopped supporting Black businesses and building Black communities, while our students' education worsened
After Hiphop began earning big money with large audiences in the early 80s...	They gave us major record deals and distribution, as well as radio airtime	BUT they began influencing the content of the music, so the audiences would gradually get dumbed down
After Blacks became interested in home ownership and the lucrative real estate business in the late 90s...	They gave us a significant rise in Black home ownership through easy-to-secure loans	BUT most of the loans were examples of predatory lending, and Blacks suffered worst as the real estate market crashed
After the people backing George W. Bush stole the first election, partly by keeping many Blacks from voting in 2000...	They gave us Condoleeza Rice, the first Black Secretary of State	BUT Rice worked against not only the interests of Blacks, but all Americans, by becoming the international face of the Bush Doctrine
After hundreds of countries throughout the world are at odds with America, even more so since the Bush presidency...	They gave us a Black president, who the world loves, hoping he'll bring about real change in American policy	...Time will tell.

If you think about it, everytime you *think* you're getting something good, it's usually another nicely packaged scam. They say you should look a gift horse in the mouth, but we can't afford not to. As I said in the first lesson of *How to Hustle and Win*, you have to inspect and investigate *everything.*

Have you ever thought you were getting over, only to learn you weren't?

Can you tell when someone who seems to be doing something you a favor is really doing the opposite?

Beware the blessings that are curses in disguise.

WHAT THE IMMIGRANT LEAVES BEHIND

Serbian filmmaker Emir Kusturica once said:

> In Serbia a lot of people hate me because they want to westernize, not understanding that the Western world is bipolar, with very good things and very bad things. Since they don't have experience of the West, they even believe that Western sh*t is pie.

Do you believe American sh*t is pie too? Don't front. You probably do. You probably think America is the best country in the world, even if you don't really like your life here.

When you think about countries in Africa and South America, you think about Black and brown people. But what else do you think? Do you think about the whole place smelling funny? Do you think about babies with skinny legs, big bellies and flies on their faces? (Why can't they swat those damn flies off?) Do you think about AIDS killing everybody? Do you think about primitive people still hunting animals for food, wearing loincloths like it's *Tarzan* or the *Jungle Book*? Do you think about those *National Geographic* specials or episodes of *Bizarre Foods*?

If you've been brainwashed enough, you may even be thinking about cannibals with bones in their noses, cooking people in a big pot while doing an ooga-booga dance…like in those Bugs Bunny cartoons.

Most of it – of course – is lies. It's their way of keeping us from finding out about our own people. In truth, the places I've been to throughout the world have modern cities, big spenders, planes, trains, and automobiles. There are cities and villages, wealthy areas and poor areas. It's just like the U.S., except people in poverty there don't believe they're "hoodrich," "ghetto fabulous," or "doin it big." Only in America, do the poor people get to be fat and download ringtones all day. Sure, there's some spots in other countries that stink because of the open sewers, but there's plenty of intersections in the U.S. where you can smell the sewer as well, not to mention all of our factory fumes. So get over yourself.

> **Did You Know?**
> Although it may seem gross to watch tribal societies eat strange foods, "bizarre foods" aren't as rare as you think. Many primitive Europeans drank blood. Ancient Romans used human urine as an ingredient in their toothpaste. And even today, insect secretions are used in making many popular American candies.

But if you've grown up thinking lowly of people on the other side of the water, you're not alone, unfortunately. Most people coming here from those other countries don't think very highly of Black people either. That includes Black Africans, Black Arabs, and even Black-ass Indians with straight hair.

But it's not their fault. They've been conditioned. First, their only exposure to Blacks in America was when they turned on CNN to see Black people wanted for crimes, turned on MTV to see 50 Cent and Ja Rule pretending to be thugs, or turned on an American movie to see all of the above, plus the coons on MadTV makin fools of themselves for white people's amusement. And that's all they knew. And they thought it was true. They figured, "Well, if Black people weren't really like that, they'd *never* let those lies get on TV." If they only knew.

Then they get here and guess what? They get conditioned some more. My parents were immigrants and they can tell you themselves that they were taught, almost as soon as they touched down, about who and what to avoid. And guess "who" are the main people to avoid?.

"From Englewood to a single hood in Botswana
I see the 'I' in 'We' my nigga, yours is my drama"
Common, "The People"

But now that you understand why people from other countries may look at you funny, I want you to remember that we are all one people. We've been torn apart and made to fight and hate each other, but we are one. Matter fact, you should go out and talk to someone from another country. If you don't know where to look, try a gas station.

Did You Know?

According to the book *America in Black and White*, the average Polish immigrant family made $41,943 a year. Not bad. The average Irish immigrant family income: $38,022. The average Cuban immigrant family income: $37,452. Looks like the numbers go down as the melanin goes up. What about Mexicans? $26,766. And that leaves American-born Blacks at dead last, making a median family income of $20,209.

When you do meet someone you can talk to, you may be surprised by some of the things you learn.

First, many immigrants are people who had money back in their home country. That's how they were able to come over and get in. That's also why they don't share the same views as the poor people of their country. While the poor want revolution and unity, the wealthy only want to make more money and enjoy American luxuries. Depending on what kind of background an immigrant comes from, he may end up bein down with you.

Second, even the poorest countries have one thing in common: They value family and traditions. Whether you're in Mexico or Zimbabwe, you'll see that everyone does what they can to help out. The young take care of the old, and entire families may live together in one home for several generations. However, Western influence is gradually changing all that, which is why some countries don't allow American TV.

Third, immigrants may come over in pursuit of the American Dream, but they often want to go back home. The reason is because America may have air-conditioning, strip clubs, and small business loans, but it is nothing like the places our ancestors come from. In America, you have to look over your shoulder everywhere you go. You can't even trust your family and friends. You can't depend on anyone to keep their word. And life here is not about family and tradition. It's about "making it," no matter whom you've got to step on to get there. And if you've ever been somewhere like Africa, South America, or Asia, you'll know how cold people here are, by comparison. That's why many immigrants choose to live among each other instead of trying to mix in with the white folks. They just can't go back home because their people back home depend on the good money they are sending from America.

It's true that the countries where Black, brown and yellow people live are mostly poor. They aren't jungles, but they aren't Chicago either. Then again, there are some parts of the Chi that remind me of the slums of India, but you get the picture. So we think we've got it made, because we're not stuck in hot-ass Africa without A/C and cable TV (both of which you can actually get in most major African cities). Meanwhile, Africans are thinking that America is a place where everybody can get rich, and life is great.

But as a wise man named Bushwick Bill said on the Geto Boys' "The World is a Ghetto":

> They call my neighbourhood a jungle/ And me an animal, like they do the people in Rwanda/ Fools fleeing their countries to come here, Black/ But see the same bullsh*t and head right back/ They find out what others already know/ The world is a ghetto

Immigrants get here, and learn quickly what they left behind. Ask any immigrant and they'll tell you. That's what inspired me to go to places like Ghana, Mexico, or Thailand. I've seen what they have – that we don't. Even if you can't go there, try talking to someone and learning what we left behind. You're realize that no matter how much you think you've got, you're missing a lot.

There are poverties worse than financial poverty. You can be poor in health, short on true friends, or just have a broke-ass spirit. But I'd rather be low on funds and high off life than rich and miserable any day.

True wealth is having a community of people who will take care of you, not a collection of material things to take care of.

The Wall: America in Black and White

"'We can change' – What ya mouths say
I'm watchin niggas work their lives out without pay

> Whatever it takes to switch places wit the bustas on top
> I'm bustin' shots to make the world stop
> They don't give a f*ck about us"
> Tupac Shakur, "They Don't Give a F*ck About Us"

In Palestine, thousands of miles from America, Yusuf Sharadi is up at 5 am, waiting in a long line with his fellow countrymen. But these poor men aren't waiting for food. They're waiting for work. They want to be selected to work for the white people of Israel to build their settlement. But the Israelis aren't building on Israeli land anymore. Now they are building further and further into land in Palestine. They want to occupy all of the holy land that the Jews occupied in the Bible. So they have pushed millions of Palestinians out of their homes, which has resulted in the battles you may see on CNN. Palestinians boys throwing rocks at tanks, while Israeli troops fire missiles into Palestinian communities.

But Yusuf's family has little money. Business is bad, and he can't find a job at home. So today, he is line to help build up the wall. The wall that keeps Palestinians out of their own land. This land is now occupied by armed Israelis. Today, Yusuf will help build the wall that keeps him out.

How different are we from Yusuf? Trapped between two worlds, Yusuf must make a decision that many of us would think is stupid. But we may not be that different. As Jay-Z raps on his mixtape cut "Young, Gifted, and Black," Black and white America are two different worlds:

> I'm America's worst nightmare/ I'm young, Black, and holdin my nuts like, "Gyeah"/ While y'all was in the pub, havin a light beer/ I was in the club, havin a fight there/ Y'all could go home, husband and wife there/ My mama at work, tryin to buy me the right gear/ Nine years old, uncle lost his life here/ I grew up thinkin life ain't fair/ How can I get a real job? China white right there/ Right in front of my sight like, "Here" Yeah/ There's your ticket out the ghetto, take flight right there/ Sell me, you go bye-bye here/ Damn, there's a different set of rules we abide by here/ You need a gun, niggas might drive-by here/ Y'all havin fun, racin all your hot rods there/ Downloadin all our music on your Ipods there/ I'm Chuck D, standin in the crosshairs here/ Y'all straight, chicks got horsehair here/ Y'all aint gotta be in fear of your bosses there/ You lose your job, your Pop rich, y'all don't care/ So I don't care, y'all actin like y'all don't hear/ All the screams from the ghetto, all the teens duckin metal here/ So they steam like a kettle here/ Tryin to take their mind to a whole different level here/ Yeah, we real close to the devil here/Gotta be a better way, somebody call a reverend here/ Yeah, y'all must really be in heaven there/ Somebody tell God that we got a couple questions here/ My lil cuz never got to see his seventh year/ And I'm so used to pain that I ain't even shed a tear…

Jay was on to something. But how different are our two worlds really? Do you have an idea? How much do you know about the other side? How much do you know about how big the gap is between our worlds?

Employment

I bet you already know that it's harder for a Black man to get a job than a white man. But people have done studies to prove just how hard it really is. When researchers sent out identical resumes to employers, they used two different names for each resume. One group had typically Black names like "Rashid" and "Diante" while the other group – with the same education and qualifications – had white names like "Prentice" and "Zachary." Guess which resumes got calls back? That's why Black leaders pushed for affirmative action, to help Black people get into jobs (and into school) in spite of racism. But did you know affirmative action actually benefits more white women than Black people? Either way, affirmative action is on its way out now, because white people are tired of letting Black people in!

Government Assistance

"They done even managed to modernize slavery
They clonin little babies, these people goin crazy
And white America's on high alert
Black America's still starvin and livin in public housin
You still eatin off your food stamps
That's why one out of every three Black boys end up in boot camp"
Trick Daddy, "The Children's Song"

Did you know there are more white people on welfare than Black people? In fact, welfare was started to help white single mothers. Also, there are many forms of welfare that are very different from the kind Black people usually experience, complete with the project housing and government cheese. One example is the kind where middle-class white families are allowed to keep their house and their current standard of living, which gets paid for by the government. Another form is corporate welfare, where million-dollar companies are given tax-breaks and other funding from the government, whether they are making money or not. In the end, the money that goes to Black people for welfare is nothing compared to the money we spend on our big corporations (or our military).

Crime and Punishment

"White cop acquitted for murder, Black cop cop a plea
That type of sh*t make me stop and think
We in chronic need of a second look at the law books
And the whole race dichotomy"
Nas, "America"

If you watch the news, you would actually think Black people commit more crime. But just as with welfare, there's also two kinds of crime. Blue Collar crime refers to the kinds of crimes poor people commit, like armed robbery, drug dealing, and pickpocketing. White Collar crime refers to the type of crimes committed by people who wear suits and ties. That means money laundering, embezzlement, fraud, and corporate theft. And guess which kind of crimes get the lightest sentences, and the nicest prisons? As Plies says, "How in the f*ck can four birds get you a life sentence?/ But give a cracker seven years for money launderin' millions?" Of course, there are also disparities with sentencing even when whites and Blacks commit the same crimes.

Education

You may think the differences are between public schools and private schools. But in a book titled *Savage Inequalities* by Jonathan Kozol, he describes the differences between public schools in poor Black communities and public schools in nearby white communities. In one word, it was "savage." But we know the school system wasn't even meant to educate Black people. Ever since they let Blacks into white schools, we ain't been learnin sh*t. That's why every high school in the hood has 1,000 or more freshman, and about 100 seniors. That means about 900 out of 1,000 didn't make it. That's why America loves people like Joe Clark, who became famous for kicking poor Black and Hispanic kids out of his high school. I could go on and on, but if you read the rest of the book, you'll get the picture.

Money, Money, Money...

Man if I gotta explain this one to you, you must need medication to stay focused. We probably all know that when people say they're tryin to "keep up with the Jones," the Jones must be some white family. Not only do poor Black people live worse than poor white people, but even middle class Blacks have it worse than middle class whites. We get sh*tted on when it's time to buy a house, when it's time to take out a loan, when we get paid at work, man just about everything is worse. And that's not just some angry rhetoric. I went to grad school remember? All the sh*t I'm sayin is based off facts and statistics!

Oh, and rich Black people aren't doin too much better. Rich Blacks don't enjoy the same freedoms as rich whites, and get discriminated against almost as badly. When millionaire entrepreneur Farrah Gray takes his seat in first class, flight attendants question whether he should be in coach. Police have stopped him for no justifiable reason. And Gray, who become a millionaire by the age of 14, recently settled out of court with a national drug store chain, where an employee grabbed him and turned him over to a security officer. The employee accused Gray of stealing cookies that had actually been given to him by the general manager of a radio station. That should tell you that just "coming up" in this game won't make life lovely. We've got to change the game, since ain't none of us REALLY winning. After all, if Bill Gates woke up one day and found out he only had Oprah money, he'd jump off a building.

The Big Picture

Throughout history, people like W.E.B. Du Bois have written about how much Black people have contributed to building this country. Really, this country would be nothing without us. At the same time, we don't enjoy any of the benefits of this place! After all, this place wasn't made FOR us…it was just made BY us. And guess who spends the most money on white America? Black America. We're no different from Yusuf, helping to build the system that destroys us…but at least Yusuf isn't doing it just to put rims on his Escalade. And as America moves on, Mexicans are now being done the same way. One day – hopefully – we'll all wake up and understand the wall we're building.

(Suggested Reading: *Marked: Race, Crime, and Finding Work in an Era of Mass Incarceration* by Devah Pager; *Felony Disenfranchisement in America: Historical Origins, Institutional Racism, and Modern Consequences* by Katherine Irene Pettus; *Black Labor, White Wealth: The Search for Power and Economic Justice* by Claud Anderson; *The Shame of the Nation: The Restoration of Apartheid Schooling in America* by Jonathan Kozol; *The Hidden Cost of Being African American: How Wealth Perpetuates Inequality* by Thomas M. Shapiro; and *The American Dream and the Power of Wealth: Choosing Schools and Inheriting Inequality in the Land of Opportunity* by Heather Beth Johnson)

We don't all live in the same world.
Our circumstances create our realities.

RACE RIOTS

Throughout America, most white people refused to live next door to Black people until after the 1940s. (see "O.P.P.") Until then, even though many Black people were poor, they were often able to build successful Black communities without the help of white people. They had Black schools which were able to produce geniuses and scholars, even though they had raggedy books and one-room shacks for schoolhouses. They provided services for each other, in place of money. And they protected each other.

In many cities, these Black communities became prosperous and powerful. Seeing Black communities growing like this made a lot of people very angry. That's when the race riots began.

"Like men we'll face the murderous, cowardly pack/ Pressed to the wall, dying, but fighting back!"
Claude McKay, "If We Must Die" (1919)

Lynchings and so-called race riots went hand in hand. I say "so-called" because these weren't spontaneous acts where everyone – Black and white – just went nuts. Typically, white mobs drove into the streets looking to spill Black blood after reading or hearing reports of Black men raping white women. In fact, there was usually no evidence of a rape having occurred, and the Black men in question were usually targeted because of their success and power.

Ida B. Wells-Barnett discovered that these bogus rape charges covered up consensual sex between Black men and white women. As with Kobe Bryant and so many others, it was actually the white women who actively pursued the Black men.

Wilmington, North Carolina (1898)

After white Democrats used inflammatory lies about Black men raping white women to draw white voters out en masse, they went even further to secure their win against the opposition supported by Black voters. Stuffing the ballot boxes with bogus votes, they stole the election from Black voters, who had turned out in record numbers. Afterwards, as if to celebrate victory, white men, many of them bankers, lawyers, merchants, and clergymen, formed vicious mobs and attacked Blacks.

Atlanta, Georgia (1906)

After local newspapers, including major papers still in publication today, boasted of lynchings and called for a revival of the Ku Klux Klan, a series of fabricated reports of Black men assaulting white women were published.

On September 22nd, thousands of whites from both the city and surrounding rural areas gathered in downtown Atlanta and began randomly attacking innocent Blacks. This happened in and near Auburn Ave., which once held slave auctions, but was now hosting more and more Black businesses. The Atlanta Race Riot ended three days later, with a total of 25 Blacks brutally murdered and hundreds of others seriously injured.

Did You Know?

The victims of race riots weren't limited exclusively to Blacks? Throughout American history, white mobs have attacked Hispanic communities, Indian communities, east Asian communities, Jewish communities, and - of course - Native Americans. For one example, try Googling "dotbusters" (not "Ghostbusters") to learn about white mob violence against east Indian immigrants.

Fifty years later, the Sweet Auburn District was rebuilt and became the wealthiest Black business district in the country.

Springfield, Illinois (1908)

A white woman accused a Black man of beating her to avoid admitting that it had really been a white man who had beat her. The ensuing violence led to deaths and injuries, but more significantly forced hundreds of Black residents to flee the city. This is another unstudied factor in how the racial makeup on many cities changed.

East St. Louis, Illinois (1917)

An aluminum plant facing a strike by its workers decided to hire Black workers. White trade unionists demanded that this be stopped, and that Blacks stop being allowed to move into the city altogether. Soon, a rumor was being circulated that a Black man had insulted white women and shot a white man in the subsequent altercation. White mobs then took to the streets and headed straight for the Black neighborhoods, where they began shooting into homes indiscriminately. 300 homes and buildings were destroyed, dozens were killed, hundreds were injured, and 6,000 Black people fled the city.

Various Cities (1919)

There were significan't race riots in Longview, Texas; Chicago, Illinois; Knoxville, Tennessee; Omaha, Nebraska; Elaine, Arkansas; and several more cities throughout the U.S. At least 26 race riots occurred in the summer of this year, earning it the name "the Red Summer of 1919." In every case, Blacks actively fought back against their white attackers but were quickly outnumbered.

Tulsa, Oklahoma (1921)

The Greenwood area of Tulsa, Oklahoma was known as the Black Wall Street of America for its many prosperous Black businesses and wealthy Blacks. When a jailed Black man was to be lynched by a mob of 2,000 whites for allegedly sexually assaulting a white woman, a group of armed Black men showed up to protect him. What followed was total chaos. The frenzied white mob went into the streets attacking innocent Blacks, soon overwhelming the Black Wall Street area and burning it down to the ground. According to Ron Wallace's *Black Wall Street: A Lost Dream*:

> The night's carnage left some 3,000 African Americans dead, and over 600 successful businesses lost. Among these were 21 churches, 21 restaurants, 30 grocery stores and two movie theaters, plus a hospital, a bank, a post office, libraries, schools, law offices, a half-dozen private airplanes and even a bus system...[In this community] the dollar circulated 36 to 1,000 times, sometimes taking a year for currency to leave the community. Now in 1995, a dollar leaves the Black community in 15 minutes...It was a time when the entire state of Oklahoma had only two airports, yet six blacks owned their own planes. It was a very fascinating community. The area encompassed over 600 businesses and 36 square blocks with a population of 15,000 African Americans. And when the lower-economic Europeans looked over and saw what the Black community created, many of them were jealous.

Did You Know?

On June 13, 2005, the majority of the U.S. Senate formally apologized for the Senate's failure to pass on almost 200 anti-lynching bills that came before it over the past several decades. During the recorded history of lynching in America, there have been at least 4,749 known victims. Not surprisingly, however, the apology was not unanimous. More than a dozen white senators, particularly those from the South, refused to co-sponsor the apology, even as almost 200 Black descendants of victims looked on from the visitor's gallery.

Amazingly, the Blacks of Greenwood, relying only upon their own resources and each other, were able to rebuild Black Wall Street, supplying the idea for The Game's record label of the same name.

When you hear about riots though, what do you think about? Probably a mob of wild Black folks tearing up their own communities, huh? In reality, the first riots involving people of color involved rabid mobs of whites attacking innocents. Their goal wasn't just to inflict harm, but to destroy strong communities and terrorize residents into fleeing. In fact, there were dozens of "Sundown Towns" throughout this country where whites told Black residents they'd have to move by sundown...or else. This is how a lot of cities became mostly white, and how other cities became even more segregated than they once were. What made these white folks so mad? They were scared of being outdone. Poor whites were outraged at the growing prosperity of their former slaves. These Blacks were doing then what you COULD be doing now...only maybe, by now, they've scared you out of it.

Beyond race riots alone, there's a lot more to the history of the "racial cleansing" of American towns. Here's some books you can check out on the topic: *Sundown Towns: A Hidden Dimension of American Racism* by James W. Loewen, *Driven Out: The Forgotten War against Chinese Americans* by Jean Pfaelzer, and *Buried in the Bitter Waters: The Hidden History of Racial Cleansing in America* by Elliot Jaspin.

People of color don't need outside help to be successful with each other...but when you do things your way, be ready to defend yourself.

MOVIE TO SEE

Rosewood

John Singleton's 1997 film *Rosewood* covers the terrible violence that, once again, followed reports from a white woman that she had been attacked by an unidentified Black man. For over two weeks, homes and churches were burnt down, hundreds of Blacks were killed or forced to flee into the swamps for safety. When the 1923 Rosewood race riot was over, a grand jury was assembled to investigate but said they could not move forward, due to "insufficient evidence."

O.P.P. (OTHER PEOPLE'S PROPERTY)

The Hustle

14-year old Reginald had been invited over by some of the boys in the neighborhood to play outside. The three boys who invited him over, Kaeshawn, Gerald, and Tay, were all his age, but they'd grown up very different. While Reginald had recently moved down to Atlanta from a much nicer town up north, the three others had lived in southwest Atlanta since birth. Once Reginald pulled up in his brand new mountain bike, the boys convinced him to come into Tay's backyard to pick peaches from a large tree. As the four boys climbed, laughed, and picked fruit together, Reginald grew thirsty. He decided to go and buy drinks for himself and his new friends. He returned to the front porch to get his bike. It was gone.

Reginald never realized how he'd been scammed. A month later, he saw Kaeshawn riding a bike that looked identical to the one he lost. Somehow, Kaeshawn *still* convinced him it wasn't his. Reginald continued being a sucker for years to come.

Would you fall for such a simple scam?

What if I told you that we're getting suckered this way as we speak?

Read the next section to see how the game works.

The Move and Remove Game

"White flight" refers to what happens when too many Blacks (or others) move into white communities, and whites respond by moving out.

Question: What percentage of Black neighbors does it take to cause "white flight"?

A. 8%　　**B.** 20%　　**C.** 35%　　**D.** 50%

I'll help you out. The answer is the seventh letter in the word "integration." With that said, let me break down how the whole game works:

Thinking life will be better, Black families who have some money move into nice white neighborhoods. ➾
White people start selling their houses at rock-bottom prices to move away from the Black people as quickly as possible. ➾
More Black people start moving in, including poor people attracted to the low house prices. ➾
The Black neighborhood's property values drop even more, and the city stops caring about the neighborhood because it is mostly Black now. ➾
These neighborhoods are called "inner city" by white people who don't want to call them "ghettoes." ➾
Black families live in poor neighborhoods in the "inner city," which are now full of drugs, crime, and failing schools. ➾
Black people who have made some money want to move out of the inner city, and into the nice white neighborhoods in the suburbs right outside the city. ➾
The white people in the suburbs flee again, this time to the suburbs even further out. ➾
Black people follow them again, thinking life will be better. ➾
Once enough Black people have moved out of the "inner city" into first-tier and second-tier suburbs, white people start buying up houses in the Black neighborhoods for almost nothing. ➾
White families start moving back into the "inner city" and begin rebuilding the area. ➾
The "inner city" is renamed "downtown living" and the houses there sell for millions. ➾
Game Over. You Lose. Player 2 Wins.

Trying to join the crowd that beat you isn't going to make your life better. Trying to do so, you often lose more than you gain.

Gentrification

Gentrification: One group of people moving into a community by displacing another group of people.

The examples of Atlanta and Tulsa show us that Black people were not only able to build strong Black communities without outside help, but they were also able to rebuild them. However, since the 1940s, as Blacks started moving their families into white neighborhoods, things have changed. As soon as the Black people began moving in, white people began running for the suburbs. This is called "white flight."

Soon, "inner cities" across America were mostly Black...and poor. Black communities and business areas like Auburn Ave. had fallen apart because Black people had wanted to be around white people more than each other. But when white people ran off to the suburbs, no one woke up and figured out that white people didn't want to be around them! So Black people followed again, and moved into the suburbs. Whites then ran even further. Black people moved out even further again, hoping for a better life and better schools, wherever the white folks were.

Finally, white people saw that enough Black people had left the "inner cities," so they moved back. With only poor Black people left, many of them living in government housing, all the white people had to do was tear down the projects and offer Section 8 housing in the suburbs. Now all the white people could move back and regain control of their cities.

This is called "gentrification." It's a dirty game.

And right now, if you live in a Black community in the "inner city," I bet there are white people slowly trickling in, buying up cheap houses.

And if you live in a predominantly white community, I bet there are more and more people of color moving out the inner city into your area.

They just want the power (over us, but away from us). We just want to be up under them. We just don't get it, do we?

**Don't keep thinking it's better with others,
when you could be *making* it better among your own.**

Policing Our Own

Bat Patrol

"Splash!" Two Atlanta police officers driving along a river in Atlanta heard the sounds of something large being dropped into the water. When they went back to investigate, they found the bodies of two young Black males.

In July of 1980, Atlanta police announced that they had linked the murders of the two males, Nathaniel Cater, and Jimmy Ray Payne. By that time, eleven Black children had disappeared or were found slain.

Over a 22-month period beginning in 1979, the bodies of 28 young Black males were found, most of them strangled to death. The serial murders soon became known as the "Atlanta child murders."

Blacks in Atlanta were panic-stricken. While the government pledged to find the killer, the murders continued. So local people began organizing to police the community themselves.

The Guardian Angels, a group of New York citizens who patrolled the streets and subways of their city to deter crime, came down to Atlanta to teach local youths how to defend themselves. Local school principals gave students whistles to wear around their necks in case they were snatched up. Muhammad Ali donated $400,000, and hundreds of thousands more were given by other athletes and celebrities. Most of this money went towards the investigation, local organizations involved in the hunt for the killer, or directly to the families of the victims.

Most importantly, a vigilante group of Blacks armed with baseball bats formed a "Bat Patrol" in the Techwood housing projects to protect Black children. Other vigilante groups sprang up in Black neighborhoods across Atlanta and formed patrols and watches. Rather than waiting for the police to stop a killer, Black people rose up and decided to defend their own communities.

Where is the Bat Patrol in your neighborhood?

Policing the Police

Speaking of policing the criminals in your community, what about the crooked cops? If we truly had community control, we wouldn't need ANY kind of cops in our communities (see "Lessons on Resistance: Jamaica"). We damn sure wouldn't need the kind of cops who come from redneck towns and suburbs *outside* of our communities, who look at our people as animals, and who see their jobs as a chance to "lock away a few more niggers." (If they don't kill them first, that is)

In some neighborhoods, police don't even come unless they're 50 deep, because the residents are known to band together and resist *aggressively*, flippin over their squad cars or pourin garbage cans full of bricks onto their windshields. But there's much more legitimate ways to deal with the police, even the corrupt ones. Working together, Black people can protect their own communities, from every type of criminal. As the Black Panther Party said in their Self-Defense Platform:

> We want an immediate end to POLICE BRUTALITY and MURDER of black people. We believe we can end police brutality in our black community by organizing black self-defense groups that are dedicated to defending our black community from racist police oppression and brutality. The second Amendment to the Constitution of the United States gives us a right to bear arms. We therefore believe that all black people should arm themselves for self-defense.

Did You Know?

In 1982, Wayne Williams, 23, was convicted of the murders of Cater and Payne, and sentenced to two consecutive life sentences. Until John Allen Muhammad, the infamous DC Sniper (another suspicious case), Wayne Williams was known as the first, and only, major Black serial killer. But popular opinion - and the evidence - says that Wayne Williams was framed. An extensive Georgia Bureau of Investigation (GBI) file containing crucial information about the possible role of the Ku Klux Klan was not released and was subsequently destroyed. The fraud was so obvious that parents of 14 of the victims asked the Justice Department to reopen the case, and look into the KKK's involvement. Charles Sanders, an active member of the KKK, told a police informant that the Klan was trying to begin a race war by killing Black children. Although Williams was convicted in 1982, children and adults were still being abducted and murdered in Atlanta - in the same pattern - until at least 1989. Wayne Williams remains behind bars, swearing his innocence.

How to Shoot a Cop

But everyone doesn't need to arm themself. On YouTube, you can find a video series titled "How to Shoot a Cop." It sounds crazy until you realize that they're talking about shooting them with a camera. In fact, since the videotaped Rodney King beating, groups like Copwatch have popped up all over the country. Their mission: To deter police misconduct by routinely filming police in action. You can even see a documentary titled *Copwatch: These Streets Are Watching* free at www.supremedesignonline.com. Oh, and in case you're illiterate, I'll repeat: I am *not* telling you to shoot *guns* at police officers.

Citizen's Review Board

Another recent development in many cities, especially since the shooting of an elderly woman in her Atlanta home by corrupt cops, is the Citizen's Review Board. Here, local community members can report misconduct and participate in reviews of police activity. It's called community involvement, if you ain't heard of it. Go try you some.

If someone in your community rapes a woman or molests a child, what will happen to them, if anything?

If the police abuse someone in your community, what will be done, if anything?

Black people don't need outside help to police their communities.

The Good Foot

Put yourself in the following scenario: You've just moved into a new neighborhood. Every time you pass this one house on the way to your house, it seems like there's always the same half-dozen ex-convicts, hot girls, and dopeboys hangin out in the front yard. On your way to the grocery store today, you're about to pass them again when you notice they're having a ghetto-ass outdoor barbecue. Same goons, same girls, same bad-ass kids running out into the street. What do you do?

A. Keep driving. Don't even look their way.
B. Drive past, but nod your head, and throw up the peace sign.
C. Stop your car and tell someone it's dangerous to let those kids run into the street.
D. Stop your car and ask if you can grab a case of beers and come hang out for a minute.

Now here's what happens, depending on the choice you made:

A: You keep driving, looking straight forward, so you miss the gestures of some of the older women who are attempting to invite you over. When you ignore big mama, you've just disrespected the entire clan. Since you're apparently not f*ckin with them, they're not f*ckin with you. Two months later, when someone's broken into your house and taken everything, they knew who was planning it before it happened. But they never talked him out of it, because you're nobody to them.

B: You nod to the crowd and show a gesture of good will. Many of them do the same. Some of the others, especially the more hardened teenagers, are like "Who the f*ck is that?" One of the boys actually wonders if you were motioning to his girlfriends, who is insanely jealous and insecure about. He can't tell what exactly you meant, so he decides to take it the wrong way. The next time you pass, he throws a rock at your car.

C: You decide to be a good Samaritan, and "teach" somebody the "right way." Isn't that what this book pushes you to do? Right. So you stop the car, step out, and educate your neighbors on the dangers of letting their children "run wild," as you say it. The women look offended, the men's stares are cold enough to freeze the Sudan, and you realize you've just insulted everyone. Turns out you have to first understand the people you want to help. Now you're trying to figure out how to save face, so you make a joke. But your joke only offends the crowd more. Someone you don't see mumbles, "Get the f*ck outta here," and you realize it's your cue to say goodbye. From this day forward, nobody gets out of the street when you're trying to drive through.

D: You stop the car, ask whether the barbecue is a family-only type of event, and explain that you're their neighbor. They respond that they've seen you plenty of times and thought you were too good to speak. Now that you've proven that's not the case, you're certainly welcome to bring some beer over and partake in the festivities. They laugh at your choice of beer when you return, but they treat you like family nonetheless. After all, you're the neighbor. The kids are still "running wild," the teenagers are either ignoring you or eyeing you suspiciously, but the folks drinking your beer think you're all right. And the more you tell them about how difficult your move has been, more and more of them offer to help somehow. From this point on, you have a new set of friends you can count on. Two months later, when someone is planning to rob your house, your neighbors tell them not to. "That's good people. You get those uppity-ass niggas across the street instead," they tell him.

The choices we make, and the paths we take, decide the kind of lives we live from day to day. You have only a few seconds to make a first impression, so be careful that you're not setting off bad relationships instead of good ones. It only takes a little bit of effort, a few friendly words, and a decent show of respect to get others to see you in a positive light. The next time you pass a group of people you normally don't speak to, talk to them. It will make all the difference in the world, though you may have never known it.

In any new relationship, do you take the necessary steps to start things out on the good foot? Are you good at introducing yourself?

Do you know how to make a good first impression...with *any* audience?

Start off every relationship the right way.

I Know What You're Afraid Of

Are you scared of white people?

Now I don't know if there's a criteria for whether someone qualifies as a "thug" or not, but it seems like anybody can say they are one. No application process, no background check, no five-day waiting period. Instant thugs. A true "thug," "goon," or "gangsta" is supposed to be someone who is fearless. Well, I don't know if they're not afraid, or they're actually more afraid than the rest of us.

Even "Monster Kody" Scott admitted, "The thing is that I was afraid [when I joined the gang]. Most bangers are. You don't want to be a victim, so you join up with something that's powerful for protection." Hmm. So maybe things ain't what they seem. And perhaps some of us really don't give a fuck, and *are* completely fearless. But I'll let you know what almost all thugs, gangstas, and even pro-Black revolutionary-type folks are equilaterally scared to death of: **white people**.

I'll explain. I've been dealing with investments and big business for quite some time now. A few years ago, I went through an experience I'd just seen in the movie *Empire*. (See "Movie to See: Empire")

The story begins when a white boy (who I thought owned a lawn-care firm) took a $1200 deposit from me to replant my front lawn. But after he killed my existing grass, he disappeared. I was dumb-struck. I looked him up on the Better Business Bureau website (www.bbb.org), and it turned out he'd done this to a lot of people. I was just about to go guerilla on him (not GO-rilla), when I had a moment of conscience. I hesitated because...and I hate to admit this, but it's a fact for many of us...he was white.

But only a few months before this experience, I'd gone to *war* with some guys from my neighborhood over a break-in and some missing cash. Serious jail-time sh*t over less than a thousand dollars. I can't even count how many felonies got committed in one night alone.

But that's not what happened with the lawnboy. Why? Why are we, as dead prez rapped, "quick to retaliate when the enemy us"? At the end of "So Long," David Banner says:

> I think for the most part our generation is filled with a bunch of motherf*cking cowards. And I say that, man, cause we beef with amongst each other, we kill and we shoot each other in our own hoods, and we bang each other. But we won't bang on the cops, you know what I'm sayin? And one thing these motherf*ckers in America know – they know we won't do sh*t…I don't understand if you don't ride for something, dog. Fight for something, fight anybody but your motherf*cking self, nigga! We sell drugs, but we only sell drugs to ourself. We bang and we only bang on ourselves. We do every f*cking negative thing and niggas is so hard – Niggas on the radio, on videos, on tapes, in movies – They got guns, they got pistols, but ain't nobody shooting at nothing but they self.

But it's deeper than the police. It's the white power structure in general…and anything that's a facet of it, including the police. Just think about it. We don't start sh*t with the white-owned businesses that treat us like dirt. We don't harass white men dating Black women (we harass the women). And for those who think that Black people actually perpetuate racism against whites, we really don't do too much besides talk shit and call them "cracka" (And that's a name that white people came up with!). Like Ludacris' character said in the movie *Crash*:

> The man [Mo Fat] steals from Black people. Only reason Black people steal from their own is 'cause they terrified of white people. Think about it. Sherman Oaks. Burbank. Santa Monica. All scary-ass places for a brother to find himself. Drop Mo Fat at a Starbucks in Toluca Lake, that nigger will run like a rabbit, soon as somebody say "decaf latte."

Scared of what? The posh poodles? The fancy silverware? Yup. Anything unfamiliar. But more than anything else, too many white folks.

Many of us are still intimidated by white people socially, intellectually, economically…damn near every way except sexually and athletically. I think all people of color experience this phenomenon. But involuntary minorities like Blacks and Hispanics don't have an effective way to cope with anxieties about white people, while other minorities just attempt to think and act like white people to avoid any cultural conflict.

> "Black men will kill each other because they have not yet chosen to challenge and neutralize on every front the widespread power of white men to rule over their lives."
> Amos N. Wilson

Think about it. In most Black neighborhoods, white people can buy cheap homes, then walk their dogs and roam freely, jogging around in their little booty shorts and all. And in the most gang-ridden, crime-infested hood! But let a young Black person from another neighborhood come through uninvited. He's in danger. If I'm lying, let me know.

> "Some say they expect Illuminati [to] take my body to sleep
> [But] niggas at the party with they shotties, just as rowdy as me
> Before I flee computer chips, I gotta deal with brothas flippin
> I don't see no devils bleedin' – Only Black blood drippin"

Tupac Shakur, "They Don't Give a F*ck About Us"

So back to the lawn guy. I found his address, but I knew nobody would drive me out there. Just imagine me asking, "Hey, can you ride me out to West Lynchville to go do a kick-door on this white guy? You can stay in the car if you'd like." I didn't think that would go over well. Imagine the news headline: "Heroes fight back: Five gang members shot by dozens of police and local civilians after attempting to kidnap and rape local church-going family." No thanks.

I finally had an idea. White people are scared of jail. Why? Cause they're finally the minority in there! So I left a voicemail for the guy (who had long ago stopped taking my calls), telling him I'd taken out a warrant for his arrest for fraud. I was bluffing, but he called back almost instantly. He begged me to cancel the warrant, pleading, "Please. I've never been in any trouble before!" I bet! Because he probably only scammed Black people who would just get mad and give up without a fight.

Within two days, he'd mailed off a check for the refund (plus some), and I was victorious. But I learned something about myself, and about a lot of us. The question I asked myself, and the question you should ask, is: Are you scared of white people? Cause a lot of thugs and revolutionaries don't REALLY stand up to nothin.

You can't be tough in one circle and a punk in another.

Movie to See (Kinda)

Empire

Although it's relevant to this story, *Empire* ain't exactly one of my favorite flicks. To begin, it had gay-ass John Leguizamo (who had just played a drag queen in *To Wong Foo*) cast as a Hispanic druglord/gangsta. Right. Very believable. Those Hollywood people really know their stuff.

But the story was aight. Leguizamo's character gets caught up tryin to flip his drug money into legitimate investments through a real smart and clean-cut white boy. He begins to trust him so much that he turns over almost all his money. Meanwhile, he starts hangin in the white boy's circles, while turning his back on his old homeys. As many of us do.

That's when the white boy turns out to be a scam artist. He runs with the money. Leguizamo's shocked. In the end, he tracks the guy down and gets gangsta on him. BUT...does this happen in real life?

The first part certainly does. I've seen A LOT of hood dudes get scammed by seemingly legitimate "business" people. Whether the scammers were white, they simply didn't know what to do. But when the scammers were Black, gunplay was proposed almost immediately.

KILLER TURNED BITCH

How much do you know about African killer bees? I heard about them some years back when they were causing a panic in Texas and Florida. The way the media made it sound, another "African" plague was threatening the innocent people of our country. All I'd heard was that the African "killer bees" were 10 times more deadly than "normal" bees. So I looked it up. After some research, I realized something:

These bees are no different from us.

The Bees: First of all, they're not purely "African." They're actually a mixed breed. In the Americas, these "Africanized" bees descended from 26 African queen bees accidentally released in Brazil by a biologist named Warwick Kerr. Kerr had been interbreeding the common Italian honey bees with bees from Tanzania in southern Africa. Hives containing these particular queens were noted to be especially defensive. Kerr was attempting to breed a strain of bees that would work better in tropical conditions than the weak European bees used in the Americas. But after their release, these 26 African queen bees mated with local bees from Europe, and their descendants have since spread throughout the Americas.

You: You see the relation yet? Who was brought here to work? Think about the Americas…and the mixture of Africans and Europeans…what (or who) did it make?

The Bees: These Africanized bees are tough. They're known for having much greater defensiveness than European honey bees. They are more likely to attack a perceived threat and, when they do so, attack in larger numbers. This is how they earned the nickname "killer bees."

You: Think some more. Think about how we respond to any threat, real or perceived. See the connection yet?

The Bees: The reasons for this ferocity go back to the roots. In central and southern Africa, bees have had to defend themselves against other aggressive insects, as well as animals that destroy hives if the bees are not sufficiently defensive. In addition, instead of beekeeping, when people wanted honey, they would seek out a bee tree and kill the colony, or at least steal its honey. The colony most likely to survive either animal or human attacks was the fiercest one. Thus the African bee naturally developed ferocity.

You: Now think about which group of people in America suffered the most abuse, and had to fight back the most. What did that do to them?

The Bees: But not all Africanized hives are defensive; some are quite gentle, which gives a beginning point for beekeepers to breed a gentler stock. This has been done in Brazil, where bee incidents are much less common than they were during the first wave of the Africanized bees' colonization.

You: Sounds like how, since slavery, the strength and aggressiveness of Blacks has been seen as a threat, leading people and institutions to cultivate weakness in young Black people. By grooming young Black people, especially men, to be "gentle," less and less people rebel and fight back against threats and abuse.

"Patience has its limits. Take it too far, and it's cowardice."
George Jackson (1941-1971)

The Bees: In places where the Africanized bee has been "re-domesticated", it is considered the bee of choice for beekeeping in Brazil. It is not only more well-adapted to the tropics, but more industrious than European bees.

You: Ah, just as the "gentle" Negro is the best Negro, right? Think about it. This new generation of passive, obedient Black men works harder (for whites), only to receive nothing, except for a pat on the head here and there.

Did You Know?
If the truth about "killer bees" makes you think about media hype, think about this: Chained dogs are 3 times more likely to bite than unchained dogs. Makes you think about prison...or people "trapped" in the ghetto.

The Bees: Still, the Africanized bee is widely feared by the public, due mostly to sensationalist movies and exaggerated media reports. In truth, the sting from a "killer" bee contains less venom than the sting from a regular bee, and they've only killed about 14 people altogether, which means that they're actually less dangerous than most venomous snakes. But as the bee spreads through southern America, officials worry that public fear may force misguided efforts to combat them.

You: The bottom line is, no matter what, you're still a nigger. You're still a dangerous, deadly nigger that needs to be exterminated. No matter how good or bad you are, you will be painted in that light, and many people will deal with you based on those perceptions.

The Bees: The strategy to reduce the "threat" is to breed "gentle" qualities into these bees until they are hard-working and strong, but no longer defensive or aggressive.

You: Same sh*t. They're making bitches out of us daily.

They made you to be tough, but then you became a threat. Then they remade you, so who are you a threat to now?

Don't keep getting made and remade.

SUPREME THE ASSHOLE ON "SPOILED ASS KIDS"

Stop buying your kids all the sh*t you couldn't have. Don't you get it, you big dummy? If you do that, they won't learn to work for sh*t! That's why 45% of the children of middle-class Black parents end up poor! Among white folks, it's only 15%! (True Story) If you have to struggle, or at least earn, the things you get, you'll not only appreciate em, but you'll always know what you gotta do to get sh*t in the future? What the f*ck do our kids know though? They know they just gotta whine, beg, or throw a tantrum to get what they want from you. How the f*ck does that help them? And how the f*ck does it help your child when you do all the thinking for them? Do you make your kids think before they say anything, do anything, or ask you anything? Why the f*ck not? You want them to be retarded? Make them think! Make them wash their own damn clothes and build their own damn toys! You ain't doin em no favors if you don't!

NEGROES WITH GUNS

"I was angry about the [MLK] assassination, but I wasn't shocked by it. I knew that change was going to take something different – not sit-ins, not peaceful coexistence."
Samuel Jackson

David Walker

> They want us for their slaves, and think nothing of murdering us…therefore, if there is an attempt made by us, kill or be killed. Now, I ask you, had you not rather be killed than to be a slave to a tyrant, who takes the life of your mother, wife, and dear little children? …Believe this, that it is no more harm for you to kill a man who is trying to kill you, than it is for you to take a drink of water when thirsty.

In September 1829, David Walker, a free Black man from the South, published **the most revolutionary anti-slavery message America had seen.**

The 76-page pamphlet was titled *Walker's Appeal, in Four Articles; Together with a Preamble, to the Coloured Citizens of the World, but in Particular, and Very Expressly, to Those of the United States of America.* Long-ass title, I know, but that's how book titles went back then. In his *Appeal*, Walker argued that Blacks in America suffered more than any other people in the history of the world, and identified 4 causes for their "wretchedness":

1. The many evils of slavery
2. A weak and submissive attitude towards whites (even among free Blacks)
3. The Christian Church
4. False help by white groups pretending to be on the side of Blacks

The pamphlet called for immediate, universal, and unconditional freedom for Blacks. No Black or white man had published anything like this before. Walker refused the idea of returning to Africa, arguing:

> Let no man of us budge one step, and let slave-holders come to beat us from our country. America is more our country, than it is the whites — we have enriched it with our blood and tears. The greatest riches in all America have arisen from our blood and tears: — and will they drive us from our property and homes, which we have earned with our blood?

He also supported slaves who used violence in self-defense against their masters and overseers, and suggested that slaves kill their masters in order to gain freedom:

> The whites have had us under them for more than three centuries, murdering, and treating us like brutes; and…they do not know, indeed, that there is an unconquerable disposition in the breasts of the blacks, which, when it is fully awakened and put in motion, will be subdued, only with the destruction of the animal existence. Get the blacks started, and if you do not have a gang of tigers and lions to deal with, I am a deceiver of the blacks and of the whites...If you commence, make sure work – do not trifle, for they will not trifle with you.

Walker got his pamphlet out to many Blacks in Northern cities, but it was much harder to get it to the slaves and free blacks in the South. The government worked to suppress it. Black men were arrested for owning it. Whites staged attacks on Walker's home.

In Savannah, Georgia, white authorities seized dozens of copies smuggled in by Black sailors. Walker had sold them jackets in Boston, and had stitched copies into the lining. It was already illegal in Georgia to teach a slave to read. Plantation owners offered big cash rewards for anyone who could stop Walker, dead or alive.

Undaunted, Walker implored his people to keep fighting, both physically and mentally:

> Men of colour, who are also of sense, for you particularly is my APPEAL designed. Our more ignorant brethren are not able to penetrate its value. I call upon you therefore to cast your eyes upon the wretchedness of your brethren, and to do your utmost to enlighten them—go to work and enlighten your brethren!—Let the Lord see you doing what you can to rescue them and yourselves from degradation.

In June 1830, not long after publishing the third edition of his *Appeal*, David Walker was found dead on the doorstep of his home. But his vision lived on. Walker's *Appeal* was one of the strongest causes behind the long legacy of slave revolts and rebellions that followed. While abolitionists like Frederick Douglass issued peaceful calls for change, Walker's strain of rebel thought continued to influence militant Blacks. And it was the actions of these militant Blacks that effectively scared whites into listening to the solutions offered by Douglass.

Ever wonder why you've never heard about this dude? Maybe because what you learn in school is meant to program you. If your only Black "role models" are the "first" Blacks to be accepted into white sports, schools, and other institutions, then it's a pretty slim chance you'll ever come up with the idea of bangin on behalf of your people. At best, you'll be tryin to "get in where you fit in."

But stories like Walker's are a major part of our legacy…and if we don't continue *that* tradition, all is lost.

Robert Williams

There's more you've missed. Robert F. Williams was raised in the small southern town of Monroe, North Carolina. An ex-Marine, he later became involved with the Monroe NAACP as a community organizer in the 1950s. After he defended two young Black boys who were jailed for kissing a white girl, Williams became famous around the world.

But Williams soon saw that peaceful tactics didn't always work. While civil rights leaders in his area were demonstrating to integrate the swimming pools, white men would threaten and shoot at them. The police did nothing to stop it.

One day, Williams and a crowd of Black women came to the Union County courthouse to protest two separate cases scheduled for the same day. At the time, Monroe's Black community was still reeling from a vicious lynching and the gang-rape of a Black college student.

The first trial was for a white railroad engineer's beating of a Black hotel maid. The same day, a married white mechanic was being tried for beating and raping a pregnant Black woman in front of her five children.

Both men were freed.

One of the men's lawyers blamed the confusion on his client being "drunk and having a little fun" at the time of the assault, while the other man was acquitted even though he failed to appear in court. The women with Williams were outraged. They turned and looked at him with disgust for failing to protect the women.

Williams had seen enough. He said, "We must meet violence with violence. Black citizens unable to enlist the support of the courts must defend themselves."

Williams then started the Black Armed Guard (with the National Rifle Association's blessings) to defend the local Black community from the Klu Klux Klan. Black residents fortified their homes with sandbags and began training with rifles in case of night raids by the Klan. Williams pushed for the use of powerful weapons instead of more traditional firearms. He wasn't without good cause. KKK membership was at about 15,000 locally and most of them had guns.

When J. Edgar Hoover and the FBI learned about Williams' tactics, they went after him. They not only claimed that he was insane, but that he should be considered "armed and dangerous." A number of civil rights leaders, including MLK, denounced Williams as well. But the burly ex-Marine wasn't shaken.

As Williams' ideas grew in popularity, even King was forced to admit:

> All societies...accept [self-defense] as moral and legal. The principle of self-defense, even involving weapons and bloodshed, has never been condemned, even by Gandhi....When the Negro uses force in self-defense he does not forfeit support – he may even win it, by the courage and self-respect it reflects.

After a violent clash, he fled for Cuba, wife and kids behind him, machine gun slung over one shoulder. There, Castro offered his full support, as he believed in freedom for Black people in America. Williams continued to speak out for the struggle, and even ran a radio station from Cuba that was heard in the U.S.

But the white people whom Williams had worked with in the Communist Party began turning against him. Seemed he was too "pro-Black" for their interests. These former "friends" began starting trouble for him in Cuba.

Williams left Cuba and traveled to North Vietnam in 1964, where he traded Harlem stories with president Ho Chi Minh and wrote anti-war propaganda aimed at Black U.S. soldiers.

In 1965, he relocated his family again to China, where Williams became friends with president Mao Tse Tung and moved in the highest circles of the Chinese government for 3 years. The Chinese treated him like a king. They, too, supported the struggle of the Black man in America. According to Chairman Mao:

> The evil system of colonialism and imperialism arose and throve with the enslavement of Negroes and the trade in Negroes. And it will surely come to its end with the complete emancipation of the Black people.

After some time, Williams' lawyer tried to persuade him to come back to the U.S., as his supporters had started a campaign to elect him president. As it turned out, Robert Williams was idolized by Blacks in the U.S., especially those tired of singing "Kumbaya" and waiting passively for change. But Williams refused to return. He knew that there were still charges against him, and he was sure to be thrown in prison as soon as he stepped off that plane.

But things changed in 1969, when the U.S. was trying to develop a better relationship with China. Williams was now seen as an asset. He was asked to serve as an advisor to the U.S. government and was allowed to return home. The state of North Carolina eventually dropped all charges against him. Williams moved on to a post at the Center for Chinese Studies at the University of Michigan.

Unlike all of the Black leaders who begged for peace, only to be murdered in cold blood, Black revolutionary Robert F. Williams was able to live out his last years in actual peace. He passed away in 1996. And he was able to see his vision come to fruition. Williams' book *Negroes with Guns* was one of the strongest forces behind Huey P. Newton's forming the Black Panther Party.

"Power concedes nothing without demand."
Frederick Douglass

How do *you* see our struggle for self-determination? Can it be won with heartfelt poems and petitions alone? What else is needed? Who'll do it?

Singing "Kumbaya" won't always cut it.
Sometimes you have to step in the streets and fight.

The Great Depression

On Biggie Smalls's classic *Ready to Die* album, he raps:

> All my life I been considered as the worst/ Lyin' to my mother, even stealin' out her purse/ Crime after crime, from drugs to extortion/ I know my mother wished she got a f*ckin' abortion/…I swear to God I just want to slit my wrists and end this bullsh*t/ Throw the Magnum to my head, threaten to pull sh*t/ And squeeze until the bed's completely red/ I'm glad I'm dead, a worthless f*ckin' buddah head

Biggie wasn't the only feelin like that. Growing up, I remember a lot of us were either depressed or full-blown suicidal by the time we were teenagers. When we played chicken by pretending to tie our shoes in incoming traffic, we weren't just being badasses. When we jumped across rooftops and scaled buildings (the origins of parkour – look it up on Youtube), we weren't just being reckless. We were making it clear that we didn't want our lives. We were all ready to die. After all, the world made us feel disposable like trash, while the elders who should've helped us didn't do much more than yell at us. But talking about depression just isn't cool among people of color. We think that's a white people problem, so we don't talk about it.

Think about the following:

- 10.4% of Blacks in America (and 12.9% of Blacks from the Caribbean) reported having MDD (Major Depressive Disorder)

- More than 1 in 10 Blacks in America has had suicidal thoughts
- 4.1% of Blacks in America have attempted suicide
- Suicide is the 3rd leading cause of death among Black youth ages 15-19
- Black youth are the fastest growing percentage of suicide victims
- Serious depression can also lead to "suicide by proxy" or "indirect suicide" meaning you *create* the circumstances that get you killed

Remember *The Wonder Years*, with Fred Savage? The show about the kid dealing with the quirky, yet comical, situations that adolescence and middle school tend to present? And everything always seemed to work out okay within about 30 minutes or so? Well, my life was nothing like that. I don't even know why I brought it up.

I'd been struggling with my home situation since my childhood. At some point in my middle school years, depression set in and gradually became an everyday reality in my life. I guess it was always there.

Looking back, I realized I'd been deeply disturbed by my almost non-existent relationship with my father, by my detached relationship with my mother, and by my parents' dysfunctional relationship with each other. It would be years before I'd have the hindsight to understand how all of it was affecting me. Before turning to alcohol with increasing dependency, several other at-risk behaviors began materializing.

For example, I (check off the ones that apply to you too):

- ❑ Got into fights and conflicts
- ❑ Stabbed kids with pencils
- ❑ Ignored the teachers
- ❑ Avoided doing work in school
- ❑ Spent a lot of time alone, feeling miserable
- ❑ Wished (out loud) for death
- ❑ Acted like a total nut

Eventually, all of this led to a series of parent-teacher conferences that ultimately produced no change at all. After all, nobody was getting to the root of the problem. So I became a class clown at school, while entertaining thoughts of suicide at home. I thought maybe I needed therapy, but when I brought it up, no one took me seriously. They had no idea. My first attempt at suicide may have convinced them. Unplanned, it probably wouldn't have succeeded anyway, but it drove my point home. I needed help. I just had no idea how I'd get it.

Over the next few years, I began reading up on depression: its symptoms, its causes, and its treatment. At 14, they'd put me on anti-depressant medication but it make me feel more like a dopehead than a regular kid, so I stopped taking it. Instead, I started reading up on the subject of depression and began treating myself. I learned that my depression resulted from having an idealized view of where I should be, and what my life should be like...and comparing that perfect picture with how f*cked up I thought I really was.

I couldn't live with myself because of it. Everything that went wrong made me hate myself. Early on, I tried praying and asking for guidance and help. *I never got it.* At first I was mad at God for giving me such pain and misery for no apparent reason. Then I realized I was talking to myself the whole time. I stopped believing in this mysterious God who answers prayers if he feels like it, and started looking at the man in the mirror.

"You cannot see the future with tears in your eyes."
Navajo proverb

I began with trashing that ideal image I had for myself. I wasn't rich, I wasn't handsome, and I wasn't the captain of the football team. I didn't have a good family, and I didn't live in a good neighborhood. I had bad days, and sometimes I had bad weeks. But I learned that was all a part of regular life. I stopped hating life, and started learning to live with it. After all, tons of people had it ten times worse than me.

The crazy thing is, once I learned to live with it, it was ten times easier to change everything. Instead of beating up on myself for having problems, I could focus on beating my problems.

I learned about why life was so hard for people like me. I learned about what people of color have been put through (slavery, exploitation, abuse, rejection, dehumanization, etc.), and I understood why I couldn't let myself fall victim to that pit of despair.

"Waste not fresh tears over old griefs."
Euripedes (485-406 B.C.)

I changed my perspective. I refused to be a victim, and I chose to be victorious. Every time I felt the thoughts of depression coming back, I reminded myself that clinical depression usually is the result of a chemical imbalance in the brain. That means it's not real. All those feelings that life wasn't worth living, that everything was terrible, that I was a failure, they weren't based on reality. So, like the hallucinations I had when I was trippin on acid that one time (another story), I ignored them when they came up. Eventually, I outgrew them. Choosing to see myself as the problem-solver instead of the problem allowed me to take control of my life, and my mind.

That was over ten years ago. **I haven't had a weak thought since.**

Don't give power to weakness. Kill it before it kills you.

Going Out with a Bang

Armand was ready to go out in a blaze of glory. As he loaded up the Mac-11, he didn't even bother to use his t-shirt to keep his prints off. He hopped on his bike and rode down to the intersection of Crenshaw and Slauson, to the parking lot of the store where he used to buy his clothes...back when he had good money. There he waited for the Brinks armored truck to make their daily pick-up. As the two guards began loading the bags onto the truck, Armand caught them by surprise. Somehow, he was able to convince both to lay down their weapons and kick them away.

Out of nowhere, almost as quickly as Armand had jumped the Brinks men, two squad cars tore into the parking lot, cornering Armand. His back against the wall, he now had four police officers aiming at him, with more on the way. They hadn't fired any shots yet. "Put your f*cking gun DOWN!" they shouted. Armand knew it was over. Cursing and screaming, he turned and pointed the Mac-11 at one of the officers. 28 shots later, it was over. Armand lay disfigured in a pool on the asphalt. He hadn't fired a single shot. In fact, his gun was empty. And he had known it.

Reactionary vs. Revolutionary Suicide

The above story is not rare. There's even a word for it nowadays, and they mention it in the movie *Phonebooth*. It's called "cop-assisted suicide." In general, it's also known as "suicide by proxy" or "indirect suicide." It's what happens when a person who doesn't know he's depressed and suicidal goes out on a mission that will almost definitely end up killing him. And dozens of us do it every day. We're killing ourselves like never before, and nobody understands why.

It's what Tupac was trying to tell us in so many of his song. For example, "So Many Tears," where he raps:

> Now I'm lost and I'm weary, so many tears/ I'm suicidal, so don't stand near me/ My every move is a calculated step, to bring me closer/ to embrace an early death, now there's nothin left/ There was no mercy on the streets, I couldn't rest/ I'm barely standin, bout to go to pieces, screamin "peace"/ And though my soul was deleted, I couldn't see it/ I had my mind full of demons, tryin to break free/ They planted seeds and they hatched, sparkin the flame/ inside my brain like a match, such a dirty game/ No memories, just a misery/ Paintin a picture of my enemies killin me, in my sleep

Well, a few of us do. I know Huey P. did. He said we kill ourselves in reaction to the misery we experience, when we should instead be giving our lives trying to destroy the bullsh*t that made us so miserable.

"The greatest tragedy in the ghetto is watching people become accustomed to the prospect of a bleak future."
Ice T

He coined the term "revolutionary suicide" to describe the actions of Black people – oppressed by racism and poverty – who risk their lives for the people, for positive change, by standing up to the system. He argued that this was very different from the "reactionary suicide" commited by so many others through drug addiction, criminal activity, and other self-destructive behaviors that result from hopelessness. He argued that "the slow suicide of life in the ghetto" should be replaced by a revolutionary struggle that would end only in victory (change of the system) or revolutionary suicide (death).

Almost poetically, he said in "I am We, or Revolutionary Suicide":

> So many of my comrades are gone now. Some tight partners, crime partners, and brothers off the block, are begging on the street. Others are in the asylum, penitentiary, or grave. They are all suicides of one kind of another...The difference lies in hope and desire. By hoping and desiring, the revolutionary suicide chooses life; he is, in the words of Nietzsche, "an arrow of longing for another shore." Both suicides despise tyranny, but the revolutionary is both a great despiser and a great adorer who longs for another shore. The reactionary suicide must learn, as his brother the revolutionary has learned, that the desert [the American nightmare] is not a circle. It is a spiral. When we have passed through the desert, nothing will be the same.

Mwalimu Baruti has written that "Black men kill themselves with their futures ahead of them, and white men when their futures are behind them." It's true. The way we give our lives is very different from everyone else. White people typically commit suicide once their company crashes or they go bankrupt. Sh*t, most of us *start out* bankrupt! Many of us feel like we were "born dead," so we don't need to lose anything in particular for us to feel like everything is lost. Having so little, and being treated like we're less than nothing...it's enough to send someone over the edge. It's not so amazing that so many of us are "damaged goods," but that so many of us somehow can still make it. As James Baldwin observed several decades ago, "All over Harlem, Negro boys and girls are growing into stunted maturity, trying desperately to find a place to stand; and the wonder is not that so many of them are ruined but that so many survive." But now our survival rate is dropping.

We're killing ourselves in dozens of ways, some of them too subtle to notice. Some of us are so unhealthy psychologicall and emotionally that we've used the endless pursuit of money as a "mask" to cover up our own illness. Even you may fit the profile. But instead of dying for nothing, dying over nothing, dying with nothing...try living FOR something...and even if you die, it won't be for nothing.

Live for something, or die for nothing.

It's All in your Head

Are you hot? Cold? Hungry? Tired? Angry? Depressed? Worried? Why? It's all in your mind! None of it is actually real. It may feel real, but it's only as real as you allow it to be. Did you just lose your job? Well, that's real. But how you deal with it is up to you. You can choose to be upset about it, or you can choose to be excited about what the future now holds. Most people, unfortunately, choose negative feelings over positive feelings. But you have to understand that there is a choice.

"You can transcend all negativity when you realize that
the only power it has over you is your belief in it.
As you experience this truth about yourself you are set free."
Eileen Caddy

When it's chilly outside, you probably complain that it's cold. That complaint only makes you feel colder. You gave it power over your mind, and now you're convinced to feel cold. But there are people who live in the Artic circle and the Himalayan mountains. They don't whine about the cold. You can say that they're used to it, but there's more to it. Many of these people are disciplined. There are monks who can set themselves on fire without screaming, so what's your problem? You're stressed because you're not getting along with someone the way you want to? You mad cause your finances ain't perfect? Get over it. Think differently. And that will make all the difference in the world.

When my stomach starts growling for food, I remind myself that many people go days without food. And I tell my body not to complain. If it's cold outside, I breathe differently and think myself warmer. If that seems out of your reach, then you've been brainwashed into believing that there is something out there more powerful than your mind. And there isn't.

This attitude is necessary for a successful life. Without it, we feel that our lives are the result of outside forces, and that we can do very little to change things. The truth is the opposite. Most of our lives are in our control, but we believe that "things happen to us" instead of "us making things happen," so we are constantly in trouble. Or at least we feel we are. I remember an inspirational poster in an office building I visited recently that said:

> Our lives are not determined by what happens to us, but how we react to what happens; not by what life brings to us, but by the attitude we bring to life. A positive attitude causes a chain reaction of positive thoughts, events, and outcomes. It is a catalyst…a spark that creates extraordinary results.

Similarly, Napoleon Hill, author of *Think and Grow Rich*, has said, "Self-discipline begins with the mastery of your thoughts. If you don't control what you think, you can't control what you do. Simply, self-discipline enables you to think first and act afterward."

"The great successful men of the world have used their imaginations.
They think ahead and create their mental picture, and they go to work
materializing that picture in all its details, filling in here, adding a little there,

altering this a bit and that a bit, but steadily building, steadily building."
Robert Collie

If you can't see life that way, you'll have a very unsuccessful life. On the other hand, once you realize that everything is in your control and life is what you make of it, even your failure becomes learning opportunities (so they're not really failures at all). Next time you think you're worried about something, think differently. Think of yourself as concerned with the future, and confident in whatever plan you develop to address your concerns.

"Three weeks from now, I will be harvesting my crops.
Imagine where you will be, and it will be so."
Gladiator

See yourself where you want to be, and then do what's necessary to get there. Don't let your negative emotions take root and become real to you. Turn them all around and think yourself towards where you really want to be. That's the *Secret*. Now you don't have to buy *that* book.

Think yourself to where you want to be in life.

Keep Hope Alive

Rats in Jars

Here's another rat-related experiment you may not want to try at home:

Two mice are placed in glass jars filled halfway with water. The water comes up so far in the jar that if the mice don't keep swimming their heads won't be above water. Both jars are then covered in black paper, to prevent any light from coming through. The only difference in the two is that the black paper on one jar is then cut to form a tiny hole where just a small beam of light shines through. The rats are left overnight. By daybreak, the rat in complete darkness is dead. The rat with the glimmer of light is still holding on scratching along the sides of the jar trying to get out.

The Red Button

In the 1980s, the United States and the Soviet Union were involved in what was known as the Cold War. It was a "cold" war because it was a war of words and ideas, and although a "hot" war involving troops and guns could have started at any time, there had been no physical attacks. People on both sides of the world feared the day when these two highly militarized world forces would go to war. They knew that if these two superpowers went to war, many more nations would become involved, and World War III would take place. Since the United States had already been the first – and only – nation to use a nuclear weapon against another country, many feared that the Soviet Union would end up using their nuclear bombs as well.

Americans were so paranoid that the president would one day "push the red button" that they prepared as if world war was inescapable. Many felt hopeless. They avoided having children, as babies wouldn't be able to survive such times. They avoided starting new businesses, as the economy was sure to completely fall apart. Many avoided buying homes, as there seemed to be no point. Many even avoided enrolling in college, as they were sure their studies would be interrupted.

But the war never happened. And all those hopeless people who hoped only to save their own lives, while not really even living life itself...they didn't have kids, they didn't build their businesses, they didn't get that house, and they didn't finish school. They gave up early, only to realize they should have never quit at what they were doing. At best, they delayed all the things they could've done much earlier.

In many ways, growing up in the ghetto is something like living in the middle of a warzone. Death may come any day, and any way. And anyway, many of us ain't expecting a better life. Some of us only hope to survive.

> "Where we call the cops the A-Team/ 'cause they hop out of vans and spray things
> And life expectancy's so low, we making our wills at 18"
> Jay-Z, "Where I'm From"

I remember being 15, not expecting to see 21. When I saw 21, I looked back, thinking, "Damn, I wish I could have talked to myself then."

As a teenager, I lived like life wasn't worth much. I lived like death was inevitable, and was in fact not far away. I lived like I wouldn't raise children, build a business, own my home, or finish college. Basically, I didn't really live at all. I was dead. A "Black Zombie" as Nas said, walking around among the living (or were we all dead?). And like a zombie, I was in survival mode. A zombie doesn't make plans for the future. He lives for today and doesn't care about tomorrow. But death *isn't* inevitable.

> "My niggas is chillin, gettin high, relaxin/ Envisionin ownin sh*t, yo it can happen"
> Nas, "Black Zombie"

I know plenty of dudes who partied their lives away, expecting to die by 20. They're now 30 and 40, stuck working at McDonalds. They shouldn't have wasted their opportunity. You may feel like you don't have much, and therefore you don't have much to live for. But you may be missing all that you *do* have. And much of what you're missing may be found *within*. But if you're a dead man walking, chances are you've never looked there. As Nas said,

> Wake up! Black zombies in a spell for more than four-hundred years!/ Ghetto niggas won't have it no more! Can I get a witness?/ Why listen

to somebody else tell you how to do it?/ When you can do it yourself? It's all in you! Do it, do it, do it…

You have a choice at this point. Make it…live by it…and *don't look back.*

Bottom line: Don't be hopeless. Life is what you make it.

HATERS AND MOTIVATORS

"Know that those who hate you are more numerous than those who love you."
Chananga (African) proverb

As Plies told *The Source Magazine* in December 2007:

> The nigga who came up with [the idea of] "street niggas," hated on everything they couldn't do. They couldn't go to college so they hated. They couldn't play ball so they hated. The sad part was the more times you been to prison, niggas wanna give you stripes. You been locked up fifteen times don't mean you gangsta. That mean's you ain't good at what you do.

What he's saying is that being a "street nigga" is not a script he's trying to stick to. The idea of a "street nigga" is something people made up to keep other people (us) in the hole where they want them to be. Either it's white America telling you how to act, or it's the dudes living next door to you telling you the same dumb sh*t.

"A man who can't dance thinks the band is no good."
Polish proverb

Now that's a hater…but you can take that hate any way you want. A smart man takes his haters and sees them as motivation to do better. After all, as Plies said, people usually hate on whatever they can't do. So look at it this way:

Haters	Motivators
A hater makes you doubt yourself.	A motivator makes you want to prove yourself.
A hater shows other people what's wrong with you.	A motivator shows you what's wrong with other people.
A hater causes you to worry about losing what you have.	A motivator causes you to work harder to have more.
A hater makes you lose sleep.	A motivator makes you not want to sleep.
A hater attacks your flaws.	A motivator shows you your weaknesses.
A hater is usually jealous of you.	A motivator may actually want the best for you.
A hater thinks they're better than you.	A motivator wants you to be better than you are.
A hater's words aren't nice or helpful.	A motivator's words may not be nice, but they can help you.
A hater wants you to give them more.	A motivator wants you to give yourself more.
A hater targets weakness.	A motivator targets weakness.
A hater will either push you or crush you.	A motivator will either push you or crush you.

For every hater you have, you have one motivator, because life is how you see it. Only the unsuccessful nobodies are free from having critics. Your critics are either going to be the worst thing in your life, or the best thing in your life. It's up to you.

"As steel sharpens steel, so one man sharpens another."
Proverbs 27:17

But to be realistic, some of us are a little too worried about imaginary haters keeping us down. In the immortal words of Soulja Slim on "Soulja Life Mentality":

> And these niggas out here, talking bout a nigga hatin on them. F*ck you talking bout? A *nigga* hatin on you? Bitch ass nigga, you know who hatin on you? The D.A. and the judge, that's who hatin on your bitch ass, nigga! The polices and all that type of sh*t, nigga. F*ck you talkin bout? A *NIGGA* hatin on you??

Steel Sharpens Steel

Haters? That was the least of my problems. Before I was even successful enough to be worthy of "haters," I had people who criticized everything from the way I walked to the shoes on my feet. Like most of the kids in my neighborhood, I grew up defensive. We learned how to defend ourselves against sticks and stones, as well as the words that certainly hurt…though we could never show it.

We learned how to "play the dozens," also known as "snappin," "roastin," or "joning," dependin on where you come from. We talked about each other until somebody said something personal, and then we were ready to fight. We protected our personal space, and didn't allow anyone to get too close to our face or to touch us if they didn't know us…even if it was accidental. We grew up like child soldiers in war-torn Sierra Leone, always looking out for any act of aggression. In many ways, we *were* soldiers. We just had no idea which side we were on. Confused and led astray, we endlessly fought against

> **Did You Know?**
>
> Wildlife expert Dr. Harry Jacobson explains that, "Buck [male deer] fighting takes place all year round. A dominance order begins to become established immediately after birth. As six month old fawns mature, a pecking order starts to take shape. Most of the fighting... involves a flailing of hooves or aggressive posturing initially until the bucks get their first sets of antlers. Once the bucks' antlers are hardened, fighting can occur in the more traditional manner with which we're familiar...When bucks spar, they are testing one another, and they're also sharpening their fighting skills without getting into full-fledged combat...Often an older buck and a younger buck will spar, and the older buck will allow the younger buck to test himself. Younger bucks begin to spar as soon as they come out of velvet as part of their maturing process. They're learning the behavior that will at some point in the future be significant to them either in breeding or not breeding."

each other. Sometimes we simply *waited* for somebody to disrespect us, just so we could show our manhood by crushing them.

Years later, I was still affected. I used to see every criticism as a personal attack. Even in college, I damn near fought professors for marking up reports that I thought were A+ material...but weren't. I couldn't hear what was really wrong. I wasn't listening. I didn't care. I felt like I was right. In many ways, I was just protecting my personal space in the way we did as kids. When I felt disrespected, I either became defensive or offensive. Either way, I was ready to attack.

Maybe I *was* insecure. Hell, we probably all are, to some extent. Growing up in this awful place, where we are constantly made to feel less than human – it does that to you. It makes you doubt your very reason for living, and at the same time, it makes you very angry at anybody who makes you doubt yourself more.

I thought any comment or suggestion was a personal attack. I looked at any critique on my views as a declaration of war. I saw any judgement passed on anything about me as putting down my whole existence. The words, "You're wrong" were almost fighting words.

It's taken me years to learn to appreciate that it takes steel to sharpen steel. You simply can't buy a knife, use it for years, and expect it to remain sharp. What keeps it sharp? Carrots?

No, you need to sharpen that knife with a material that is as hard, or harder. The reason most of us are so dull is because we fear another man improving us. When someone says we're wrong, we could go back and try to figure out why they said that, and then work on fixing the problem...but we don't. We practice something known to psychologists as "cognitive dissonance." Cognitive dissonance means that, when faced with a view that goes against what we're doing, we do one of 3 things:

1. We change our behavior.
2. We ignore what we're being told by changing what we think about the person telling us.
3. We justify our behavior by making excuses.

If it's not obvious, the first response is the rarest. People don't change like that. They'd rather change their relationship with you before they'll change something that may be wrong with them. Fortunately, I've grown out of that. I respect – and even desire – for other people to tell me where I'm slipping. The way I see it, it only makes me better.

Can you handle criticism? Or are you defensive? Or offensive?

Do you ask people for advice on how you can step your game up?

Do you attempt to first see yourself (find something in common) in the people *you* seek to criticize? Are you always completely unalike?

Steel sharpens steel. Let criticism improve you.

CHANNEL YOUR ENERGY

Eternal Blackness

The basic building block of all matter is known as the atom. Depending on its properties, an atom represents a certain element. For example, the most basic atom is hydrogen, which is known for having only 1 proton and 1 electron. The sixth element in the periodic table is carbon, which has 6 protons, 6 neutrons, and 6 electrons. Every living thing on earth is made up mostly of carbon, so we are known as carbon-based life forms.

Carbon, by the way, is black. You've seen carbon before. You seen coal? That's carbon. Seen oil (the black kind)? Carbon. The black substance that makes us "Black" as people is made up of carbon as well. It's called melanin. Melanin and its close relative melatonin get their names from the Greek "mela," which means Black.

For years, white scientists ignored melanin and melatonin and acted like they didn't matter. Now we know that melanin and melatonin, which Black people produce naturally, are necessary for a healthy life. Now white people go to GNC and buy melatonin pills to get their minds right. They have to, because they can't really produce it on their own. In white skin, there's very little melanin. And if you don't have melanin, your body can't use sunlight to make vitamin D. So, as Prodigy raps on "My World is Empty Without You":

> Yo, they feeding us bullsh*t with all these books/ We didn't ask to be here, we got took/ Enslaved, and killed, we was raped and hung/ We was lied to, and forced to build America/ We was robbed of our technology, and knowledge of self/ The Black man is the original man of this earth/ We can live under the sun, it give us strength/ The white man gets sunburn, and cancer of the skin

So many white people have to buy melatonin, milk (vitamin D), and sunscreen, just to feel "normal."

Melanin is not just in your skin, though. In fact, within the human brain stem, there are 12 centers of black melanin. More importantly, the pineal gland, which sits right behind your forehead, is responsible for producing melatonin as well as the melanin your brain needs, neuromelanin. The ancient Egyptians and Indians called the pineal gland the "third eye" or the "mind of God." In white people, the pineal gland is 85% calcified, which means it doesn't really work the same. In Black people, it's only 5% calcified.

Today, modern science has learned that melanin was fundamental to the evolution of life on Earth. Scientists now know that "black substances, starting from very simple composites of carbon, subjected to natural forces like temperature, electrical discharges, and radiation evolved into complex structures." Huh? In plain English, Black matter evolved from basic carbon to more complex melanin and eventually to complicated motherf*ckers like you and me. Deep, ain't it? Astrophysicists have even found that melanin is present in the blackness of space.

Okay, so what's my point so far?

Black is deep. Black is everywhere. Black is you. Got that, right? Let's go further. If all life, including your Black ass, began with the simplest Black substances, down to a simple-ass Black atom known as carbon, then that Blackness has recycled and regenerated itself for billions of years…to now.

Today, we are fighting a war in Iraq over that same eternal Blackness. I know I lost you just now. I'll explain. Most of our energy comes from natural resources known as fossil fuels. From the oil that becomes gasoline, to the coal that powers our factories, we depend on fossil fuels for energy. A "fossil fuel" is the byproduct of a living thing that has been dead for so long that its body has broken down and turned back into a more basic substance like oil or coal. That oil or coal is then pulled from the Earth and used to make stuff like gasoline, kerosene, sytrofoam, plastic, and all the other petroleum-based products. That means that right now, you could be driving a car powered by the remains of one of your ancestors from a million years ago. His Black ass became the oil that made the gasoline that you put in that Chevy. Or maybe he became the coal that burned to make the electricity that's charging your cellphone right now. Or maybe he became a sh*tty ass plastic diaper that will never decompose and go back to the earth. Or maybe he became a diamond.

After all, coal – when subjected to enough heat and pressure – forms diamonds. In fact, anything made of carbon can become a diamond under the right conditions, even peanut butter. In fact, a company named Lifegem can convert the carbon in cremated human remains into a high-quality diamond…for a price.

Now I want you to meditate on how significant the simple Blackness of your skin is. Even if you're light-skinned, homey. You've got melanin too. In a nutshell, YOU are what the universe is made of, and your essence is timeless.

You are the eternal, everlasting force that keeps this universe moving. So act like it.

How to REALLY Recycle

"Energy cannot be created or destroyed. It only changes form."
Albert Einstein

Now you know I'm not about philosophy and ideas you can't use. So let's apply this new understanding to the way we live our lives.

That same Blackness that formed this universe, that formed all life, that forms your Black ass…is being pulled from the Earth, right? It then changes forms and becomes something else, right? Either it becomes another form of energy, like electricity, or it becomes dead weight, like a plastic bottle. Energy can keep turning into more energy. But a plastic bottle will never go back to the earth and become energy again. Enough plastic bottles and Styrofoam cups and it's over for the Earth.

So what is the most powerful natural resource on this planet? You! And more specifically, that Black mind of yours – the most untapped natural resource on the planet today…and the most powerful. They can destroy everything around you, even your body, but they can't do anything to your mind…unless you let them.

Oops, I forgot how much we let them. Like the fossil fuels they use to make the chemicals that destroy our planet, our own beautiful Black minds are being used to destroy us.

"The most potent weapon in the hands of the oppressor is the mind of the oppressed."
Steve Biko

But you have a choice. You may not be able to decide what they do with all that oil, but you can choose where your Black ass goes. You can do what they want you to do, or do what you want to do. Either you channel your thoughts and energy into a positive and productive outlet, or a negative and unproductive outlet. Your energy either produces more energy, or death and destruction. A diamond or a diaper.

When we are frustrated, angry, depressed, or confused, we have a choice. We either channel that energy constructively or destructively. We can either build or destroy, and most of us choose to destroy. But we don't destroy the system that made us so miserable. Instead, we destroy ourselves and each other. We make things worse for everyone…except the ones we are so mad with.

But a few of us – only a few – learn to channel that rage and become outspoken. We know we're going to go through hell in this life anyway, so we choose to go out fighting against what we know is wrong. These people take their pain and frustration and write the kind of incredible music that inspires others...or give the kind of speeches that move people to act...or they write books that inspire revolutions.

The choice is yours. If you don't have a positive outlet for your energy, find one. Pick up a pen. Pick up a mic. Pick up a paintbrush. Sh*t, pick up a couple dollars and go learn a martial art. All that negative energy in you will either be channeled in a positive direction so it can build you up...or it will build up inside you and destroy you.

Find a way to channel your energy for the greater good.

Bumps on your Face

Normally, you get pimples and acne when you're finishing up puberty. But I've been seeing more and more people in their 20s and 30s with bumps on their faces like connect-the-dots. My brother Lord Diligent gave me a theory on why that is. He admitted that whenever he held things in, like frustration, pain, sadness, or worry, he would notice that he would start breaking out. Once he started finding ways to channel that energy and get it out of his system, he would clear right up. It made sense. When I meet people who are cool and stress-free, they have clean complexions. When I meet people with f*cked-up faces, they're usually pretty f*cked up in the head too. Sometimes, people are able to hide it so well that no one can tell how miserable they are. But your face tells it all. Your eyes give away the pain on your mind, and your skin gives away how long you've been holding it in. Learn how to channel that energy and watch how quickly your eyes get brighter, teeth get whiter, and your skin gets clearer. Oh, sorry, but your breath won't smell better until you start eating right.

Pain and Pleasure

Everyone says Black men are better in bed. White women love Black men. Asian women love Black men. Even some Black women still love Black men. It's not just about size either. I've heard from plenty of women about the many Black men who just "didn't measure up" to the myth that all Black men are bigger. So what is it? It's the energy. The same energy that most of us bottle up until we have headaches and bumps on our face. That same energy that came from 400 years of oppressive slavery, followed by 100 more years of modern-day slavery in a racist country like this one. That builds up into an explosive force, and when it comes out, it is powerful. That's why Black men can fight better. That's why Blacks dominate boxing, and men like Kimbo Slice and "Rampage" Jackson are a threat, even in no-holds barred fighting. That's why Blacks continue to produce the best and most moving music, of any type. And that's why Black men can f*ck the dog sh*t out of almost anybody. That's 500 years of pain in that passion, honey.

KEEP A JOURNAL

Need a place to transfer your thoughts and energy? Then do what dozens of great people have been doing since we invented paper: Start keeping a journal.

It doesn't matter whether you draw in it, write lyrics, or detail everything that's happened that day and how you feel about it, but it's one of the best things you can do to improve yourself. Years later, you can look back at your old writing and see how much you've grown, as well as what mistakes you made in the past so you won't repeat them. Not only that, but there's many times when releasing your frustration by writing about it will save your life.

"Behave like the chameleon: Look forward and observe behind."
Malagasy (African) proverb

For example, here's two entries from my own journal, one from when I was 14, the other from ten years later.

Journal Entry: March 2, 1995

F*ck school. I'm glad I got expelled. I've been wantin to drop out since I was ten anyway. And I've got plenty of reasons. It ain't just that those crackas at my school don't like me. Sh*t, all I did was rob a white boy! It ain't like I killed somebody! But it's bigger than that. I'm just not feelin school period.

Man, school don't guarantee sh*t. The richest people in the world ain't college educated, and people with high-school diplomas and college degrees ain't guaranteed a job no matter how good their grades were. Anyway, most schools generally don't want a mothaf*cka like me in there in the first place…cause I think how I want to think, not how you tell me to.

None of that matters though. Sh*t is hopeless for someone like me. Jersey City ain't got sh*t to offer me in terms of a future, whether I'm educated or not. Really, education and school ain't even the same sh*t. I can educate myself. School is being controlled and regurgitating bullsh*t information. I've known the school curriculum was bullsh*t since they taught that lesson on the "great" Christopher Columbus in sixth grade. How the hell do you "discover" a land where there's millions of people already living…and then you TAKE the sh*t from them? THAT makes you a great person in history? Bullsh*t.

That's why I've been reading up on things myself, outside of school. I realized the sh*t they teach you in school is lies. I stopped saying the Pledge of Allegiance the same year, after we learned about slavery. "Land of the Free," my ass. I stopped even recognizing the American flag as "my flag" around the time we memorized the Star Spangled

Banner in Music class. Our nation's anthem is a celebration of war and destruction. How f*cked up is that?

I refuse to try to assimilate into the American Dream. And if school is a major part of being a f*cking pawn, or a "productive citizen," I don't need that either. I'm smart enough to make my way without a high school diploma. I'ma be successful one way or the other. *Scarface* showed me there's other ways to make it to the top. I could do that. Or I could just do nothing at all. I can't see too much in my future besides a little bit of money and a gunshot before the curtains close any damn way. So I'm better off not wasting my time on useless sh*t like Algebra and Biology. I'm *glad* they put me out.

Journal Entry: November 20, 2004

I just looked back at something I wrote after being expelled from high school. All I could think was, "Damn, I really wrote that huh?" Ten years is a long time, and it's amazing how much change one can undergo in that amount of time. I really *was* ready to drop out for good back then. Who would've thought that I'd be working on my doctoral degree ten years later? Definitely not the people who expelled me. Not the teachers who failed me. Not the guidance counselor who told me I wasn't college material. Not even my friends at the time. All that turned out to be great motivation! But the number one person who I was up against...who I just had to prove wrong...who had to see it to believe it...was me. Ten years ago I was ready to end my life, either by my own hands, or by putting myself in the wrong situation at the right time...and now here I am. Eatin good, makin good money, feelin good about life, and with a beautiful female who's head over heels for me...literally. I'm glad I never gave up.

Keep a journal. What you learn when you keep track of your growth and experiences may surprise you.

THE FORK IN THE ROAD

Tenisha held Dwayne tightly against her as he grinded his hips into hers. Stripped down to their underwear, their writhing bodies were wrapped around each other like two ropes tangled together. They looked like they were in love, even though they had just met earlier today. Tenisha was laid on her back on Dwayne's bed and Dwayne was on top of her, kissing her passionately. Her brown skin glistened with sweat as her soft thighs wrapped around Dwayne's legs. Dwayne knew he didn't have a condom, but he had gone a little further than he should. He felt like he couldn't stop now. As he attempted to enter Tenisha, she screamed, "Stop! Wait! What are you doing? We can't!" Dwayne pretended not to understand. "Why?"

"Because you don't have a condom! I'm not doing that!"

Dwayne was still in between her legs, his body begging for satisfaction. He had a choice.

He could accept Tenisha's refusal, push up off of her, put his clothes back on, and show some serious self-discipline.	OR	He could give in to his urges, go full steam ahead, and ignore her screaming, crying, and begging for him to stop.

Dwayne decided to take the second route. In fact, he didn't even know he had made a choice. He just went with instinct and said, "F*ck it." Tenisha did plead for him to stop, but she didn't scream loud enough for Dwayne to think he was raping her. He kept going til he was done, worrying almost right away about whether he had gotten this stranger pregnant.

Dwayne's decision was life-altering. This wouldn't be the last time he raped a girl. After the first time, it became easier for him to do it again, even under stronger resistance. Dwayne stopped seeing women as fully human, and more so as a means to satisfy his urges. He stopped taking no for an answer on other things as well. As the years passed, Dwayne Redmond became the type of person who only cared about his own wants and desires, and pleasing himself at any cost. It wasn't long before 26-year-old Dwayne was behind bars for statutory rape of a 14-year-old, whom he had picked up walking home from school. When the prison blood-tested him, Dwayne learned that – somewhere along the line – he had contracted HIV.

"It is difficult to overcome one's passions, and impossible to satisfy them."
Marguerite de La Sabliere (late 17th century)

If there were such a thing as alternate realities or parallel universes, we would be able to follow the course Dwayne's life, had he chosen the first option. Maybe we would learn that Dwayne discovered the power of self-control and discipline in denying the urge to f*ck Tenisha that night. Maybe we would learn that Dwayne continued to make choices where he denied his desires and lusts, and put careful thought into every decision he made. Maybe we would learn that Dwayne eventually disciplined himself into the kind of man we often only read about: a man who denies himself in the best interests of others, works more than he plays, and accomplishes good for all instead of only pursuing self-gratification. That one choice could have sent Dwayne's life in two entirely different directions, but unfortunately we only know what really happened, and not what could have.

> "To win or lose, to love or hate, to try or quit, to risk or withdraw, to accelerate or hesitate, to dream or stagnate, to open or close, to succeed or fail, to live or die – Every one of these starts with a CHOICE."
>
> Snowden McFall

There are several points in your life when you will be faced with a fork in the road. Many times you won't even know that's what it is. But the choices you make at these junctures are life-altering. They are the type of events that, once you pass that point, you cannot go back and start over. In life we take a path, and these are our forks in the road. The way you go can set you on a course that will be incredibly difficult to change.

Think of these forks in the road like the picture below.

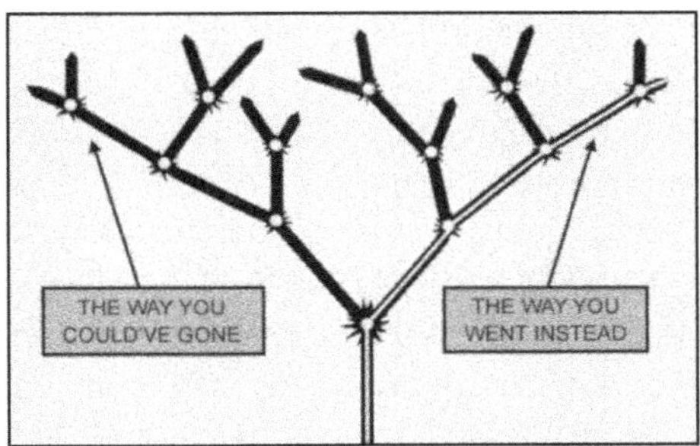

The idea is this: If you start out on one path, and one day, venture off that path at a crucial juncture (like the decision to rape someone), you may veer so far off your original course that it will take hundreds of turns in the opposite direction to get back. If you're old, there's a chance you may never even get back near that old path. So be careful. The choices you make in life ultimately determine your destiny.

When Dwayne made his choice, he flipped a switch within himself that made it easy to do the same thing in every similar situation. Self-control was soon no longer even on his plate. Before long, Dwayne's "choice" became the way he lived his whole life.

So...how will you know when you hit a fork in the road? And will you consider the consequences of the choice you make?

**The choices you make determine the path you take.
At every point, you must choose wisely.**

The War on Terror

The War on Terror did not begin on September 11, 2001. There have been plenty of wars with different names, each of them fighting an imaginary force, in some imaginary place, with no boundaries, and no end in sight.

In recent years, we've seen it called a War on Drugs. Sometimes, it was called the War on Poverty. In urban areas like Los Angeles, it's been called a War on Crime or a War on Gang Violence. There's even a continuing War on Illegal Immigration. Each time, these wars against abstract ideas result in thousands of casualties…and each time it's Black and brown people dead or in jail.

Before the 1980s, there was the War on Communism, which worked the same way. Hundreds of Black, brown, and yellow countries (and American groups) were targeted and destroyed.

This is nothing new.

Even in the earliest moments of Western Civilization, there were wars against "outsiders." In ancient times, it was the Greco-Roman empires versus foreign "barbarians" like the Persians and the Carthaginians, when Black armies were attacked endlessly until they gave up their lands. Watch *Lord of the Rings* or *300* to get an idea of how ancient whites envisioned their "epic" battle against the rest of the world.

A few centuries later, it was Christianity vs. Islam, and we had the Crusades, where Christian knights beheaded Black Muslims in mid-prayer, in order to spread Christianity and regain control of Moorish Europe. As Black and brown people united through Islam, religion started becoming an important part of why to go to war.

A few centuries after that, European Christians were pitting themselves against the "heathen savages" of Africa, Asia, and later South America. Their goal was to clear the path for white settlers to come in and take over the land. Thus, religion became a highly useful tool in *how* to go to war.

Then the British Empire was on a quest to take over the whole world, and the wars weren't only about land and religion. They were also about indirect economic control.

And look at what America was built on. Starting with Columbus, they did their best to destroy every Indian and take his land. Starting with Captain John Hawkins, they did their best to destroy every African by making him a slave in America, while leaving the ones back home fighting each other til none were left.

Even the presidents were clear about what they were trying to do. Our first President, George Washington, predicted at the end of the U.S. Revolutionary War, "...the gradual extension of our settlements will as certainly cause the savage [Indian], as the wolf, to retire [disappear]; both being beast of prey, tho' they differ in shape."

President Thomas Jefferson said "...if ever we are constrained to lift the hatchet against any tribe, we will never lay it down till that tribe is exterminated, or driven beyond..."

President John Quincy Adams said the United States took control of the land that became Florida and fought the Seminole Wars to confront the danger of "mingled hordes of lawless Indians and Negroes."

And Theodore Roosevelt was just one of the many presidents who spoke of establishing the permanent rule of "dominant world races" (white people), declaring, "The most ultimately righteous of all wars is a war with savages."

Today, the word "savages" has been replaced by "terrorists" and "immigrants," and "lawless Indians and Negroes" has been replaced with "criminals" and "gang members." You know who those words refer to. Different day, same sh*t.

Today, the last remaining place on Earth where white people have not been able to take control is in the Middle East. There, the Muslim Arabs who have the oil, money, and power, are not interested in white America and what it has to offer. They charge what they want for oil, and they don't let white people tell them what to do.

According to Davey D, the royalty of Saudi Arabia are more gangster than your favorite gangster rapper. The princes there not only have more money than our president, but they can tell him "F*ck you" and get away with it.

So it's only natural that the next war for control is with the Middle East. By creating bogus links between terrorism, Islam, and the Middle East, the U.S. and Europe are able to trick the people into buying into this new set of wars. The truth is, there are plenty of white terrorist groups out there (like the ETA, the IRA, and the hundreds of white supremacist militias throughout America), but we don't hear about them. Christians commit the same acts, but we don't hear about them. European countries do much more dirt than many of those Arab countries, but we don't hear about them.

We hear what they want us to hear, and we hear that the war is against those crazy Arab Muslims.

But what does this have to do with us?

Let's look at the high-profile terrorism suspects who have been arrested since 9/11:

- Zacarias Moussaoui, a Black North African (accused of planning the 9/11 attacks, even though he was

Did You Know?

Beginning in April 2003, one month after the invasion of Iraq, and continuing for over a year, the United States Federal Reserve shipped $12 billion in US currency to Iraq. The US military delivered the bank notes to the US-run Coalition Provisional Authority, to be dispensed for Iraqi reconstruction. At least $9 billion was unaccounted for due to a complete lack of oversight. How do you lose track of 9 billion dollars in cash? Easy, you don't.

protected – and possibly trained – by the United States government)

- Richard Reid, a Jamaican (accused of a failed attempt to light a "shoe bomb" in a plane)
- Jose Padilla, a Puerto Rican ex-gang member (accused of planning to build a "dirty bomb" and arrested, even though he hadn't actually committed any wrongdoing)
- John Allen Muhammad, an ex-Nation of Islam follower (the DC Sniper who, along with a young protégé, shot innocent Blacks and whites in what he confessed was a "secret mission" orchestrated by the U.S. government)
- A group of Black Muslims in London (accused of a train and bus bombing that occurred under highly questionable circumstances, and which later resulted in a Brazilian man being targeted and killed publicly by London police)
- A group of dreadlocked Haitians in Miami (entrapped by federal agents who offered the poor members millions of dollars to stage an attack)

They even got a Chinese dude at one point. And they also made a big deal out of John Walker Lindh, the "American Taliban." He was a suburban white boy who had gotten into Islam through listening to hiphop and studying the Five Percenters. Even though they treated him a lot better than they did the others (they said he was just "confused), his arrest was a stern warning to all those white boys who want to be down with Black and brown people.

So you tell me what's REALLY going on? Consider this: The fear created by the government after 9/11 allowed them to pass bills known as the PATRIOT Act. The PATRIOT Act began denying us our constitutional rights on the basis of "homeland security." So who suffers the most under this new legislation?

Not only can you be targeted and jailed JUST for speaking out about the government now, but you can be held indefinitely and without promise of a lawyer or a trial. How different is that from the countries the U.S. talks so bad about?

It gets worse. The wiretaps, government agents, and warrantless searches allow law enforcement to do things they could never get away with in the past. As a result, thousands of drug dealers, gang members, and hustlers have been caught across the country. If the government hasn't been able to "get you" using the ordinary laws, they can always put you away with the Patriot Act. Again, young Black and brown men (and women) must lose in order for "them" to win.

Which side are you on? Or do you feel privileged enough not to have to take a side? Do you believe you're exempt somehow? If not, what are you gonna do about it? Or are we too busy squabbling with our own?

The Black man has been and will always be...the enemy. So figure out which side you're on.

REVIEW

The principle for this chapter was **"Kill Yourself So You Can Live":** This means: Eliminate the weaknesses in yourself and the world around you, while developing the strength and discipline it will take to do so.

Here are the principles and lessons we covered:

Channeling your Energy
Find a way to channel your energy for the greater good.
Keep a journal. What you learn when you keep track of your growth and experiences may surprise you.
You are the eternal, everlasting force that keeps this universe moving. So act like it.
Choosing the Course
Beware the blessings that are curses in disguise.
Bottom line: Don't be hopeless. Life is what you make it.
Choose your strategy according to your situation.
The choices you make determine the path you take. At every point, you must choose wisely.
Think yourself to where you want to be in life.
We don't all live in the same world. Our circumstances create our realities.
You can't serve two masters.
Community Organizing
Be careful who you consider your "friends."
Black people don't need outside help to police their communities.
Don't keep thinking it's better with others, When you could be making it better among your own.
Get in where you fit in, or do something about it.
People of color don't need outside help to be successful with each other... but when you do things your way, be ready to defend yourself.
Start off every relationship the right way.
True wealth is having a community of people who will take care of you, Not a collection of material things to take care of.
Trying to join the crowd that beat you isn't going to make your life better. Trying to do so, you often lose more than you gain.
Whatever you do, help others enough so that becomes your legacy.
Embracing the Struggle
Everyone can be a part of the same struggle. But everyone's role will different.
Live for something, or die for nothing.
Persistence overcomes resistance.

What doesn't kill you only makes you stronger.
Singing "Kumbaya" won't always cut it. Sometimes you have to step in the streets and fight.
The Black man has been and will always be...the enemy. So figure out which side you're on.
Use pressure to your advantage. Focus, don't fold.
You can't be tough in one circle and a punk in another.
The Process of Perfection
Don't give power to weakness. Kill it before it kills you.
Don't keep getting made and remade.
Inner peace is one of life's greatest – and rarest – accomplishments. Find it, and you won't chase anything else.
Keeping pace with a slow crowd only makes you another loser. Think clearer, move faster, do better.
Live like you cherish life, not like you're anxious for death.
Never give in to being broken, no matter what the costs.
Steel sharpens steel. Let criticism improve you.
You may first need to get away and cut all ties in order to find and develop your true strength.
You may need to resist and refuse any and every attempt to change your vision, even as others give up around you.

N O I G Q L L J R Y R A T I L O S C T A

F Y S L A E P P A Y M E G G S O Y M D I

Y Y T I R A P S I D T L N C U L Y Y V Y

Y T O R T U R E Q Q E I U U H L A K B N

Y T F R E E D O M H C R N Y U V T J P U

Z R I U R Z J A U N I E R A N O S I R P

M A Z R J L Y H E S I L S F M F M X O W

S N N N A U J T Q E L N I E V U H N B G

I S Q O B D N T N H L A D S Q C H Z A M

V F B E I E I S J E T O V U T W M N T P

I O E D S T R L M I M R R E S W W K I C

D R N U J F A X O K R H A A R T J I O U

I M F T U D C Z R S J M S P P Y R M N M

C A A I L K J V I U E O D I R U P I E B

E T A V A Y L L U N N B M L N L S C A X

R I B R B X P P D L I T D Z E U L Y G L

Q O S E O Y K M M K Y M Y X Z C P C U L

E N E S R G E I J O G D E G L J P L G C

E I N Q V N X S R E H T A F T E B E P P

A N T R T U B X Y J K U H S I Q M S Y I

The Finished Product

ACCOMPLISH YOUR GOALS

"Those who refuse to place limitations upon themselves will always succeed...Success waits patiently for anyone who has the determination and strength to seize it."

Will you reach your goals? Who knows?

You do. It's all on you. But you can't win it all. At least not alone. For one of us to fully succeed, there must be success for all. And "success" isn't a one-time deal like the lottery.

You can be very successful in one area of life, but a complete and total failure in another. You can fail miserably to reach a goal a dozen times, but be incredibly successful on the very next attempt.

Not having the thought patterns that lead to achievement puts you completely at the mercy of chance and circumstance...the formula for failure in any venture. By leaving the results up to anything other than your own will and intention, you can almost guarantee that things won't go right.

By taking your life into your own hands, you complete one part of a two-step process to being successful. The other step is to apply the right follow-through. There are many people who have the right ideas and the right mindset to make them happen, but lack the discipline or desire to take the steps that come next.

Ideas are like living things that need air to live. When an idea or a goal emerges in your consciousness, if you don't "put it out there" within a certain timeframe, it will inevitably die. Without follow-through of some sort, all ideas – even the best ones – die.

So if you want success, you've got to stop just thinking about it. Even if you can't do everything, do some damn thing. Success will come.

Quiz Nine: Potential for Success

1. Do come up with ideas, plans, or goals that you never seem to take beyond the thinking stage? Yes No

2. Do you normally put in the extra energy, time, and/or money that it takes to execute difficult ideas, plans, or goals? Yes No

3. Do you truly see yourself as a person with the characteristics needed to KEEP whatever your goal is, if you were to succeed in getting it? Yes No

4. Do you often visualize yourself as already having attained the outcome, seeing and feeling success in advance, as opposed to worrying about things not working out? Yes No

5. Are you incredibly determined to succeed, completely willing to make even dramatic changes in your lifestyle to reach your goals? Yes No

6. Do you really, honestly feel confident that you'll reach your objective in the time you've given yourself? Is your time-frame realistic? Yes No

7. Are you totally committed to continuing the daily actions, both big and small, that achieving your goal requires? Yes No

8. Are you truly enjoying the challenge of reaching your goal? Is it fun, or does it feel like you just have to keep pushing yourself into something you don't enjoy? Yes No

9. Are you taking all the time that's required to learn the new skills and/or steps necessary to reach your goal? Yes No

10. When set-backs and delays occur, do they feel insignificant, not slowing your progress at all? Yes No

11. Do you find it truly easy to give up your habits or the things associated with your old way of doing things? Yes No

12. Are you at complete ease with accepting the new life, habits, foods, routine or responsibilities associated with reaching your goal? Yes No

13. How many goals have you set for yourself and accomplished?

Explanation

This was a test of how much "hustle" and "grind" you really have in you. Your answers tell whether you're likely to achieve your goals or not. Now, because each of these issues "weighs" differently, it would be impossible to grade this quiz by the number of yeses you checked off.

Instead, look at your answers and consider how you feel about them. Spend 5-10 seconds meditating on each one, noticing how it feels knowing that this is the truth about you, and thinking about what it means. Unless you lied. In that case, do it over.

After taking this quiz, only about 2 in every 10 quiz takers report feeling very optimistic about reaching their objective. And this is probably bloated, because statistics show that, if the goal will take any longer than a month to achieve, only about 1 in 20 people will actually reach it on their next attempt. So after you evaluate your quiz, if you feel optimistic about your chances, congratulations.

If you feel depressed, then think long and hard about what you can change and how you can change it. It's possible that you still have a lot more to change than you know. You may have to kill yourself so you can live. Put the gun down. It's a metaphor.

The Ninth Principle

"Seal the Deal" means: Choose the best paths, envision the future, ensure survival, and achieve success.

What You'll Learn

* What Rick Ross, Noriega, and Saddam Hussein have in common.
* Why the South African government killed revolutionary Steve Biko.
* How Malcolm X escaped from prison.
* Why you like white girls and can't help it.
* Why rappers and celebrities are being targeted for their activism.
* How to get (and keep) a job, or make legit money without one.
* Why you should go to college, or what you can do if you don't.
* What Hurricane Katrina has to do with Michael Vick.
* What it takes for hustlers to change their lives.
* Which changes can happen overnight, and which take lifetimes.
* Why revolution is the *only* answer to our problems.

Cry Freedom

> The logic behind white domination is to prepare the Black man for the subservient role in this country. Not so long ago this used to be freely said in parliament, even about the educational system of the Black

> people. It is still said even today, although in a much more sophisticated language.
>
> To a large extent the evil-doers have succeeded in producing at the output end of their machine a kind of Black man who is man only in form. This is the extent to which the process of dehumanization has advanced.

These are the words of South African activist Steve Biko, in a speech he gave in the 1970s, titled "We Blacks." It's amazing how much of his words ring true for Blacks everywhere, especially in the United States, even now. Biko's words and works gave birth to a movement that fueled the fires of Black consciousness throughout the world. But that may never have happened.

Steve Biko was once just a college student, trying to find a way to make a change for his people under South Africa's racist apartheid system. Under apartheid, a small minority of white foreigners controlled most of South Africa, as well as the lives of the Blacks and Indians living there.

Biko joined an organization promoting racial unity as a way to change the cruel system of South African government. But he soon realized that simply wouldn't work.

He became convinced that Black and Indian students needed an organization of their own, and he helped found the South African Students' Organization (SASO) in 1968. The SASO didn't preach a "multiracial" solution to the problems of South Africa. Instead, they began promoting an identity that was unified in its separateness from whites, and they succeeded in attracting thousands of Black and Indian youths throughout South Africa.

The SASO then evolved into the even more powerful Black Consciousness Movement (BCM). As part of the BCM, Biko's writings and programs empowered Blacks, and he became famous for his slogan "Black is beautiful." Biko saw the struggle to restore Black consciousness as having two stages, "Psychological liberation" and "Physical liberation." He knew he had to first change his people's minds before they could change their conditions.

As a result of this work, Steve Biko was banned by the government in March of 1973. This meant: (a) He was not allowed to speak to more than one person at a time; (b) He was restricted to isolated rural areas; (c) He could make no public speeches; and (d) No one could quote anything he said, including past speeches or even simple conversations.

Nonetheless, Biko and the BCM were able to continue building. There were eventually able to organize several protests, which built up to the Soweto Uprising of June 16, 1976. This rebellion was crushed by heavily-armed South African police shooting 700 protesting school children. After that day, the authorities were intent on destroying Biko once and for all.

On August 18, 1977, Biko was arrested at a police roadblock under the Terrorism Act No. 83 of 1967. This was long before the "War on Terror," but just goes to show how much the game plan hasn't changed. The police clubbed him in the head and chained him to a window grille for a full day.

A few weeks later, police threw him, naked, into the back of a Land Rover and began the long drive to Pretoria prison. He died soon after arriving there. First, the police claimed his death was the result of a hunger strike. After his massive head injuries were found, the police claimed Biko had bashed his own head, attempting suicide. The Attorney-General stated that he would not prosecute any police involved in the arrest and detention of Biko. Steve Biko may have physically died at the hands of his enemy, but his work helped give birth to the Black Consciousness movement in America. Without him, a lot of future activists and revolutionaries wouldn't have known what their calling was in life.

What does this have to do with you?

Like Che Guevarra, Martin Delany, and Frantz Fanon, Biko originally studied medicine, and could have been a successful doctor.

But like Fanon and the others, Biko developed an intense concern for the development of a revolutionary mentality among all people of color. He, like the others, realized that would be the only way to change the awful conditions experienced by Black and brown people throughout the world.

Did You Know?

Almost thirty years after Steve Biko's death, public demands led the government to reopen the investigation. On October 7, 2003, the South African Justice Ministry again decided that the policemen who killed Biko would not be prosecuted because of insufficient evidence and the fact that the time span for prosecution had passed.

But Biko could have chosen to be a doctor! He could have become very wealthy, doing good work, and probably wouldn't have been killed by the police. He could have saved himself from the racist evil of his country by making enough money to move away...but to where?

"If I had to die for something, let it be for the truth."
Medgar Evers

Where is there that Blacks are free? Certainly not America. And Biko was in Africa, home of Black people! But almost everywhere in Africa, whites still had the money and power. So Biko made his choice, and his choice put him in the history books. Biko could have lived a good life as a rich doctor, which must have seemed great to someone coming from a poor background. But he decided to give his life to a greater cause. Instead of healing a hundred bodies, he chose to heal millions of minds.

And if Biko, Gueverra, Fanon, Delany, and many others had not made the choices to follow the paths they took, the world would be a very, very different place, and we would be much, much worse off today. As Steve Biko said himself, "It is better to die for an idea that will live, than to live for an idea that will die."

"Destiny is not a matter of chance, it is a matter of choice;
it is not a thing to be waited for, it is a thing to be achieved."
William Jennings Bryan

I'm not recommending that you drop out of school. What I *am* saying is that you should look at what path you REALLY want to take in life, and make the choices to actually take it. At some point, you may come to a life-changing fork in the road, and go the way no one else thought you should…and it will make all the difference.

I was a talented graphic artist in college and received several awards. I could have gone into graphic design as a career and made a lot of money. I was already working with rappers, models, and big companies like GE, and it would have been easy to keep following that path.

But one day I realized my calling. And I made the choice to become who I am today. I haven't been killed…yet, but no matter what happens I don't have to wonder what I "could have" done with my life. I can feel good about myself at the end of the day, because I didn't follow the path towards money and luxury, and instead committed myself to the struggle for freedom…and I still get paid in full!

So please don't think it can't be done. Anyway, what else is really worth doing? If all you do is live, buy a few things, and die…what was the point of you even being here? Even if you have a family, what if all you empower them to do is live, buy a few things, and die as well? Without an agenda you're willing to die for, your life ain't bout much. So, by all

Did You Know?

Toussaint was just like us. In fact, he had it better than most of us. He wasn't even involved in the fighting to begin with. Because he was well-provided for by his overseer, he commented:

"We went to labor in the fields, my wife and I, hand in hand. Scarcely were we conscious of the fatigues of the day. Heaven always blessed our toil. Not only we swam in abundance, but we had the pleasure of giving food to blacks who needed it."

In fact, Toussaint, like many other revolutionaries, could be con-sidered middle-class (given the context). Like Steve Biko, Frantz Fanon, and Che Guevara, he was a doctor before he became a rebel leader!

Toussaint wasn't suffering in the fields, but his people were. He knew right from wrong. And he decided to give his life, and all within his power to make things right. So what's your excuse?

means, do school, do you, do whatever...but when the opportunity presents itself, do something worth doing.

A life not worth dying for isn't worth living for. Find your calling.

TEN YEARS FOR A BLOWJOB

In 2003, Genarlow Wilson was a 17-year-old senior at Douglas County High School in Georgia. He had a 3.2 GPA and football skills that had caught the attention of a several Ivy League schools. He was popular among students and teachers and had been voted Homecoming King.

All that changed after a New Year's Eve party, which he and his friends videotaped. After the party, 17-year-old Michelle had her mother pick her up. When her mother smelled weed and alcohol on her, she claimed she had no idea what had happened. "I think they raped me" she explained to her mother. This led to an investigation.

When police came to the hotel room, they found the video. On it, it's clear that Michelle was not raped. It's also clear that another girl, Tracy, is going around the room, sucking several of the boys off.

She was 15, and it was obvious that she wasn't being held against her will. But at the time the boys were charged, Georgia law stipulated that it was "a misdemeanor for teenagers less than 3 years apart to have sexual intercourse." Sure, it was a misdemeanor to have regular sex, but it was a *felony* for them to have *oral sex*.

According to Chandra Wilson's article in *Atlanta Magazine*:

> Four of the teens buckled and signed documents—some without even their parents' knowledge—accepting pleas to lesser charges in exchange for lighter prison terms. The pleas varied, but there were some commonalities: None would serve the mandatory 10 years in prison for aggravated child molestation (for having oral sex with 15-year-old Tracy), but all would be registered sex offenders forever. Cheryl Arnold, Ryan Barnwell's aunt, says prosecutors used scare tactics to pressure the kids into accepting plea deals. "He was scared, they made him think that they would get 30 years in prison if they went to trial."

But Genarlow Wilson stood his ground. His lone codefendant, Frankie soon took a plea as well. Still, Genarlow stood firm. At his trial, Genarlow was found guilty of aggravated child molestation, which carried a mandatory ten years behind bars. Ten years for a blowjob.

It caused such an uproar that the law was changed after his conviction. But the Legislature refused to make the new law retroactive, leaving Wilson stuck in prison.

Oh…Did I mention that the 15 year old girl was white, and Genarlow Wilson was a young Black ballplayer with dreads? Make sense now?

Genarlow's codefendants all pled guilty and were released after a few months. But Genarlow still refused to budge. He knew he had done nothing wrong. He had never even been in trouble with the law before. He turned down two plea bargain deals, stating, "What's right is right. I'm just standing up for what I believe in."

People thought he was crazy. But he understood something his friends didn't. If he pled guilty, he would be branded with child molestor status. That meant that he'd have to move far away from any school zone, making life nearly impossible, and he'd have to report his status everywhere he lived and everywhere he worked.

So Genarlow Wilson chose to stick to his guns and continue to fight for his freedom. As news of his story spread, people joined in his fight with him. Protestors, lawyers, and rappers came to his defense. Even comedian Ricky Smiley got involved in the fight for Genarlow's freedom. In October of 2007, Genarlow Wilson's conviction was overturned and he was freed. He'd sacrificed a few years of his life to prison, but he saved himself many more years of being labeled a child molestor.

What would you have done in his shoes? Cop a plea? Give up? Stand your ground? I've got brothers in prison doing 23-hours a day in lockdown because they won't stop identifying as Five Percent. The prisons have targeted Gods and thrown hundreds of them in solitary until they sign a little piece of paper saying they're not God. But they won't budge. Why? Because they stand for something *that tough.* And they known their fight is worth fighting. They know they're not wrong, so they're not admitting guilt, just as Genarlow Wilson wouldn't.

What Do You Stand For?

Before we can even answer that question, we have to ask this one: What do you REALLY want out of life? I hope its not money, or wealth, or financial security, or whatever they call it now. Money comes and goes, but there are more important things in life that we often miss in the pursuit of money. I am learning to dedicate myself to the pursuit of freedom.

Yes, freedom. Are you free? Probably not. You don't need to be living on your own island to be free, but I'm sure that 90% of the people who read this aren't truly free. You aren't even free to be yourself in this society, because certain things aren't "acceptable," or perhaps you're just scared to be your own person.

- ❑ Do you follow trends? Not free.
- ❑ Taking a path set for you by others (peers, parents, etc.), but which you don't really want for yourself? Not free.
- ❑ Afraid to deny the ridiculous beliefs of your religion because you're scared of going to some childish conception of Hell? Not free.
- ❑ Smoke weed daily? Not free (chew on why).
- ❑ Student loans? Yup.
- ❑ Negative friends who drain you? Ditto.
- ❑ A job you hate? Of course.

So what's free? Think about it. Your mind. As Jay-Z rapped, "Lock my body, [but you] can't trap my mind."

As I evolve, my pursuit of that millior dollar [pipe] dream has almost vanished. Of course, some remnants remain like popcorn flakes stuck between your teeth. And you know, if you don't floss that stuff out, your breath gets pretty bad pretty fast.

The same with the dominant ideology. Let it go. All of it. Maybe not cold turkey, but all of them devils have to die ONE day.

I talk to people who say they don't eat pork...but they eat a little bacon here and there. You're a nincompoop. You eat pork. Will it kill you? Nope. Neither will a little bit of cocaine. Or a little bit of gay sex. Or a little bit of child porn.

But dammit, stand for something and stand your ground. Take a stand on issues and be about it. There are some things in life you need to be against *and* have a rationale for *why*. It wasn't until I knew what was really wrong with the American Dream that I could honestly say it was worth it to be completely against it. Otherwise you'll be just like Whitney Houston. Lots of crack, then just a little bit, then eventually, back to a lot.

I've adopted the same attitude towards a lot of meaningful things that otherwise meaningless people don't find meaning in. Maybe the world would be a better place if we all found something to live for...something with meaning....a meaning for life...instead of just meaning to live. The meaning of life? To live like you mean it.

What do you stand for? How far are you willing to go for it? What will you stick to your guns for, no matter what?

What will people say about your life when it's all over? Will anyone know what you stood for, or fought for?

Will you be an inspiration or just another blip on the radar?

Have you watered yourself down or given up ground to please others?

Are you and your views getting stronger or weaker daily?

Stand your ground.
Give an inch a day, and in two weeks you've lost a foot.

You Want a White Girl, Don't Ya?

You know about Genarlow Wilson. You know about Kobe Bryant. You know about O.J. You know about the reasons behind most of the lynchings and race riots in American history. You may have heard Ice Cube rap on "Cave Bitch":

> Why everytime we get famous/ You wanna play us like Andy and Amos?/ The devil sent you to try and tame us/...Cuz everytime I turn on the TV/ I see several brothers with she-devils/ Smilin' cuz you out on a date/ But sooner or later, the bitch'll yell rape

But do you get it?

If you don't, I don't blame you. Every day, we're bombarded with images that tell us white women are the best thing crackin. In fact, most Black women feel the same way. Not only are white women still the standard of beauty in the country, but young Black girls still don't really see enough Black images of beauty to aspire to. After all, Black female celebrities start looking more and more like white women the moment they become famous. It's so bad that even someone light-skinned like Beyonce was airbrushed on the cover of *Vanity Fair* to look even lighter. Just take a look at the "White Girls" video on the *How to Hustle and Win* Youtube page and tell me you don't see it. In their defense, it's not always their fault. They're just as easily influenced as the rest of us. Plus, they're told that these changes are something they *have* to do. Care to wonder why?

Back to you. Check yourself. Just pick True or False:

T F White women take better care of men than Black women.

T F White women will listen to you more.
T F Halle Berry is prettier than than Nia Long.
T F African women are usually unattractive.
T F White girls are better at sex.

If you answered True on at least 3 out of 5 of those questions, then you may like white women more than you want to admit. Maybe you've been conditioned to think even white turds are better than brown ones. Think about it. I bet you've never seen a young Black man walk through the mall holding hands with a Black woman...but if he's got a white girl, he's not letting her go. Or maybe we're conditioned to hate ourselves. Maybe you're just like Yung Berg, and you don't care for "dark butt" women because they "look like monkeys."

Do you really believe the myths? Don't believe the hype. My brother Dominant put it this way:

> Everybody wants a white girl cause they think she gonna be more submissive, more nasty, more everything, with less arguing and less drama. That's where you f*ck up. You only THINK she's down with whatever you say and do. She's only f*ckin with you up to a certain point. She'll dump you when she done with you. And trust me homey, she ain't with you cause of the sh*t you stand for. She gonna get with a strong nigga just so she can break him down, real slow and sneaky. By the time she's done with him, he'll be so f*cked up, he won't even know how he ended up all weak and stupid.

How many brothas do you know who are with white women...who are on some real dedicated Black community sh*t? I've never seen one stick to that script once they start coming home to Becky and her friends. So you can believe that you've got the power if you want to. In *Why Black Men Love White Women*, author Rajen Persaud explains it well. At one point, Persaud recalls an interview where Bryant Gumbel was showing off his white fiance:

> The body language states: "This is my white woman." The *my* in the dialogue represents ownership; it is in that illusion of ownership where the power lies. But there really isn't much control happening, and in cases where he is in control, it is by permission. At any given point the white woman can give the command to turn him off.

Check out Persaud's book. Once you're done, check out Michael Eric Dyson's *Why I Love Black Women*. In the meantime, stop chasing them white girls!

True Freedom

While we're talking about freedom, we need to be clear on what freedom really means. In *Young Gifted and Black*, Theresa Perry writes:

> For the slaves, literacy was more than a symbol of freedom; it was freedom. It affirmed their humanity, their personhood. To be able to

> read and write was an intrinsic good, as well as a mighty weapon in the slave's struggle for freedom. Literate slaves filed legal petitions, protesting and challenging their enslavement; they forged passes for themselves and others, thus allowing escape from the horrors of slavery. Literate slaves read newspapers and pamphlet's and kept themselves and the slave community informed about the antislavery movement and the war. Denmark Vesey, David Walker, Nat Turner, and other literate slaves led rebellions and wrote pamphlets and tracts denouncing and exposing the slave system. They read the Bible, interpreting its message in a way that supported resistance and rebellions.

> While learning to read was an individual achievement, it was fundamentally a communal act. For the slaves, literacy affirmed not only their individual freedom but also the freedom of their people.

Tupac Shakur, after serving time in a New York prison, revealed that had built with "every" Five Percenter in the prison. However, he wasn't fully sold on their idea of God. He said, "If you're God, open this gate for me. Let me out of here." Tupac, although a very brilliant man, had missed the point. He didn't understand freedom the way the slaves saw it in the 1820s, or the way Malcolm X had seen it in the 1950s, or the way the Gods do in the present era. To the Gods, like the others, "freedom" was only real, if it meant a "free dome" (a free mind).

In the *Autobiography of Malcolm X*, Malcolm tells about when he was arrested in Boston and sentenced to prison. There, he learned about the teachings of the Nation of Islam. This is when the hustler known on the streets of Boston as Shorty Red began his transformation. But it wasn't an easy process. Though he was smart, Malcolm had lost interest in school long ago and dropped out in the ninth grade. In order to join the Nation of Islam, every aspiring member had to write a one-page letter to leader Elijah Muhammad. Little did he know that the simple act of writing would prove to be one of the most difficult tasks a successful hustler like Malcolm had ever attempted: "I must have written that one-page letter to him over and over. I was trying to make it both legible and understandable…It shames me even to remember it…The things I felt I was pitifully unable to express…"

But Malcolm kept at it, determined to improve:

> I became increasingly frustrated at not being able to express what I wanted to convey in the letters that I wrote, especially those to Elijah Muhammad. In the street, I had been the most articulate hustler out there – I had commanded attention when I said something. But now,

> trying to write simple English, I not only wasn't articulate, I wasn't even functioning.

Malcolm studied the writing of others, read and copied the entire dictionary, and read books on every subject under the sun. He also continued writing, and as he improved, he became bolder with who he wrote to, and what he wrote about:

> I have never been one for inaction. Everything I have ever felt strongly about, I have done something about. I guess that's why, unable to do anything else, I soon began to write people I had known in the hustling world, such as Sammy the Pimp, John Hughes, the gambling house owner, and the thief, Jump Steady, and several dope peddlers. I wrote them all about Allah and Islam, and Mr. Elijah Muhammad...Later on, I even wrote to the major of Boston, to the governor of Massachusetts, and to [President] Harry S. Truman...I hand scratched to them how the white man's society was responsible for the Black man's condition in this wilderness of North America. It was because of my letters that I happened to stumble upon starting some kind of home-made education.

Before long, Malcolm was the most well-read prisoner in the jail. It was through his self-education, that Malcolm freed himself from prison. After being transferred to a prison facility with a much larger library, he remarked, "Months passed without my even thinking about being imprisoned. In fact, up to then, I had never been so truly free in my life." Malcolm X, still physically in prison, was now aware of a world he had never seen before. He realized that, in the streets, he had still been held behind walls that he could not see:

> Ten guards and the wardens couldn't have torn me out of those books. Not even Elijah Muhammad could have been more eloquent than those books in providing indisputable proof that the collective white man had acted like a devil in virtually every contact he had with the world's collective non-white man...I have often reflected upon the new vistas that reading opened for me. I knew right there in prison that reading had changed forever the course of my life...My home-made education gave me, with every additional book that I read, a little bit more sensitivity to the deafness, and blindness that was affecting the Black race in America.

Malcolm used his new-found intelligence and eloquence to successfully argue for his parole. Even once he was physically free, Malcolm X continued to find a greater freedom in knowledge and awareness:

> If I weren't out here every day, battling the white man, I could spend the rest of my life just reading, just satisfying my curiosity – because you can hardly mention anything I am not curious about.

Sure, you're reading *this* book, but is study a major part of your life? If not, why not? No time? Bad excuse. Even 2,000 years ago, the famous Rabbi Hillel told his followers, "Do not say, 'When I have free time, I will study,' because you may never have free time." The quality of your life is determined by the quality of your mind. Without knowledge and understanding, your life is guaranteed to be more problematic. Even if it's cool for the short-term, it's definitely gonna suck for the long-term.

So read (and write) more. When people ask how I could possibly know about all this stuff that I write about, I just tell them, "I read." Even when I was drunk, depressed, homeless, or stressed…I was reading and writing. And between that and the many beautiful struggles of my life, I found true freedom like Malcolm. Not only did I find my own answers, I found a formula that could free us all. Now it's your turn.

> "[If I had my own country] school would not be optional. It would mandatory. Because I do not like unintelligent people; it's a pet peeve. If you dumb, you not around me, so that says a lot about the people you see around me, because I hate dumb people."
> Lil Wayne, *GQ Magazine* interview

Start by creating a reading list for yourself. If you need help, try the recommendations in this book and *How to Hustle and Win, Part One.*

What you take into your mind determines what it puts out. The quality of your thought determines the quality of your life.

I Am What You Ain't

I AM...	I am NOT...
A soldier, because I can take pain...and I not only know how to give orders, but how to take them.	A goon, because a goon (by definition) only takes orders from a boss.
A warrior, because I will continue fighting even when alone.	A thug, because I fight for something, not over nothing.
A boss, because I'm on top of my affairs.	A punk, pussy, bitch, or hoe, because I will F*CK YOU UP if you cross that line.
The lord of all worlds, because I can master any domain.	Religious, because I am bigger than a label and a list of things someone tells me to believe.
A man, because I'm grown and mature.	A boy, because I am not engaged in childish desires, thoughts, or actions.
Victorious, because I've survived a lot and come out on top.	A victim, because I don't need your pity or a handout.
A role model, because if you are looking, I can show you.	Weak, because it takes great strength to do what's right in this world.
A thinker, because I take time to decide which directions I take.	A follower, because I don't trust my life in the hands of a stranger.
A student, because I stay learnin. A day I don't learn is a day wasted.	Perfect, because only liars and fakes have no flaws.
A poor righteous teacher, because I walk the earth in humility	A leader, because I show people how to make their own decisions.
The people, because I am one of many, and I am not alone.	Elite, because I am not snobbish or stuck-up.
A freedom fighter, because there is	An "armchair philosopher," because I'd

a war out there, and we're losing.	rather put in work than debate ideas.
A revolutionary, because the system is unjust, and the people deserve change.	A nigga, because I am too much of a man to call myself by a name made for slaves.
Invincible, because I'm only human.	Immortal, because my works and ideas will outlive me.
[fill in the blank]	[fill in the blank]

THE REAL RICK ROSS

At the height of his reign, "Freeway" Ricky Ross was pulling in $2-3 million weekly and had close ties to some of the most notorious international drug smugglers on the scene. With thousands of employees, Ross operated drug sales not only in Los Angeles, but in cities across the country including St. Louis, New Orleans, Texas, Kansas City, Oklahoma, Indiana, Cincinnati, Baltimore, Cleveland and Seattle.

Ricky was once a high school dropout in South Central Los Angeles. Though he was a very talented tennis player, the future didn't look promising. Functionally illiterate, and scraping by with little money, Ricky saw an opportunity to prosper when an older teacher at a job center turned him on to cocaine. Ricky, 19 at the time, looked up to the man and started dealing for him.

The money was good. Eventually, Ricky decided to go solo. He met a character named Oscar Danilo Blandon Reyes, who would begin supplying him. Their business relationship grew into a friendship, and Ricky would enjoy spending time at Blandon's home, far from the hellish ghettoes of L.A.

Blandon schooled young Ricky in the art of staying "low key" and taught him how to market large quantities of cocaine at bargain-basement prices. "At first we were just getting eight ounces or so worth $16,000," Ross explained. "As time went on Blandon started supplying kilos (worth tens of millions of dollars). I don't know how it was possible. I didn't question him. Just took it as a blessing."

By 1984, "Freeway Ricky" was a kingpin, with over a dozen crack houses in South Central L.A., churning out $20,000 to $40,000 a day in profits. His network of drug dealers peddled an unbelievable 500,000 rocks daily. Ricky was using cashiers' checks to buy close to $6 million in property – motels, tire shops, junk yards, apartment buildings, houses.

One day Blandon brought Ricky a brand new Uzi submachine gun and a .22 with a silencer. Ricky and a partner then added gun dealing to their resumés… selling the Uzis, AK-47s, and AR-15 assault rifles that became the trademark of bloody gang wars and drive-by shootings throughout the 1980s. Most of it fueled by beef over the growing drug trade. Freeway Ricky's drug trade. All of this was made possible through Blandon. Blandon even once tried to sell Ricky a *grenade launcher.*

For ten years, "Freeway" Ricky Ross operated his drug empire with zero harassment from the police, the DEA, or any other agencies. Whenever ambitious local police planned to shut him down, other government agencies told them to back off. It wouldn't last forever though.

"Soon as you get your money right, they hit you with conspiracy."
Young Jeezy, "Crazy World"

Finally, once the crack epidemic had fully saturated every Black community in America, Ricky was no longer needed. He was, of course, *disposable.* In 1996, Ricky was set up and convicted of conspiring to buy more than 100 kilograms of cocaine from a police informant. The government's star witness against him: His old friend, Oscar Danilo Blandon Reyes. On Blandon's testimony, Ricky and two other men were convicted by an all-white jury. Ricky was eventually sentenced to 20 years in prison.

What happened to Blandon, you ask? Well, records show that he received $45,000 in government rewards and expenses for "assisting" with Ricky's arrest. Blandon only received a 24-month sentence for his drug trafficking charges, and following his release, was *hired* by the DEA, where he was salaried at over $40,000 a year! And now? His current whereabouts are unknown. Probably somewhere on an island, chillin.

Ricky's eyes were teary as he described Blandon's testimony to an interviewer, following his conviction:

> It was like he was killing me. It was nothing I could do but sit there and take it. There's a tape they played in court where (Blandon) said, "I hate niggers, but they pay cash."…I would have died for him. He's the worst. When I see how (the government) twists the rules for him and they want to give me a life sentence, to me it's sickening.

It's even more sickening that some of us still can't see the game for what it is. But Ricky was blinded by the fast money, and the lure of success…not to mention that he was really *good* at this sh*t. Sometimes, distracting factors like that can blind you to the big picture. In fact, in an interview right before his sentencing, Ricky still only felt "partially responsible" for the destruction crack had done, for the crack babies and drug-addicted prostitutes dying slowly throughout Black communities across America, and for the young Black men killing each other and dying in jail trying to get – to quote Lil Wayne – "rich like a white man." Ricky, still young, explained that the consequences of his actions had not crossed his mind at the time.

As he matured, with more than enough time to sit, think, and read, Ricky began seeing the big picture, something most of us miss when we're moving too fast.

He later explained why he didn't feel totally responsible, "I took the drugs and I transferred them from [Blandon's] hands to their hands. I feel that I was a 'strawberry' (a crack whore) too. I was manipulated. I was just like the prostitute." Ultimately, he said, the U.S. government is responsible for the crack epidemic. "They put it in our hands. They financed it. It was their planes that brought it over here," he told the *Final Call Newspaper* for their article, "A Pawn in the CIA Drug Game." "Their guy, Oscar Danilo Blandon, he set up the market. They picked me." You can look at him as a villain or a victim, but there is a great deal of truth to Ricky's allegations.

During the 1980s, President Reagan openly supported the Nicaraguan Contras in their fight against the Sandanistas. The Sandanistas were Nicaragua's ruling party and they represented the interests of the common people. They were also allies of Fidel Castro's Cuba, and the United States wanted them out of power.

"Can't you tell that I came from the dope game
Blame Reagan for making me into a monster
Blame Oliver North and Iran-Contra
I ran contraband that they sponsored
Before this rhyming stuff, we was in concert"
Jay-Z, "Blue Magic"

The Contras were being funded by the shipments cocaine into Los Angeles dealers with the CIA's full knowledge and assistance. CIA officials were even the ones unloading and refueling the planes.

"First they give us the white, then they throw us in jail"
Young Jeezy, "Soul Survivor"

In August 1996, the *San Jose Mercury* published Gary Webb's infamous "Dark Alliance" article, an expose detailing how the CIA had assisted Contras in supplying large quantities of cocaine to Los Angeles dealers like "Freeway" Ricky Ross. The article also offered plenty of evidence on the CIA's role in aiding and protecting the dealers themselves in supplying crack cocaine to Black communities. The author, Gary Webb, was found dead in 2004. Two shotgun blasts and they ruled it a suicide. Right.

Anyway, it should be a given by now that the illegal drug trade in this country is designed just for US…to fall victim. But some of us still won't see it until it's too late. We're like rats in a windowless house, goin after the cheese, not understanding how the trap works.

> "The ghetto is a nigga trap, take the cheese
> Soon as you do it, here come the po-lice
> Invented and designed fo' us to fail
> Where you gon' end up? Dead or in jail"
> Ice Cube, "The Nigga Trapp"

Today, Ricky Ross is a dedicated anti-drug advocate. With his upcoming autobiography, he hopes to dispel some of the myths involved with the dope game, including the illusion that you can actually WIN it. And who better to tell you about it? If you can't learn game from someone who was literally on the very top of it, no f*ckin body can save you.

No matter where you stand in life, do you see where you fit in the big picture? Are you somehow part of the machine that keeps us all down?

Can you push past your pursuit of prosperity to prevent the problems it produces in poor populations? Can you say that three times fast?

The relentless pursuit of prosperity is often our biggest problem, instead of a solution. Look at the big picture.

TOILET PAPER HUSTLERS

Manuel Noriega

Born in Panama City, Panama in 1934, the "real" Noriega was a career soldier. By the early 1960s, Noriega had risen quickly through the ranks in both the military…and the cocaine business.

By 1971, the U.S. had "hard evidence" of his heavy involvement in drug trafficking, "sufficient for indictment." But Noriega had been on the U.S. government's payroll since the 1950s. By the 1970s, he was a CIA asset, receiving more than $100,000 per year. In 1976, CIA Director George Bush even gave him a VIP tour of CIA headquarters in Washington. But Noriega was making way more than $100K a year. From 1981-1983, Noriega expanded his empire and engaged in extensive drug trafficking and money laundering with the Medellin, a powerful Colombia cocaine cartel. By August of 1983, Noriega enhanced his position in Panama by promoting himself to full general, effectively making him the de facto ruler. In November of that same year, he visited with his people at the White House, the State Department, and the Pentagon, including CIA Director William Casey.

Throughout the early 80s, the U.S. government loved him for spying on Fidel Castro and other anti-U.S. leaders, as well as allowing the U.S. to set up listening posts for Central America. Noriega was also aiding the American military against rebels in El Salvador and against the government of Nicaragua. Noriega was a major player in helping the

CIA funnel coke out of the country, while bringing in guns and funds for the U.S.-supported Contras. (See "Che Guevara")

BUT at the same time, Manuel Noriega was also spying for Fidel Castro and others. He was also helping Cuba get over on the US economic embargos. He was even helping get weapons for the Sandinistas (who were fighting the Contras) and the rebels in El Salvador. Whose side was this motherf*cker on? One side, homey: Greed. Manuel Noriega was all about whoever was paying.

In 1984, the CIA and the Medellin cartel helped finance the campaign of Noriega's candidate for President, Nicolas Barletta. Barletta was declared the winner 10 days after the election, even though Barletta had really been defeated by at least 4,000 votes.

Around this time, a few self-motivated DEA agents and US Attorneys began under-the-radar investigations into Noriega's drug activities.

In 1986, after the *New York Times* publishes the most detailed and damning report on Noriega to ever appear in the U.S. media, the Reagan administration told him not to worry! High-ranking U.S. law enforcement officials, including the head of the DEA began advising Noriega on how to achieve "a better public image."

By 1988, Noriega's main "protectors" in the U.S. government were gone (or dead). Noriega was finally indicted on Federal drug charges, and no one stepped up to save his ass this time. In fact, the next year, the CIA turned their back on their old asset and provided more than $10 million in aid to Noriega's opposition. When the ballot count started coming up short for Noriega's side (again), he stopped the electoral process and sent the goons out against the opposition. This time however, Washington condemned the "fraudulent election." Ain't that crazy?

In December of that year, the US invaded Panama in order to "capture Noriega." The body count totaled 3,000-5,000 Panamanians (mainly civilians) dead, plus over 3,000 wounded, and 20,000-30,000 left homeless.

In 1990, after putting Noriega in prison (where he remains), the U.S. installed another puppet named Guillermo Endara as president. Ironically, the new president, vice president, and the attorney general ALL have links to drug trafficking and money laundering as well. It just don't stop. Within a year, Colombian drug cartels and associates of Noriega once again turned Panama into a narcotics transshipment center. Today there are far more cocaine production facilities than ever existed under Noriega, and drug use in Panama is at all-time highs.

Get it yet? If not, keep reading. You will.

Saddam Hussein

Before being falsely associated with WMD, 9/11, and Al Qaeda, Saddam Hussein first came into prominence as a CIA asset during the Reagan administration. At the time, the U.S. was very interested in getting Iran's leader, Ayatollah Khomeini, out of power. They figured removing the Ayatollah would give them better control of the Middle East, a region rich in oil and resources, but run by Muslims who couldn't stand American interests. With the full support of the U.S. government (particularly the CIA), and supplied with American weapons, Saddam took Iraq to war with its neighbor Iran.

The bloody eight-year war ended in a stalemate. There were hundreds of thousands of casualties with estimates of up to one million dead for both sides. Both economies, previously healthy and expanding, were left in ruins. Saddam, in his attempt to force a surrender, had employed chemical weapons that he had been sold by the U.S.

The Reagan administration had lent Iraq $40 billion to fight this war – on credit. In addition, Saddam had borrowed from other Arab countries, bringing Iraq's total debt to at least $75 billion. Saddam was sh*tfaced. The U.S. now wanted him to pay up for a war *they* had pushed him to fight. But Saddam wasn't bowing down any further.

Ignoring the demands of his "handlers" in the CIA, Saddam resumed running Iraq as he saw fit. A CIA plot emerged, involving a young Kuwaiti woman falsely testifying that she and thousands of others were being tortured and abused by Saddam's forces. This was used to justify the U.S.'s first invasion of Iraq. After the short show of force by the U.S., Saddam still refused to fully cooperate. Bush Sr. was pissed.

So, years later, as tensions rode high following the attacks on September 11th, Bush Jr. reported that Iraq "possesses and produces chemical and biological weapons. It is seeking nuclear weapons." Soon, Americans were led to believe that Saddam had something to do with 9/11.

Alleging that Iraq had "Weapons of Mass Destruction" (which it didn't), the Bushes again invaded Iraq in 2003. Saddam's sons and 14-year old grandson were found and executed first, their blood-soaked faces proudly displayed on American media. Then Saddam was captured and sent to trial where he was branded a madman. Why? He was blaming the U.S. for pushing him to do the sh*t he was being accused of.

On December 30, 2006, Saddam, former CIA asset, was hanged. Used, abused, and discarded. That's the way they do you.

To read more about Saddam and his friends in the U.S. Government, you can check out *Spider's Web: The Secret History of How the White House*

Illegally Armed Iraq by Alan Friedman, or look it up online at www.whatreallyhappened.com

Osama Bin Laden

Osama is a bad guy. He wants to hurt innocent people. So, yes, he's bad. I know you're glad I got that out of the way. Now, I can say this:

Osama bin Laden wasn't responsible for 9/11. You can find 500 books and 400 videos telling you who really did it (and how and why), so I won't waste 300 pages on that.

To keep it short, Bin Laden started out a militant Muslim with a wealthy family. Nobody *that* special. But *one day*...our government decided they weren't going to let the Soviet Union take over Afghanistan, which was valuable, because it provided access to oil, and produced lots and lots of heroin. And the U.S. loves its oil and dope, you know.

So they trained and funded Bin Laden to go to war against the Soviets. Bin Laden and his Mujahideen whupped some Russian ass, and they held Afghanistan down. But Bin Laden started noticing that his bosses were trying to take over a bit too much. Having some very strong views, Bin Laden didn't like what Western influence was doing to Muslim lands. He saw that wherever Americans had not taken over by force, they were taking over by spreading their culture. It seemed that everywhere America went, porn, pork, pollution, and poverty followed. Not to mention that American interests were taking control of the region's rich resources, as well as building military bases on the land, which they'd use to attack Arab nations.

So he switched sides. He turned against the U.S. He went hard, bombing sh*t and taking full credit, like – for example – when he blew up a U.S. embassy in Africa.

But when 9/11 went down, the government and the news said it was Bin Laden almost right after the attacks. They just knew. At least, that's how it seemed to us. The truth is, it was all part of the plan.

Bin Laden swore he didn't do it, but then a video popped up where it appears that he says he did it. That's all they needed! The U.S. went into Afghanistan and took over, claiming it was all about finding Bin Laden.

Did You Know?

According to the FBI, "Bin Laden has not been formally charged in connection to 9/11." Rex Tomb, Chief of Investigative Publicity for the FBI said, "The reason why 9/11 is not mentioned on Osama bin Laden's Most Wanted page is because the FBI has no hard evidence connecting bin Laden to 9/11." And as far as the "confession" video, not one document has been released that demonstrates the authenticity of the videotape or that it even went through an authentication process. In fact, if you look closely...ah, forget it...nobody looks closely nowadays, do they?

Then they wanted to hit Iraq, claiming Bin Laden was one of Saddam's homies. When they told Colin Powell to make the case for an Iraqi invasion, he threw the papers in the air and said, "I'm not saying this sh*t!" Colin Powell had played puppet for long enough. This was the turning point where he decided he was done acting as official house Negro, and would later resign. But since he never broke his silence, he still hasn't been targeted. But they didn't really need Powell. They had Condoleeza. She said what they told her to, and the next thing you know, we were terrorizing Iraq worse than Saddam ever could.

Years later, we still don't know where Bin Laden is, and Bush said he didn't care. But everytime they want to get you riled up, they'll produce a "new" video of Bin Laden talking sh*t. You'll get scared, and they'll use your fear to let them do whatever they want. Meanwhile, the real Bin Laden has probably been in a CIA freezer for the past five years.

What does any of this have to do with you? Ah, don't tell me you haven't figured out how to "find yourself" in this book yet. Here's how you do it: You look at the lesson, then you look back at the story, and then you think about what parts of your life the lesson can apply to, based on the lives of the people in the story. So for this one, think about whether you've been working for or helping someone else, and you thought you were benefiting...only to find out that they were just using you for the short-term. Well, look at what happens! There's the lesson!

And you don't have to be a CIA asset to be a toilet paper hustler. Everywhere you look, Black celebrities, musicians, athletes, politicians, gangsters, and businessmen are being taken down from the pedestals they *thought* they had. As soon as you've fulfilled their purposes, or you become a liability by going against the grain, you're *out*...and usually in the most embarrassing way. As Ice Cube raps on "Hood Mentality"

> I'm gon' be that little fool comin' in your living room/ Starting point guard nigga, fresh out of middle school/ Either it's the NBA or it's the NFL/ I don't know what else I can do to keep my ass up out of jail/...I wanna be all broke up, movin' all old and slow/ I wanna be an alcoholic, just like Broadway Joe/ I wanna be a sideshow, kinda like Iron Mike/ Used to have a few Bentleys, now I just ride a bike

I shouldn't even have to explain how actual hustlers are the most used and quickly discarded, but a quote from Killer Mike sums it up:

> Big schemes, big dreams, yeah I'm with it folk/ But 20 years of dealin dope is just a f*ckin joke/ And so what [if] you 'the man' with that white, man?/ Probation got you answerin to a white man.

Plies made the same realization: "I don't know if 25 years worth 2 years of ballin/ That's a big pill to take and I ain't tryna swallow it."

Matter fact, I think most hustlers understand that their time is limited. They know they can get taken down at any time, so they live it up while they're on top, not realizing that they could transition their money into legit business if they could just slow down on all the material excess.

But I'm not mad at the hustlers who understand this. I'm upset with those of you living "clean" lives who *don't.* Don't you know that your life remains in the balance as well? Your job ain't guaranteed. Your freedom ain't promised. If they feel like outsourcing your position, bankrupting your company, and foreclosing your house, they *can.* And if they want to lock your ass up, they *will.* I should know. I didn't get hit with felony charges *until* I completely cleaned up and started doing the right thing.

So who's using you? I mean, who's taking care of you? For how long?

Once you're done being used, you get discarded.

WATCH WHAT YOU SAY

Will Smith on Black Oppression

People typically think of Will Smith as a soft celebrity, like Michael Jordan, careful not to make waves and take any unpopular political stances. What more would you expect from the guy who made "Summertime" and "Parents Just Don't Understand" before going on to star as the *Fresh Prince of Bel Air*? But you're mistaken. Will Smith is *not* a sellout. He just plays one on TV.

In an August 9, 2004 interview with a major German newspaper, the former Fresh Prince said some pretty controversial things he probably would never have said around the U.S. media. When asked if 9/11 had changed anything for him personally, Smith answered:

> No. Absolutely not. When you grow up black in America you have a completely different view of the world than white Americans. We blacks live with a constant feeling of unease. And whether you are wounded in an attack by a racist cop or in a terrorist attack, I'm sorry, it makes no difference. In the 60s, blacks were continuously the victims of terrorist attacks. It was civil terrorism, but terrorism nonetheless.

Smith then talked about building with Kofi Annan, former head of the United Nations and a fellow critic of Bush. I can just imagine what those two brothers admitted in privacy. Smith also revealed feeling "lied to" by President Bush, and said he hoped the film *Fahrenheit 9/11* "contributes to more people waking up and looking into things and drawing their own conclusions." And I guess he figured that was tame.

Not tame enough.

> **Did You Know?**
> It seems that if you're down with Black people, you're a nigger by association. For example, the Venezuelan elite has used racial slurs to taint Hugo Chávez, denouncing him as a black monkey. According to author Tariq Ali, "A puppet show to this effect with a monkey playing Chávez was even organized at the U.S. Embassy in Caracas. But Colin Powell was not amused and the Ambassador was compelled to issue an apology." The attacks continued when Venezuelan media referred to the Minister of Education, Aristobulo Isturiz, who is black, as "a monkey" and "an ape." Meanwhile, analysts have remarked upon the racial undertones of political conflict in Chávez's Venezuela. "Class and skin color differences," remarks Wilpert, "clearly correlate very highly at demonstrations, such that the darker skinned (and presumably lower class) support the Chávez government and the lighter skinned (and presumably middle and upper class) oppose the Chávez government." Willie Lynch Syndrome is bigger than America.

Once white Americans found out what their favorite Negro action hero was saying behind their backs in Germany, they were in an uproar. The group Patriotic Americans Boycotting Anti-American Hollywood added Smith to its list of "banned" stars and began leading a boycott of his films. Patriotic Americans founder Jon Alvarez said: "I've always been a huge fan. But now I'm not going to put a dime in Will Smith's pockets." Since then, Will Smith has learned to keep quiet about what he really thinks, both at home and abroad.

Danny Glover on White Terrorism

Shortly after the 9/11 attacks, Danny Glover said that the U.S. was in "no position" to pass moral judgment on terrorists. "One of the main purveyors of violence in this world," said Glover, "has been this country, whether it's been against Nicaragua, Vietnam, or wherever." Criticizing blind patriotism, Glover stated, "It's basically this rabid [American] nationalism that has its own kind of potential of being maniacal, in some sense. As we march down and wave the flags, we must be sure of what we're waving them for."

Needless to say, white folks were pissed.

But Glover wasn't scared. In 2003, white people threatened to boycott MCI, in an attempt to force them to dump Glover as their pitchman. This time it was because of views he'd expressed about Cuba and the war in Iraq.

He still didn't give a f*ck. Later, he added his signature and support to "The Conscience of the World," a public letter signed by 160 artists which condemned the War in Iraq, and pledged support for the Communist dictatorship of Cuba. He also supported the group Not In Our Name, which pledges "resistance to endless war, detentions and roundups, [and] attacks on civil liberties," and is directed by members of the Revolutionary Communist Party.

Glover is also among a number of high-profile U.S. supporters of Hugo Chavez. The group also includes singer Harry Belafonte and Princeton University scholar Cornel West, who have defended the Venezuelan president against accusations of democratic abuses.

This has led many Americans to boycott Glover's work, including one who declared:

> While Danny Glover has every right to embrace Hugo Chavez's communist/socialist dictatorship, I in turn have every right to refuse to watch his damned movies, and I shall. I've had enough of Danny Glover, Harry Belafonte, and Cornel West, and others like them.

Translation: These damn niggers are going crazy with this revolution sh*t!

> **Did You Know?**
>
> A lot of other famous Black celebrities have much stronger views than you'd think? In fact, one major Black film star – who I'll leave nameless – was recently in a storm of trouble for trying to build a paramilitary training camp for a Black guerrilla army!

Recently, Venezuela's Congress approved several million dollars in financing for two films, with Glover as executive producer. First in line was *The General in His Labyrinth*, which deals with the life of South American liberator Simon Bolivar. The other is *Toussaint*, which Glover will also direct, documenting the life of Haitian revolution leader Toussaint L' Ouverture.

Of course, white folks are doing their best to shut *that* down. Although *Toussaint* is set to star big names like Don Cheadle, Mos Def, Angela Bassett and Chiwetel Ejiofor, it still hasn't received any more funding for its $30 million budget, beyond the $18 million kicked in by Hugo Chavez. Glover visited nearly every studio and producer in the U.S. and Europe, only to hear: "Where are the white people in it? What about white people? Who would see this?"

Of course these people wouldn't put out a film on Black revolution! People seeing the story of Toussaint might set some sh*t off, you know!

But, for just a minute, forget about the white people trying to keep the film from seeing daylight. Where are the rich rappers, the A-list celebrities, the superstar athletes, and the big-time CEOs? Can *anyone* chip in? Ah…either (a) they're really NOT as rich and powerful as they seem and they *can't*…or (b) they're clueless and they don't care...or (c) they're punks and they're scared. Or (d) all of the above. I say D.

Dave Chappelle on the Refusal to Coon

Almost everyone knows Dave's story by now. He had one of the funniest shows ever to hit cable TV, but the best part about his comedy was that it gave you the truth. Dave was telling the truth about a lot of things, but especially about white people. Over time, Dave felt that he was being pushed to make Black people the joke, instead of white America. Dave wanted to tell it like it was, but the white executives wanted him to do more "cooning." Dave was the star of the show, but with his new $50 million dollar deal, the people in power were going to tell him how to do it. In interviews, he revealed:

> I felt in a lot of instances I was deliberately being put through stress because when you're a guy who generates money, people have a vested interested in controlling you…I was doing sketches that were funny, but socially irresponsible. It was encouraged…I would go to work on the show and I felt awful everyday…I felt like some kind of prostitute or something. If I feel so bad, why keep on showing up to this place? I'm going to Africa. The hardest thing to do is to be true to yourself, especially when everybody is watching.

So he pulled a George W. Bush, and said "F*ck yall niggas, I'm outta here," and went to South Africa to be with some of his Muslim brothers (did you know he's Muslim?). There, he got away from all the attention and pressure, and found freedom and peace of mind. Meanwhile, the white media said he'd gone insane. I guess, in their eyes, anyone who won't suck their dicks for a dollar *must* be crazy. In the end, Dave ditched the show. And he's *still* rich, bitch!

Jadakiss on the 9/11 Conspiracy

Rappers aren't free to say whatever they'd like either. As long as they're talking about murder (but only if the victims are Black too) and buying up jewelry (but only if the jeweler is white or a Jew), they're okay. After all, they're helping further what American wants for Black people.

But when a rapper like Jadakiss asked, "Why did Bush knock down the towers?" on his single "Why?" the media went nuts. Jada was criticized endlessly, that line was censored from almost all radio and video airplay, and Jada was instructed to backpedal and clear up what he "really meant" by the line. According to Anthony Cutajar in *USA Today*:

> Over the years, the rapper Jadakiss has depicted a world of drug dealing, murder and other assorted mayhem without raising many eyebrows. But seven words in his new song Why – "Why did Bush knock down the towers?" – has gotten Jadakiss the most mainstream attention, and criticism, of his career.

In his first interview about the lyrics, Jadakiss told Billboard.com, "I just felt he [Bush] had something to do with it. That's why I put it in there like that. A lot of my people felt he had something to do with it." But after media pressure persuaded his label to do some "coaching," Jada had to change his story. The new explanation, according to Cutajar, was:

> Jadakiss doesn't really believe Bush ordered the towers destroyed — he says the line is a metaphor, and that Bush should take the blame for the terrorist attack because his administration didn't do enough to stop it.

This is how they did Plies for calling out "crackas" on "100 Years," how they did Wu Tang for calling white people "devils," and how they did Kanye when he started his career saying "crack dealer buys Jordans, crackhead buys crack/ and the white man gets paid offa all of dat."

All them "tough" dudes got checked. The game ain't changed. Even Billie Holliday suffered a backlash in 1939 for "Strange Fruit."

There are just *certain things* your gangsta ass ain't allowed to talk about. So with salt like this in the game, it's no wonder that we don't hear more controversial material from new artists...or established ones. Everyone is scared to death of upsetting the *real* gangsters in charge.

For example, have you ever heard the song, "I'm Black" by Jadakiss's partner Styles P? If not, I'm sure I know why. In an era where you can hear somebody whisperin. "Bitch, wait til you see my dick" on the radio while you drive your kids home from school, a song about being proud to be Black was quickly swept off the airwaves...even though people said they liked it! I bet *that'll* discourage anybody. No wonder so many of us are scared to tell the truth!

Saigon on the Refusal to Sell Out

Sometimes, saying too much can get your whole career sidetracked. Especially if you work in a corrupt industry. Saigon is another example. He explained to *XXL* how his immense talent still didn't keep his project from getting shelved indefinitely:

> My vision was, since you're gonna market my music to children anyway, let me give them something beneficial. I'm not gonna make a single about getting oral sex or distributing kilos, but I will make a song about the importance of education in order to make a living, or how not to fall a victim to genocide.

Bad idea. The Atlantic Records label execs told him he could put his album out on their subdivision Asylum (a smaller label), even though he had signed to Atlantic. As he rapped on "Believe It":

> I tried to help the label see the vision/ But they lowered me to a subdivision, you gotta be f*ckin kiddin/ They'd rather me pretend I'm something I'm not/ I'm the new Public Enemy, I'm different from Yung Joc

But apparently, Yung Joc gets the major promotional push, and somebody like Saigon needs to drum up all of his publicity on YouTube. What's the answer? There's the soft route and the hard route.

Soft route: Keep your views to yourself until you have enough money and power to do and say what the f*ck you want, so long as you don't need any *more* of their money. (eg. Ice Cube, Paul Mooney, etc.) As Ice Cube rapped on "It Takes a Nation of Niggas to Hold Us Back":

> A lunatic, y'all know what I represent/ The only rapper that wanna fist-fight the president/...Hollywood, they thought they could tame this/ Pitbull, but I know what the game is/...My style never change in 22 summers/ Straight independent and doing my numbers/ This sh*t don't sell, you know I'm still paid/ So sour-puss niggas, can drink lemonade

Hard route: Stop depending on people who hate you for your paycheck. Matter fact, stop depending on anyone who ain't with the program. Do you, and find other people who share your views to help you do it. Eventually, a grassroots movement will arise. (eg. **Me**)

What you do, if anything, is up to you. But until then, keep this in mind:

The people who pay for you own you.
Be aware that your leash isn't as long as you think it is.

Movie to See

Long Kiss Goodnight

If you look at Samuel Jackson's body of work, he's goin hard against a corrupt government in almost all of his films. For an early example, check out *Long Kiss Goodnight.* About 90 minutes into the film, a CIA man hints that the 1993 World Trade Center bombing was aided by the CIA to get the government to raise their funds to fight terrorism. (Which is true! In fact, the "Arab" they paid $1 million to do it, Emad Salem, proved it to the media because he'd recorded their conversations! Google him!) Anyway, in the film they have a new plan. The exact lines are: "You're telling me that you're going to fake some terrorist thing just to scare some money out of Congress?" The agent replies, "Well, unfortunately, Mr. Henessey, I have no idea how to fake killing 4,000 people. So we're just going to have to do it for real. Oh, and blame it on the Muslims...naturally." Sound familiar? Think!

You're the Enemy

The Federal Emergency Management Agency (FEMA) has a $6 billion plus budget. But only about 6% of that budget goes into the relief effort. And if you remember Hurricane Katrina, you know FEMA doesn't do a damn thing for real disasters. So where's the money go?

> **Did You Know?**
>
> In case of an "emergency," the President can suspend the US Constitution by enacting any of the following "Executive Orders": 10990 Allows the government to take control over all modes of transportation, highways, and seaports. 10995 Allows the government to seize and control the communication media. 10997 Allows the government to take over all electrical power, gas, petroleum, fuels, and minerals. 10998 Allows the government to take over all food resources and farms. 11000 Allows the government to mobilize civilians into work brigades under government supervision. 11001 Allows the government to take over all health, education, and welfare functions. 11002 Designates the Postmaster General to operate national registration of all persons. 11003 Allows the government to take over all airports and aircraft, including commercial aircraft. 11004 Allows the Housing and Finance Authority to relocate communities, build new housing with public funds, designate areas to be abandoned, and establish new locations for populations. 11005 Allows the government to take over railroads, inland waterways, and public storage facilities. 11051 Specifies the responsibility of the Office of Emergency Planning and gives authorization to put all Executive Orders into effect in times of increased international tensions and economic or financial crisis. 11310 Grants authority to the Department of Justice to enforce the plans set out in Executive Orders, to institute industrial support, to establish judicial and legislative liaison, to control all aliens, to operate penal and correctional institutions, and to advise and assist the President. 11049 Assigns emergency preparedness function to federal departments and agencies, consolidating 21 operative Executive Orders issued over a fifteen year period. 11921 Allows the Federal Emergency Preparedness Agency to develop plans to establish control over the mechanisms of production and distribution, of energy sources, wages, salaries, credit and flow of money in the U.S.A. financial institution in any undefined national emergency. It also provides that when a state of emergency is declared by the President, Congress cannot review the action for 6 months.

In 1984 (remember the book?), President Reagan authorized a secret national readiness exercise, code named REX 84. The REX 84 Program was established on the reasoning that if thousands of illegal aliens crossed the Mexican/US border at once (how?), they would be quickly rounded up and detained in detention centers by FEMA. So REX 84 allowed for military bases to be closed down and to be turned into prisons. REX 84 was so highly guarded that special metal doors were installed on the 5th floor of the FEMA building in D.C.

The real purpose of the REX 84 exercise was to test FEMA's ability to assume military authority. The exercise required the following: (1) Suspension of the Constitution of the United States; (2) Turning control of the government over to FEMA; (3) Appointment of military commanders to run state and local governments; and (4) Declaration of Martial Law. And we all know that whether it's called immigration or terrorism, the war is against Black and brown people. Since 9/11, terrorism became a more popular target (since it scares people more than losing their jobs to immigrants), so REX 84 and similar policies were redesigned around the new threat.

A form of Martial Law already exists in the U.S. It's been in place since shortly after the September 11 attacks, when Bush issued Military Order

Number One, which empowered him to detain any noncitizen as an international terrorist or enemy combatant. Today that order extends to U.S. citizens as well! Yes, you. You can get Guantanamo'ed too!

Beginning in 1999, the government has entered into a series of exclusive contracts with Halliburton subsidiary KBR to build detention camps at undisclosed locations within the United States. The government has also contracted with several companies to build thousands of railcars, some reportedly equipped with shackles, presumably to transport detainees. And in 2008, for the first time an active military unit, Northcom, has been given a dedicated US assignment for "civil unrest containment." According to diplomat and author Peter Dale Scott, the KBR contract is part of a Homeland Security plan titled ENDGAME, which sets as its goal the removal of "all removable aliens" and "potential terrorists."

"Potential" terrorists, huh? You get it yet?

There are now over 600 prison camps in the United States, all fully operational and ready to receive prisoners. They are all staffed and even surrounded by full-time guards, but remain empty. These camps are to be operated by FEMA. The camps all have railroad facilities as well as roads leading to and from the detention facilities. Many also have an airport nearby. The majority of the camps can house a population of 20,000 prisoners. Currently, the largest of these facilities is just outside of Fairbanks, Alaska. The Alaskan facility is a massive "mental health" facility and can hold approximately 2 million people.

Well, who's gonna go in all those detention centers and prison camps? You are.

The *Washington Post* reported in 2006 that the National Counterterrorism Center's central repository holds the names of 325,000 "terror suspects," a 400% increase since Fall of 2003. According to author Naomi Wolf, the most recent estimate is now at 775,000, with the number increasing by 20,000 per month.

But who fits the definition of a ""terror suspect"? You do.

Did You Know?

You may soon have a microchip embedded somewhere under your skin? The Verichip, also known as the RFID chip, continues to be proposed as an effective way to keep track of human beings. It's already being used successfully with animals, and is promised to change the way everyone on the planet does business. Your whole life will be on the chip. This is *real*, not movie sh*t. Look it up.

A Pentagon official said the Counterintelligence Field Activity's TALON program has tons of files on antiwar protesters. But other groups in the crosshairs could include anti-abortion protesters, anti-tax agitators, immigration activists, animal activists, environmentalists, peace demonstrators, Second Amendment rights supporters...and, of course, "crazy niggas" like you. Simply readin up on revolutionary ideas is dangerous, homey. Let me continue.

The Violent Radicalization and Homegrown Terrorism Prevention Act (H.R. 1955) passed on October 23, 2007, by a vote of 404–6. The resulting agencies would study and propose legislation to prevent the threat of "radicalization" of Americans. The act seeks to prevent "the potential rise of self-radicalized, unaffiliated terrorists domestically." That means anyone who "could" be against the system…in any way. And we're not talking about Islam anymore. In a 2005 RAND report titled "Trends in Terrorism," an entire chapter is devoted entirely to a non-Muslim "homegrown terrorist" threat – the threat of people working against the global status quo. To prevent the spread of radical thinking, this act sought to "police thought," specifically targeting the Internet and other information sources as "tools of radicalization."

Whether you like it or not, you're either their bitch or their enemy. So which one is it?

If you're not a supporter of the oppressor, you are its enemy.

Did You Know?

Leeland Eisenberg ran up in Hillary Clinton's campaign headquarters, claiming to be strapped with a bomb, taking hostages, and making demands on the government. He wasn't a terrorist. Amy Bishop killed minority professors, some of whom were from other countries. She wasn't a terrorist. Joseph Stack flew a plane into an IRS building, as an intentional attack on the US government. He wasn't a terrorist. What makes them immune? They have something known as white privilege. With white privilege you can do whatever the hell you want, and nobody will make your crime reflect a collective. In fact, you'll probably get away with it somehow. But if *your* Black/brown/yellow ass gets into a fistfight on your next Delta flight, you're going to Guatanamo Bay!

MOVIE TO SEE

Fahrenheit 9/11

On second thought, skip that. As Immortal Technique said, "Fahrenheit 9/11, that's just scratching the surface." For something deeper, look out for films like (1) *Revealed: The Path to War;* (2) *Hijacking Catastrophe: 9/11, Fear & the Selling of American Empire;* (3) *Loose Change: Final Cut*; (4) *Unconstitutional: The War on Our Civil Liberties*; (5) *American Dictators;* (6) *America: From Freedom to Fascism*; (7) *Police State 3: Total Enslavement*; and (8) *ENDGAME: Blueprint for Global Enslavement.* And there's probably many more! But *all* of these mind-blowing documentaries above can be found free online at www.supremedesignonline.com. There's so much evidence on this sh*t that I still don't understand how people can act all stupid and clueless. And if you want to keep up with what's really going on from day to day, check out the regular updates at sites like www.infowars.com or www.whatreallyhappened.com

IGNORANCE AND GREED

While sending over missionaries to gain the trust and admiration of the African people, Europeans also set up trading posts in the continent. European goods that were offered for trade were usually of the poorest quality, but of new varieties which the African rulers found attractive. Kinda like the products they sell us in the stores they set up in the hood.

For example, African weapons were beautiful and effective, and conflicts involving them did not end in many fatalities. However, crude European guns became the new obsession as some chiefs discovered their killing power, prompting rival chiefs to also need guns to respond to the threat. Kinda like how our communities got flooded with guns.

Estaban Montejo, an African slave who fled a Cuban plantation in the 1800s, recalled how some of his people were enticed into slavery:

> It was the scarlet which did it for the Africans; both the kings and the rest surrendered without a struggle. When the kings saw that the whites were taking these scarlet handkerchiefs as if they were waving, the told the Blacks, "Go on then, go and get a scarlet handkerchief" and the blacks were so excited by the scarlet they ran down to the ships like sheep and there they were captured.

What?! You mean we fell for that? We let people lead us into a lifelong imprisonment…in pursuit of some material bullsh*t? Ah, who would be dumb enough to fall for that? Oh. Oh yeah. Damn.

Well anyway…before long, the African desire for European goods became immensely widespread and profitable. And the Europeans only traded for slaves, not for any African goods. To boost business, the Europeans intensified class divisions and ethnic division in African societies, leading to perpetual conflicts and warfare. The resulting wars provided the captives that would be sold into slavery for goods like rum, pots, and guns. Kinda like how the rise of gang rivalries led to sky-high rates of gun violence and incarceration for us.

What do you want most? Why? How does pursuing it affect you?

How will getting it affect you? Will it help anyone besides you?

When you don't know better, the things you think you want are often the things that will destroy you.

HOW TO GET A JOB

It'll be different for everyone, but here's a Step-by-Step Process to get you started on the road to legitimate, stable employment:

1. First, you need to take stock of what exactly you're good at. Don't sell yourself short and say "nothing." Everyone has skills and abilities.

2. Look at what kinds of jobs your skills are best suited for. If all you can do is manual labor, then that's where you need to look. Even an inventory boy can work his way up to manager (it's been done thousands of times), so don't obsess over starting out small.
3. Start talking to people. Ask everyone you know who's hiring. Walk into businesses and ask if they have openings. Find managers and ask if they need help. Start conversations with strangers. When white people do it, it's called networking.
4. Look for jobs on websites like *Craigslist* or *Monster*. Check the newspapers. (Watch out for scams that *cost* you money, though) You can also register with temp agencies and businesses that hire people with little experience (like movie theaters, restaurants, supermarkets, retail stores, shipping and inventory positions, and factory work).
5. Emphasize your strong points. Sell yourself like you're promoting a rapper. Just don't overdo it.
6. Get your appearance together. Put on a shirt and tie (that fit). Make sure your hair and nails are clean and cut. More importantly, put together a resume (that looks legit). Get help if you need to.
7. The same way you're going to dress up, dress up that resume if you don't have enough experience. Everyone does it…just have family members or others agree to answering the phone in the name of whatever businesses you named on your resume to say you worked there…and you're great.
8. Get used to rejection. Just like with women, it's a numbers game. Would you go gay after you got turned down by ten women in a row? No, right? (I hope) You'd go after number 11, 12, maybe even 487…until you got what you wanted. Persistance pays off.
9. For your interview, show up early, but not too early, and be prepared to talk about what *you* can offer *them*, not the other way around.
10. Make sure you have references and people who can support the fact that you can be trusted and depended upon.
11. Learn whatever you need to know before you show up for any interviews, including answers to any questions they might ask. Do your background research on the company and what they're all about.
12. Have a firm (but not too firm) handshake. Make (and maintain) eye contact. Sit up straight. Talk in your whitest voice possible, and sit up straight. Basically, do your best to look like a super-duper good guy.

If you get a job, don't take off any days or show up late for at least the first two weeks. Otherwise…the next list is probably the one for you:

Top 12 Ways to Lose your Job

1. Do what you're not supposed to do.
2. Don't do what you *are* supposed to do.
3. Do too little.
4. Do too much.
5. Do it too late.
6. Do *you*.
7. Don't show up.
8. Don't know your role.
9. Don't get permission.
10. Don't respect positions.
11. Do something offensive.
12. Do somebody you work with.

Supreme the Asshole on "Can't Do Rights"

Now I know some of you mothaf*ckas hate the idea of working from 9 to 5 and having a boss over you, telling you what to do. Get over it! If you ain't got a legitimate, successful hustle of your own yet, stop complaining and sweep that floor like you're supposed to! It's always the ones saying they can't deal with being told what to do for 8 hours...who will be the same people to do dumb sh*t to get money and end up in jail, being told what to do all goddamn 24 hours.

If your job is lifting boxes, lift them damn boxes. Lift them better than anyone else, and one day you'll be the dude telling everybody else to lift boxes. But nooooo...these "Can't Do Right" mothaf*ckas lose job after job because they can't take orders, can't show up on time, and can't work instead of goofing off. That's a little kid mindset. A grown man don't give a f*ck what kind of job he's got. He knows the job is either something he does just to keep his bills paid and stay out of the streets, OR he's using his free time OUTSIDE of that job to CREATE his own job. Grow the f*ck up and lift that damn box.

The Science of Hustle

"Hustling" has nothing to do with whether an activitiy is legal or not. Hustling is defined by how you go about any activity. It refers to any aggressive attempt at improving your condition, especially so when the odds are against you. The slaves hustled for freedom. Dr. King hustled for Civil Rights. You're probably hustling for a promotion or a better job right now. But the media presents you with a stereotype of what it means to hustle. As a result, you don't realize how necessary it is to hustle. How else would you change your conditions? If you keep doing the same thing, won't you keep getting the same thing? If you work at a dead-end job (or a high-end job with a glass ceiling), you'll be forever stuck in your rut unless you *hustle*. How do you think Bill Gates, Donald Trump, and all our other favorite white folks made it? Even the street hustlers selling drugs are simply striving to succeed against the odds, and transcend their desperate conditions. As Plies raps on "Rich Folk":

> When a nigga tell you he likes sellin dope, he a damn lie/ Cause if he did, then he'd sell dope for no price/ We just willin to take chances and get by/ Ain't like we *like* to do it, we gotta sell pies/ Cause if you don't, there's a good chance you gon to die/ All we need is a lil money and we

> alright/ Cause most niggas just want a piece of the good life/ The worst feelin is the sh*t you can't buy/ What's filet mignon when you ain't got the money to try?/ All that miracle sh*t don't work for my kind

Jay-Z takes it further on "Say Hello":

> We ain't thugs for the sake of just being thugs/ Nobody do dat where we grew at, nigga, duh!/ The poverty line: we not above/ So out come the mask and glove, cause we ain't feelin' the love/ We ain't doing crime for the sake of doing crime/ We movin' dimes cause we ain't doin' fine/ One out of three of us is locked up, doing time/ You know what that type of sh*t can do to a nigga mind?/ My mind on my money, money on my mind/ If you owe me ten dollars, you ain't giving me nine/ Ya'll ain't give me 40 acres and a mule/ So I got my Glock 40, now I'm cool

What does this tell us? That anyone who has the odds against them must either hustle hard or submit to their conditions. Basically, you either it shake it or take it. So considering how bad our global economy is right, I think we might all be considering whether we need to start on a hustle.

A 9 to 5 job isn't for everyone. There's an easy way to tell: *See if you can be successful without one.* Of course, most people who think they can hustle on their own actually can't. Even I spent many years trying to find out if I had what it took.

When I was a kid, I used to take everything apart, trying to understand how things worked. By the time I was ten, I figured I could drop out of school and be an inventor. I hadn't exactly been able to make anything – or fix any of the sh*t I took apart – but I figured I was on my way. After all, Thomas Edison had done it. Why couldn't I? Right.

Life started getting pretty rough around that time. By the time I was 14, I'd been expelled from school, and I was never home. I spent most of my time in the streets, still not knowing what I'd do with my life. But by this time, I was sure that school wouldn't have anything to do with it.

I ended up running with a little crew of stick-up kids and petty thieves. Robbing people didn't pay the bills, but it seemed fun at first. The power we had over those people was just a feeling I had never felt before. But it wore out after a while. After that one time when we literally knocked a kid's eye out of its socket, I started feeling guilty.

As time passed, almost all my old friends grew out of strong-arming and moved into drug-dealing. I held off for as long as I could, but I gave in too. Still, I realized pretty fast that drugs wouldn't be my "golden ticket" out the hood. How? Easy. I watched *everyone* fail around me.

Once I was back in school, people kept telling me to stick to this education thing. I barely planned to finish high school, until my Crisis

Intervention Counselor forced me into this special program. Through the program, I ended up getting into college…barely.

Once I was there, I went right back to trying to find my million-dollar hustle.

- ❒ I tried bein a rapper, but I wasn't into dancing around on stage or dealing with industry politics. So that didn't work.
- ❒ I tried sellin stunguns to college girls, but they were too big for their cute little purses. That didn't work out either.
- ❒ I tried running a graphic design company, but I didn't know sh*t about business management. Another failure.
- ❒ I tried selling guns, but the ATF cracked my man, and I figured I was next. I quit *that* one before I took the fall.
- ❒ I tried using my graphics skills to forge documents, but that actually ended up making me homeless (long story).
- ❒ I tried real estate, but without training, I was losing thousands more than I was making. After ruining my credit, I finally got out.
- ❒ I even tried pimpin to make ends meet, but beatin the girls up to increase productivity wasn't for me.

Somewhere along the way, life got so hectic I started keeping a journal again. I hadn't written in a journal since I was stressed and depressed in middle school, but I figured it couldn't hurt. It didn't hurt at all, actually. In fact, it helped a lot. It helped me sort out my present affairs, but it also helped me look back at my old mistakes so I wouldn't repeat them. As I wrote, I'd go back and read and trip out over all the crazy sh*t I'd done. It was really entertaining.

When MySpace came along, I started journaling on my blog as well. People thought I was entertaining too, but they also loved the way I "broke everything down." I analyzed everything that was happening in my life, and it turned out a lot of people don't do that when they look at their lives. Sh*t, some people don't even like looking at their own lives at all. But people said they learned a lot from what I wrote, and that I was helping them in ways I wouldn't realize until much later.

That's when the idea hit me. I'd write a book.

I talked to a few people who I could count on for guidance and good advice. They all said I should be writing an educational book. They felt that I could use my life experiences to explain things about life to people who just couldn't see those things for themselves yet.

The result was the book you're reading now. I found my hustle. It's not a million-dollar hustle, because I could care less about money nowadays

(Don't worry, I'm not broke). But it's a hustle I can live with at the end of the day, and feel good about it. No hoes to slap, no ATF to duck, and no eyeballs to pop out. This is my hustle. And if you really want to, you can find yours.

Just keep in mind that you don't quit your day job until your side hustle starts paying off (enough to support you). And you don't risk LOSING your day job by trying to work your side hustle while you SHOULD be on your day job. For more insight, you should check out Hotep's *Hustle While You Work: Using your 9-5 to Jumpstart your 5-9.*

And once you've got a hustle you're good at, don't forget to diversify. In this economy, you need to have as many sources of income as possible.

If you can't find a job, make one.

---

10 Reasons to Go to College...and 6 Not to

College doesn't guarantee you a better life, but it can damn sure help. Here are 10 reasons to fill out that long-ass application:

1. It's basically free. And I don't mean only if you get a scholarship, either. Considering that the average college graduate earns thousands more than the average person without a degree, you'll earn back whatever it cost you pretty fast. A college degree opens up a world of opportunities many non-graduates don't have. I'm not saying that you can't do well without the degree, only that a degree can make things a lot easier. For example, college graduates usually earn higher salaries, get better jobs, are approved faster for loans, and are less likely to go to jail. Anyway, student loans are easier to repay than a car loan any day.

2. The girls. If you can't pull a decent girl on a college campus, you seriously need to step your game up. They're everywhere, and they come in every shape, size, complexion, and IQ level. If you're just trying to get you some, there's plenty who are there for that too. Another thing is that if a girl can afford to go to college, she's either got her head on straight, or daddy is paying the bills. Either way, it's worth your time. Not to mention that college girls just seem to be cuter. Just don't overdo it and flunk out.

3. The social life. And yeah, there's gonna be a party somewhere almost everyday. The valedictorian of my graduating class would complete all of his work before 7 pm every day so he could hit the parties and social events later that night. Then there's the brotherhood. Some of my closest friends, even now, are people I went to college with years ago. We went through a lot of sh*t together, and learned to have each other's backs. Places like college, prison, and the ghetto have a few things in common. One is that if you don't learn how to join up with others and develop solidarity, it is very hard to survive alone.

4. Networking. Speaking of meeting people, college is the ultimate place to network. It's here that you can meet everyone you'll need later on in life. As David Banner told *Look Magazine*:

> College is the only think tank that we have as black people and we don't even use it as that. When you go to college you might have a friend who's an accounting major, a friend who wants to be a dentist or a homegirl who might be an attorney. Ya'll should come together and start thinking about the future instead of the present. Then you can network.

You'll need these folks later on, so build your bonds now. Get every full name and email address you can.

5. Freedom and Independence. It's not like high school. They don't decide when your classes start. You can schedule all of your classes on 3 days of the week, and be off the other four. Or you can take mostly afternoon and evening classes, and sleep in. No one tells you what to do. The most anyone can do is make suggestions. Either you do what you're supposed to, or you waste your tuition money. That's bad for you irresponsible folks, but for the rest of us, it's a chance to finally do things our way.

6. Leaving home. Whether you're trying to get away from a f*cked-up neighborhood or a f*cked-up family, college allows you to spend at least 9 months of the year somewhere else. Usually, it's somewhere nice, since most college towns are decent places. Even if your home base is okay, at 18, it's about time to spread your wings and fly on your own, baby bird. Only way to do that is by leaving the nest, and having no safety net to fall back on. You want to learn to be a man? Leave home and see if you can handle 12 credit hours, a part-time job, and a social life. You'll be a man in no time. Of course, a lot of people leave home

Did You Know?

Hopefully, you won't run into a college professor like Amy Bishop. In February 2010, Bishop tried to kill nearly everyone at the faculty meeting where she was being reviewed for tenure. The news media tried to give her a break, saying she was stressed out from being denied tenure. As if that makes it okay to kill 3 important professors. The media told all about Bishop's life, and barely described the victims. Why? Bishop is white. Her victims were all people of color. Had it been the other way around, you know how it would have gone down. But when white people kill people, there's always a sob story involved. They're said to suffer from psychological problems. But when people of color kill people, there's none of that. We're just the animals they say we are. What's worse is that Bishop had already murdered her brother, and tried to mailbomb another professor, and was cleared both times...and allowed to keep teaching! Only white people.

and come to a college campus as a completely different person. Schoolboys become thugs. Sluts become churchgirls. Lames become part of popular fraternities. But you can also do the opposite. You can leave behind all the bad sh*t in your past as well, moving on to do better things, and be a better person.

7. Finding yourself. If you grew up like me, your neighborhood doesn't allow for many opportunities to discover who you really are. There's probably not a lot of people "on your level" to talk to, so you end up doing the same sh*t with the same people more than you'd really like to admit. In college, you'll meet plenty of idiots, but you can also meet a lot of people who are on the same page as you. Also, most colleges nowadays have a Black Studies department. Beyond just finding yourself on a personal level, attending an HBCU gives you the chance to learn about your people. It may be the first time that you actually hear a teacher say some real sh*t about Black people, and not the watered-down bullsh*t they told us on Black History Month.

8. A well-rounded education. I know a lot of educated dummies, but I also know a lot of people I can't have a conversation with because they don't know sh*t that damn near everyone else in the world knows. You shouldn't be 30 and not know who Napoleon was, or not know the laws of physics. Being that uneducated is just another way of saying, "Hey world, take advantage of me and my ignorance." Just make sure you study a field that you actually plan to use in real life!

9. Sports and entertainment. I know a lot of ballplayers that got into the game once they hit the college track, and even more that took their skills from high school and got full scholarships. The chances of going pro straight from high school aren't good, but they're better if you're playing college ball. Keep in mind that there's international leagues that also recruit from college campuses. Same thing with the music industry, or film or television...college is a great place to develop your skills, make your connections, and get your name known.

10. The difference. Sure, you might be the only person there from your neighborhood. But I doubt it. There's almost always gonna be a bunch of people who ain't that different from you. And there are clubs and organizations for y'all to come together. Even if you do attend a small college where you're one of the only five people from DC, it just makes you that much more attractive and interesting to other people. Anyway, you didn't come to a completely different environment to surround yourself with the same old sh*t. Get around people who are different from you, and learn something new.

"There are two educations. One should teach us how to make a living and the other how to live."
John Adams

So, I gave you ten reasons to go. But I have to be fair…and real…and offer six reasons on the other side of the coin.

1. It's not for everyone. Some people try their best, and can never fully adjust to a college environment. It's no different from someone who's been in prison to long, and can't get back acclimated to the outside. If all you know is party and bullsh*t, you may not be able to handle all the responsibilities.

2. It can be expensive. And the financial aid process can be a pain in the ass. While I still think it pays off in the long run, you may run into several financial roadblocks throughout the course of your matriculation (look it up). When the funds get low, a lot of folks go.

3. It's not a promissory note. No matter what they tell you freshman year, a college degree doesn't guarantee you a job. It just improves your odds. But jobs are scarce right now, and – even with a degree – you'll still have to hustle hard to get in where you fit in. Don't believe that you've got it made just because you got a degree.

4. You STILL have to find your path. College starts you off with a broad range of general studies, but then you have to specialize and choose a major. I'd suggest choosing one that you not only enjoy, but that you know will get you employed. A bachelor's degree in History won't get you a job doing anything but teaching High School History.

5. There are other forms of education. In fact, some of you may do better in a vocational or technical school. You may fare better at a culinary institute, a nursing school, or an art school. Hell, you may want to learn how to do electrical work. A liberal arts education is just ONE way, not THE way.

6. You don't NEED it. You don't need a college degree to have a good-paying job these days. Just ask Bill Gates and a dozen other dropout millionaires. Of course, you still need some kind of education, but it may only be a few months of training in a particular skill. For example, a registered nurse (RN) only needs an associate's degree in nursing (ADN), a bachelor's of science degree in nursing (BSN), or a certificate from a diploma program in nursing to make an average yearly salary of $60,000. A dental hygienist only needs an

> **Did You Know?**
> Considering today's economy, if you are college bound, you may want to choose wisely regarding where you'll attend. Private colleges are often much more expensive than state universities. If you don't expect much of a difference, it may be safer, financially at least, to attend a state university… especially since student loans can become a heavy burden that even bankruptcy won't relieve.

associate's degree or certificate in dental hygiene for an average salary of over $64,000. And police supervisor can make over $75,000 with just a high school diploma! Here are 22 other high-paying, no-bachelors-degree-required jobs, from Harlow Unger's book *But What If I Don't Want to Go to College? A Guide to Success through Alternative Education*:

Air traffic controller	Nuclear technician
Funeral director	First-line supervisor of fire fighting
Operations manager	Elevator installer and repairer
Industrial production manager	Sales rep. (scientific products)
Transportation manager	Radiation therapist
Storage and distribution manager	Nuclear medicine technologist
Computer technical support specialist	Power plant distributor and dispatcher
Gaming manager	Fashion designer (if you're successful)
Nuclear power reactor operator	Ship engineer
Computer specialist	Detective and criminal investigator
First-line, non-retail supervisor	Commercial pilot

Whatever you do, wherever you go, pursue education.

How to Survive School

1. Have a determined idea. Have a reason for being there, and a goal in mind. If you feel like you're only there because you "have to be," you'll be outta there in no time. Find a purpose, even if all you want is that degree. And plan out your classes and your study habits so you can get there in four years or less.

2. Be personable. Get to know your teachers, so you're a human being to them, and not just a name on a piece of paper. That will help a lot when you need help or need an extension on a deadline. Let them know where you're coming from, and that you might have a hard time, but you're serious about passing.

3. Don't overdo it. Being a brown-noser or a suck-up won't help at all. You'll lose respect from fellow students and even the teacher. There's nothing wrong with asking for extra credit work on the low, but don't be the jackass that reminds the teacher to give out homework when she forgets.

4. Stick to a schedule. Once you're out of elementary school, time management is major. You have to know what's due, when it's due, and how long it will take you to do it. You have to budget your time like it's money. I know you want a social life too, and you can have one, if you spend your time wisely.

5. Prioritize. I know a lot of dudes who failed out of school chasing pussy, and I'd hate for you to be one. If you want to smoke, drink, f*ck, or look at videos on YouTube, cool...but do that sh*t after you've handled your business. I don't know anybody who can make it in life, whether legally or illegally, if they can't get their priorities in order.

6. Consider consequences. Before you act, think. During my sophomore year of college, I got locked up for fighting in a club, right before my mid-term exams. I could've failed out of school. Fortunately, I had a good relationship with the teachers and they let me take the exams a little later. On the other hand, I know plenty of dudes who got in some kind of trouble and never got back on track. Just keep in mind that you have a goal, and you can't blow it over petty sh*t.

7. Keep the end in mind. You've got to keep your eyes on the prize. A lot of sh*t will frustrate you and stress you out, but you've got to keep it moving and not quit. Dropping out may seem like an easy way out of a situation that's headed nowhere but the reality is different. For every two people who became successful after dropping out, there are twenty who didn't.

8. Be your own man. You may get clowned for being a school-boy, but you have to be your own man. That means you're either going to be weak and try so hard to fit in and be accepted that you'll dumb yourself down…or you'll be strong and confident enough so that people will have to respect you. I had a couple partners back in high school that got straight As and Bs, but no one ever tried them because they were also knockin brothers out. As for me, everybody thought I was the one who would "do good" and come back and "save" everybody back home. I tried, actually, but you know how that went.

9. Find the relevance. Yeah, I know they teach bullsh*t in schools. It's the white man's education. But you live in the white man's country and are probably trying to make some of that white man's money. So deal with it. Black people have been everywhere in the world at every time, and if you want to know what something in class has to do with you, it's up to you to go look it up. And yes, there's plenty of classes that seem completely irrelevant, teaching skills or ideas you feel you surely won't need in life, but the teachers usually know that. So sometimes, if you just show them you're doing your best, they'll probably pass you even if you didn't technically pass.

10. Teach yourself. Like I said, one only learns what one teaches oneself. If you want it to stick, read it for yourself. Look it up online. Find a video on YouTube. Learning sh*t is easier than ever before.

11. Find help. If you find it hard to figure something out on your own, get help. I bet there's a smart girl somewhere who wouldn't mind "tutoring" you. And even if you are gonna smash, smash afterwards.

12. Use your resources. There's other resources out there. There's counselors and other people at every school who can help you out with getting scholarships, jobs, and other benefits. All you have to do is seek it and you'll find it. Laziness gets nothing.

Stacks on Deck

Working for the Mafia, Parnell "Stacks" Edwards went from petty theft, to credit card fraud, to participating in one of **the biggest heists in American history**. He also got himself killed being stupid.

Stacks' vocal support of the Black Panther Party and his increasing addiction to heroin made him seem like more of an asshole than he already was. But his boss Jimmy Burke tolerated him and used him as best he could. But Stacks' final screw-up would push Burke and his fellow gangsters to the edge.

In 1978, Henry Hill told Jimmy Burke about massive sums of cash being held overnight in a safe at the Lufthansa cargo terminal in New York. The money was in the millions and was in totally untraceable money. "Sweeeet," they thought. Burke devised a plan to steal it.

Stacks' job was to take the panel truck used in the heist and drive it to a junkyard in New Jersey, where Mafia contacts would crush it and the evidence would be destroyed. The heist worked out better than Burke could have imagined, but Stacks neglected his duty and started celebrating early. He got high as a kite on cocaine and marijuana, visited his girlfriend, partied some more, had sex with her, and fell asleep.

Unfortunately for him, the police found the panel truck. It was sitting in a no parking zone, with a muddy boot print which they matched to a pair of shoes owned by Stacks! Plus there were fingerprints still on the steering wheel, and a Lufthansa employee's wallet was left inside! I couldn't make this sh*t up if I wanted to!

Though it seemed that things for Stacks could get no worse, he made them worse. In *Wiseguy: Life in a Mafia Family*, mobster Henry Hill recalled Stacks' presence at a Christmas party following the heist:

> We were all having a good time when "Stacks" sees my amount of money on me, and started to do his "Black dude" number, "How come I'm f*cking broke and all you whities got the money?" And then Edwards would persist in making racial jokes about the "May-fia guys who got all those millions from the airport".

I'm serious. Dude not only came to the party, but he talked sh*t, even police had found the panel truck he was supposed to get rid of! Hill later recalled, "I knew that Stacks had signed his death warrant that day."

Indeed he had. Stacks went into hiding, but his dumb ass didn't go far. He was eating breakfast when hitman Tommy DeSimone walked in and fired several bullets into Stacks' head and chest with a .32 caliber silencer-equipped pistol. Stacks finally did something the way he was supposed to. He died instantly.

"Misspending a man's time is a kind of self-homicide."
George Savile (1633-1695)

What killed Stacks? Was it the mob? Nah. If you understood this lesson, you'll know he killed *himself* by f*cking around and doing bullsh*t, when he had priorities to attend to…especially when the odds he was gambling with were life or death Many young men are just like Stacks. As Young Jeezy rapped in "Don't Get Caught": "And I don't believe in wastin' time/ We'll catch them hoes later, stay on your grind/ Got a low tolerance for ignorance/ You thinkin' pleasure, I'm thinkin' business."

How many of us put pleasure before business?

How many of us will die that way?

How many of us will waste our lives (the same as death) that way?

Don't waste your life f*ckin around. Have your priorities in order.

SUPREME THE ASSHOLE ON "IT WAS SOME BULLSH*T"

I asked my man Darnell how he got shot. He started off with, "It was some bullsh*t." Later on, I found out it was over a girl who was sleepin with him, another three dudes, and possibly her own uncle. I asked my man Terrence why he lost his job. He hit me with, "Man, it was some bullsh*t." Turns out, he was stealing office supplies. If you ask Bill Clinton why he almost got impeached, he'll probably say, "It was some bullsh*t."

Anytime somebody starts a story with "It was some bullsh*t," they're either gonna tell you the really dumb sh*t they did to f*ck up bad, or they'll lie and leave out the dumb sh*t they did. Basically, "It was some bullsh*t" translates to "I was on some bullsh*t." So stop lyin! Be real with people, and they'll be real with you!

KATRINA VICKTIMS

"While white folks focus on dogs and yoga
My people on the low end tryin' to ball and get over"
Common, "The People"

Mike Vick

It was July 26, 2007. The courthouse was surrounded by a swarm of protestors that wanted a pound of Michael Vick's flesh – people screaming for the Atlanta Falcons quarterback to "burn in hell" and holding signs calling for his murder, torture and neutering.

How many of these people were Atlanta Falcons fans, fans of #7 himself, only a few months earlier cheering Vick on? Of course, those people didn't care for Vick as a person. He was just a player, known for the number on his jersey and the number of points he helped score. And so long as a Black man is occupied with the entertainment of white people, they don't really see him as Black. But today, these people were judging Mick Vick as they really saw him.

As they yelled those awful threats, with – I'm sure – a few calls of "nigger!" here and there, they revealed how they really felt about Black men like Mike Vick.

According to Dan Wetzel's *Yahoo! Sports* article "Racial Divide," there were a few Black people there as well. As a matter of fact, almost all of the people supporting Vick or holding signs pleading for "due process" and "innocence until proven guilty" were Black.

But on the other side was an "emotional, angry, passionate anti-Vick group" that was overwhelmingly white. Presenting themselves as animal-rights supporters, they verbally attacked Vick more than they did the idea of dog-fighting, a crime for which Vick had not even begun trial.

"Burn in hell you (expletive) (expletive)," repeatedly screamed one woman. "Die like those dogs," shouted another. It was clear. It was a modern-day lynching. How much had really changed?

Of course, there was – as always – the resident Negro on hand for his expert opinion: "I wouldn't say it's a racial thing," said David Williams, an African American, in a hopeful tone, "It's not racial." Right. But as the wise Dick Gregory has said, "Being a Negro makes you no more an expert on the race situation than being sick makes you an expert on medicine."

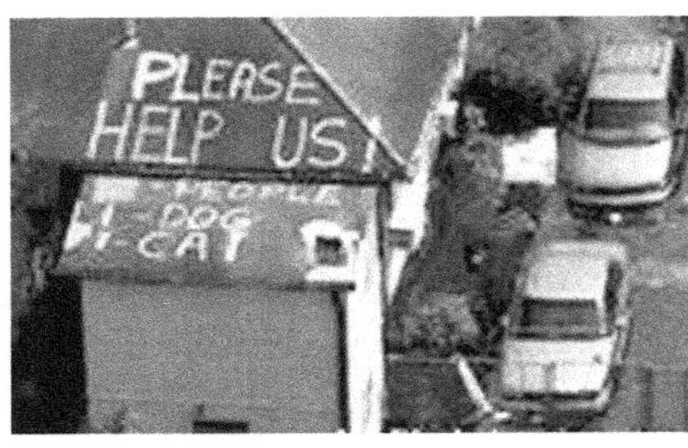

Hurricane Katrina

Imagining these white people ready to rip a Black man limb from limb, a Black man who many of them had rallied behind as a football star, made me think. I thought about how quickly things can change for us. I thought about how we're never trained in what exactly "not" to do. Finally, I thought about Hurricane Katrina, where whites went about rescuing pets while Blacks stood on their rooftops screaming for help.

As a matter of fact, as of October 2006, all fifty states will be required to help evacuate pets during a natural disaster such as a hurricane or earthquake, or risk losing federal money under a bill signed by President Bush. The bill was supposedly prompted by reports that thousands of pets were stranded during Hurricane Katrina. Forget the fact that it took five whole days for them to save all the Black families…and hundreds died anyway. Instead…what are the rescue agencies being criticized for? A "no pets" policy that required pet owners, most of them white, to abandon their animals while being rescued.

Of course, the idea behind the policy was to make room for other people. But people who'd rather save an iguana than let another wild-haired Negro on board didn't see it that way. So what did some of these white folks do? They defied evacuation orders and stayed in the disaster area with their cats and dogs and hamsters.

What does this tell you?

1. First, white people *love* animals.
2. Second, most white people don't give a rat's ass about Black people.

At the very least, white people love animals more than your Black ass. I mean, rich white folks were spending big bucks flying in choppers and rescuing animals from the zoo, rescuing dogs and horses from flooded areas, rescuing any little critter, while scores of Black humans died in watery graves. Can you imagine being stuck on a rooftop for days before you finally see a helicopter…and it passes you because there's four sheepdogs on board?

> **Did You Know?**
> There is plenty of evidence that Hurricane Katrina was a planned catastrophe. Even Lil Wayne raps about it on "Georgia (Bush)":
> "So what happened to the levees, why wasn't they steady?/ Why wasn't they able to control this?/ I know some folk that live by the levees/ that keep on tellin me they heard explosions/ Same sh*t happened back in Hurricane Betsy/ 1965, I ain't too young to know this/ That was President Johnson/ but now it's president (Geeoorrgiaa) Bush!"

What about the "Good Ones"?

Thinking about this made me think about the white people who don't fit the "racist" profile, or the "conservative" profile. These are the politically conscious, vegetarian, dreadlock-wearing white folks that want to "Save the Planet." But what do they want to save when they campaign in Africa? The starving children? No, let Oprah do that, there's something more important. People with AIDS? No, let Alicia Keys do that, there's something more important. What, then? A f*cking ring-tailed lemur. Apparently there's only 88,000 of them left.

Ignoring the hundreds of thousands of Black, brown, and yellow people who need clean water in the Third World (let Jay-Z do that), white people are out to save a whale, some poisonous frog, or maybe even a stankin ass plant. **White people will save a chipmunk before your**

Black ass. Do you know why so many white people are vegetarian? Because they don't think those poor chickens, cows, fish, and crabs should die. I've even met some white people who are fruitarians. They won't even eat vegetables because the plants die when you pick the vegetables. That's how much they love ANY living thing EXCEPT Black, brown, or yellow people. If you ask one of those white "activist" folks what they're fighting for, I guarantee it will be *anything* but you.

"It's water water everywhere and babies dead in the streets
It's enough to make you holler out
Like, where the f*ck is Sir Bono and his famous friends now?
Don't get it twisted man, I dig U2
But if you ain't about the ghetto, then f*ck you too"
Mos Def, "Dollar Day"

But maybe there's a more sinister agenda. After all, why don't animal-rights activists and environmentalists work to preserve the ENTIRE region? That means saving the land, the animals, AND the native people. But no.

In *White Lies, White Power,* Michael Novick addresses "racist environmentalism." To put it simply, many of the organizations that appear to be about saving the Earth are fronts for white supremacist organizations who want to clean up the Earth for themselves to enjoy, while eliminating people like you. According to one white supremacist organization, whites have a "duty to restore the world back to its original balance alongside with our ultimate goal…of preserving the pure Aryan race." Another organization member added:

> The way to do this is to make ourselves known as environmentalists and wildlife advocates. There are many groups out there helping wildlife and the environment. They are not necessarily white power advocates like ourselves, but if we make contributions to these groups, we achieve two things, (1) we break out of our media stereotype…and (2) we gain recognition.

"You want to save the planet? F*ck that! Save *us*, dammit!"
Killer Mike, "Pressure"

Maybe the efforts being made to save the lemurs are actually part of an effort to get rid of the people living near the lemurs. It seems disturbing that some white people would envision a green Earth with happy dolphins and pretty flowers and no terrible Negroes. But remember, the same white folks who kiss their dogs in the mouth daily may still have a hard time shaking your hand. People of color normally don't even keep our dogs in the house. On the other hand, there's enough white people having *intimate relationships* with their dogs for it to have its own section in the adult video stores in New York.

I guess that's why an eBay auction for 22 Mike Vick football cards, chewed up and slobbered on by two Missouri dogs, ended with the winning bidder shelling out $7,400. That's thousands more than any other Vick item has ever sold for. Says a lot, doesn't it? I bet none of the bidders ever gave a dollar to a charity helping urban children.

I'd probably love animals too, if it was their warmth and protection that helped me survive Europe in the caveman days. But that's not my story. As for me, I'd rather rescue one Haitian refugee than 10,000 lab rats. Sure, some of these white folks may sincerely want to save the slew-footed sloth, but what are they also doing in the process? They're expressing their unconscious (or conscious) disregard for the millions of people of color who suffer daily. They're dedicating themselves to a fruitless cause as well. Because if you don't work to tackle white supremacy and its careless destruction of the Earth, you're not getting to the root of things, and all those bunnies are gonna die either way.

Do you love animals (or just certain animals)? Why or why not?

Did You Know?

Everything you've learned about HIV and AIDS may not be true? Although you were probably told that AIDS came from Africa, there's a lot of evidence suggesting AIDS is manmade, and was designed specifically to destroy the Black and gay population of the U.S. Its' success here seems to have been duplicated to destroy Black and brown populations, wherever they are largest, throughout the world. There is also no evidence that the HIV virus causes the AIDS disease, and other factors lead to the disease itself, including the medications many people are taking for HIV infections. Some scientists say that HIV can be treated naturally, and doctors in Africa have already found a way to destroy the virus. But, if you know how happy the people in power are about the spread of AIDS, you know a "cure" won't come out anytime soon.

What about insects? Why or why not? What's the difference?

What about bacteria and viruses? Don't they deserve love?

If you could start a charity, would you dedicate it to poor people or poor animals? Why?

Who you help tells a lot about who you are.

LAW AND PORN

Lawrence Burton, Esq., directs porn films. Well, not exactly. He directs and produces straight-to-video "documentaries" about the adult entertainment industry. They're not really porn flicks, because he's just interviewing adult film stars and documenting different aspects of "the life." Sometimes, there's some pretty wild stuff that he just can't help but catch on film. But he also tosses in footage of up-and-coming rappers and interviews with well-known celebrities. To accomplish all this, he spends a lot of time at industry parties and other crazy events.

Most of the time it's just him, his camera, and a media pass for the event he's attending. It's safe to say he enjoys his job.

But Burton wasn't always a film producer. He graduated from law school sometime in the early 90s. He went on to work in corporate law, which he hated. But one of Burton's "special" clients eventually realized he also had strengths in criminal law. Burton was called for a series of small cases where he performed extremely well. Eventually he was retained as a full-time attorney for a very exclusive group of people – the Mafia. He worked like a slave for them. They always had cases, always needed counsel, always needed their dirt dressed up to "look legit." Although Burton saw plenty of trash bags full of cash over the years, he still hated his job. He had gone from helping slimy companies get away with murder – financially – to helping slimy individuals get away with murder – literally.

But after putting 10 years into a profession he never cared for, he had saved up a ton of money. Now he could finally move on to a profession he loved. Matter fact, he never had to make any money off his films – though he did – because he had saved enough while slaving away to be set for life. And he had a hell of a life now too. He had gone from working 16-hour days to working at his computer when he felt like it. The rest of the time he could audition "new talent," that is, some fine young girl trying to get into "the life" through him. And he had kept things good with the mob guys, so if he ever needed any "assistance," he had plenty of connections. It had taken 10 years, but Burton had put in his work with the end in mind.

Pursuing instant gratification kills your chances for long-term success. The best rewards take time.

Black Mafia

One of the most sophisticated, corporate-like, structured, organized crime groups outside of the Italian mafia was The Young Boys Inc. (or YBI). Founded by a small group of teen-aged friends on Detroit's west side in the mid 1970s, Young Boys Incorporated was the first Black drug cartel operating openly on street corners.

In less than two years, YBI took over the majority of southeast Michigan's heroin trade with absolutely no interference from any other crime groups. At the height of their drug business in the early 1980s YBI was making an estimated $300,000 a day, and more money per month than the nearly bankrupted Chrysler Corporation.

The murder of one of the founders, Dwayne Davis (AKA Wonderful Wayne) and a series of federal indictments on 2 of the remaining bosses and 40 of the top lieutenants crippled YBI in 1982. There were a few lieutenants who survived and carried the organization in Detroit and Boston, Massachusetts, through the late 1980s until crack cocaine became the drug of choice over heroin.

YBI had such an incredibly organized and structured drug ring that after their downfall other African-American Detroit drug cartels copied their strategy and rose to prominence such as "Best Friends", "Pony Down", "Black Mafia Family" and even "The Chambers Brothers." YBI's reputation and system of organization impacted and influenced drug gangs nationally during the 1980s and 1990s.

The Black Mafia in Philadelphia took over the heroin trade and became so powerful it extorted even the Italian Mafia itself. The Black Mafia's success led to a younger group paying homage to the Black Mafia naming themselves the "Junior Black Mafia" (whose name spawned the rap group Junior M.A.F.I.A.).

The Junior Black Mafia were also heavily involved in drug trafficking, specifically crack-cocaine, during the Mid 1980s to early 1990s. The Black Mafia name was resuscissitated again in recent years with the rise of the Black Mafia Family, a multi-state organization operating out of Michigan, California, Georgia, and Florida.

Ultimately, however, every last one of these organizations produced nothing that lasted but death and destruction in the Black community. While their members enjoyed periods of success and lavish spending, most were dead or doing long sentences before their 40th birthdays. Meanwhile, the money had dried up, members' children were poor again, and the community was worse than it had been before each group had hit the scene. Countless people dead or in prison, and thousands of people hooked on addictions that would wreck their lives, so millions of dollars could change hands...but who did it go to?

In every instance, the formula contained the same elements:

effective organization + strong leadership +
constant expansion - conscious agenda =
expansion + incredible profits + constant surveillance =
deaths and incarceration + destruction of the community

If we were going to copy someone else's formula, what if we had copied something else? What if we had copied Garvey's formula for the UNIA? What if we had resusscitated Che Gueverra's idea for guerrilla revolution? What if we brought back the methods of David Walker or Tecumseh?

You can create a plan or structure so strong that it will be duplicated for generations to come. Some of the products and techniques we use today were invented by Black people hundreds of years ago (see "Black Inventors"). Many of the ideas we hear about now aren't new, but reinventions of old ideas that have been around for ages. The lesson here is to produce something that is so strong and effective people will want to follow in your footsteps. Knowing that you can do this, you must also make sure that the formula you are producing or reintroducing is one that will build us all up, not destroy us further.

Organize...the right way, and for the right reasons.

Old School Whips and Wasted Money

This was the fifth old car I'd bought in the past three months. The first three had sold pretty quickly, but the fourth had been too much work. I didn't know that when I'd bought it at the salvage auction because I hadn't brought any of my mechanic friends with me. But I learned my lesson: Impulsive decisions lead to bullsh*t conditions. But I'd only spent about $200 on that car, so it wasn't a big loss.

I'd dropped a little more on Number Five. But $1500 didn't seem too bad for an '83 Oldsmobile Cutlass with a good 350 motor, working transmission, clean body, and spotless interior. I planned to double my money on the sale.

The first thing I did after buying it was getting it a full tune-up: new sparkplugs and wires, oil change, and all fluids flushed and replaced. I put in a new headliner because the old one was sagging like old lady titties, and started shopping for a cheap set of rims. I found a set of 22-inch chrome rims with low-profile tires for $600. With those on the car, it was already starting to look like a winner. I was going to drive it for a while until I sold it, so I thought about all the other things I could do to upgrade it even further.

I was on the way to getting it sprayed with a custom paint-scheme when my brakes stopped working. I barely managed to pull off the road in time. Closer examination revealed that the whole brake system was rusted. The brakeline had snapped. The car had been somewhere up north, where rain and snow create rust in places I normally didn't look.

After a couple hundred dollars of repairs, I got the car painted for a great price and found two more deals I couldn't pass up. The first was for a sound system, complete with woofers, 6x9s, a 1000-watt amp, and a digital in-dash stereo. The second was a roof-mount monitor for

DVDs. It cost me extra to install the in-dash stereo into the old-school dashboard of the cutlass, but it looked (and sounded) good when it was done. But after I got the monitor put in, I had to upgrade my car battery to handle all the new power it needed. But I still felt like I wasn't doing too bad.

Then one day I noticed the new paint job peeling along the car body's corners and edges. Turns out that cheap paint job didn't include them laying down a coat of primer to secure the new paint. Even with all the money I was constantly spending, I figured I could still sell the car soon and make a profit. That is, until the day I was trying to pull out of a parking space and realized that my transmission was shot.

Those big wheels were wearing away at the transmission, and they had finally worked it past the point of no return. I needed a new transmission. I probably shouldn't have to tell you that when I finally sold the car, I didn't make a profit. Not even close.

**Whatever you put your time or energy into,
make sure you will get out more than you put in.**

CHANGE THE GAME

The seeds were planted in Martin Delany long before he was even born. Delany was born free in Virginia in 1812, though his father was a slave. Delany's maternal grandparents were born in Africa and his grandfather was rumored to have been a prince. Greatness was written into his blood. Delany was born to change the norms, and everyone who knew him knew it.

We knew it when Delany's mother was able to argue successfully in court for her family's freedom, at a time when this was unheard of, especially by a Black woman. We knew it when he attended his first Negro Conference at 23, and he first came up with an idea to set up a "Black Israel" on the East coast of Africa. But lacking the money and support he needed, Delany worked on other things and became involved with organizations that helped fugitive slaves stay free. We knew it when the dark-skinned Delany was one of the first Blacks accepted to Harvard University's medical school. But a month after arriving, white students argued against the admission of a Black man. They said they had "no objection to the education and elevation of Blacks but do decidedly remonstrate against their presence in college with us."

After this, Delany realized that intellectual arguments could not succeed in persuading the white ruling class to do what was right for people of color. Whites were not interested in helping, or even allowing, Black people to rise up. Afterwards, Delany's ideas became more radical and revolutionary. He argued that there was no future for Blacks in the United States of America. He was convinced that Blacks should leave and build a new nation elsewhere.

This upset most white abolitionists, but not as much as Delany's calling them out as hypocrites who preached racial "equality" but refusing to hire Blacks in their own businesses. By this time, Delany had given up on white people and America as a whole. Delany tried for a while to bring Blacks back to Africa, but now the white missionaries in Africa were the ones working against him.

Determined to bring about change, he made several attempts before ultimately deciding to return to America to help free the slaves. During the Civil War, he was one of the few Blacks who was able to meet with Abraham Lincoln, who thought he was "a most extraordinary and intelligent man," and perhaps even smarter than Frederick Douglass.

Delany thought of a way to bring about freedom for the slaves. He proposed a corps of Black men led by Black officers who would serve to win over Southern Blacks. His plan worked, and the Civil War was won, with Delany serving as the first Black line field officer in the U.S. Army.

Martin Delany was ahead of his time. Before Blacks were attending Harvard, leading U.S. troops, debating with presidents, or publishing revolutionary literature, Delany was doing all of those things...*in the 1800s.*

Delany, like Jesus, Buddha, Allah (Clarence 13X), and hundreds of others, was one of those men possessed with a determined idea to change society. They were *born* with this mind, in fact, the seeds were planted in them before they took their first breath. Every great revolutionary is born from the struggle of his people. They are not privileged people in terms of money, but they are privileged by the wisdom they possess. They can see things in ways others cannot, they can explain things in ways others cannot, and they accomplish change even after their physical deaths.

One of most valuable lessons one can draw from the life of Martin Delany is the way he went against the grain of everything that was expected of him. Delany "flipped the script" so to speak. Delany didn't accept what everyone else accepted, so he took what was given to everyone and changed it to suit his needs. Before Blacks in America even knew a game was being played on them, Delany was trying to "change the game."

When Delany put out his novel *Blake: Or the Huts of America*, it was the first book published by a Black man in America. The novel was about a

Black man traveling through slave communities, planting the seeds for rebellions and uprisings. Delany's novel also called for Black separatism. The novel contained several reworkings of "Plantation Songs" where Delany flipped demeaning minstrel-show material into revolutionary material. For example, where the original "Old Uncle Ned" mourned the death of a slave:

> Den lay down de shubble and de hoe
> Hang up de fiddle and de bow –
> No more hard work for pool old Ned
> He's gone whar de good darkeys go

Delany turned this bullsh*t into a song of rebellion *celebrating* the death of a slavemaster:

> Hang up the shovel and thee hoe-o-o-o!
> I don't care whether I work or no!
> Old master's gone to the slaveholders' rest –
> He's gone where they all ought to go!

Delany's new version wasn't about being a happy slave like the original. It was exactly the opposite. From the work he did, to the words he wrote, Martin Delany wanted revolution for Black people. In his novel, Delany took popular bullsh*t and transformed it into revolutionary material. Today, most of our revolutionary ideas from the 60s and 70s have been perverted into McDonald's commercials, postage stamps, and $30 t-shirts. If only we knew we had the power to turn the tables again. We could make all the right things popular again.

Since Delany, plenty of people have been able to take regular bullsh*t and flip the script to change the game. Dave Chappelle did it with the truths he showed the world (through comedy) on the *Chappelle Show*. Aaron McGruder was doing it with *The Boondocks* comic strip, and now he's still doing it with the TV show. Osa Odiase did it with Live Mechanics, a line of socially-conscious urban clothing. Dozens of actors and rappers are turning the game around right now, as you read this. (Can't you tell by all these lyrics I'm quotin?) In fact, *you* could do it. Delany was just one man. But that's all it takes. And it's not impossible.

> "The artist must elect to fight for freedom or for slavery."
> Paul Robeson

It could begin with making intelligence respectable in the hood again. It's as simple as carrying a book around, and being ready to whup somebody's ass if they disrespect the fact that you're reading a book. Or you could be putting out hot music that sounds like the sh*t that's popular now…except it's talking about something very different. There's hundred of ways to turn poison into antidotes and viruses into vaccines. **The power to make the change is in your hands**.

Don't quit and run away. Change the game.

SEEDS WILL GROW

When the Seed Is Planted

Diligent grew up in South Central Los Angeles. As a young child, Diligent had a Japanese friend named Jason. Jason's family wasn't rich by any means, but Diligent could tell they were doing much better than his own. While Jason introduced Diligent to his first experiences with CapriSuns and Slip N Slides, Diligent went home to a house where he wasn't even comfortable taking a bath. Depending on how you grew up, you may know the feeling. So Diligent made an effort to spend as much time at Jason's as possible, eating dinner there almost every night, and getting treated like a member of the family.

Did You Know?

Genetic use restriction technology, also known as terminator technology, is the name given to methods for limiting the use of genetically modified plants by causing second generation seeds to be sterile. That means that terminator seeds would only produce one crop. The seeds that come from that crop would not produce more crops. The spread of this terminator seed technology would effectively keep people from growing their own food. Instead, farmers will always have to buy seeds from companies like Monsanto.

One night, seated at the table with Jason, his parents, his aunt, and his grandmother Edna, Diligent ended up sitting next to Grandma Edna's purse. While no one was looking, he rummaged through it and found $300 in cash, which he quickly put in his pocket. It wasn't out of the ordinary for Diligent. Where Diligent came from, even the 6-year olds knew how to steal, con, and hustle on a come up. And maybe it was his youth, or perhaps the idea that Jason's family could handle the loss, but it didn't seem like a big deal to steal the money.

Unbeknownst to him, Jason's family was devastated. Not only were they set back financially by the loss, they were hurt that a child they had treated like their own had violated their trust like this.

Diligent returned to Jason's house another day and Jason sadly turned him away at the door. "I can't come out and play with you, and you can't come in the house anymore," Jason said. "Why?" Diligent asked, still confused in his childish innocence.

"Because you stole money." Diligent was crushed. In that moment, he swears he could

Did You Know?

The "Doomsday Vault" is the name given to a vast underground vault storing millions of seeds from around the world. This seed bank, built in 2004, is located on a remote island near the Arctic Ocean, over 400 feet inside of a frozen mountain. The Doomsday Vault is considered the ultimate safety net for the world's seed collections, in case of a "doomsday" - type of event.

feel the guilt of a grown man. It was as though a thousand years of wrong-doing became clear in that one moment of conscience. As a little kid, he was determined never to steal again.

Have you ever burnt a bridge you can't repair?

What did you learn from it?

Have you ever sworn off something in your youth?

Did you stick to your oath? Why or why not?

Some bonds, once broken, can never be repaired. Let those be learning experiences.

When the Plant Matures

"Lessons learned, sessions turned to life reflected
And everything I found real in life, know I kept it
They say life's a teacher, you're gonna get tested
When a nigga changed, they keep saying that nigga strange
Couldn't see how my mind won't be the lame
Ahead of my time, I caught up with the game
Making good music, making paper, making change"
Common, on T.I.'s "Goodlife"

When I met Diligent, he was 19 or 20 and doing pretty well for himself. I had just arrived in Atlanta as a teenager and Diligent was one of the brothers I looked up to. When I was short on money, Diligent always seemed to have some. Pretty soon, I asked him about what he did. Before long, I was doing it too. And guess what? It wasn't dope. **But we damn sure were hustlers.**

We would take trips downtown to a small storefront business that looked as though it had been abandoned years ago. On the outside, there hung an old, faded sign that only read "Panda Trading Co." Once you got inside, it felt as if you had traveled into a whole different world. It didn't even look like Atlanta inside. The air even smelled different. It was like you were in the Third World, as if you had tunneled straight into China. Not Chinatown, but *China.*

There were shiny things everywhere you looked. Chains, medallions, diamonds, rings, bracelets, watches, earrings, everything. And it was all fake, or "slum" as we called it. And it was for sale at wholesale prices. You could buy a diamond necklace for five dollars, or a Movado watch for twelve. While two men worked the counters, armed with pistols in holsters, several Asians milled around in the back areas or sat on crates behind the counter.

Meanwhile, the kind of customers who would come into the slum shop were of a different breed. Everyone from jewelry-slingers who looked like pimps to pimps who were also jewelry-slingers, to two-dollar hustlers who looked more like bums than anything else. And then there was us. There are a few classes to hustlers. There are the wholesalers, who only make moves by the cases. Below that there are the retailers. Among the retailers, you have your first class hustlers, who'll spend at least $300 every trip to the slum shop and make back anywhere from $1000-3000 guaranteed on hand to hand sales. Below that, you have your tourist hustlers who work malls and downtown areas and make a decent bit of change. Below that you have your petty hustlers – the type who work the bus stop down the block from the slum shop, selling the chain right off their neck. Those are the ones who only make enough to get by from day to day.

Diligent was of the first class of hustlers. With him, I would go out of town to malls in the Carolinas or Tennessee, places that had never seen the kind of merchandise we were pushing. We'd go to a legit jewelry store, get in good with a female worker who would give us a jewelry bag or two, and use the bags to make our fake sh*t look legitimate. Sometimes, we even had fake receipts printed.

When Diligent was in town, he would only market Rolexes and Breitlings to industry heads and club owners, strictly an A-List of clients who he would have to burn within a few days of meeting them. One day, he'd be partying with them in the club, the next day he'd be hoping never to see them again.

It made good money, but it was all a scam. And Diligent couldn't shake the idea that he was taking advantage of decent people. I felt the same way, especially after a trip where I sold a Rolex (which cost me $20) to a young Muslim dude – a family man – for about $400. I thought about that man's family, and how he probably thought he was making a good investment – maybe he'd try to sell it and get more money – but he had basically wasted a grip of money that he could have spent on his kids. The money was good, but it wasn't something I felt too good about doing. I needed a clear conscience, so I got out.

Eventually, the slum business got oversaturated and played out in the big cities. Soon, slum was so widespread enough that people got hip in the small towns as well. Today, you can't even get someone's attention with a watch or chain, much less sell one for a good profit.

Diligent didn't disappear with the slum game though. He simply transferred his energy to a slightly different hustle. He began working festivals and concerts with a now-legit hustler named Ahmed. This time they had booths and stands, still selling watches, but now at reasonable prices. What he lost in per-item-profit he made up for in sales volume. Working the festivals eventually led him to doing T-shirts. The shirts cost less than two dollars each and sold for ten or twenty, but there was always the risk of getting arrested and your merchandise confiscated. Plus, besides Ahmed, he was consistently running into people he couldn't trust. Diligent kept being reminded that "when you hustle in the streets, loyalty and credibility are hard to come by."

Finally, he ran into Ice, a fellow hustler. Only Ice wasn't a fellow "hustler." Ice was a merchandiser. There's a big difference between a hustler and a merchandiser. Every merchandiser is a hustler, but every hustler isn't a merchandiser. To begin with, while a hustler naturally preys on the weaknesses of the consumer, a merchandiser doesn't have to take advantage of anyone, because people come to him requesting his services. Second, while a hustler can operate alone without any bonds of loyalty, a merchandiser relies on partnerships with people who are legitimate and trustworthy because the industry is cutthroat.

Almost ten years after I met Diligent as a hustler preying on people's desires for shiny things, he's now an inside merchandiser, producing and marketing everything from dogtags to t-shirts for the biggest names in entertainment. It took some years for the seeds of integrity to come into full bloom for my brother Diligent, but it's been the most "diligent" move he's ever made.

Which ideas have taken years for you to fully embrace?

Which ideas are still slowly developing?

Some seeds sprout quickly, while others take time to grow.
It takes open eyes to learn every lesson that life presents.

RAISE YOUR DAMN KIDS

"Niggas be a father, you're killin your son"
Jay-Z, "Meet the Parents"

At 17, Tyreek wasn't givin his baby mama, Misha, nothin. He actually did his best to steer clear of Misha's triflin ass. But one day, almost three years later, Misha was at the beauty salon getting her hair done, when her stylist said, "Girl, you ain't getting no money from him? No good nigga! You better take him to court!" The wheels started turning in her head, and she went hard. She took Tyreek to court. Now, he owed for every year that he hadn't paid. He was 20, owing $8,000. Tyreek ended up going to jail for child support the next year. It was only then that he wondered if he could have avoided all this by not avoiding his child.

Tyreek's story isn't rare. The lesson here should be to be careful where you stick your dick, but once you have a seed, there's no turning back the wheels of time and making a smarter decision. So you have a baby now. What are you doing?

"A hundred years from now it will not matter what your back account was, the sort of house you lived in, or the kind of car you drove ...but the world may be different because you were important in the life of a child."
Anonymous

Answer these questions, and if you're happy with the answers, you're probably doing a good job as a parent. It's hard to be a good parent when you're still young yourself, but it can be done. The same way, there's 30 and 40 year olds that couldn't raise a baby turtle right.

Questions for Fathers Not Living With Their Children

1.) How much time – in hours per day – do you spend with your child? (A child needs to regularly see both parents to feel like he or she actually HAS two parents. You shouldn't have time for 3 girlfriends and 4 habits if you don't have time for your own seed)

2.) How much money do you spend on your child or give to your child's mother? Is it enough to pay for food, clothes, childcare, medical care, and educational needs? (Babies are expensive, and $20 a week doesn't even pay for gas money these days. If you can afford to drink, smoke, and club, you should have plenty set aside for your child)

"The most important thing that parents can teach their children is how to get along without them."
Frank A. Clark (1911)

3.) Can you be trusted to take care of your child on your own for longer than a day? How often do you do it? (And don't be stupid enough to call it babysitting since it is YOUR child too)

4.) How much do you know about how your child is doing in school? How much do you do to help with their education? (If their teachers don't know you by name, you ain't doin much)

5.) Are you living your life in such a way that you will be there for your child as they grow up? Will you be able to send your child to college, or will you expect them to see you on visiting days?

6.) Why do you want to see your child when you do see them? Do you only talk about seeing your child when you want some from their mom?

7.) Out of all the times you call your child's mother, how many times do you ask to speak to your child? What do you talk about?

8.) When you *do* talk to your child, do you sound like a responsible parent? Do you know how to give good, child-friendly advice?

9.) No matter how crazy you think your child's mother is, are you able to compromise and get along reasonably for the sake of your child?

10.) Do you get angry or jealous about the idea of another man being in your child's life – no matter whether he's positive or not?

Questions for All Parents

"Cops are just as crooked as the niggas they chasin'
Lookin' for role models, our father figures is basers"
Tupac Shakur, "They Don't Give a F*ck About Us"

1.) What are you teaching your child, and how will it help them to be successful in life? (Doing cute dances and singing along to the radio ain' sh*t) Do you depend solely on the school system to educate your child?

2.) Do you argue with the child's other parent in front of the child? Do you say and do things to the child's other parent that negatively affect the child? (Remember, everything you do has long-lasting effects)

3.) What are the rules and expectations you have for your child? How are you preparing him for adult life? Will he one day be running for governor, or running from the police?

4.) What do you spend your money on when you spend money on your child? (You shouldn't spend $500 on Christmas gifts when your lights keep getting cut off, and you shouldn't be buying the RocaWear collection when he's 6 and can't spell his own name)

5.) Do you teach your children about their culture, their history, their heritage, and the legacy they must live up to? Do you show them as well? As Bill Cosby said recently, "Explain Black pride, and you start when you're breast feeding...The drug dealer is not in your culture, nor is the prostitute, nor is the glorified pimp if you teach Black pride."

6.) When people tell you that your child's done something wrong, do you take it personally? Do you immediately jump to the defense of your child? Does your child know that you'll always take their side?

7.) Do you overcompensate for other shortcomings by caving into the demands that you CAN provide for your child? Or do you overcompensate for the things YOU weren't provided as a child?

8.) Do you require your child to think critically, or do you expect them to follow and obey without understanding why? Do you encourage or discourage them asking questions?

9.) Does your child have all the skills and knowledge expected for them at their age? Do you know what those expectations are?

10.) Do you regularly put aside your own personal desires for the benefit of your child? Or do you regularly pass off your child to someone else?

There's probably 5,000 other questions worth asking, but hopefully this gets you started on a process of seriously examining yourself and your relationships. If you have children, that's one of the most (if not THE most) important relationships you can have. So do it right.

As hard as it may be, you MUST put 100% into raising your children.

THE REVOLUTION WILL NOT BE TELEVISED

"We are fighting for the preservation of life. We refuse to be brainwashed by comic-book notions that distort the real situation. The only way that the world is ever going to be free is when the youth of this country moves with every principle of human respect and with every soft spot we have in our hearts for human life. We know that as a people, we must seize our time."
Bobby Seale

When I went to Japan, I saw dozens of guys with hiphop gear on, sagging pants, gold teeth, and even dreadlocks. The girls looked like they'd fell out of a Beyonce video, except they didn't have any ass. And many of them had darker skin than the older Japanese, which I learned was because many young Japanese people tan their skin to be dark like Black Americans.

When I went to the Dominican Republic, I heard Reggaeton for the first time, and watched as young dudes in the barrios (ghettos) threw up their sets and freestyled on street corners. Even in Africa, where many people are now so ashamed to be Black that they pray to a white Jesus and the women bleach their skin, I saw how the younger generation emulates Black Americans. They wore the same styles, listened to rap music, and said "What's up NIGGER?!" like it was something cool to do.

When I saw a Benz drive past on 20-inch rims, with the Asian driver hanging out the window in sunglasses, a low fade, and a platinum grill – in Bangkok, Thailand – I knew it was "bigger than hiphop."

These people were into more than just the music. Some of them can't even understand English well enough to get the lyrics. They're into the lifestyle and the culture, but on a deeper level, they're into *you.*

Throughout the world, everyone wants to be you. And not because they think you're rich. They don't want it because they think you're happy. They want to know what it's like to be you because you are the greatest and most important people on the planet right now. The whole world is watching the Black man in America…just waiting to see what you do.

You see, the world really *is* a ghetto. It's a daily struggle for many people just to eat, just to survive, just to make it to another day. But they see something in you that gives them inspiration and hope for the future. Most of them don't even know exactly what it is. But some of them do. They want to be part of the struggle, your struggle, your revolution. They don't just want to be "down" with you…**they want to rise up**

with you. But it seems that you're the only ones who don't want to be part of your own revolution.

David Walker knew it would come to this. So did Malcolm X *and* MLK. Even historian Alexander de Tocqueville wrote in *Democracy in America*:

> If there ever are great revolutions there [in the West], they will be caused by the presence of the Blacks upon American soil. That is to say, it will not be the equality of social conditions but rather their inequality which may give rise thereto.

The rest of the world is waiting on you. From Palestine to South Africa to Latin America, the seeds of revolution are growing…and spreading. Even rappers are starting to wake up to the call for global change. As self-described "revolutionary Black Power Fista" Bun B rapped on MIA's "Paper Planes" remix:

> Now one thing's for certain, and two are for sure/ Being poor is a disease, you gotta hustle up a cure/ Start with your head homey, then use your hands/ If you try it in reverse, you don't even have a chance/ We worldwide worried with the hunger and the thirst/ From the 3rd world countries to the 2nd and the 1st/ It sounds like a verse but it's more like a plan/ Get your Robin Hood on, *put some pressure on the man!*

Take some time to think about the following…and what they mean:

South African Strike

In an area of South Africa, poor Black workers went on strike. They were demanding a pay raise of only ten cents, but the company heads weren't having it. If you didn't know, South Africa is mostly run by white people who are more racist than the average Nazi. When the word spread about the strike, Black people throughout the area went on strike as well, in order to show solidarity. With half of the city going on strike, or boycotting, the South African economy was hurting for its Black dollars. The workers got their raise.

The Attica Riots

You ever heard of the Attica prison uprising? No? Google it or Youtube it. Or read the story about it in Michael Knight's *The Five Percenters.* Attica's just one example of what happens when Black and Hispanic people come together to fight back…instead of fighting each other. I'll tell it to you as quick as I can. In 1971, 85% of Attica's prisoners were Black and Hispanic. This was also an era of increased social awareness among inmates, coming from groups such as the Five Percenters, the Black Panthers, the Young Lords and the Nation of Islam. When news came that the state had killed political prisoner George Jackson at San Quentin Prison, Attica inmates organized a hunger strike. Then the prisoners of D Block took over, seizing prison guards as hostages to

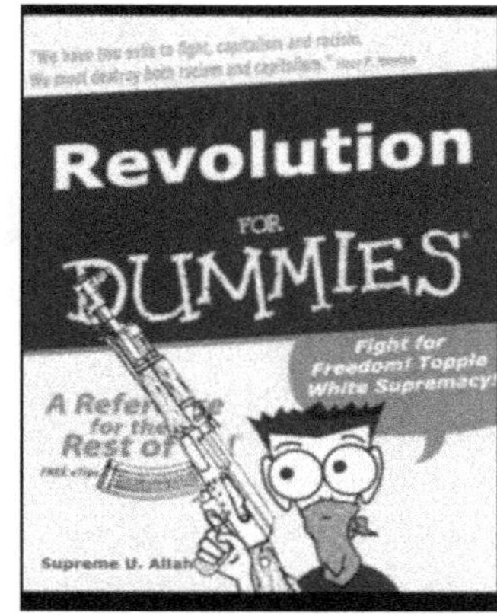

force the state to address their demands. According to Judi Cheng, all the prisoners - Black, Latino and white - stood united. A number of politically conscious white prisoners, some of them in Attica for crimes of opposition to the Vietnam war, recognized the leadership of the Black and Latino brothers, many of whom already united as Five Percenters. They presented a list of demands covering legal rights and repression, work, food and hygiene, and other crucial issues regarding prison conditions. On Sept. 12 the prisoners announced there could be a peaceful resolution to the conflict if Rockefeller would open negotiations with them. The next day, Rockefeller ordered a military attack on the prison. A thousand state troopers, sheriff's deputies, and prison guards armed with automatic weapons and nausea gas stormed the prison. After 15 minutes, the assault had left 28 people lying dead and hundreds wounded. Ten of the dead were prison guards. State officials used the media to put out the lie that the prisoners had slashed the throats of guards who died. Autopsies later proved that, like the 18 murdered prisoners, they had all been killed by gunshots from the state's assault. Anything to stop us.

Shooting Down Santa

Just before Christmas of 2007, Santa was shot down over the slums of Brazil. Well, not really. Every year, a man dressed as Santa is flown by helicopter to a nearby community to get poor children excited about Christmas. However, the neighborhood they fly over is one of the favelas, or ghettoes, of Brazil, where even the police don;t go unless they are coming in armored trucks to do massive raids. The local gangs and drug dealers simply do not allow a police presence until it's time for a full-scale battle. So when they saw a helicopter flying over their territory, they thought it was the police…**and they let them AKs rip**. And they know how to take a chopper down with a rifle. While it may not be nice to shoot down Santa, this story is a reminder that – throughout the world – people ain'tt scared, and are taking complete control of their communities – for better or worse.

A New Kind of Riot

In November of 1994, Black residents in Lexington, Kentucky, took to the streets to show their outrage after a white police officer fatally shot a Black teenager. The Black residents didn't start destroying their own homes and businesses, though. Instead the news reported that they "released their anger by overturning police cars and throwing rocks at whites." That's different.

Lakota Indians

Recently, the Lakota Indians of the Northwest U.S. announced that they were seceding from the United States. That means they are cancelling the contracts they signed with white settlers over 150 years ago, and reclaiming the land as their own. They are welcoming anybody to come join them in what they are calling a new nation covering a large part of the northwestern United States. They're basically saying, "F*ck you paleface, we're doing our own thing now."

And Here We Are

The poem "Harlem" by Langston Hughes captures the spirit of how these f*cked-up conditions must – one day – lead to revolution:

> What happens to a dream deferred?
> Does it dry up
> like a raisin in the sun?
> Or fester like a sore –
> And then run?
> Does it stink like rotten meat?
> Or crust and sugar over –
> like a syrupy sweet?
> Maybe it just sags
> like a heavy load
> Or does it EXPLODE?

Think about what he's saying. The American Dream was deferred for us, meaning we didn't benefit from it, while white folks did. As Mary J. Blige sang on Big Boi's "Something's Gotta Give," "They been sellin us a dream/ Tellin us we're on the same team" So what happens to those of us who dreamed of a better life? Me, personally, I'd rather explode than dry up, fester, run, rot, sugar over, or sag in misery.

While you're thinking about poetry and revolution, there's a dozen artists that come to mind, from the Last Poets to Amiri Baraka, but here's a recent one I like. In Amaris Howard's "Where Is Our Revolution?" (myspace.com/amarishoward) she spits:

> I mean, what is revolution?/ I just can't seem to spell it/ See, every time they try to sell it/ They tell me it's not letting no white people call you nigger/ Or Halle Berry winning an award for starring in a soft porn with a white man/ Or MTV playing artists that look like me/ Or Black Entertainment being booty-shaking arrangements/ Instead of Black Elevation/ Or 50 Cent getting album of the year for being shot 9 times/ Or Blacks going to college to learn how to be slaves…to the system…/ And they say don't talk about it, be about it/ so see, I'm no

> revolutionary/ A poet maybe, if even that, but the fact is, revolution is a battle/ And there will be causalities, whether you choose to fight or not/ And I always hear people say "I don't know how they did it back in those slave days"/ but I do...They did it JUST LIKE YOU/ Everyday our lives are stolen due to the justice system and police brutality/ but we sit quietly for Massa/ or we whisper/ But revolution is loud/ acting and not pretending to be something we're not/ but doing something about what we are/ or not allowing someone else to define who we are/...You can't be afraid to lose if you're already losing/ Time to start choosing a way out instead of a way to fit in/ But how do we begin to see the need for revolution?/ How about when there are more Black youth in prison than in schools?/ or when your brother gets shot for reaching for his phone?/ or when your children's' future is gone before it's begun?/ See revolution ain't no fun but it's necessary/ Like the air you breathe or like the sleep you need/ So everyday I wake up and say "Good Morning"/ and before I start yawning/ I pray for revolution/ because today the Black nation is dying/ today the nation is dying/ but revolution is coming...tomorrow...

So who you wit? Change is coming, and it ain't gonna come from the top down. True change has gotta come from the bottom up. Everywhere around the world, revolution has been a part of our people's history. Wherever people have been held down for long enough, they eventually grow the mind to rise up. Since the world's in pretty bad shape wherever you go, you have more allies than you think.

Once at the bottom, there's nowhere left to go but up.
The revolution is mounting...with or without you.

N.I.G.G.A.

Tupac said that "N.I.G.G.A." – as in his album *Strictly 4 My N.I.G.G.A.s* – stood for "Never Ignorant, Getting Goals Accomplished." The same way Pac had flipped the meaning of "Thug Life" into a revolutionary statement, he was able to transform "nigga" into a meaningful idea...at least for a little while. If only Pac had lived past 25, we may have seen the long-term results of his full gameplan. But he was cut down before he could grow into the full measure of his potential.

But not you. You're still here, and you have time. What are you doing? What are you planning to do? You may not be ignorant, but are you gonna get your goals accomplished?

Think about the goals you have for yourself. Now think about how you plan on getting there. Trouble is, we can see a pot of gold at the end of the rainbow, but we don't know how to get to the end of a rainbow. Well, you actually can't because the rainbow is basically an illusion. Kind of like the dreams many of us waste our best years chasing.

If you want to be successful at accomplishing your goals, you have to be realistic about both your goals themselves AND how you plan on getting there. Anything is possible, but life isn't a fairy tale either. You COULD go from the projects to a mansion, but do you know how much planning and hard work it would take?

You can start by thinking backwards. Start with the end result in mind, and imagine yourself traveling backwards in time. Look at all the steps you'd have to go through. Don't forget that things can go wrong along the way, and they usually do.

Once you've imagined all the way backwards to the present, come up with a roadmap. The same way a GPS system plans out a route to get to a destination, or a good chess player plans out a strategy to win, you have to plan for your goals. And both a GPS system and a good chess player know how to factor in for detours and unexpected changes.

You can start even smaller, by starting a habit of goal-setting. Write down a few of you big goals, like quitting smoking, getting a degree, starting a successful business, or becoming a teacher. The write down some of the smaller goals that it will take to get there. If you're accomplishing your smaller goals, then you know you're on your way. If you're not making progress on the little things, you need to rethink your strategy and maybe reconsider your goals.

So, are you setting some goals today? If so, good for you. That's the first step on a long road of progress...as long as you keep it up. If not, why not? Are you a procrastinator? Do you constantly put off until tomorrow what you can do today...only to NOT do it tomorrow either? You gotta change that gameplan...or be just another "nigga."

What are your goals for today? Do you have a set of goals every day? How often do you accomplish all of them? What are your goals for the next 5 years? What hard steps are you taking to accomplish them?

Set your goals today and start working towards them.

SMALL BATTLES

Double Consciousness

"Revolution is not an event. It is a process."
Mao Tse Tung

> ...The Negro is a sort of seventh son, born with a veil, and gifted with second-sight in this American world – a world which yields him no true self-consciousness, but only let's him see himself through the revelation

> of the other world. It is a peculiar sensation, this double-consciousness, this sense of always looking at one's self through the eyes of others, of measuring one's soul by the tape of a world that looks on in amused contempt and pity. One ever feels his twoness – an American, a Negro; two souls, two thoughts, two unreconciled strivings; two warring ideals in one dark body, whose dogged strength alone keeps it from being torn asunder. The history of the American Negro is the history of this strife – this longing to attain self-conscious manhood, to merge his double self into a better and truer self. In this merging he wishes neither of the older selves to be lost.

The quote above comes from *The Souls of Black Folk*, a groundbreaking book by W. E. B. Du Bois. Just three years after the end of slavery in America, Du Bois was born a free Black man in Massachusetts. He was privileged enough to receive his bachelor's degree from Harvard University, followed by the esteemed University of Berlin, until he returned to Harvard University for his Ph.D. Du Bois was no sharecropper. He would eventually become one of the most respected Black thinkers of his time. His words were sharp and calculated, conveying some of the most profound statements made at the time.

Did You Know?

Elders and shamans in West Africa have said that, as the slave trade progressed, the "very best" of their people were sent to *intentionally* be captured by the slave traders. Their intention was that these people would produce a lineage of greatness that would one day emerge to redeem its right place in the world.

In fact, Du Bois was the one who correctly predicted that the problem of our present era would continue to be "the problem of the color-line." Du Bois also described the "double consciousness" of Blacks living in America, where Blacks could neither be both "Black" and "American," nor could they only be one.

A smart man. But he had his issues. Born free in the North, he had trouble relating to the problems Blacks faced in the post-slavery South. To some extent, he had problems relating to many Blacks, period.

"The distance doesn't matter; it is only the first step that is difficult."
Marie de Vichy-Chamrond (1697-1780)

From 1897 onwards, he argued against a number of Black leaders. One rival was Booker T. Washington, an ex-slave who called for Southern Blacks to learn trades and continue to work with their hands to rebuild their lives and communities. Du Bois considered him a new-age slave, and criticized him and his schools every chance he had. Du Bois didn't see the point in Blacks learning trades. Instead, he pushed the intellectual agenda hard, identifying a "talented tenth," a small percentage of educated Blacks in America, as the saviors of all Blacks.

Du Bois even hated on Marcus Garvey, who the light-skinned Du Bois called a "gorilla." Du Bois claimed Garvey's plans to return to Africa were even more stupid than Washington's calls to rebuild the South. Du Bois was an instrumental "tool" in stopping Garvey and the UNIA, one of the strongest grassroots movements ever.

In response to these attacks, many of Du Bois' critics regarded him a sell-out. Considering his elitist views, and the fact that he was living off the money of white "sponsors," they may have been right.

But, over the years, Du Bois' views were changing. By his late 20s, he became interested in Black Nationalism and socialism. He began advocating Pan-Africanism, which sought to unify Blacks in America, Africa, and throughout the world under one Red, Black, and Green flag. Du Bois, then 32, organized the first Pan-African Conference in 1900.

But Du Bois was no revolutionary. He still believed in America, and he still certainly believed in white people. In 1909, Du Bois helped found the NAACP, which consisted of both Blacks and whites. The NAACP promised change, but hoped to argue things intellectually at a time when other Black leaders were calling for action.

Over time, Du Bois began to realize that a group economy among Blacks was a good way to fight discrimination and poverty. With collective economics, Blacks could prevail. In 1912, he joined the Socialist party at 44, though only for a short time. A few years later, he organized another Pan-African conference, this time with less white influence.

In 1920, he released *Darkwater: Voices from Within the Veil*, a highly controversial book, where he began commenting on the crushing forces of white supremacy, and his prayers for the rise of a Black Messiah. *Darkwater* makes the ever-popular *Souls of Black Folk*, which Du Bois had written 17 years before, seem tame and conservative by comparison. *Darkwater* was (and still is) revolutionary and unconventional in both its

Did You Know?

The most celebrated works of Black literature are often those that are considered the most accommodating towards white people, even when the authors have written other (often better) books that were more revolutionary. For example, Du Bois is known for *Souls of Black Folk,* but not *Darkwater.* Martin Delaney's *Blake* is unknown. Frederick Douglass is known for promoting nonviolent abolition, but his only fiction novel, *The Heroic Slave,* advocated physical confrontation and revolt. Bet you've never heard of it. Even Harriet Beecher Stowe, who was criticized heavily for the passivity in *Uncle Tom's Cabin*, followed up with a book called *Dred: Tales of a Dismal Swamp*, which also promoted violent revolution. *Dred* even sold better, but you've probably never heard of it.

content and style of presentation, addressing topics ranging from the plight of Black women to outright revolution.

Du Bois also began to change his vision for the NAACP. He now argued that they should focus on Black economic development instead of simply fighting discrimination. In 1934, Du Bois, now 56, resigned as editor of the NAACP's journal, *The Crisis*.

Five years later, he founded a more "radical" journal on racial issues. As a result of these new views, he was forced to resign from Atlanta University. He returned to the NAACP at 76 as a researcher, but his new views led to more disagreements with their leadership. Both the whites and Blacks in charge agreed to dismiss him in 1948.

In 1951, the government finally targeted him. Du Bois and four others were indicted under the Foreign Agents Registration Act. He was accused of acting on behalf of a foreign nation due to his words on Pan-Africanism and socialism. Even though he was acquitted, his views were now much stronger than the Black civil rights leaders who once called him a sell-out, and they avoided him. In 1961, he finally gave up on America and renounced his U.S. citizenship. He was 91. He moved to Ghana, the home of revolutionary Pan-African leaders like Kwame Nkrumah. He became a Ghanaian citizen before dying there in 1963. Du Bois, once a "sell-out" and now a Pan-African, had chosen to have his body buried in Africa.

Has the way you think about life changed gradually over the years? Can you tell which direction you're moving in?

Did you once argue against some of the same ideas you now argue for? Does this help you understand other people who are where you once were? What helped you find your path and stick to it?

Is your journey complete? How do you know?

**Every day is a small battle to reclaim your mind and freedom.
Some wars may take nearly a hundred years to win.**

The Battle of Mogadishu

Some battles are won much quicker. When U.S. troops came into Somalia for a "peace-keeping mission," (of course that's not what it was really about) they underestimated the effectiveness of the African guerrilla fighters. Here's what happened:

October 3, 1993: Day One

14:49 Military Time (2:49 PM Civilian Time) — Two principal targets, Somali rebel clan leaders, are located at a residence in central Mogadishu, Somalia.

15:32 — The American force launches: 19 aircraft, 12 vehicles, 160 men.

15:42 — Official assault beginning. American soldiers hit the target house. Four Rangers fast-rope in. One Ranger, Private First Class Todd Blackburn, misses the rope and falls 70 feet to the street.

15:47 — Large crowds of Somali guerrillas and citizens begin converging on the target area.

15:58 — One of the American vehicles, a five-ton truck, is hit and disabled by a guerrilla's rocket-propelled grenade, several American soldiers are wounded.

16:00 — Groups of armed Somalis begin converging on the target area from all over Mogadishu.

16:02 — Targets acquired: assault force reports both clan leaders and about 21 others in custody. As the force prepares to pull out, 3 vehicles are detached to rush the wounded Private Blackburn back to the base.

16:15 — The convoy is delayed and does not move out, due to confusion about the loading of prisoners. Delta is waiting for the convoy to signal them, while the *convoy* is waiting for Delta to signal *them.*

16:20 — First helicopter crash: Black Hawk Super 61 is hit by another guerrilla's rocket-propelled grenade and crashes 5 blocks northeast of the target building.

16:22 — Crowds of armed Somalis start racing toward the Super 61 crash site.

16:26 — Convoy starts moving, late. Prisoners loaded, the convoy and ground forces all begin moving toward the crashed helicopter. Black Hawk Super 64 takes the place of Super 61 in orbit over the city.

16:28 — Search and rescue team ropes in to assist the crew of the crashed Super 61 helicopter. Both pilot and co-pilot are dead.

16:35 — Convoy makes wrong turn and begins driving lost through city streets, sustaining heavy casualties by Somali snipers and armed militia.

16:40 — Second helicopter crash: The replacement helicopter, Black Hawk Super 64, is hit by another guerrilla's rocket-propelled grenade, and crashes about a mile southwest of the target building. Hostile crowds of Somalis begin moving toward it as well.

16:42 — As the afternoon sun begins to set, 2 Delta Force snipers are inserted by helicopter to help protect the injured pilot and his crew.

16:54 — The Lost Convoy, with more than half of its force wounded or dead, abandons its search for the first downed Black Hawk and begins fighting its way back to the base.

17:03 — A Quick Reaction Force [QRF] convoy is dispatched from Command and Control in an attempt to rescue the men stranded at the Super 64 crash site. It encounters immediate attacks.

17:34 — The QRF and the Lost Convoy, both having sustained heavy casualties, link up and abandon the effort to break through to save the pilot of the Super 64. The remainder of the ground force of Rangers and commandos are converging around the first crash site, sustaining many casualties. Ranger Corporal Jamie Smith is among those shot.

17:40 — Somali crowds overrun the Super 64 crash site, killing two snipers and every member of the crew, except the pilot, Mike Durant, who is carried off by militia through the city.

17:45 — Both convoys return to the base. 99 men remain trapped and surrounded in the city around the first downed Super 64. Corporal Smith is bleeding heavily, medic requests immediate evacuation.

19:08 — Black Hawk Super 66 comes and drops water, ammunition, and medical supplies to the trapped force. It is badly damaged, and cannot land to evacuate. Ranger Corporal Smith limps back to base.

20:27 — As the night sky darkens, Ranger Corporal Jamie Smith dies.

21:00 — 2 companies of 10th Mt. Division troops, along with the remainder of Task Force Rangers call for the aid of Pakistani tanks, and Malaysian armored vehicles. The new Rescue Convoy forms at Mogadishu's New Port, and begins planning the rescue.

23:23 — The Rescue Convoy moves out in the darkness of night.

October 4, 1993: Day Two

At Midnight 00:00 (24:00), the Rangers are still trapped inside Mogadishu without essential equipment like night vision.

01:55 — Rescue Convoy reaches the trapped Ranger force. A second half of the convoy finally reaches the site of Durant's downed Black Hawk 64. Durant and his crew are missing.

03:00 — Forces still struggling to remove the pinned body of Cliff Wolcott, pilot of downed Super 61.

05:30 — Rangers start moving from the city to the Pakistani Stadium, on foot: Wolcott's body is finally recovered. Vehicles roll out of the city. Elements of the Rangers are left to run out of the city, on foot, through gunfire. The road they take is known as the Mogadishu Mile.

06:30 — The force makes it back to the Pakistani Stadium. 18 Americans are dead or mortally wounded, 73 injured, and 1 captured. The Battle of Mogadishu is over. The Somalis have won.

In just two days, a decisive battle was fought and won. Several wars and battles have ended just as quickly, although they were still significant enough to affect the course of history and world politics for years to come. Similarly, you may one day arrive at a climactic event that can change your life. It may only last an hour, but it could make all the difference in the world. So don't run from conflicts and disagreements. One may become the "epiphany" that opens your eyes to life as you never saw it before. On the other hand, you may be able to do the same for someone else. So don't disregard any interaction, exchange, or conversation as trivial or meaningless. You can find meaning anywhere.

How long does it take to change someone's life? What about your own?

How long would it take to change your hood? This society? This world?

And once the process of change has begun, then what?

Some battles can be won in only a day.
But the fight does not end there.

What Now?

Hopefully, this book has pushed you in the right direction. Wherever you're headed now, it was already there. I'm just here to provide the spark for the fire. Whatever you do, don't let that fire burn out and die. At times, the game will be frustrating, and may even seem hopeless. But it's not. It's a beautiful struggle, and there's a solution for every problem. As you begin, or continue, your own individual path towards revolution, keep in mind that everything you do is part of a bigger struggle. If you're not helping, you're hurting. Here's a few pieces of advice to help you get everything in perspective. I've based them on real problems that readers presented to me after reading Part One.

Problem: You still haven't figured out what you want to do with the rest of your life?

Solution: Join the club. Nearly everyone from age 15 to 51 has that problem. Why? Well, we grow up in a world that doesn't encourage living with meaning…so most of us wonder for years about the meaning of life…and then we finally give up, and give in, to whatever the system tells us is best. But reread this book a few times, and I bet you'll find your calling. The hard part, however, is sticking to it.

Problem: Today's youth running wild with no direction or hope for the future?

Solution: Of course they are. This world doesn't promise much. So take a few under your wing and break the cycle of neglect. Mentoring is easier than it looks. It only requires time, dedication, and a listening ear.

Problem: You're out-of-touch with what's going on in the hood, or among the "common people"?

Solution: It's not hard to get a feel for the pulse of our people. But if you don't do it, you'll never be able to reach the ones you need most. Above all, we must respect everyone's experiences, because it's self-destructive for us to think we're better than each other. If you want to know what's happenin in the hood, start getting your hair cut/done in a hood barbershop/salon from now on. Talk to the young people you pass by daily. Watch BET and listen to urban radio, just to see what the people are into. Finally, stop listening to the out-of-touch "experts."

Problem: Your relationships keeping you from doing more with your life?

Solution: Your relationships either inspire you or suffocate you. When your mindset changes, often your relationships will have to change as well. Do it early, or regret it for the rest of your life.

Problem: The "industry" keeps people who tell the truth out of the mainstream?

Solution: Forget the mainstream. Most major deals rape the artists anyway. Sell your music independently and say what needs to be said. Start an underground movement.

Problem: Illegal enterprise seems more enticing than legal money?

Solution: Use your brain and crunch the numbers. Statistically, your chances of "winning the game" are about as good as your chance of hitting the lottery. You're much more likely to fail and fall. Instead, apply whatever you know from the street game to hustle legitimately. It's more work, but less risk, and more long-term benefit.

Problem: You're not a hustler – you're more of a worker?

Solution: Work your ass off then. Make good money. And then kick as much as you can into movements that matter. Fund the struggle.

Problem: The people in power have too much power, and all seems hopeless?

Solution: People have won armed struggles using mud and bamboo, and changed entire political climates through basement meetings. Never underestimate the potential of the common people. We outnumber the people in power 1,000 to 1. Spread word and build solidarity. Change is brewing.

Problem: This book can change lives, but people don't read?

Solution: Read it to em. Buy em a copy. Or simply spread the word. Everyone doesn't have to read the message in order to see the vision.

Problem: "The struggle" seems too vague and ambiguous – you can't figure out where and how to begin?

Solution: Every step you take to create change in our world is a contribution to the struggle. Find your angle. If you do music, tell the truth in your music. If you're a teacher, teach them how to think critically and change their situations. Lawyer? Fight for the right side. If your enterprise is strictly about money, fund a worthwhile program, mentor some teenagers, or use your free time to push a bigger agenda.

Problem: People don't seem to want to change, and it's frustrating to keep trying to change them?

Solution: You can't change anyone else. But you can get them to see something they may have missed. However, it may take ten or twenty exchanges before you see any changes. The older people are, the more set they are in their ways. But given enough motivation and information, anyone can change.

Problem: People are blind and won't accept the truth, even when it seems crystal clear?

Solution: What worked for you may not work for others. Remember that people are motivated by different things, and it takes different methods to reach us all. Some of us are followers by nature. When it's clear we can't teach someone to think for themselves, we simply have to give them something powerful and meaningful to follow instead of whatever they're currently into. Even then, we have to add on more than we take away.

Problem: People seem too scared to speak up or fight for change?

Solution: It will take those of us who are strong, who are examples of success, to be the first to step forward without fear. Those of us who are financially secure, emotionally stable, and intellectually strong will have to step out of our comfort zones and speak first, and speak loudest. Others will follow the lead.

Problem: All revolutionaries seem to die before the mission is accomplished?

Solution: We all die. You can either live on your knees, sit on your ass, or die standing up. And there's plenty of revolutionaries, activists, and educators, who have died of old age, surrounded by the many who loved them. And there's thousands more who have supported the struggle without putting themselves at its forefront. And the "mission" isn't some imagined victory that will miraculously occur one day soon. Our mission – our obligation to our children and the generations who follow – is doing our part to better the future.

Even in the dictionary, there is very little separating a victim from a victor. How you interpret your struggle makes all the difference.

REVIEW

The principle for this chapter was **"Seal the Deal"** This means: Choose the best paths, envision the future, ensure survival, and achieve success.

Here are the principles and lessons we covered:

Goal-Setting and Accomplishment
Don't waste your life f*ckin around. Have your priorities in order.
If you can't find a job, make one
Set your goals today and start working towards them.
Whatever you do, wherever you go, pursue education.
When you don't know better, the things you think you want are often the things that will destroy you.
Investing Time and Energy
As hard as it may be, you MUST put 100% into raising your children.
Pursuing instant gratification kills your chances for long-term success. The best rewards take time.
Whatever you put your time or energy into, make sure you will get out more than you put in.
Revolution
Don't quit and run away. Change the game.
Every day is a small battle to reclaim your mind and freedom. Some wars may take nearly a hundred years to win.
If you're not a supporter of the oppressor, you are its enemy.
Once at the bottom, there's nowhere left to go but up. The revolution is mounting...with or without you.
Some battles can be won in only a day. But the fight does not end there.
Stand your ground. Give an inch a day, and in two weeks you've lost a foot.
True Success
A life not worth dying for isn't worth living for.
Once you're done being used, you get discarded.
The people who pay for you own you. Be aware that your leash isn't as long as you think it is.
Wealth alone doesn't make you a hero.

Before we close this experience out, let me leave you with these words from author Ayi Kwei Armah:

> *"Endless our struggle must seem to those whose vision reaches only to the end of today. The present is where we get lost – if we forget our past and have no vision of the future.*
>
> *A healer needs to see beyond the present and tomorrow. He needs to see years and decades ahead. Because healers work for results so firm they may not be wholly visible till centuries have*

flowed into millennia. Those willing to do this necessary work, they are the healers of our people."

In other words, this is not the end. The journey's far from over. I'm going to leave you with a few more quotes to keep that fire burning. Dig into what they mean, and the fearless lives of the people who said them.

"I have freed many slaves, and could have freed thousands more if they only knew they were slaves." - Harriet Tubman,

"If you are deaf, dumb, and blind to what's happening in the world, you're under no obligation to do anything. But if you know what's happening and you don't do anything but sit on your ass, then you're nothing but a punk." - Assata Shakur

"The real servant of the people must live among them, think with them, feel for them, and die for them." - Carter G. Woodson

"It does not require a majority to prevail, but rather an irate, tireless minority keen to set brush fires in people's minds." - Samuel Adams

"The objector and the rebel who raises his voice against what he believes to be the injustice of the present and the wrongs of the past is the one who hunches the world along." - Clarence S. Darrow

"Stand before the people you fear and speak your mind - even if your voice shakes." – Maggie Kuhn

"When a man decides to do something he must go all the way, but he must take responsibility for what he does. No matter what does, he must know first why he is doing it, and then he must proceed with his actions without having doubts or remorse about them." - Don Juan

"I wish to die a slave to principles, not to men." - Emiliano Zapata

"There are only two mistakes one can make along the road to truth; not going all the way, and not starting." - The Buddha

"First they ignore you, then they laugh at you, then they fight you, then you win." – Mahatma Ghandhi

Afterword

MWALIMU BARUTI

Any people, conscious of being threatened or attacked, mobilizes for defense and retaliation to school the attacker. It is only a submissive, pacified, vanquished people who do not consciously respond to being violated by others.

People who fear standing up often try to find some imaginable "humanity" in their destroyers as a means of lessening and rationalizing their terror of the daily assault against their mental, physical and spiritual being. They make sacred promises not to retaliate against those who have committed, and continue to perpetrate, every imaginable evil against them. But, at no point in history, is there any credible evidence that this works to empower such cowards. Tactics such as these, by people who see themselves as impotent, only serve to encourage the barbarians to further destroy them.

Warriorhood calls for a completely different approach toward the enemies of our people. It demands that we act against them as we know, deep down in our hearts and souls, warriors do. It is different if we don't know, or are afraid. And we know that fearfulness is not in a warrior's character, for fear cannot carry the burden of war.

But we do know and are not fearful. That this knowing and intrepidation is characteristic of us makes it impossible for us to seek the back road to a delusional peace. It forces us to stand in the face of our enemies and command victory and justice. There is no other way. There is no gray area to hide or sleep in, between us and them. There is only victimization or victory for warriors with just cause.

Knowing this, and having read and deeply considered the revolutionary thoughts presented in this book, *Rap, Race and Revolution*, the question, for members of the warrior class – male and female – becomes where to from here? In other words, now that everyone who has reached this point knows better, what do we do? Besides further reading (beginning with the texts recommended at the back of this book and its prequel, *How to Hustle and Win*)...there is only one simple answer: **Act on what we know.**

- Mwalimu K. Bomani Baruti,

Author of *Asafo: A Warrior's Guide to Manhood* and *Nyansasem: A Calendar of Revolutionary Daily Thoughts*

www.AkobenHouse.com

Mwalimu K. Bomani Baruti is the co-founder and co-director of Akoben Institute, an independent Afrikan-centered school, and author of 14 self-published books, including:

Excuses, Excuses: The Politics of Interracial Coupling in European Culture

Chess Primer: An Introduction to the Game of Chess

The Sex Imperative: Homosexuality and the Effeminization of Afrikan Males

Complementarity: Thoughts for Afrikan Warrior Couples

Mentacide and other essays

Kebuka! Remembering the Middle Passage Through the Eyes of Our Ancestors

Eureason: An Afrikan Centered Critique of Eurocentric Social Science

Battle Plan: Notes Toward Higher Ideals in Afrikan Intellectual Liberation

Bro. Baruti has been featured in *The Faith Tribune, Frontline, The Ghetto Tymz, Nex Generation, XXL, EM (Ebony Man), The Final Call,* the *Atlanta Daily World, The Atlanta Voice,* the *Journal of Social and Behavioral Sciences* and dozens of radio shows, television programs and websites. Also considered a voice worthy of our youth's attention, samplings of his lectures and interviews can be found in the music of hip hop artists such as dead prez and Nas.

Descriptions of Bro. Baruti's books, along with CDs of his radio interviews and DVDs of his lectures, classes and interviews may be found at **www.AkobenHouse.com**

Appendixes

OTHER STUFF YOU NEED TO KNOW

So here's all the stuff that I couldn't fit anywhere else. It's all useful.

MOVIES TO SEE

There are so many flicks worth seeing that I couldn't give them all their own "Movie to See" box! So here's the rest. Try em all. As you already know, many of the documentaries (marked with a *) can be seen free at www.supremedesignonline.com

4 Little Girls
A Hero Ain't Nothin but a Sandwich
A Soldier's Story
All Power to the People*
American Blackout*
American Drug War: The Last White Hope*
American History X
Antwone Fisher
Apocalypto
Baraka*
Black Caesar
Black Gunn
Black Like Me
Blow
Bowling for Columbine*
Brothers
Choices
Claudine
Cocaine Country*
Cornbread, Earl and Me
Cosmic Slop
Do the Right Thing
Esoteric Agenda*
Fabled Enemies*
Five on the Black Hand Side
Four Little Girls
Fred Hampton*
Glory
God Grew Tired of Us*
Goodbye Uncle Tom*
Gordon's War
Hand of God*
Higher Learning
Hoop Dreams*
In Lies We Trust*
Invisible Children*
KIDS
Lackawanna Blues
Learning Tree
Letter to the President*
Lion of the Desert
Ludicrous Diversion*
Matrix of Evil*
Men of Honor
Paid In Full
Powers of Ten*
Pride
Prisoners of Katrina*
Putney Swope
Quilumbo
Sankofa
School Daze
Second Coming
Shaka Zulu
She Hate Me
Sicko*
Slumdog Millionaire
St. Louis Blues
Sweet Misery: A Poisoned World*
The Book of Numbers
The Boys of Baraka
The Century of the Self*
The Education of Sonny Carson
The FBI's War on Black America*
The Great Debaters
The Hate that Hate Produced*
The Hurricane
The Man
The Meeting
The Merchants of Cool*
The Message
The Origins of AIDS*
The Other Side of AIDS*
The Secrets of the CIA*
The True Story of Blackhawk Down*
The Warriors
The Weather Underground*
Torture of Mothers
Torture: America's Brutal Prisons*
Traitor
Trouble Man
Tupac: Resurrection*
Unreported World*
When the Levees Broke*
When We Were Kings*
Willie Dynamite

BLACK INVENTORS (L-Z)

L. Bell	Locomotive smoke stack. Patent# 115,153	May 23, 1871
Ellijah McCoy	Lubricating Cup	Nov. 15, 1895
James Robinson	Lunch Pail	1887
Peter Walker	Machine for Cleaning Seed Cotton	
Paul L. Downing	Mail Box	Oct. 27, 1891
Henry Blair	Mechanical Corn Harvester	
Henry Blair	Mechanical Seed Planter	1830
Joan Clark	Medicine Tray	1987
Thomas Stewart	Mop	June 11, 1893
Fred M. Jones	Motor	June 27, 1939
Granville Woods	Multiplex Telegraph System (Allowed Messages To Be Sent And Received From Moving Trains)	1887
I.O. Carter	Nursery Chair	1960
J. A. Joyce	Ore Bucket. Patent # 603,143	April 26, 1898
Folarin Sosan	Package-Park (Solves Package Delivery Dilemma)	1997
John Parker	Parker Pulverizer Screw for Tobacco Presses	Sep. 2, 1884
Anna M. Mangin	Pastry fork	March 1, 1892
J. Hawkins	Gridiron	March 3, 1845
J.L. Love	Pencil Sharpener	Nov. 23, 1897
Daniel H.Williams	Performed First Open Heart Surgery	1893
Majorie Joyner	Permanent hair wave machine. Patent # 1693515	Nov. 27, 1928
G.W. Murray	Planter. Patent # 520,887	June 5, 1894
D. McCree	Portable Fire Escape. Patent # 440,322	Nov. 11, 1890
Bessie V. Griffin	Portable Receptacle	1951
J. H. Hunter	Portable Weighing Scales. Patent # 570,533	Nov. 3, 1896
Frederick Jones	Portable X-Ray Machine	
William Barry	Postmarking and Canceling machine	
Joseph Jackson	Programmable Remote Control	
T. J. Byrd	Rail car coupling . Patent# 157,370	Dec. 1, 1874
O.B. Clare	Rail Tresle. Patent # 390,753	Oct. 9, 1888
Granville Woods	Railway Air Brakes (First Safe Method Of Stopping Trains)	1903
W. F. Burr	Railway Switching device . Patent # 636,197	Oct.31,1899
Tom Carrington	Range Oven	1876
H. Grenon	Razor Stropping Device. Patent # 554,867	Feb. 18, 1896
J. H. Dickenson	Record Player Arm	Jan. 8, 1819
A.P. Abourne	Refining of coconut oil.	July 27, 1980
John Standard	Refrigerator. Patent# 304,552	July 14, 1894
W.D. Davis	Riding Saddles	Oct. 6, 1895
John W. Reed	Rolling Pin	1864
James Forten	Sailing Apparatus	1850
Marie V.B. Brown	Security System. Patent # 3,482,037	Dec. 2, 1969
C. W. Allen	Self Leveling table. Patent # 613,436	Nov. 1, 1898

W.S. Campbell	Self-setting animal trap. Patent # 246,369	Aug. 30, 1881
C.O. Bailiff	Shampoo Headrest	Oct. 11, 1898
George Tolivar	Ship's propeller	
Onesimus	Small Pox Inoculation (He brought this method from Africa where advanced medical practices were in use long before Europeans had any medical knowledge)	1721
Wm. Harwell	Space shuttle arm used to capture satellites	
Edmond Berger	Spark Plug	Feb. 2, 1839
A. B. Blackburn	Spring seat for chairs. Patent # 380,420	April 3, 1888
Frederick Jones	Starter Generator. Patent # 2475842	July 12, 1949
Granville Woods	Steam Boiler/Radiator	1884
G.W. Kelley	Steam Table	1897
Imhotep	Stethoscope	Ancient Egypt
T.A. Carrington	Stove	July 25, 1876
C. J. Walker	Straightening Comb	Approx. 1905
Charles Brooks	Street Sweeper	Mar. 17, 1890
Norbett Rillieux	Sugar Refining System	Dec. 10, 1846
Joseph Gammel	Supercharge System for Combustion Engine	
Granville Woods	Telephone (His Telephone Was Superior To Bell's)	Dec. 2, 1884
W. A. Lovette	The Advance Printing Press	
W.B. Purvis	The Fountain Pen Patent # 419,065	Jan 7, 1890
Madeline Turner	The Fruit Press	1916
Fred M. Jones	Thermostat Control	Feb. 23, 1960
Granville Woods	Third Rail (Subway)	
Frederick Jones	Ticket Dispensing Machine. Patent # 2163754	June 27, 1939
Lewis Temple	Toggle Harpoon (revolutionized whaling industry)	1848
T. Elkins	Toilet	Jan. 3, 1897
R.A. Butler	Train alarm. Patent #157,370	June 15, 1897
M.A. Cherry	Tricycle	May 6, 1886
Granville Woods	Trolley Car	1888
Frederick Jones	Two-Cycle gasoline Engine. Patent # 2523273	Nov. 28, 1950
L.S. Burridge & N.R. Marsham	Typewriter	April 7, 1885
George W. Carver	Variety of 300 products from peanuts, 118 products from sweet potato, and 75 from pecan	1900-1943
A.L. Lewis	Window Cleaner	1892
H. H. Reynolds	Window Ventilator for Railroad Cars	April 3, 1883
Otis F. Boykin	Wire Type Precision Resistor	June 16, 1959
Lydia Holmes	Wood Toys. Patent # 2,529,692	Nov. 14, 1950
Philip Emeagwali	World's Fastest Computer	1989
John A. Johnson	Wrench	

About the Author

Supreme Understanding is a community activist, educator, and expert on the socio-economical and psychological struggles of oppressed people.

Supreme received his bachelor's degree in world history from Morehouse College, followed by a master's degree in urban education from Georgia State University. At 26, he received his doctorate in education from Argosy University, where he focused his research on the benefits of non-formal education with at-risk youth and disadvantaged populations.

In 2000, Supreme co-founded Show and Prove Youth Outreach, a non-profit organization dedicated to the education and empowerment of at-risk teens. In 2006, Supreme Design, LLC was incorporated to design and publish materials and literature for Show and Prove.

Supreme Understanding's work has brought him to Ghana, Mexico, the Dominican Republic, India, Japan, Thailand, the Czech Republic, Austria, Germany, England, the Caribbean, and dozens of cities throughout the United States. The author's travels have provided him in-depth opportunities to learn about the struggles of oppressed people throughout the world, and their similarities with the struggles of people of color in the U.S.

Supreme is a highly sought-after lecturer, and his multimedia presentations have engaged diverse audiences of both youth and adults. Supreme has presented on a variety of topics with organizations as diverse as the ACLU, the Urban League, 100 Black Men, the Japanese Ministry of Education, and the U.S. Social Forum.

As the author of *How to Hustle and Win: A Survival Guide for the Ghetto*, Supreme's message has reached scores of young urban readers, many of who would write in stating that this had been the first book they'd read in several years. Even with it's deliberately "different" title, *How to Hustle and Win* was extremely well-received by both the general public and the media.

Supreme's work continues as the curriculum director of Show and Prove Youth Outreach, CEO of Supreme Design, traveling lecturer and consultant for numerous organizations and agencies, and author of several upcoming books on overcoming the odds of oppression and disadvantage.

Recommended Reading (Part Two)

Makes Me Wanna Holler by Nathan McCall

Making of the Whiteman by Paul Lawrence Guthrie

Malcolm X Speaks by George Breitman

Malcolm X: The Man and His Times by John H. Clarke

Man, God, and Civilization by John G. Jackson

Marcus Garvey and the Vision of Africa by John Henrik Clarke

Medical Apartheid: The Dark History of Medical Experimentation on Black Americans from Colonial Times to the Present by Harriet A. Washington

Melanin: The Black Key to Freedom by Richard King

Melanin: The Chemical Key to Black Greatness by Carol Barnes

Men are from Mars, Women are from Venus by Dr. Richard Gray

Message to the Blackman by The Honorable Elijah Muhammad

Metu Neter (Pt. 1) by Ra Un Nefer Amen

Monster: The Cody Scott Story by Sanyika Shakur

Nationbuilding by Kwame Agyei Akoto

Neo-Colonialism: The Last Stage of Imperialism by Kwame Nkrumah

Nile Valley Civilizations by Ivan Van Sertima

Nile Valley Contributions to Civilization by Anthony T. Browder

Our Savior Has Arrived by The Honorable Elijah Muhammad

Pedagogy of the Oppressed by Paolo Friere

Perpetual Prisoner Machine: How America Profits From Crime by Joel Dyer

Poverty Traps by Samuel Bowles

Powernomics: The National Plan to Empower Black America by Claud Anderson, Ed.D.

Race First: by Tony Martin

Rich Dad, Poor Dad by Robert Kiyosaki

Roots by Alex Haley

Second-Rate Nation: From the American Dream to the American Myth by Sam D. Sieber

Selections from the Husia: Sacred Wisdom of Ancient Egypt by Maulana Karenga

Sex and Race Vol. 1, 2, 3 by J.A. Rogers

Soledad Brother by George Jackson

Somebody's Trying to Kill You by Dr. Harry X. Davidson

Stolen Legacy by George G. M. James

Stupid White Men by Michael Moore

Taking Another Look by Asiba Tupihaci

The 33 Strategies of War by Robert Greene

The 48 Laws of Power by Robert Greene

The African Genius by Basil Davidson

The African Origin of Civilization: Myth or Reality by Cheikh Anta Diop

The African Slave Trade by Basil Davidson

The Art of Mackin' by Tariq Nasheed

The Art of War by Sun Tzu

The Autobiography of Malcolm X by Alex Haley and Malcolm X

The Bandana Republic edited by Bruce George and Louis Reyes Rivera

The Black Man's Burden by Hubert Harrison

The Black Presence in the Bible by Rev. Walter McCray

The Book Your Church Doesn't Want You to Read by

The Debt by Randall Robinson

The Destruction of Black Civilization by Chancellor Williams

The Developmental Psychology of the Black Child by Amos Wilson

The Dust Rose like Smoke: The Subjugation of the Zulu and the Sioux by James O. Gump

The Egyptian Philosophers by Molefi Kete Asante

The Encyclopedia of Black America by W. Augustus Low Virgil A. Clift

The End of White Supremacy by Benjamin Goodman

The Fall of America by The Honorable Elijah Muhammad

The Falsification of Afrikan Consciousness by Amos N. Wilson

The Five Percenters by Michael Muhammad Knight

The Hip Hop Generation: Young Blacks and the Crisis in African American Culture by Bakari Kitwana

The Hustler's 10 Commandments by Hotep

The Iceman Inheritance by Michael Bradley

The Isis Papers by Frances Cress Welsing

The Maafa and Beyond by Erriel D. Robertson

The Mark of Oppression by Dr. Abraham Kardiner

The Maroon Within Us by Asa Hilliard

The Miseducation of the Negro by Dr. Carter G. Woodson

The Mob by Virgil Peterson

The Negro and Nation by Hubert Harrison

The Negro in the Making of America by Benjamin Quarles

The New World Order by A.R. Epperson

The Philosophy and Opinions of Marcus Garvey by Amy Jacques Garvey

The Power of Intention by Wayne Dyer

The Prison Industrial Complex by Attorney Alton Maddox

The Seven Spiritual Laws of Success by Deepak Chopra

The Shaping of Black America by Lerone Bennett, Jr.

The Teaching of Buddha by Bukkyo Dendo Ryokai

The World's Sixteen Crucified Saviors by Kersey Graves

The Wretched of the Earth by Dr. Franz Fanon

Theology of Time by Elijah Muhammad

There is a River by Vincent Harding

They Came Before Columbus by Dr. Ivan Van Sertima

Think and Grow Rich: A Black Choice by Dennis Kimbro

To Be a Slave by Julius Lester

Toms, Coons, Mulattoes, Mammies, and Bucks by Donald Bogle

Towards Colonial Freedom: Africa in the Struggle against World Imperialism by Kwame Nkrumah

Two Thousand Seasons by Ayi K. Armah

Vitamin Bible by Earl Mindells

War of the Bloods in my Veins by Dashaun "Jiwe" Morris

We Took the Streets: Fighting for Latino Rights with the Young Lords by Miguel Melendez

West Africa before the Colonial Era: A History to 1850 by Basil Davidson

What They Never Told You in History Class by Indus Khamit Kush

When Africa Awakes by Hubert Harrison

Who Betrayed the African World Revolution by John Henrik Clarke

Why Are So Many Black Men in Prison? by Demico Boothe

Why Black Men Love White Women by Rajen Persaud

Why I Love Black Women by Michael Eric Dyson

Worlds Great Men of Color Vol.1, 2 by J.A. Rogers

Yurugu: An African-Centered Critique of European Cultural Thought and Behavior by Marimba Ani

The Prisoner's Handbook

By "A Hundred Years Down"

A prison psychology specialist suggested that I write a little 'handbook' or guide for prisoners who are new to jail. After some thought, I got together with a few other "old-heads." Between us we've got over 100 years in Pennsylvania hell-holes. We know our sh*t! We came up with this little list of suggestions for the tens of thousands of young men who are being railroaded into prison, Pennsylvania's fastest growing business. If you have a husband, son or friend who's been thrown into prison in the past year or so, I suggest that you print out this handbook and send it to him. - Penn Pete

General Rules

Rule 1: Never double-cell with a friend. If the Man (the guards, the administration) makes you live in a cell with another man, cell with a person with whom you can get along. It should be a man you're able to adjust to.

Rule 2: It's very, very difficult to live in a bathroom with another person. It would be difficult even if the other person was your wife. When you share long hours in the cell with another man, nerves are sure to get frayed. Be tolerant and talk with your cell-partner.

Rule 3: Give your cell-partner at least an hour a day of solitary cell-time. Men need time alone. You need it. Your cell-partner needs it. Each day, make sure that your cell-partner has an hour alone in the cell. Demand the same for yourself. For God's sake, use some of the time to play with yourself and some to unwind.

Rule 4: Respect your cell-partner's property. Don't read his papers or his mail. Don't eat his food. Don't disturb the little bit he has. Of course, insist that he give you the same respect.

Rule 5: Don't talk about your cell-partner to anyone else. You have to live with your cell-partner. You've got faults, he's got faults. Keep your problems in the cell. Work out your problems between yourselves. Don't bad-mouth your cell-partner to other prisoners.

Rule 6: Don't comment on your cell-partner's personal habits. Farts, snoring, toilet practices and so forth are personal traits which you must learn to tolerate, or you must change cell-partners. Criticizing personal habits is, generally speaking, counter productive. Remember that you have personal habits which irritate your cell-partner. Talking about them just adds to the irritation.

Rule 7: The exception to the above is disease and cleanliness. You must insist that your cell-partner keeps his diseases to himself. That's true whether it's the flu or the genital herpes (that my one-time Egyptian cell-partner tried to share.)

Rule 8: Don't play your radio or television loud enough for men in other cells to hear it. Nothing is quite as annoying as having some kid play his "music" so loud that the other guy has to listen to it. You aren't important enough to decide for your neighbours what they should hear.

Rule 9: Mind your own business. Don't look into other men's cells unless you intend to steal something, and then you deserve whatever happens to you. What's in your neighbour's cell is none of your business and what he's doing there is none of your business. Peekers get punched out.

Rule 10: Cell-thieves are universally detested. You don't steal from other prisoners. Steal from the Man. Steal from the kitchen. Steal from the state. Steal the keys, the guard's hat, the counselor's watch, but you don't steal from another prisoner.

Rule 11: Don't talk about other prisoners' families. Especially, don't talk about another man's wife or girlfriend. Never write such a person and never phone her. Families are all that most men have. Don't invade that security.

Rule 12: Don't talk about or brag about what you have. Don't flaunt your property. Don't tempt other men to covet and so to steal from you. What you have is your business. Keep it to yourself. There are a lot of criminals in prison. You shouldn't be surprised if they behave badly.

Rule 13: Help those prisoners that you find you are able to help. Share your criminal skills with them. After all, that's what prison is all about: education in crime. But, where you're able, go beyond grooming the other guy to be a more skilled crook. If you can help him read or write, or work on the law, try to do those things. Conversely, never belittle or make fun of the thousands of prisoners who can't read, can't write and can't perform simple intellectual chores. In most cases, if the guys could read and write, they wouldn't be in prison in the first place.

Rule 14: Avoid the faggots. Don't rape other prisoners, and don't expose yourself. Nobody cares about your dick or your butt and there's always somebody who's bigger. Faggots aren't women. They aren't good as substitutes for women. What they are is dangerous. Of course, they are disease carriers, but worse, otherwise sane men forget that a faggot is just another man. Men get so serious about faggots that "lovers" often kill one another. Dumb! Don't rape. If you need to feel like a big-ship, fight someone. If you're horny (and aren't we all?) beat-off.

Rule 15: Fight the Man. Don't fight other prisoners. The guy with the keys is the enemy. He's the one who takes your freedom and your dignity. The Man stays in control by keeping prisoners divided. As long as prisoners are fighting among themselves, the Man is free to screw us all. If you have a beef, take it to the Man. Of course, physical combat is always foolish. The Man has the National Guard, for God's sake. Fight him with paper and with words. Don't cooperate in your own destruction. Nothing about prison is for your good. Conversely, the Man is NOT your friend. Befriend the devil before you befriend the bull. The guard, the prison administrator, the "treatment staff" are leeches who make their living from your suffering. The Man's not your pal. Screw him before he screws you.

Rule 16: Do your own time. Don't involve yourself in gangs, cliques, groups, crowds. If the gang goes down you go down. Be your own man, keep your own counsel and limit the numbers of kinds of people you associate with. "Walkies" and "Roadies" and "Homies" must be kept to a minimum.

Rule 17: Don't snitch. Don't rat out a fellow prisoner to the Man. But, also, remember that given the chance the other guy will snitch on you. Don't let anyone know anything you don't want the Man to know. If you know a snitch, feed him false information. It will confuse the Man and it will discredit the snitch.

Rule 18: Trust in yourself. Take care of yourself. Don't trust the Man to keep you safe or healthy or clothed. The Man lives off you, not for you. Your well-being means nothing to him. When you get sick, INSIST on treatment. If the prison is unsafe (and if you're in a Pennsylvania prison, it's unsafe) don't trust the good-heart of the Man to improve things. In all ways and at all times the Man must be forced. He's "guard," after all and you are less important to him than Rover the police dog.

Rule 19: The important thing in prison is getting out. Never lose sight of that goal. Do everything you can to get out, any program, any behaviour, any reform, whatever. Your objects must be to (1) survive, and to (2) get free. It is your duty to yourself as a living human being.

Rule 20: Do one day at a time. It's an old cliche, but it's true. Live for today. Chances are that tomorrow will come.

The 48 Laws of Power

By Robert Greene

I shouldn't even have to tell you about this book.

Law 1: Never Outshine the Master

Law 2: Never put too Much Trust in Friends, Learn how to use Enemies

Law 3: Conceal your Intentions

Law 4: Always Say Less than Necessary

Law 5: So Much Depends on Reputation – Guard it with your Life

Law 6: Court Attention at all Cost

Law 7: Get others to do the Work for you, but Always Take the Credit

Law 8: Make Other People Come to you – Use Bait if Necessary

Law 9: Win through your Actions, Never through Argument

Law 10: Infection: Avoid the Unhappy and Unlucky

Law 11: Learn to Keep People Dependent on You

Law 12: Use Selective Honesty and Generosity to Disarm your Victim

Law 13: When Asking for Help, Appeal to People's Self-Interest, Never to their Mercy or Gratitude

Law 14: Pose as a Friend, Work as a Spy

Law 15: Crush your Enemy Totally

Law 16: Use Absence to Increase Respect and Honor

Law 17: Keep Others in Suspended Terror: Cultivate an Air of Unpredictability

Law 18: Do Not Build Fortresses to Protect Yourself – Isolation is Dangerous

Law 19: Know Who You're Dealing with – Do Not Offend the Wrong Person

Law 20: Do Not Commit to Anyone

Law 21: Play a Sucker to Catch a Sucker – Seem Dumber than your Mark

Law 22: Use the Surrender Tactic: Transform Weakness into Power

Law 23: Concentrate your Forces

Law 24: Play the Perfect Courtier

Law 25: Re-Create Yourself

Law 26: Keep your Hands Clean

Law 27: Play on People's Need to Believe to Create a Cultlike Following

Law 28: Enter Action with Boldness

Law 29: Plan All the Way to the End

Law 30: Make your Accomplishments Seem Effortless

Law 31: Control the Options: Get Others to Play with the Cards you Deal

Law 32: Play to People's Fantasies

Law 33: Discover Each Man's Thumbscrew

Law 34: Be Royal in your Own Fashion; Act Like a King to be Treated Like One

Law 35: Master the Art of Timing

Law 36: Disdain Things you Cannot Have: Ignoring Them is the Best Revenge

Law 37: Create Compelling Spectacles

Law 38: Think as you Like, but Behave Like Others

Law 39: Stir up Waters to Catch Fish

Law 40: Despise the Free Lunch

Law 41: Avoid Stepping into a Great Man's Shoes

Law 42: Strike the Shepherd and the Sheep will Scatter

Law 43: Work on the Hearts and Minds of Others

Law 44: Disarm and Infuriate with the Mirror Effect

Law 45: Preach the Need for Change, but Never Reform Too Much at Once

Law 46: Never Appear Too Perfect

Law 47: Do Not Go Past the Mark you Aimed for; In Victory, Learn When to Stop

Law 48: Assume Formlessness

THE SEVEN SPIRITUAL LAWS OF SUCCESS

By Deepak Chopra

I wanted to suggest this book because it deals with personal development more than it does with "getting what you want" from other people. The following is a brief summary from the author addressing the seven laws, which are:

1. The Law of Pure Potentiality. The source of all creation is pure consciousness...pure potentiality seeking expression from the unmanifest to the manifest. And when we realize that our true Self is one of pure potentiality, we align with the power that manifests everything in the universe.

2. The Law of Giving. The universe operates through dynamic exchange…giving and receiving are different aspects of the flow of energy in the universe. And in our willingness to give that which we seek, we keep the abundance of the universe circulating in our lives.

3. The Law of "Karma" or Cause and Effect. Every action generates a force of energy that returns to us in like kind…what we sow is what we reap. And when we choose actions that bring happiness and success to others, the fruit of our karma is happiness and success.

4. The Law of Least Effort. Nature's intelligence functions with effortless ease…with carefreeness, harmony, and love. And when we harness the forces of harmony, joy, and love, we create success and good fortune with effortless ease.

5. The Law of Intention and Desire. Inherent in every intention and desire is the mechanics for its fulfillment…intention and desire in the field of pure potentiality have infinite organizing power. And when we introduce an intention in the fertile ground of pure potentiality, we put this infinite organizing power to work for us.

6. The Law of Detachment. In detachment lies the wisdom of uncertainty…in the wisdom of uncertainty lies the freedom from our past, from the known, which is the prison of past conditioning. And in our willingness to step into the unknown, the field of all possibilities, we surrender ourselves to the creative mind that orchestrates the dance of the universe.

7. The Law of "Dharma" or Purpose in Life. Everyone has a purpose in life…a unique gift or special talent to give to others. And when we blend this unique talent with service to others, we experience the ecstasy and exultation of our own spirit, which is the ultimate goal of all goals.

What Do You Do Now?

You've completed the journey. Or maybe you're just beginning. If you haven't read *How to Hustle and Win, Part One,* now is definitely the time. Without the first half, you're missing a lot. If you're done with both parts, now it's time to put these ideas to work. Here's how you can start:

- Spread the word about this book and the ideas in it, and encourage them to buy copies (or buy copies for them).
- Develop a long-term plan for how you're going to create changes in your life and the world around you. Make realistic short-term goals as well. Above all, start *DOING* what you *know* you should be doing.
- Begin by eliminating your bad/weak habits, beginning with those most destructive to you.
- Keep asking questions and thinking critically about *everything.*
- Find a pursuit or activity that will empower you, while allowing you to begin creating positive change in the world.
- Choose someone to mentor, and begin actively educating as many people as you can. Don't hold back.
- Start organizing groups of people to work for the greater good.
- If organizing isn't your thing, find a group or organization that you want to be involved with. But make sure they're for real first.
- Send us your praise, comments, or suggestions for improvement, or email your success stories to us, so we can post them online!
- Help spread the word further by leaving positive reviews of the book at Amazon.com and other sites.
- Pick up *Knowledge of Self: A Collection of Wisdom on the Science of Everything in Life*

You can reach us by mail at:

Supreme Design, LLC

P.O. Box 10887

Atlanta, GA 30310

Or you can visit us online at **www.SupremeUnderstanding.com**

www.SupremeDesignOnline.com www.youtube.com/SupremeUTV

Or www.idratherjustkeepdownloadingporninsteadofbetteringmyself.com

KNOWLEDGE OF SELF

A COLLECTION OF WISDOM ON THE SCIENCE OF EVERYTHING IN LIFE

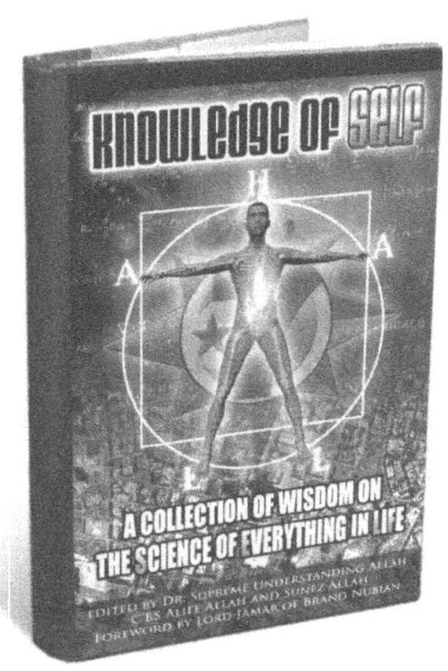

Although self-actualization is the highest of all human needs, it is said that only 5% of people ever attain this goal. In the culture of the Nation of Gods and Earths, commonly known as the Five Percent, students are instructed that they must first learn themselves, then their worlds, and then what they must do in order to transform their world for the better. This often intense process has produced thousands of revolutionary thinkers in otherwise desperate environments, where poverty and hopelessness dominate.

Until now, few mainstream publications have captured the brilliant yet practical perspectives of these luminary men and women. *Knowledge of Self: A Collection of Writings on the Science of Everything in Life* presents the thoughts of over 50 Five Percenters, both young and old, male and female, from all over the globe, in their own words. Through essays, poems, and even how-to articles, this anthology presents readers with an accurate portrait of what the Five Percent study and teach.

EXCERPT FROM KNOWLEDGE OF SELF

Love, Hell or Right by Intelligent Tarref Allah

...I ended up in C-74, the Adolescent Reception Detention Center, on the world's largest penal colony—Riker's Island. Someone coined the phrase "C-74, adolescents at war." It fit perfectly for the single building that caged some of the most dangerous 16-to-19-year-olds in New York City. I knew some of the outlaws from my stay at Spofford, others had stomped through the streets with me. My ties to old associates and the new thugs I was introduced to made my ride relatively safe. Unfortunately, most new faces in C-74 crashed head-first into injuries and extortion. I had my share of drama, but I navigated the maze of madness without a homemade icepick puncturing my body or a razor gracing my face.

My body was locked up, but my mind was in society. My family were supportive and certain that I would be vindicated in court, because I had defended myself. Their thoughts were destroyed when we found out that the gun the deceased had possessed never made it to the precinct evidence locker. Possibly, one of the deceased's friends had taken it, or it was removed by the deceased's uncle, who worked in the precinct. The deck was stacked against me. I would end up pleading guilty to murder and receive 19 years to life.

My brother and a few guys from my crew had been visiting me regularly on Riker's Island. Several months after I was arrested, they had become members of The Nation of Gods and Earths, a God-centered cultural group commonly known as The Five Percent Nation. My brother told me not to call him Moe anymore, because his new name was Uneeke Understanding Allah. The rest of my crew had adopted names like Wise and Victorious that reflected positive attributes of themselves.

"I'm trying to keep a low profile," my brother told me inside of the crowded visiting room. He leaned back in the small red chair and said, "I'm on another level now. I'm God."

I held back my laughter and wondered if he had lost his mind. To me, anything involving God was insane. I switched the subject to avoid debate.

After the visit my mind remained on my brother, so when I got back to my dorm I mentioned him to Sharief. Sha, as we called the older brother for short, was also a member of The Nation. He began explaining how The Nation was started by a man who was an understudy of Malcolm X in the Nation of Islam. His name was Clarence 13X, but he changed it to Allah and was known as The Father after leaving the Nation of Islam. He parted from the group based on Master Fard Muhammad being considered the sole personification of God, though Elijah Muhammad also taught, to a lesser degree, that all Black men were God. I immediately remembered the time in Spofford when I was confused by the Nation of Islam's conflicting views on God.

"Ain't no God," I told Sha, as I leaned back on my bed, staring at Sha's narrow light-skinned face. "Not the Black man or Master Fard Muhammad. And it definitely ain't nobody in the sky that's controlling everything."

Sha smiled, as he sat on the small locker connected to my bed. "You don't believe in a supernatural God, right?"

"You know that," I responded to the rhetorical question.

"So who or what is greater than man?"

I replied, "Nothing."

Sha smiled again, nodding his bald head. "So if there is nothing greater than man, what does that make man?"

"What?" I shrugged my shoulders.

"Listen," Sha said, "God means the supreme being. Supreme means the most high. Being means to exist. So if you don't believe in something that exists that is on a higher level than man, then subconsciously, you already understand that man is God. The Black man. They say that God is the originator. Well, anthropology and history proves that the Black man was the first on the planet. They say that God created man. Well, science proves that all races derive from the Black man. They say God gave us land to live on and fruit for food. Well, the Black man was the first to have thriving civilizations where we cultivated the land and lived off it." Sha kept going for at least ten minutes, quoting book after book to support his claims. He even made reference to the Bible mentioning "Ye are gods."

I was silent, pondering what Sha said and how he could quote so much history and science. I had known other members of The Nation, but I had never heard anyone expound on their concept of God in such simple and logical terms.

"So if the Black man is God," I said, "what's up with the white man?"

Sha asked, "Do you know what duality is?" …

* * *

Are You a Reluctant Messiah? by Supreme Understanding Allah

What kind of a mind manufactured this world? It's ours. And it's still at work. Psychoanalysts like Carl Jung have tried to describe the collective consciousness of humanity that we describe as the superconscious mind. Jung called it the unconscious mind, because for white people, it is. Just as the pineal gland (the "third eye") is 85% calcified in whites, and mostly clear among us! This mind goes much deeper, and is much more expansive in scope and the magnetic conscious (the mind we fully share) and the infinite conscious (the mind that extends beyond space and time, and designed this universe). For us, these advanced stages of consciousness are the reason why Original People throughout the world have come up with similar inventions and ideas without any evidence of cultural contact or exchange! They are also what allow us to sense what each other is thinking. And returning to the topic of Dr. King and Jesus, this mind is the force that produces great leaders among us. Every time period and civilization has its messiahs, and this Blackmind is the source of all their inspiration. Should you be able to fully tap into it, you may be one yourself. But are you ready for it?

The Bible tells us about Moses, who had killed a man in anger, fled for his life, and lived with self-doubt. His stuttering made him so self-conscious that when the Lord called on him to lead, he attempted to decline. The Lord promised that he would empower Moses to do whatever was needed, and a reluctant Messiah was born. There are several reluctant figures in the Bible who channel the divine energy described as God to accomplish great things. This list includes men like Jeremiah, who most certainly didn't want the job of Prophet, but later explained, "If I say I will not mention him or speak any more in his name, there is in my heart as it were a burning fire shut up in my bones and I am not able to hold it in." (Jeremiah 10:9). When you have tapped into your true calling, it takes a LOT to turn it down.

What does this have to do with you? Everything.

When I would wonder how an uneducated (schoolwise, at least) brother from Danville, Virginia…who kept company with tons of shady characters…who had troubles of his own…and who'd never met any prophet from the East…could come to such an incredible realization that he would eventually produce a culture that would effectively change the consciousness of the world…I am in awe. How did Allah come to realize the mathematical principles that govern the universe…and then give them to us in a way that would not only survive, but spread? How did Allah design this culture in such a way that we didn't die off or get destroyed like almost EVERY other Black organization of that era? How did this man know in 1968 that he would be gone the next year (that's recorded in his FBI files)…and understand how to prepare us to survive?

Simple. He tapped into what was naturally his. And ours. That infinite consciousness that wrote the programming for this entire universe, mapped out its history in advance, and produced Messiahs from ordinary men for hundreds of thousands of years…

* * *

EM-POWER-U by Mecca Wise

…Since change starts within us, we must begin to love and appreciate ourselves and our sisters. Many of us have the same struggles and fears. Realize we are powerful and beautiful. Set boundaries in relationships with everyone, whether male or female. If you don't value you, then who will? Realize that we are so much more than sexual beings. Pursue meaningful relationships of longevity based on values and strong foundations. Look at what we want to change about us whether mentally or physically. The changes won't occur overnight, but even small steps will help us reach our goals. Have confidence in ourselves and the courage to overcome our fears. Changing our minds isn't easy but it is the first step to changing our lives.

Women, are we willing to break the cycle, change our thoughts, use our brain power vs. our sexual power, learn the beauty of who we really are, start a new journey, and get the knowledge of ourselves? Let us begin…

For more, visit www.supremedesignonline.com, where you can read dozens of pages of free excerpts from *any* of our books.

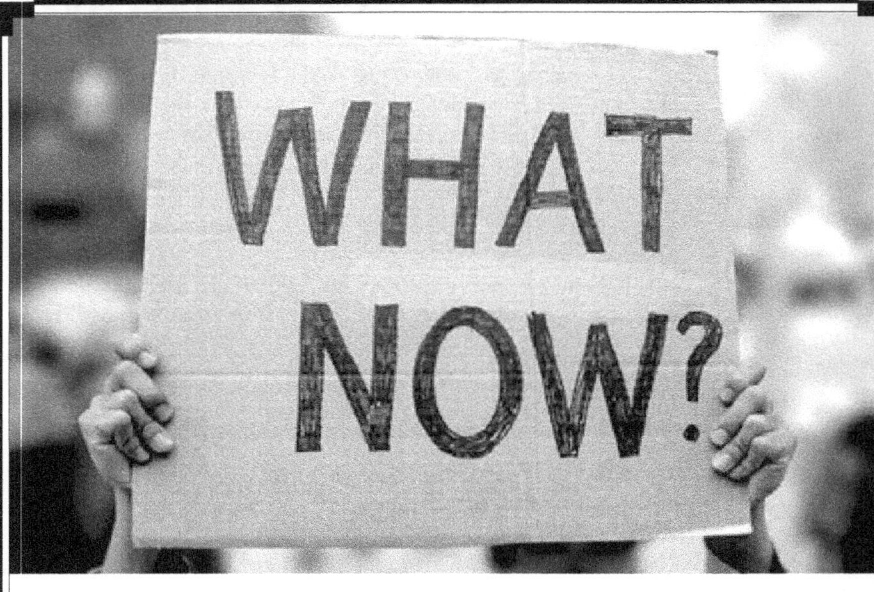

What should you do now that you're done reading?
Here are some suggestions:

- ❑ Complete any activities mentioned in this book, especially the discussions. See any of the films mentioned, but with others.
- ❑ Tell somebody about this book and what you've learned. Invite them to come read it. Don't let them steal the book.
- ❑ As another option, let them steal the book. It might help them.
- ❑ Mentor some young people or teach a class using this book as a handbook or reference.
- ❑ Talk about this book online, but don't stay on the Net forever.
- ❑ Join an organization or group that discusses concepts like the ones in this book and get into those discussions.
- ❑ Leave this book away somewhere it will be picked up and read.
- ❑ Identify the people in your community who could use a copy of this book. If they're people would want to buy a book like this, let em read a few pages and see if they can afford to buy a copy.
- ❑ If they're people who don't normally buy books – but you know that givin em a copy could change their life – give em a copy and tell em to come see you when they're ready for another one. This is why you can order copies at wholesale rates at our site.

We hope this helps you keep the knowledge contagious.

ALSO FROM OUR COMPANY

How to Hustle and Win, Part 1: A Survival Guide for the Ghetto

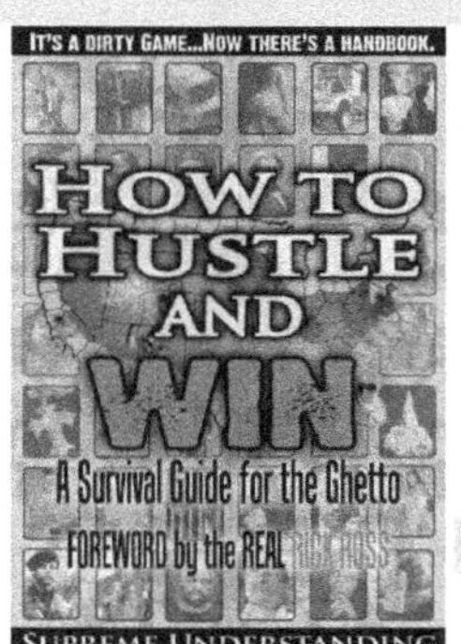

By Supreme Understanding
Foreword by the Real Rick Ross

This is the book that started it all. Now an international bestseller, this book has revolutionized the way people think of "urban literature." It offers a street-based analysis of social problems, plus practical solutions that anyone can put to use.

CLASS	PAGES	RETAIL	RELEASE
I-1	336	$19.95	Jun. 2008

ISBN: 978-0-9816170-0-8

How to Hustle and Win, Part 2: Rap, Race, and Revolution

By Supreme Understanding
Foreword by Stic.man of Dead Prez

Seen here in its original green cover, the controversial follow-up to *How to Hustle and Win* digs even deeper into the problems we face, and how we can solve them. Part One focused on personal change, and Part Two explores the bigger picture of changing the entire hood.

CLASS	PAGES	RETAIL	RELEASE
I-1	384	$19.95	Apr. 2009

ISBN: 978-0-9816170-9-1

Knowledge of Self: A Collection of Wisdom on the Science of Everything in Life

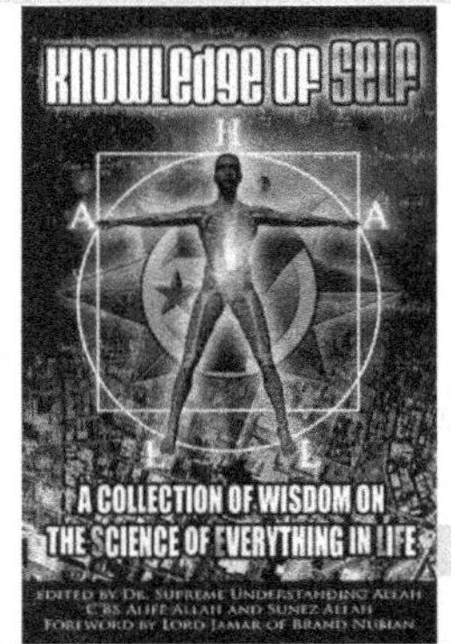

Edited by Supreme Understanding, C'BS Alife Allah, and Sunez Allah, Foreword by Lord Jamar of Brand Nubian

Who are the Five Percent? Why are they here? In this book, over 50 Five Percenters from around the world speak for themselves, providing a comprehensive introduction to the esoteric teachings of the Nation of Gods and Earths.

CLASS	PAGES	RETAIL	RELEASE
I-2	256	$19.95	Jul. 2009

ISBN: 978-0-9816170-2-2

The Hood Health Handbook, Volume One (Physical Health)

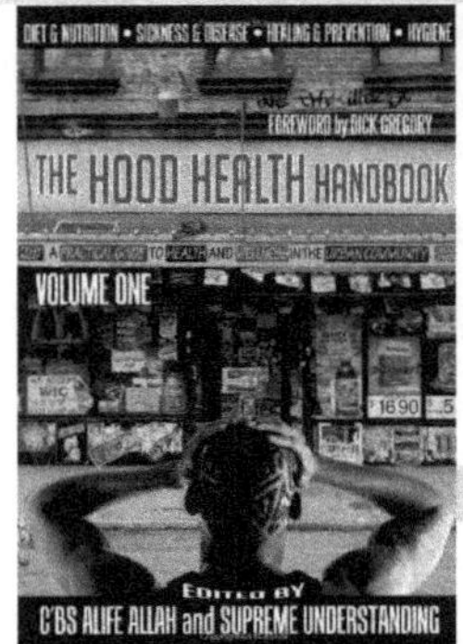

Edited by Supreme Understanding and C'BS Alife Allah, Foreword by Dick Gregory

Want to know why Black and brown people are so sick? This book covers the many "unnatural causes" behind our poor health, and offers hundreds of affordable and easy-to-implement solutions.

CLASS	PAGES	RETAIL	RELEASE
PH-1	480	$19.95	Nov. 2010

ISBN: 978-1-935721-32-1

The Hood Health Handbook, Volume Two (Mental Health)

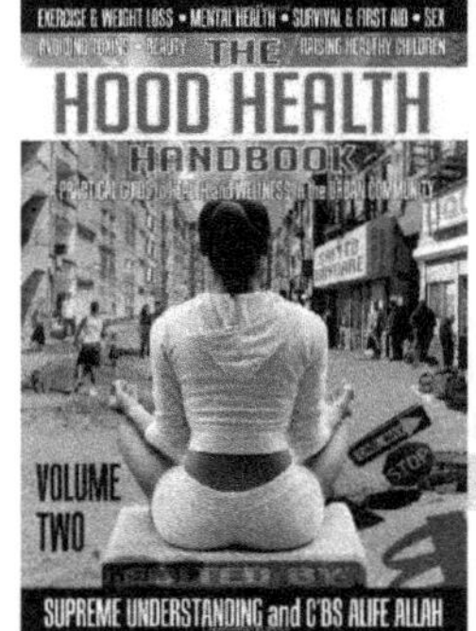

Edited by Supreme Understanding and C'BS Alife Allah

This volume covers mental health, how to keep a healthy home, raising healthy children, environmental issues, and dozens of other issues, all from the same down-to-earth perspective as Volume One.

CLASS	PAGES	RETAIL	RELEASE
MH-1	480	$19.95	Nov. 2010

ISBN: 978-1-935721-33-8

A Taste of Life: 1,000 Vegetarian Recipes from Around the World

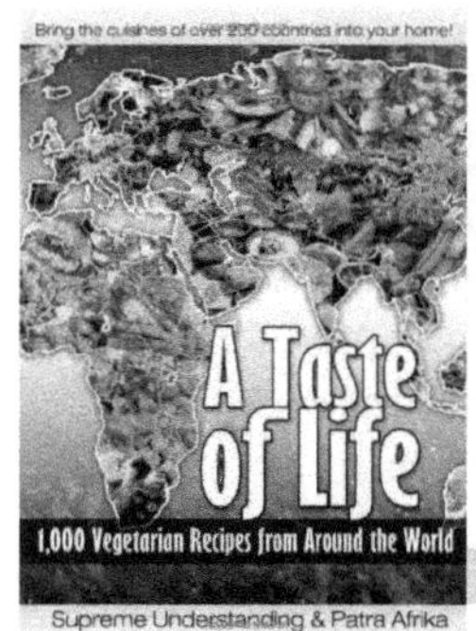

Edited by Supreme Understanding and Patra Afrika

This cookbook makes it easy to become vegetarian. In addition to over 1,000 recipes from everywhere you can think of, plus over 100 drink and smoothie recipes, this book also teaches how to transition your diet, what to shop for, how to cook, as well as a guide to nutrients and vitamins.

CLASS	PAGES	RETAIL	RELEASE
W-1	400	$19.95	Jun. 2011

ISBN: 978-1-935721-10-9

La Brega: Como Sobrevivir En El Barrio

By Supreme Understanding

Thanks to strong demand coming from Spanish-speaking countries, we translated our groundbreaking How to Hustle and Win into Spanish, and added new content specific to Latin America. Because this book's language is easy to follow, it can also be used to brush up on your Spanish.

CLASS	PAGES	RETAIL	RELEASE
0-1	336	$14.95	Jul. 2009

ISBN: 978-0981617-08-4

Locked Up but Not Locked Down: A Guide to Surviving the American Prison System

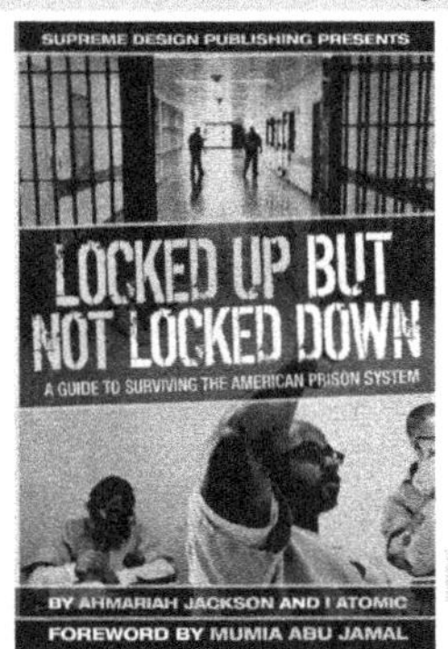

By Ahmariah Jackson and IAtomic Allah
Foreword by Mumia Abu Jamal

This book covers what it's like on the inside, how to make the most of your time, what to do once you're out, and how to stay out. Features contributions from over 50 insiders, covering city jails, state and federal prisons, women's prisons, juvenile detention, and international prisons.

CLASS	PAGES	RETAIL	RELEASE
J-1	288	$24.95	Jul. 2012

ISBN: 978-1935721-00-0

The Science of Self: Man, God, and the Mathematical Language of Nature

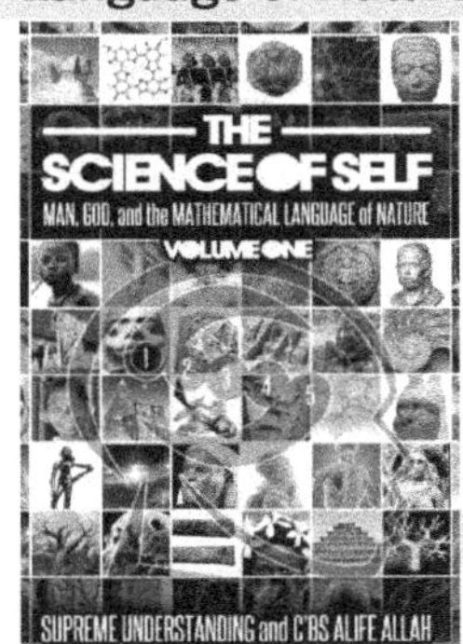

By Supreme Understanding and C'BS Alife Allah

How did the universe begin? Is there a pattern to everything that happens? What's the meaning of life? What does science tell us about the depths of our SELF? Who and what is God? This may be one of the deepest books you can read.

CLASS	PAGES	RETAIL	RELEASE
I-4	360	$29.95	Jun. 2012

ISBN: 978-1935721-67-3

When the World was Black, Part One: Prehistoric Cultures

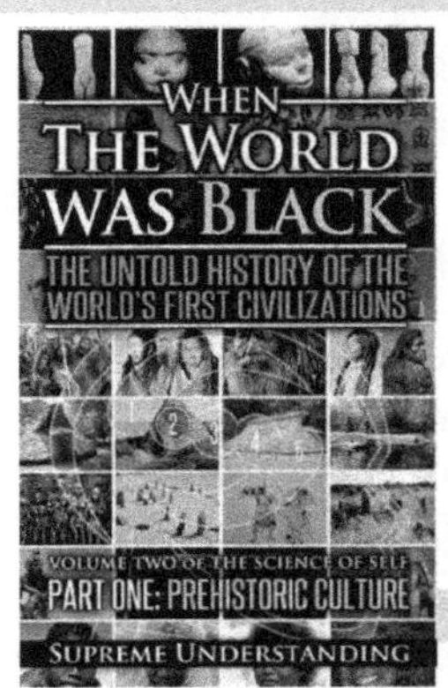

By Supreme Understanding
Foreword by Runoko Rashid

When does Black history begin? Certainly not with slavery. In two volumes, historian Supreme Understanding explores over 200,000 years of Black history from every corner of the globe. Part One covers the first Black communities to settle the world, establishing its first cultures and traditions. Their stories are remarkable.

CLASS	PAGES	RETAIL	RELEASE
I-3	400	$24.95	Feb. 2013

ISBN: 978-1-935721-04-8

When the World Was Black, Part Two: Ancient Civilizations

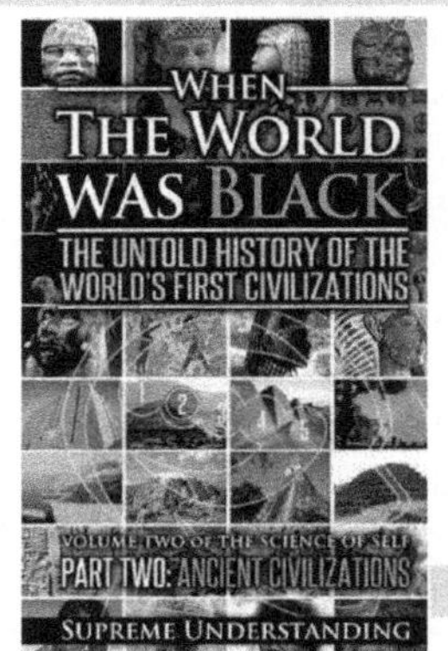

By Supreme Understanding

Part Two covers the ancient Black civilizations that gave birth to the modern world. Black people built the first urban civilizations in Africa, Asia, Europe, and the Americas. And every claim in these books is thoroughly documented with reputable sources. Do you want to know the story of your ancestors? You should. We study the past to see what the future will bring.

CLASS	PAGES	RETAIL	RELEASE
I-3	400	$24.95	Feb. 2013

ISBN: 978-1-935721-05-5

When the World was Black, Parts One and Two (Hardcover)

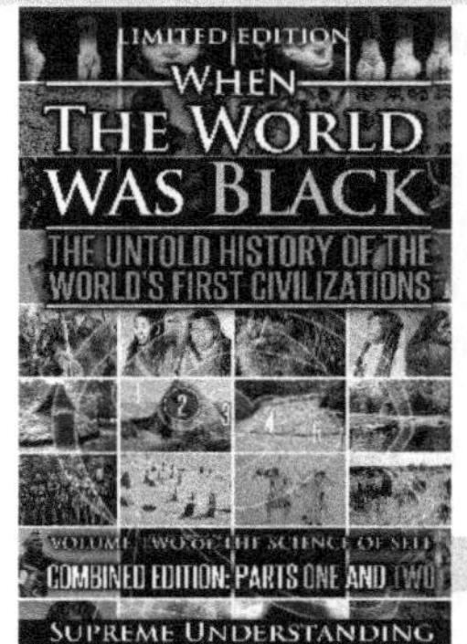

By Supreme Understanding

An incredible limited edition that combines Part One and Part Two into a single book, cased in an embossed clothbound hardcover and dust jacket. Autographed and numbered, this collector's item also includes both sets of full-color inserts.

CLASS	PAGES	RETAIL	RELEASE
I-3	800	$74.95	Dec. 2013

Only available direct from publisher.

Black Rebellion: Eyewitness Accounts of Major Slave Revolts

Edited by Dr. Sujan Dass

Who will tell the stories of those who refused to be slaves? What about those who fought so effectively that they forced their slavers to give up? Black Rebellion is a collection of historical "eyewitness" accounts of dozens of major revolts and uprisings, from the U.S. to the Caribbean, as well as a history of slavery and revolt.

CLASS	PAGES	RETAIL	RELEASE
P-3	272	$19.95	May 2010

ISBN: 978-0-981617-04-6

The Heroic Slave

By Frederick Douglass

Most people don't know that Douglass wrote a novel...or that, in this short novel, he promoted the idea of violent revolt. By this time in his life, the renowned abolitionist was seeing things differently. This important piece of history comes with *David Walker's Appeal*, all in one book.

CLASS	PAGES	RETAIL	RELEASE
P-3	160	$19.95	Apr. 2011

ISBN: 978-1-935721-27-7

David Walker's Appeal

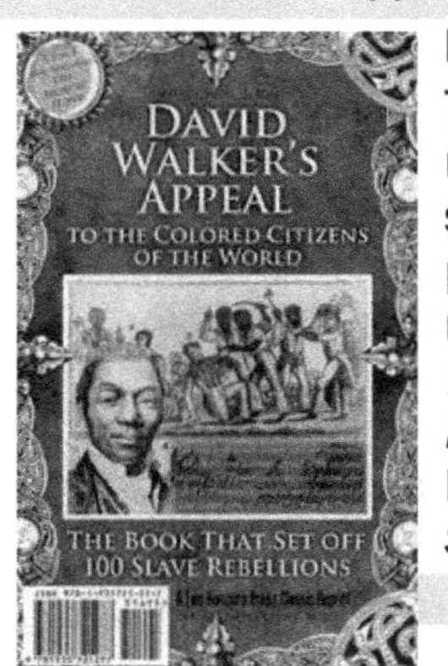

By David Walker

This is one of the most important, and radical, works ever published against slavery. Rather than call for an end by peaceful means, Walker called for outright revolution. His calls may have led to over 100 revolts, including those described in *Black Rebellion*. This important piece of history comes with Douglass' *The Heroic Slave*, which it may have helped inspire.

CLASS	PAGES	RETAIL	RELEASE
P-3	160	$19.95	Apr. 2011

ISBN: 978-1-935721-27-7

Darkwater: Voices from Within the Veil, Annotated Edition

By W.E.B. Du Bois

This book makes Du Bois' previous work, like *Souls of Black Folk*, seem tame by comparison. *Darkwater* is revolutionary, uncompromising, and unconventional in both its content and style, addressing the plight of Black women, the rise of a Black Messiah, a critical analysis of white folks, and the need for outright revolution.

CLASS	PAGES	RETAIL	RELEASE
I-4	240	$19.95	Jun. 2011

ISBN: 978-0-981617-07-7

The African Abroad: The Black Man's Evolution in Western Civilization, Volume One

By William Henry Ferris

Who would think a book written in 1911 could cover so much? Ferris, chairman of the UNIA, speaks up for the Black man's role in Western civilization. He discusses a wealth of history, as well as some revolutionary Black theology, exploring the idea of man as God and God as man.

CLASS	PAGES	RETAIL	RELEASE
I-5	570	$29.95	Oct. 2012

ISBN: 978-1935721-66-6

The African Abroad: Volume Two

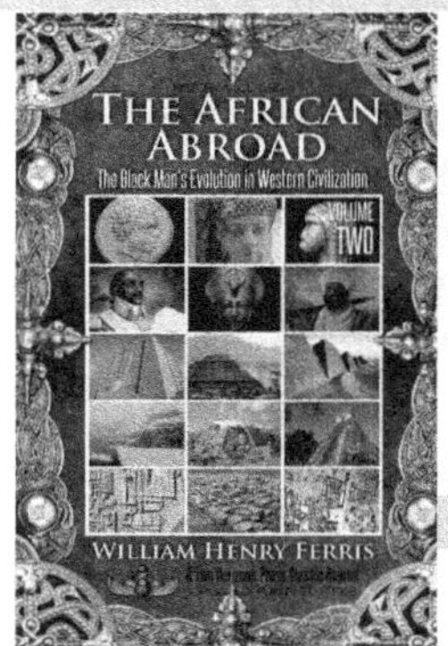

By William Henry Ferris

The second volume of Ferris' epic covers important Black biographies of great leaders, ancient and modern. He tells the stories of forty "Black Immortals." He also identifies the African origins of many of the world's civilizations, including ancient Egypt, Akkad, Sumer, India, and Europe.

CLASS	PAGES	RETAIL	RELEASE
I-5	330	$19.95	Oct. 2012

ISBN: 978-1-935721-69-7

From Poverty to Power: The Realization of Prosperity and Peace

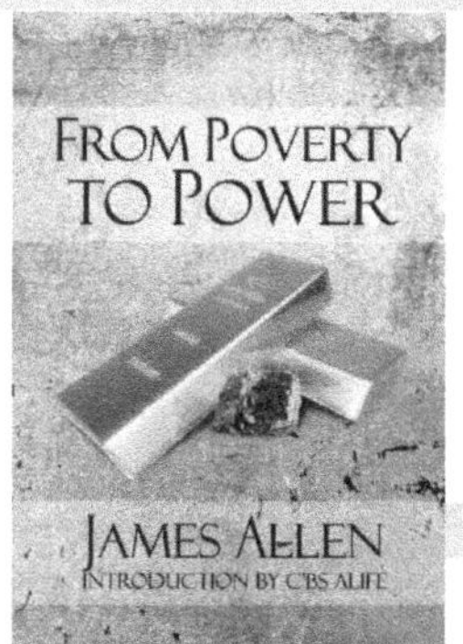

By James Allen

Want to transform your life? James Allen, the author of the classic *As a Man Thinketh,* explores how we can turn struggle and adversity into power and prosperity. This inspirational text teaches readers about their innate strength and the immense power of the conscious mind.

CLASS	PAGES	RETAIL	RELEASE
I-3	144	$19.95	May 2010

ISBN: 978-0-981617-05-3

Daily Meditations: A Year of Guidance on the Meaning of Life

By James Allen

Need a guidebook to a productive and healthy year? This is it. James Allen delivers another great work in this book, this time offering 365 days of inspiration and guidance on life's greatest challenges. This book includes sections for daily notes.

CLASS	PAGES	RETAIL	RELEASE
C-3	208	$19.95	Apr. 2013

ISBN: 978-1-935721-08-6

The Kybalion: The Seven Ancient Egyptian Laws _

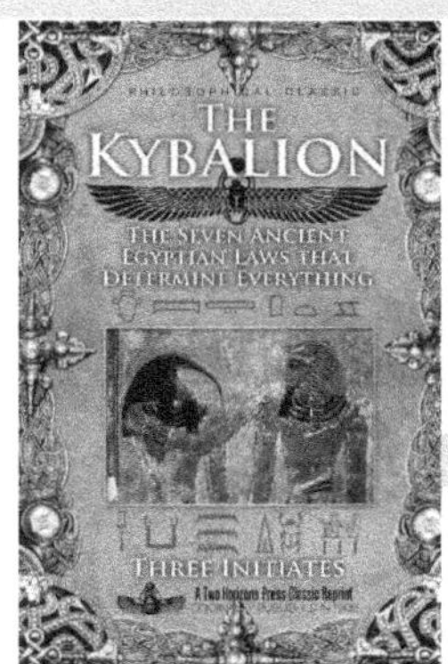

By the Three Initiates

Thousands of years ago, the ancients figured out a set of principles that govern the universe. In *The Kybalion*, these laws are explored and explained. This edition includes research into the authorship of the book, and where the laws came from.

CLASS	PAGES	RETAIL	RELEASE
C-4	130	$19.95	Oct. 2012

ISBN: 978-1-935721-25-3

Real Life is No Fairy Tale (w/ Companion CD)

By Sujan Dass and Lord Williams

Looking for a children's book that teaches about struggle? Written for school age children, this full-color hardcover book is composed entirely in rhyme, and the images are as real as they get. Includes a CD with an audio book, animated video, review questions, and printable worksheets and activities.

CLASS	PGS	RETAIL	RELEASE
CD-4	36+	$16.95	Jun. 2010

ISBN: 978-0-9816170-2-2

Aesop's Fables: 101 Classic Tales and Timeless Lessons

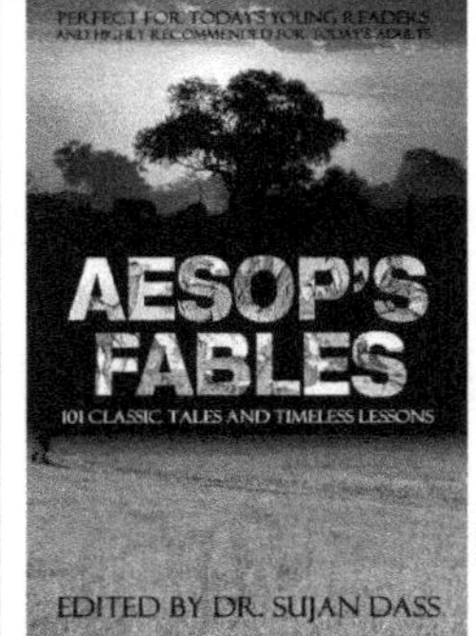

Edited by Dr. Sujan Dass

What's better to teach our children than life lessons? This easy-to-read collection of classic tales told by an African storyteller uses animals to teach valuable moral lessons. This edition includes dozens of black-and-white images to accompany the timeless fables. Color them in!

CLASS	PAGES	RETAIL	RELEASE
CD-3	112	$14.95	Feb. 2013

ISBN: 978-1-935721-07-9

Heritage Playing Cards (w/ Companion Booklet)

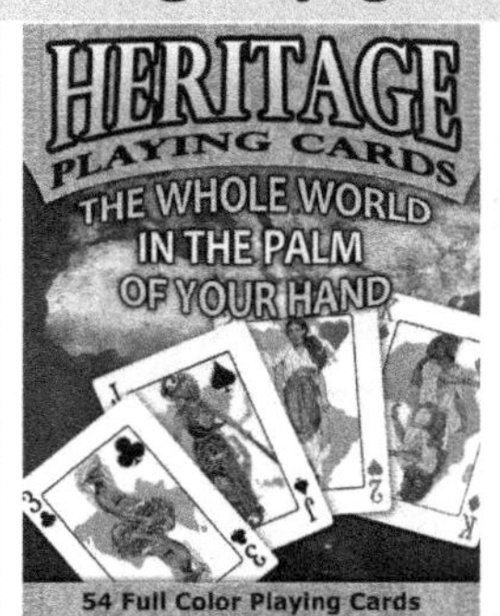

Designed by Sujan Dass

No more European royalty! This beautiful deck of playing cards features 54 full-color characters from around the world and a 16-page educational booklet on international card games and the ethnic backgrounds of the people on the cards.

CLASS	PGS	RETAIL	RELEASE
CD-2	16+	$14.95	May 2010

UPC: 05105-38587

Black God: An Introduction to the World's Religions and their Black Gods

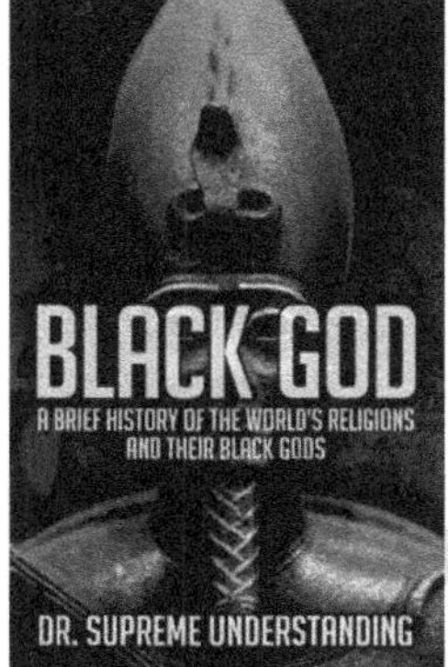

By Supreme Understanding

Have you ever heard that Christ was Black? What about the Buddha? They weren't alone. This book explores the many Black gods of the ancient world, from Africa to Europe, Asia, and Australia, all the way to the Americas. Who were they? Why were they worshipped? And what does this mean for us today?

CLASS	PAGES	RETAIL	RELEASE
C-3	200	$19.95	Jan. 2014

ISBN: 978-1-935721-12-3

Black People Invented Everything

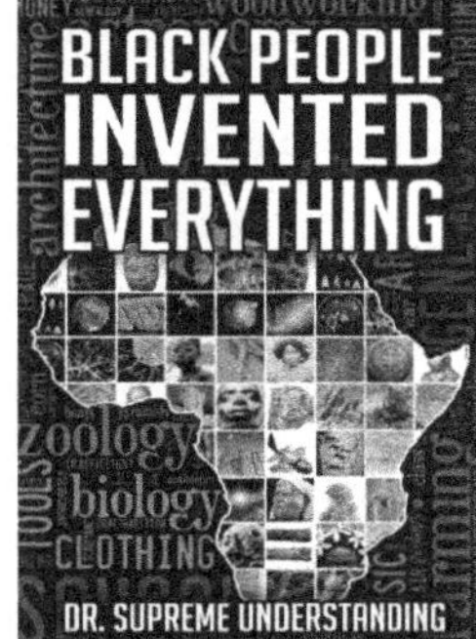

By Supreme Understanding

In *The Science of Self* we began exploring the origins of everything that modern civilization depends on today. In this book, we get into specifics, showing how Black people invented everything from agriculture to zoology, with dozens of pictures and references to prove it!

CLASS	PAGES	RETAIL	RELEASE
I-3	256	$29.95	Feb. 2020

ISBN: 978-1-935721-13-0

The Yogi Science of Breath: A Complete Manual of the Ancient Philosophy of the East

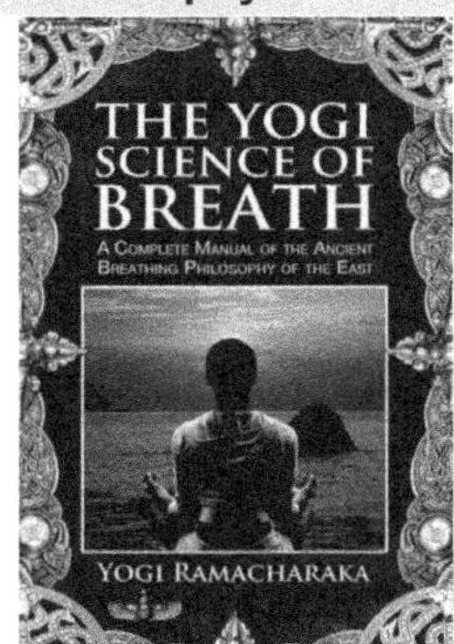

By Yogi Ramacharaka

A classic text on the science of breathing, one of the most ignored, yet important, aspects of our physical and emotional health. This book has been used by both martial arts experts and legendary jazz musicians. This edition explores the "secret science" of breath, and where its mysterious author learned such teachings.

CLASS	PAGES	RETAIL	RELEASE
PH-4	112	$14.95	Apr. 2012

ISBN: 978-1-935721-34-5

How to Get Our Books

To better serve our readers, we've streamlined the way we handle book orders. Here are some of the ways you can find our books.

In Stores

You can find our books in just about any Black bookstore or independent bookseller. If you don't find our titles on the shelves, just request them by name and publisher. Most bookstores can order our titles directly from us (via our site) or from the distributors listed below. We also provide a listing of retailers who carry our books at www.bestblackbooks.com

Online (Wholesale)

Now, you can visit our sites (like www.supremeunderstanding.com or www.bestblackbooks.com) to order wholesale quantities direct from us, the publisher. From our site, we ship heavily discounted case quantities to distributors, wholesalers, retailers, and local independent resellers (like yourself – just try it!). The discounts are so deep, you can afford to GIVE books away if you're not into making money.

Online (Retail)

If you're interested in single "retail" copies, you can now find them online at Amazon.com, or you can order them via mail order by contacting one of the mail order distributors listed below. You can also find many of our titles as eBooks in the Amazon Kindle, Nook, or Apple iBooks systems. You may also find full-length videobook or audiobook files available, but nothing beats the pass-around potential of a real book!

By Mail Order

Please contact any of the following Black-owned distributors to order our books! For others, visit our site.

Afrikan World Books
2217 Pennsylvania Ave.
Baltimore, MD 21217
(410) 383-2006

Lushena Books
607 Country Club Dr
Bensenville, IL 60106
(800) 785-1545

Special Needs X-Press
927 Old Nepperhan Ave
Yonkers, NY 10703
(914) 623-7007

www.ingramcontent.com/pod-product-compliance
Lightning Source LLC
Chambersburg PA
CBHW031231090426
42742CB00007B/150